Hegel's *Encyclopedia of the Philosophical Sciences*

Hegel regarded his *Encyclopedia of the Philosophical Sciences* as the work which most fully presented the scope of his philosophical system and its method. It is somewhat surprising, therefore, that some scholars regularly accord it only a secondary status. This Critical Guide seeks to change that, with sixteen newly written essays from an international group of Hegel scholars that shed much-needed light on both the whole and the parts of the *Encyclopedia* system. Topics include the structure and aim of the *Encyclopedia* system as a whole, the differences between the greater and lesser *Logics*, the role of nature in Hegel's thinking, Hegel's account of the relationship between body and soul, theory and praxis, mind and matter, his account of rational politics and the shapes of absolute spirit as art, religion and philosophy. This book will be invaluable to all students and scholars with an interest in Hegel and the history of philosophy.

SEBASTIAN STEIN is a Lecturer and Research Associate at Ruprecht-Karls-Universität Heidelberg. He is co-editor of *Hegel's Political Philosophy* (with Thom Brooks, 2017) and *Hegel and Contemporary Practical Philosophy* (with James Gledhill, 2019), and is the author of several journal articles and book chapters on Aristotle, Kant and post-Kantian idealism.

JOSHUA I. WRETZEL is Assistant Teaching Professor at Pennsylvania State University. He has published numerous articles on the German philosophical tradition in journals including the *European Journal of Philosophy*, the *International Journal of Philosophical Studies* and *Hegel Bulletin*.

(Continued after the Index)

HEGEL'S
Encyclopedia of the Philosophical Sciences

A Critical Guide

EDITED BY

SEBASTIAN STEIN
Ruprecht-Karls-Universität Heidelberg

JOSHUA I. WRETZEL
Pennsylvania State University

CAMBRIDGE
UNIVERSITY PRESS

Shaftesbury Road, Cambridge CB2 8EA, United Kingdom

One Liberty Plaza, 20th Floor, New York, NY 10006, USA

477 Williamstown Road, Port Melbourne, VIC 3207, Australia

314–321, 3rd Floor, Plot 3, Splendor Forum, Jasola District Centre, New Delhi – 110025, India

103 Penang Road, #05–06/07, Visioncrest Commercial, Singapore 238467

Cambridge University Press is part of Cambridge University Press & Assessment, a department of the University of Cambridge.

We share the University's mission to contribute to society through the pursuit of education, learning and research at the highest international levels of excellence.

www.cambridge.org
Information on this title: www.cambridge.org/9781108458900

DOI: 10.1017/9781108592000

First published 2021
First paperback edition 2023

A catalogue record for this publication is available from the British Library

Library of Congress Cataloging-in-Publication data
NAMES: Stein, Sebastian, 1980– editor. | Wretzel, Joshua, editor.
TITLE: Hegel's Encyclopedia of the philosophical sciences : a critical guide / edited by Sebastian Stein, Eberhard-Karls-Universität Tübingen, GermanyJoshua Wretzel, Pennsylvania State University.
OTHER TITLES: Encyclopedia of the philosophical sciences
DESCRIPTION: Cambridge, United Kingdom ; New York, NY, USA : Cambridge University Press, [2021] | Series: Cambridge critical guides | Includes bibliographical references and index.
IDENTIFIERS: LCCN 2021024835 (print) | LCCN 2021024836 (ebook) | ISBN 9781108471985 (hardback) | ISBN 9781108592000 (ebook)
SUBJECTS: LCSH: Hegel, Georg Wilhelm Friedrich, 1770–1831. Encyklopädie der philosophischen Wissenschaften. | BISAC: PHILOSOPHY / History & Surveys / Modern | PHILOSOPHY / History & Surveys / Modern
CLASSIFICATION: LCC B2919 .H38 2021 (print) | LCC B2919 (ebook) | DDC 193–dc23
LC record available at https://lccn.loc.gov/2021024835
LC ebook record available at https://lccn.loc.gov/2021024836

ISBN   978-1-108-47198-5   Hardback
ISBN   978-1-108-45890-0   Paperback

Contents

v

Contributors

THOM BROOKS is Professor of Law and Government at Durham University.

JANE DRYDEN is Associate Professor of Philosophy at Mount Allison University.

STEPHEN HOULGATE is Professor of Philosophy at the University of Warwick.

RALPH M. KAUFMANN is Professor of Mathematics at Purdue University.

JEAN-FRANÇOIS KERVÉGAN is Emeritus Professor of Philosophy at the Université Paris 1 Panthéon-Sorbonne.

ANSGAR LYSSY is a researcher at the Universität Heidelberg.

CHRISTIAN MARTIN is Senior Associate Professor of Philosophy at the Ludwig-Maximilians-Universität München.

DEAN MOYAR is Professor of Philosophy at The Johns Hopkins University.

TERRY PINKARD is Professor of Philosophy at Georgetown University.

ROBERT B. PIPPIN is the Evelyn Stefansson Nef Distinguished Service Professor at the University of Chicago.

PAUL REDDING is Professor Emeritus of Philosophy at the University of Sydney.

SALLY SEDGWICK is Professor of Philosophy at Boston University.

SEBASTIAN STEIN is Research Fellow at the Ruprecht-Karls-Universität Heidelberg.

IOANNIS TRISOKKAS is Assistant Professor of German Philosophy at the National and Kapodistrian University of Athens, Greece.

ROBERTO VINCO is Assistant Professor at the Ruprecht-Karls-Universität Heidelberg.

JOSHUA I. WRETZEL is Assistant Teaching Professor in Philosophy at Pennsylvania State University.

CHRISTOPHER YEOMANS is Professor of Philosophy at Purdue University.

Introduction

Sebastian Stein and Joshua I. Wretzel

> The prophet's voice possessed of god
> requires no ornament, no sweetening of tone,
> but carries over a thousand years.
>
> Heraclitus (535–475 BC)

In 1817, Hegel published a condensed articulation of his basic philosophical commitments, designed to help make his notoriously difficult lectures a bit easier to follow. He titled this compendium the *Encyclopedia of the Philosophical Sciences in Basic Outline* and, for the rest of his life, made consistent use of it in his classes, constantly amending it until its last, more detailed version was published in 1830. That Hegel called this text an "encyclopedia" was as bold a choice as it was strange. For on the one hand, it of course suggests that Hegel saw his own knowledge and system of philosophy as encyclopedic. But on the other hand, the text also bears no structural resemblance to any other encyclopedia.

This uniqueness is due to its method. Hegel presents his work in three parts – *Logic*, *Philosophy of Nature*, and *Philosophy of Spirit* (or *Geist*) – and argues that his *Encyclopedia* proceeds "according to a method that will some day be recognized, I hope, as the only true method" (Hegel 2010a). But what is this method and how does it define the *Encyclopedia*?

According to Hegel, the structuring principle (Hegel 2010a: §§17&18, 45–6) of all philosophical knowledge is 'the concept' (Hegel 2010a: 507). Synonymous with reason, it defines reality and all thought about reality and functions as the common denominator for the categories of philosophy. These categories define thought and being in general, nature and all mind-related and spiritual life, that is, *Geist* (Hegel 1986: 17), and their shared origin in the concept gives definition and unity to their sequence.

The sum of philosophy's categories and their relations thus define philosophical knowledge. Tracking the concept's activity, this knowledge takes a circular form: the *Encyclopedia*'s categories form a "circle of circles" (Hegel 2010a: §15, 43), where each category is justified by its predecessors and prepares its successors. Strictly speaking, there is thus no beginning and no end to philosophical knowledge, as each category is defined in relation to all other categories without there being a sequentially first or a last point. This is true even if we, as finite thinkers, prefer to proceed from the concept's most abstract to its most concrete categorial determinations (Hegel 1991c: 29–32).

Still, if read in a linear manner, the *Encyclopedia* presents its concept-engendered categories as a 'progress' from the *Logic*'s greatest possible abstraction to the most concrete account of 'philosophy' as truth's self-comprehension. Each category addresses a contradiction in its predecessor and provides a new question that its successor sets out to answer until the category "philosophy" provokes the question "what does philosophical knowledge consist in?" and thereby leads back into the *Logic*'s 'beginning' with 'undetermined being'.

In the *Encyclopedia*'s first part, the '*Logic*', Hegel deduces the concept and argues that the more abstract categories that precede it already *are* the concept, albeit in a self-inadequate form (Hegel 2010a: 509). Once the 'subjective concept' has been deduced, it is shown to turn itself into objectivity and to then unite itself with this objectivity to become the living and manifest ontological truth that Hegel calls "the idea" (Hegel 2010a: §18, 46). This idea has three forms and each major section of the *Encyclopedia* represents one of them, thus defining the entirety of concep-tual truth.

What kind of knowledge do the *Encyclopedia*'s propositions represent? Hegel argues that there is an intellectual desire in every mind-possessing being for the most profound kind of knowledge (Hegel 1991c: 28). Such desire grows out of *Geist*'s eternal need to know itself, its thought and the world (Hegel 1986a: 13, 24). It reaches for answers that are deeper than a collection or even a systematic interpretation of patterns amongst empir-ical facts and events of the past and present or a speculation about the future. It is a curiosity about principles that are unconditioned and unchanging (Hegel 1986a: 14).

These principles enable empirical reality and its changes (Hegel 1986a: 14) they define the eternal 'now' and always have been, are and always will be true (Hegel 1986a: 21). They constitute the origin and the final end of all that empirically exists, function as the absolute condition of all possibility and actuality and define the meaning of life. They even enable the intellectual overcoming of death: to think philosophical truth means to participate in the eternity of its content and in eternal truth's self-contemplation.

When philosophy succeeds in satisfying the thinkers' desire for such ultimate principles, Hegel argues, it speaks with the voice of eternal truth that comprehends itself (Hegel 1986a: 13). Philosophy thus empowers thinkers to comprehend the eternity in which they always already participate and to "enjoy" their own participation in it:

> [In philosophy,] the eternal Idea, the Idea that is in and for itself, eternally remains active, engenders and enjoys itself as absolute [*Geist*]. (Hegel 2007c: §577, 276)

Crucially, the knowledge that philosophy affords is also always *our* knowledge. While the truth thinks itself through us, it also needs us to think itself. Hegel's finite philosopher lets the truth speak for itself, and yet, it takes the philosopher to have it spoken (Hegel 2010a: 10). Despite its unconditionality, philosophical truth is thus available to and enabled by us as self-determining thinkers that are confronted by specific empirical circumstances (Hegel 2008b: 16). Philosophy thus enables the thinker to think through an empirical context and comprehend the reality-immanent, yet unconditioned truth (Hegel 2010a: §236, 299).

While some empirical circumstances might make it more difficult or even impossible for some thinkers to comprehend the truth that governs the empirical world, and while philosophical truth expresses itself through finite means, truth's eternity is not dependent on finitude but vice versa: the empirical world is the 'appearance' of the truth that the philosophers seek to express (Hegel 2010a: §209, 280–1).

To Hegel, philosophical comprehension is thus the closest that a mind-equipped being can ever hope to come to freeing itself from its own finitude as it cleanses the thinker of the influence of irrational historical, social and cultural conditioning and sets her or him free of prejudice, assumptions, stereotypes and dogma (Hegel 2010a: 8–9), stripping away everything that is mere "ephemeral existence, external contingency, opinion, unsubstantial appearance, untruth, illusion" (Hegel 2008b: §1, 17).

Philosophical insight includes the realization that all philosophical thought of the past, present and future is part of the articulation of the one truth. Finite philosophers, including Hegel, thus aspire to be truth's messengers and to relate what they are able to grasp of it (Hegel 1986a: 20). This requires a free act of will on the part of the thinker: one must independently decide to keep philosophy and its truth alive. In an effort to avoid dogmatism, the philosopher must accordingly scrutinize and test every supposedly true statement. This requires a mental attitude that, unlike scepticism, is consciously directed at the truth while allowing for the falsehood as much as for the truthfulness of thought. Philosophical propositions thus have to be constantly tested, potentially reformulated and regained in order for the truth they carry to stay alive and to have actual impact on the contemporary world (Hegel 1986: 22).

Every philosophical proposition or system might thus turn out to be false or to be true only in part and thus stand in need of revision. This includes Hegel's *Encyclopedia* (Hegel 2010a: 33), making it a summons for thinkers to think for themselves and to express in their own language whatever they find to be true in Hegel's and in their own thought. Hegel's readers are supposed to be humbled by and stand in the service of truth, not of Hegel, and appropriate from the *Encyclopedia* only what is true in it: they must reject or reformulate the statements they find to fail the standard of truth.

The *Encyclopedia*'s standing as a most fundamental account of philosophical truth also defines its relationship to Hegel's other works. His lectures on religion, art, history and philosophy discuss the myriad empirical forms that the truth, which the *Encyclopedia* seeks to describe has taken throughout history: by philosophically defining truth in all its forms, the *Encyclopedia* uncovers the rational purpose of the historical manifestations that the lectures discuss in more detail (Hegel 1986: 58).

The *Encyclopedia* thus not only differs from Hegel's other works by virtue of the unity of its presentation, its systematicity and its reach. It also holds the key to a properly systematic comprehension of the entirety of Hegel's philosophical thought and, by extension, to his non-philosophical thought as a whole.

* * * *

The volume offers chapters on each of the *Encyclopedia*'s three sections.

Section 1:   System and the *Logic*

These chapters deal with the *Encyclopedia*'s method and its most fundamental and abstract description of the categories of thought/being. They provide contextualized discussions of the individual parts of the *Logic*, the foundations of Hegel's method and how and why everything in the *Encyclopedia* hangs together in the way it does.

Robert B. Pippin's contribution, "Logical and Natural Life: One Aspect of the Relation between Hegel's *Science of Logic* and His *Encyclopedia* in His *Science of Logic*", addresses the concept of 'life' in Hegel's *Encyclopedia*.

Pippin focuses on the notion that life is a *pure* concept that is knowable non-empirically. But as Hegel also offers two different accounts of life in the *Encyclopedia* – in the *Logic* and in the *Philosophy of Nature* – there arises a question of what the two different treatments say about the concept's purity. Pippin employs the oft-used term "relatively *a priori*" to describe this status of life and thematizes it as a means for grasping the place of the *Science of Logic* within the *Encyclopedia* more broadly.

Sally Sedgwick's piece, "Hegel's *Encyclopedia* as the Science of Freedom", considers the claim made in Hegel's *Logic* that philosophy as a whole can be understood as "the science of freedom" (Hegel 2010a: §5). Sedgwick argues that this fittingly describes his project because it relies on free subjectivity and its feature of generating its own form.

Stephen Houlgate's "Essence in Hegel's *Encyclopedia* and *Science of Logic*: The Problem of Form" addresses differences between the so-called "greater" (*The Science of Logic*) and "lesser" (*The Encyclopedia Logic*) *logics*. Houlgate focuses on the categories of form, matter and content and shows how Hegel's statements in both works are compatible with the notion that he is committed to a single and consistent logical programme.

With a related focus, "The Concept's Freedom", by Jean-François Kervégan offers an "onto-logical" view of the *Logic* as a whole: the *Logic*'s 'concept' is subjectivity and thus freedom. Since objectivity and idea are products of the concept's activity and the *Logic* ends with the absolute idea, the *Logic* ultimately describes (forms of) the concept's freedom.

Section 2: Philosophy of Nature

These contributions are meant to shed light on this relatively dark corner of Hegel's thought, his *Philosophy of Nature*. They do much to give structure to what might seem to be an account long disproven by scientific progress.

Christian Martin's "From Logic to Nature" studies the crucial moments of transition from the first to the second part of the *Encyclopedia* system. He offers two general theses about them. The first is that there is a difference between the *transitional* relation between a *Science of Logic* and a *Philosophy of Nature* and between logic and nature more broadly. Secondly, Martin shows what it means to say that "the concept" is "immanent" within nature: nature exhibits certain regularities and forms that allow it to be known by intellects like ours.

The section's final chapter, "Hegel's Philosophy of Nature: The Expansion of Particularity as the Filling of Space and Time", by Ralph Kaufmann, Ansgar Lyssy and Christopher Yeomans, defends an interpretive framework for the three main parts of Hegel's *Philosophy of Nature* that focuses on space, time and the differences between mechanical, physical and organic processes, finding that mechanical processes 'fill' the space-time continuum in a non-directional manner; physics displays directional processes while organic processes are cyclical in kind.

Section 3:   Philosophy of *Geist*

The *Philosophy of Spirit* consists of three parts, each of which is further divisible into three subsections: (1) "Subjective Spirit" consists of the "Anthropology", "Phenomenology of Spirit" and "Psychology"; (2) "Objective Spirit" of "Right", "Morality" and "Ethical Life"; and (3) "Absolute Spirit" of "Art", "Religion" and "Philosophy". Each of its parts has more than one chapter dedicated to it, with a focus on the section on absolute *Geist* and its three forms: art, religion and philosophy.

In "Hegel's *Anthropology*: Transforming the Body", Jane Dryden addresses an increasingly popular section of Hegel's *Encyclopedia* system through a contemporary lens. She focuses on Hegel's theory of the body as "ownership" and his subsequent association between "nature" and "unfreedom", and discusses the implications of these facets of Hegel's thought for race, gender and disability.

Joshua Wretzel's piece, "Hegel's Critique of Materialism", deals with the opening sections of the "Anthropology" and provides a means to understanding Hegel's metaphysics of mind within the larger context of the *Encyclopedia* system. It develops a "minimalist critique of materialism", a "minimalist conception of immaterialism" and a "transformational conception of materialism" to show how Hegel's metaphysics provides a viable alternative to the "disenchanted" view of materialist philosophy.

Dean Moyar's "Hegel's Psychology: The Unity of Theoretical and Practical Mind" offers an inferentialist take on Hegel's philosophy of mind. Focusing on the theory of "free mind", Moyar argues that this refers to a *capacity to make valid practical inferences*. He shows how this notion connects with Hegel's accounts of theoretical and practical spirit, and also to the logical 'concept' itself.

Paul Redding's "Political Ontology and Rational Syllogistic in Hegel's Objective Spirit" argues that the principles of singular subjectivity that Hegel establishes in the *Logic* also inform his view of political normativity:

his account of modern political life is defined by freedom-informed, critical engagement with social norms in a manner that had to escape classical authors due to their reliance on (quasi-)Aristotelian forms of logic.

In his chapter "Taking the System Seriously: Hegel's Objective Spirit and Its Importance for the *Philosophy of Right*", Thom Brooks defends and illustrates the systematic approach to Hegel's political philosophy. He stresses that it is only by appreciating the *Encyclopedia*'s account of objective spirit and its relationship to the rest of the system that the content of the *Philosophy of Right* can be adequately appreciated. This includes Hegel's accounts of the free will and of the architecture of the *Philosophy of Right* and several of its key concepts.

Turning to the *Encyclopedia*'s final section, on "absolute spirit", Terry Pinkard's "Art as a Form of Absolute Spirit" considers the development of Hegel's thought about art, its relationship to religion and how his statements in the *Encyclopedia* and in the lectures on the subject attempted to capture the rationality that inheres in these. While the development of Hegel's thought on the matter is found to display a consistent concern with the importance of religious art and places religion over art with regard to its ability to function as a stabilizing social force, Hegel's optimism about religion-based progress is found to have possibly been unduly informed by the features of his historical period.

While Pinkard's piece takes a broad view on Hegel's encyclopedic philosophy of art and its connections to other works, Ioannis Trisokkas focuses on what he calls "The Stubbornness of Nature in Art". This refers to the way that nature resists formation by and thereby a complete unity with thought. Trisokkas argues that this is evident in three elements of nature that are all present in art: materiality, natural form and genius. This "stubbornness" gives rise to Hegel's claim that art is absolute spirit only implicitly.

Roberto Vinco's piece, "The *Encyclopedia*'s Notion of Religion", shows how religion is woven into the fabric of Hegel's thought in the encyclopedic system. Vinco contends that Hegel's notion of absolute idealism is, ultimately, a philosophical articulation of a religious worldview, that the Hegelian conception of revealed religion is a modern counterpart to Scholastic theology and that speculative thinking can be regarded as a *cultus* or, in Hegel's terms, a "divine service".

Finally, Sebastian Stein's chapter "Hegel's Concept of Philosophy: Spinozism in Disguise?" analyses Hegel's concept of philosophy to find out in what sense, if any, Hegel could be called a 'Spinozist'. Stein argues that, despite the thinkers' common commitment to the notion that philosophy is "the self-comprehension of unconditioned truth", Hegel thinks that Spinoza's account renders the finite philosophers dependent on truth's self-causing. In contrast, Hegel's concept-metaphysics enables him to argue that individual philosophers still exert control over their thought and remain free in their acts of channelling truth.

This concludes the volume's discussion of Hegel's most systematic work. Its authors and editors are looking forward to continued exchanges about its content with all interested parties and hope the volume will contribute to a wider discussion about the possibility, nature and form of philosophical truth.

CHAPTER I

Logical and Natural Life
One Aspect of the Relation between Hegel's Science of Logic and His Encyclopedia

Robert B. Pippin

1.1 The Logical and the Extra-logical

The least ambitious way to characterize how Hegel wants us to understand the relationship between the *Logic* and the *Philosophies of Nature*
and *of Spirit* in the *Encyclopedia* is that that relation itself entails that the
conceptual structure of any interrogation of nature or spirit cannot be
coherently understood as wholly empirically determined.[1] Each depends
in some way on a non-derived conceptual structure manifested in its pure
form in the SL. This characterization of dependence is not incorrect, but
it does not yet distinguish how Hegel thinks of that relationship in a way
that will exclude the commonsense notion of an empty, subjective pure
form being filled in by objective empirical experience, or imposed on an
extra-logical material. This cannot be right because on Hegel's approach
any such conceptual structure already determines the concrete possibility
of determinately intelligible empirical content. It does not determine or
derive or deduce the content itself (this is clearly denied in §250 of the
PN), but it does determine the inseparable form of any such content as
the intelligible content it is. As he says in the penultimate paragraph of
the EL:

> The method is not an external form but the soul and concept of the content,
> from which it is distinguished only insofar as the moments of the *concept*,

[1] Hegel's works are cited, insofar as it is possible, from the edition of his *Gesammelte Werke* (GW)
(Hegel 1968–). For the *Science of Logic* (SL), the volume number and page are cited. The Cambridge
translation of the *Logic*, by George di Giovanni (Hegel 2010b), has helpfully listed the volume and
page number of the GW in the margins, and his translation is the one used, although I have often
altered it in cases of disagreement. For the *Encyclopedia Logic* (EL) and the *Philosophy of Nature* (PN)
and *Philosophy of Spirit*, I have used volumes 8–10 in the *Werke* (Hegel 1970–1). Passages are cited by
paragraph number. The translation of the EL used is that by T. F. Geraets, W. A. Suchting, and
H. S. Harris (Hegel 1991b).

9

even in *themselves*, in their [respective] *determinacy*, come to appear as the totality of the concept.

Die Methode ist auf diese Weise nicht äußerliche Form, sondern die Seele und der Begriff des Inhalts, von welchem sie nur unterschieden ist, insofern die Momente des *Begriffs* auch an *ihnen selbst* in ihrer *Bestimmtheit* dazu kommen, als die Totalität des Begriffs zu erscheinen. (EL §243)

Contrary to idealisms which hold that external objects depend for their existence or their sense on the subject, Hegel's idealism holds that there is an identity of form between thought and being, and much interpretive energy has been spent trying to understand such an identity.

But in the move to the *Encyclopedia Philosophies of Nature* and *of Spirit*, this all must mean that we should also attend to logical form now understood as in some way inflected by attention to the form of what is wholly other than pure thought in space and time, and the form of human action in the world, including collective human action. Said another way, the *Philosophies of Nature* and *of Spirit* remain *philosophy*. The conceptual structures laid out in both parts still aspire to a kind of conceptual or a priori truth, even if the results of the empirical sciences are everywhere incorporated. But, as already noted, this is not because Hegel thinks of either part as a result of a simple application of the moments of a *Seins- und Wesenslogik* to an external, indifferent, material *Stoff*. In these parts of the *Encyclopedia* too, the method "is not an external form but the soul and concept of the content" (*ist auf diese Weise nicht äußerliche Form, sondern die Seele und der Begriff des Inhalts*). So what is the right way to understand the bearing of the logical, as Hegel understands it, on the extra-logical? In what way are the philosophies of nature and spirit a priori sciences?

1.2 A Transition That Is Not a Transition

Hegel cautions us that the turn to *Realphilosophie* should not be understood as a "transition" in the sense we have become used to within the *Logic*. He writes instead something somewhat mysterious. He writes that the logical idea "freely discharges" or releases (*entläßt*) itself (12.253). He means that the logician can understand this bearing of relevance of the *Logic* on the extra-logical without any qualification on the self-sufficiency and philosophical priority of the absolute idea, even with respect to the "externality of space and time absolutely existing for itself without subject-ivity" (*die absolut für sich selbst ohne Subjectivität seyende Aeusserlichkeit des Raums und der Zeit*) (12.253). This self-sufficiency and priority is not qualified by such a "release." There is no deficiency that the *Realphilosophie* must sublate and correct. Nothing will qualify the logical fact that every-thing intelligible "remains in and for itself the totality of the concept" (12.253). But he does indicate the partiality and so limitation of this speculative truth:

> Secondly this idea is still logical; it is shut up in pure thought [*in den reinen Gedanken eingeschlossen*], the science only of the divine concept. Its system-atic exposition is of course itself a realization, but one confined within the same sphere. Because the pure idea of cognition is to this extent shut up within subjectivity, it is the impulse [*Trieb*] to sublate it, and pure truth becomes as final result also the beginning of another sphere and science.

> Zweytens ist diese Idee noch logisch, sie ist in den reinen Gedanken eingeschlossen, die Wissenschaft nur des göttlichen Begriffs. Die system-atische Ausführung ist zwar selbst eine Realisation, aber innerhalb derselben Sphäre gehalten. Weil die reine Idee des Erkennens insofern in die Subjectivität eingeschlossen ist, ist sie Trieb, diese aufzuheben, und die reine Wahrheit wird als letztes Resultat auch der Anfang einer andern Sphäre und Wissenschaft. (12.253)

This is the problem I would like to address, and I propose to do so by examining the differences between his treatment of the pure concept of life in the SL and the role played by the concept in the PN. Unfortunately, that issue is nested inside many other controversial issues that must be addressed first. So I propose a brief summary of the project of the task of a speculative Logic, and the way life is treated as a pure concept. I will assume that for the most part, the SL is the best source for Hegel's views on the issue, although often the *Encyclopedia* version is illuminating.

1.3   A *Science of Logic*

The SL is the science of pure thinking. By thinking, the German idealists all meant paradigmatically *judging*, judgments being the basic truth-bearers. Kant had argued, and Hegel follows him, that pure thinking's object, that is to say, its direct object, is not the world or any "really real world," but itself, where that first of all means: an inquiry into what it is to be thinking (judging to be the case) at all (what Kant called "General Logic"), the violation of which is not thinking poorly or incorrectly, but not thinking at all. What interested Hegel about any such delimitation is what interested Kant too; the general idea of the suitability of such absolutely universal forms of sense, no matter our actual theory of logic, for a determination of the general features of all possible objects of veridical thought; in Kant the relation between General and Transcendental Logic. This involves the immediate bearing of such logical form on the question of possible objects; the bearing, say, of the subject–predicate form on the claim that objects must sustain a distinction between substances and properties; the bearing of antecedent–consequence relations on there being necessary connections among events. The very idea of such an immediate bearing is proposed by Kant independently of any transcendental deduction, although he thought it was preliminary, what he called only a "clue." It could only be such a clue or potentially guiding thread (a *Leitfaden*) because, for Kant, General Logic is merely formal, and "empty of content." A relation to all possible objects could be established only by appeal to the pure forms of intuition, a restriction that introduced a kind of provinciality in Kant's results, limited as they were to human knowers. This is why Hegel makes his famous remark:

> Critical philosophy did indeed already turn *metaphysics* into *logic* but, like the subsequent idealism, it gave to the logical determinations an essentially subjective significance out of fear of the object ...

> Die kritische Philosophie machte zwar bereits die *Metaphysik* zur *Logik*, aber Sie, wie der spätere Idealismus gab, wie vorhin erinnert worden, aus Angst vor den Objekt den logischen Bestimmung eine wesentlich subjective Bedeutung. (SL 21.35)

But Hegel was willing to claim without qualification:

> Thus *logic* coincides with *metaphysics*, with the science of *things* grasped in *thoughts*, which used to be taken to express the *essentialities of the things*.

> Die *Logik* fällt daher mit der *Metaphysik* zusammen, der Wissenschaft der *Dinge* in *Gedanken* gefaßt, welche dafür galten, die *Wesenheiten der Dinge* auszudrücken. (EL §24)

And,

> The objective logic thus takes the place rather of the former metaphysics which was supposed to be the scientific edifice of the world as constructed by thoughts alone.

> Die objective Logik tritt damit viehmehr an die Stelle der vormaligen Metaphysik, als welche das wissenschaftliche Gebäude über die Welt war, das nur durch Gedanken ausgeführt seyn sollte. (21.48)

There is an immense complication here that would take several essays to sort out. It concerns the notion of "logic" in Kant and then in Hegel. As is well known, Hegel has little confidence that relying on a generally accepted table of logical forms, supposedly handed down by the tradition, is a suitable source for a philosophical theory of pure concepts, and so he relies neither on the standard rules for judgment formation and inference, nor on any modern notion of rules for well-formed formulas and truth-preserving inferences. (His actual claim is to *arrive* at such judgmental and inferential rules at the conclusion of his developmental logic, in the *Concept Logic*, rather than rely on them from the start.) So Hegel's logic is a theory of pure concepts, "thought determinations" (*Denkbestimmungen*), without which thought could not be onto objects at all, or it is from the start an "objective logic," which he tells us means that it could be considered (again already, without any *Leitfaden*) what Kant called a transcendental logic. This can be confusing because in later neo-Kantianism, especially its Marburg variety, Kant's reliance on the usual notion of logic is continued, which, together with their common denial of reliance on a separate faculty of sensible intuition, generated the problem of the bearing of such pure forms of thinking on the sensible world. That is not Hegel's problem because he does not think that, when suitably understood, there is any gap between pure thought and the objective world to be overcome or bridged. But in this context, we must leave the issue at that.

Hegel himself tells us often how to begin thinking about his claim. He does not direct us to Spinoza or neo-Platonism or Christian theology but tells us he is following Aristotle here. The basic unit of sense-making, in Aristotle, in Kant, and in a revised way in Hegel, is the predicative act. In making sense of this way of sense-making, judging, its presuppositions and implications, we are just thereby making sense of what there is, the only sense anything could make as what it distinctly is. (A phrase of Ariyeh Kosman's in discussing Aristotle is relevant here: "predication is nothing but the logical or discursive face of being."[2]) What there is must be determinate, and at the metaphysical level, its "determinations" are just the general predicates without which any specific determination would not be possible, the forms of any such possible specific determination.

As with Aristotle, this link between the order of thinking and the order of being is not an inference; it does not face a gap that must be closed by an inference, or reliance on the intellectual intuition of the rationalist tradition. (His position is not Spinoza's either, for whom there is also no gap to be bridged because there is only one object in the universe, substance; thought and being appear distinct only because of the limitations of

---

[2] Kosman (2013: 127).

finitude.) Properly understood, as noted earlier, the relation is one of identity, albeit an identity that does not confuse judging that Socrates is white with Socrates being white. The identity is an identity of logical form, and is compatible with a difference between an act of judging and a fact. Hegel calls it a speculative identity. This strategy obviously places an enormous amount of weight on properly determining, with necessity, the moments necessary for thinking to be thinking of determinate objects, and this developmental derivation is in effect the Hegelian alternative to Kant's Deduction. It is an argument form that establishes those and just those determinations without which a judging could not be a judging of objects and just thereby also establishes the determinations of objects in their knowability. So the claim for developmental necessity is the *nervus probandi* of the whole project.

It is also important to note this constant debt to Aristotle because it helps to keep clear that the metaphysics Hegel is interested in is not modern rationalist dogmatic metaphysics; it does not concern a "supersensible" reality knowable only by pure reason. In many respects it is a metaphysics of the ordinary; standard sensible objects, especially organic living beings and artifacts. Hegel's project has much more to do with this neo-Aristotelian enterprise than either a neo-Platonist theory of reality, or an attempt to determine the furniture of the universe available only to pure reason, like a monistic substance or monads or ideas. He is reanimating the oldest principle in Western rationalism: to be is to be intelligible. More simply: being is to be treated in the only way it can be treated – in its possible knowability.

But there is also a crucial difference between Hegel and Aristotle, and here Kant re-enters the picture, a picture that then grows much more complicated than it was in Aristotle. Thinking, for Hegel, is in no sense a kind of perceiving. It is a productive power, what Kant called *Spontaneität*. This claim has, in the first place, a logical significance. It means that to judge something to be the case is not to assume an attitude toward a logically structured, independent item, like a proposition. This means that a science of logic cannot be said simply to be transparent to the noetic structure of the world, as if read off the world by pure reason, as in the Wolffian and medieval tradition. Thinking is exclusively discursive. There is no *nous pathetikos*. The categorical structure of being is not simply noetically available to, transparent to, the light of reason. So in saying that pure thinking's object is pure thinking itself, we do not mean that thinking attends to a special object or event. We have to say that it determines its own possibility, and that possibility is a productive power. The interrogation of thinking occurs *by* thinking; just as we know what we believe not by inspecting beliefs, but by being believers. Understanding its metaphysical dimension cannot be understanding it as mirroring the noetic structure of its "other," the real, or the "really real."

1.4 Life as a Logical Concept

In the *Concept Logic*, Hegel treats the concept of life as a pure or logical concept. In his account, this means that we know what it is to be alive, or how we should think about the difference between living and non-living beings, non-empirically. We know it as a result of a general reflection on what is involved in self-consciously judging something to be the case, or somewhat more broadly: in the rendering intelligible of any object or event. This means that any account of what it is to judge self-consciously about objects that did not make possible a priori a distinction between living and non-living beings would be incomplete and thus inadequate. Formulated a different way: if restricted to empirical experience alone, we could make no categorical difference between an iron blade rusting in the moist air and a plant dying for lack of water. Explaining the two events empirically would have the same logical form (and, as I have noted, for Hegel this is equivalent to saying that *the events* have the same form). There clearly is a difference (iron blades don't die), and insisting it's all the same is just foot-stamping dogmatism. So Hegel rejects this identification. In the latter case, the plant is said "not to agree with its concept," not to be functioning as a plant should, and that involves a different logical form. This form is not a heuristic for organizing the results of empirical observation, and not regulative in the Kantian sense and so not subjective in the Kantian sense.

Hegel is fully aware of the skepticism that his proposal will encounter:

> The idea of life has to do with a subject matter so concrete, and if you will so real, that in dealing with it one may seem according to the common notion of logic to have overstepped its boundaries.

> Die Idee des Lebens betrifft einen so concreten und, wenn man will, reellen Gegenstand, daß mit derselben nach der gewöhnlichen Vorstellung der Logik ihr Gebiet überschritten zu werden scheinen kann. (12.179)

As a consequence of this exploration of logical form alone, we are supposed to know that there must be distinct forms of thought specific to the intelligibility of self-organized beings, of perceiving and desiring, self-organized beings, and of self-conscious and rational, perceiving, and desiring self-organized beings, or specific to plants, animals, and human animals. We know what it is to be a living being in a way that cannot depend on discovering this empirically. So how do we know it? This generates a task that is more ambitious than delimiting the features of *that* special logical form required for the intelligibility of living beings or actions or human practices. This demarcation is of crucial importance to Hegel, but he wants also to treat the question in a way that responds to the question Kant raised in the third *Critique*: granted there is this logical difference, *what is its status?* Does the teleological form designate a realm of being that is explicable only by appeal to such a form? Hegel answers yes to the last question; he claims that such distinctive conceptual forms have a necessity that *descends* from his general inquiry into the intelligibility of objects at all (by which, I should note again, I mean: the possibility of self-consciously judging what is the case). The argument is that objects and events would not be available to us in their full intelligibility, if the distinction between living and non-living could not be made. This means that accounts given of non-living beings would be insufficient on their own terms without a distinction between living and non-living.

This desideratum is difficult to state properly, and raises a very large issue immediately. First, just as Kant did not attempt to deduce the necessary *existence* of events in causal relations, but sought to show that any event that did exist must stand in a necessary relation to some prior event, and just as Kant did not try to deduce the necessary existence of living beings, but tried to show that any world that required mechanistic explanations of what exists, or any world in which change is a matter of efficient causation, must also allow, cannot rule out, that there are changes like gestation, birth, growth, reproduction, disease, and death, which cannot be properly accounted for by the logical form appropriate for non-living beings, so Hegel is not out to deduce a priori the necessary existence of living beings, but has an ambition similar to Kant's (that is, such changes cannot be properly accounted for by the logical form appropriate for non-living beings) but much more ambitious because he denies that teleological explanations are merely subjectively necessary.

Hegel's objections to Kant are clear and they bear directly on Kant's skepticism about the objectivity of the concept of life. For Kant a living being requires us to think something we cannot know, how the whole causes the parts which cause it. Over and over again in the *Kritik der Urteilskraft* (KU), Kant insists that it is the absence of any acceptable model of teleological causation, and the absurdity of any backwards causation, that makes it impossible for teleological explanation to have any objective status. But for Hegel, this simply assumes not just the *distinguishability* of whole and parts but their temporal *separability*, and that is Kant's basic confusion. However, a living being's reproduction according to kind makes clear that in such reproduction there is no puzzle about the production of parts which make a whole possible, which *then* also makes the parts possible by causing them. The generation of whole and parts is simultaneous, as in all cases of final causality. The reciprocal relation between whole and parts exists from the moment of conception, and the only real causation at work in the world is efficient causation, internally in the organism's processes and generatively. These causal series, however, cannot explain reproduction according to kind, the unity of an organism, the regularity of the occurrences of the series, the self-maintenance of an organism, illness, or even the lawfulness of nature. We therefore propose judgments about the series; we systematize the series in a way that need not presuppose a creator or bizarre temporal relations, but must see them as rule or norm bound to avoid unmanageable contingency.[3] We have of course a much better understanding of how the DNA "blueprint" is actualized, but the sequences alone still require us to think of what is happening as a defined process with a beginning and end, as the growth of an individual of a kind. Thinking we can understand the parts causing the whole and in a separate moment, some sort of backward causation moment, the whole causing the parts is not the discovery of a problem but its question-begging invention, question-begging with regard to final cause explanation that does not rely on a designer, or on forwards and backwards causation. It is an explanation that explains, in Hegel's terms, by reference to a concept. ("Because that is what leukocytes are for.")[4] Kant's argument is that we would not even understand what we are claiming

---

[3] I am agreeing here with Ginsborg:

> This is what I think Kant has in mind when he says that the "concept of connections and forms of nature according to purposes" serves as a principle "for bringing nature's appearances under rules where the laws of causality according to the mere mechanism of nature do not suffice" (§61, 5:360). It is only by interpreting organic phenomena in normative terms – as conforming (or failing to conform) to rules of the proper functioning of organic beings – that we can bring lawlike order to the otherwise incomprehensible diversity of the organic world. This is why we need the concept of purpose as a heuristic principle or guiding thread for the observation and investigation of organisms, independently of any questions that might be asked about how organisms came to be. (Ginsborg 2001: 254)

The question for Kant remains why, if this is so, the teleological principle remains a heuristic.

[4] There is a clear analysis of the importance of reproduction according to kind, and so "the intimate relation of taken and type" in Kreines (2015: 97–100). See also Kreines (2008) on the importance of Aristotle for Hegel's account.

unless we were making appeal to an entity "as if designed," but that argument rests on his invocation of a form of causality we cannot understand except by analogy with design according to concepts, and Hegel sees no reason for such a commitment in understanding living beings.[5] There is a whole because of the parts by virtue of efficient causation. But there are parts because of the whole in a different sense of "because" that is just as objective because just as necessary for the event's intelligibility, given the basic premises of the *Logic*. The thing's concept is necessary for its specification as the thing-kind it is, and without this concept, we could not even identify the parts as parts. This is not an equivocation; it is doing justice to the two sorts of dependence in their joint realization.

But the substantive case for the necessity of the concept of life is a kind of logical foreshadowing of the issue we are pursuing. (That is, its structure foreshadows the structure of the PN.) It concerns the incompleteness of the concepts of mechanism and chemism, and the attempt to show that they require the concept of life in order to be fully coherent themselves. I turn to a brief summary of that argument.

1.5   The Necessity of Life

The section on Objectivity in the *Concept Logic* raises many interpretive questions and is embedded in the complex project we have only crudely sketched. But it is clear that Hegel is treating each of the three main divisions as candidates for what counts as *The* Concept, each as an a priori claim about what renders the world sufficiently intelligible, counts as the comprehensibility of the whole. Another way to put this would be to say that mechanism and chemism are to be treated as metaphysical claims, not merely models of explanation. Explanation is one thing; a genuine understanding or comprehension, one that takes a stand on what there is, is another. (In philosophy of science this is the difference between positivist and realist philosophies of science; between being satisfied with causal laws that support robust counterfactuals, and appealing to the fundamental

---

[5] See Ginsborg (1997: 332–3). As Ginsborg suggests, we could invoke "conformity to normative law" as what distinguishes teleological explanation without a commitment to an alien form of causality (Ginsborg 1997: 339). This would still, for Kant, push the question back to a reformulation; whether such normativities are "real." For that, on Kantian premises, we would need to appeal to a nonmaterial substrate or a designing God, neither of which we will ever be entitled to. See Kreines (2015: 85–91). (I don't see that it helps much to point out, as Kreines does (Kreines 2015: 90), that Kant's skepticism can be stated without a global commitment to efficient causation, because he can appeal to a "supersensible real ground of nature" (KU 409). *All* that is knowable, however, is efficient causation, and that suffices to rule out *knowledge* of final causality.)

forces of nature. Mechanism claims to be a full account because it assumes that all there really is dynamical matter in motion.) The full claim in mechanism is that, paradigmatically, Newtonian mechanics, the calculation of the effects of dynamical matter in motion, counts as such sufficiency in comprehension or rendering intelligible. But Hegel points out that these interactions are treated as "indifferent" relations of matter in motion, and the regularity of the attractive and repulsive forces is wholly a matter of contingency, even when such regularities are so regular that such a claim for mere constantly repeated contingency can seem like magical thinking and is implausible.

Some material bodies have to be understood as having "natures" of some sort that allow and prohibit such interactions, paradigmatically the presence of chemical compounds. Appeals to such chemical natures ground and explain such combinability in ways mechanism never could.

Yet chemism too faces a limit. Mechanical and chemical accounts cannot sufficiently explain the workings of artifacts. Hegel appears to think that we led to such a notion by the simple co-presence of both mechanical and chemical explanations, the regular unity of which is as inexplicable or as merely and implausibly contingent as in the mechanism case. He is thinking of being led to explanations like "the gear does that because it is a watch gear and the watch should keep correct time" and of being unable to account for it in mechanical or chemical terms. This is the concept of simple, "external" or designer-made purposive wholes, and he tries to show how one would be led from such a teleology to "internal" teleology, where the combined mechanical and chemical relations do not sufficiently explain, say, the workings of the kidney, and where no reference to an intentional designer is possible. This introduces the concept of life, said to be the "immediate" manifestation of the idea itself. This is important for our purposes, since it is at the heart of Hegel's explanation of the difference between what he calls "logical life," or life as it is studied by Logic, and life as a concept in the philosophy of nature and in the philosophy of spirit.

For life as a pure concept, what is important is that organic beings reproduce according to kind; their life-activity in general, including reproduction, is "for" its concept, for its specific form of life, and such activity can go well or poorly. This process of striving self-realization, never more than this process, but always in the process of living, means that a being's life is never simply "achieved." The life form, though, itself perdures beyond the death of any individual, and this will be a valuable element in understanding the absolute idea.

So, a living being is "for" its kind (it does what it does to realize the life form it is), and its mere individuality is "sublated" even while still real. (No living being can lead its life as individually determined, as if everything about its life were "up to it." It *is* the life form it is, the universal.)

In sum, life is the immediate manifestation of the Idea because its distinctive modality of being at work, its *energeia* or substantial form, is an immediate form of self-determination. A living being is, while not self-consciously, determining for itself its life process. It leads its life we say, seeking its food, avoiding its predators, reproducing in its way, etc. And this is the beginning of the different treatments in the philosophy of nature and of spirit.

That is, the SL is a theory of *pure* thinking, and in that context, we seek the *pure concepts*, thinking's a priori determination of its own norms, without which any object could not be determined to be what it is, could not be what it is. This is Hegel's account of first philosophy. But first philosophy does not exhaust philosophy. First philosophy distinguishes the first-order question "what is it?" from the question "What is it to say what something is?" and tries to answer the latter. The former question can be empirical ("What is electricity?") But it need not be. ("What is *Geist*?" is a philosophical question, but not a topic in a SL.) This is his version of the distinction between general and regional ontology. How to pose and pursue the latter sort of questions is a topic unto itself. In first philosophy, pure thinking's determination of itself, not just *qua* the truth of objects, but as itself, represents, ultimately, Hegel's unconditioned; pure and absolute, self-conscious intelligibility; the intelligibility of intelligibility itself, the Absolute, *noesis noesios*.

1.6 The Logic of a Philosophy of Nature

But what is the nature of still philosophical but not purely logical questions? By comparison, in Kant's system, once the critical project had delimited the subjective conditions for the possibility of experience, morality and the realm of *Zweckmäßigkeit*, the "transition" to a metaphysics of nature (*Die metaphysiche Anfangsgründe der Naturwissenschaft*) and a metaphysics of, in effect, *Geist* (*Die Metaphysik der Moral*) is made unsystematically. Kant needs only one material concept, matter in motion, to achieve the former, and a concept of human finitude with two dimensions (that we cannot achieve our ends without aid, and that we must develop our talents to be able to make use of them) to achieve the latter. Hegel of course rejects the whole model of transcendental philosophy, subjective conditions, the unsystematic importation of an empirical concept, and the application of conditions to the empirical world. (What I want to argue, however, is that Hegel's conception of a philosophy of nature and of spirit is, surprisingly, as unsystematic as Kant's but in a very different sense.) The comparison with Kant only sharpens the question of how *Hegel* thinks of his own notion of thought's "release" from the "self-enclosed" world of pure thinking, what he had mysteriously called the *Reich der Schatten*. (He continues such characterizations in the *Philosophy of Nature*, by the way, pointing out that the richness and vitality of nature become, "in the quietude of thought" or in terms of its logical status, rather like a "dull northern fog" (PN §246, Z) (*zu gestaltlosen Allgemeinheiten, die einem trüben nördlichen Nebel gleichen*)).

In the introductory discussion of Life in the SL, he begins such a discussion with the following offhand remark:

> A comment may be in order here to differentiate the logical view of life from any other scientific view of it, though this is not the place to concern ourselves with how life is treated in non-philosophical sciences but only with how to differentiate logical life as idea from natural life as treated in the philosophy of nature, and from life insofar as it is bound to spirit.

> Es kann nur etwa zu bemerken seyn, inwiefern die logische Ansicht des Lebens von anderer wissenschaftlicher Ansicht desselben unterschieden ist; jedoch gehört sicher nicht, wie in unphilosophischen Wissenschaften von ihm gehandelt wird, sondern nur wie das logische Leben als reine Idee, von dem Naturleben, das in der Naturphilosophie betrachtet wird, und von dem Leben, insofern es mit dem Geiste in Verbindung steht, zu unterscheiden ist. (12.180)

The distinctness of the logical treatment of life is something we have already discussed and which he stresses here by comparison: "In the idea of life the moments of life's reality do not receive the shape of external actuality but remain enveloped [*eingeschlossen*] in conceptual form." (*Eben so erhalten in der Idee des Lebens die Momente seiner Realität nicht die Gestalt äusserlicher Wirklichkeit, sondern bleiben in die Form des Begriffes eingeschlossen.*) (12.180). About life as treated by the philosophy of nature, he says: "As treated in the philosophy of nature, as the life of nature and to that extent exposed to the externality of existence, life is conditioned by inorganic nature and its moments as idea are a manifold of actual shapes." (*Das Leben, insofern es in die Äusserlichkeit des Bestehens hinausgeworfen ist, an der unorganischen Natur seine Bedingung hat, und wie die Momente der Idee eine Mannigfaltigkeit wirklicher Gestaltungen ist.*) (12.180).

This difference with logical life also means that, contrary to logic as a whole, in the philosophy of nature, its end is not its beginning, but a limit in which it sublates itself, that is, becomes the philosophy of spirit. Finally: "In nature life appears as the highest stage that nature's externality can attain by withdrawing into itself and sublating itself in subjectivity." (*In der Natur erscheint das Leben als die höchste Stufe, welche von ihrer Aeusserlichkeit dadurch erreicht wird, daß sie in sich gegangen ist, und sich in der Subjectivität aufhebt.*) (12.180).

These are all fragmentary hints at an explanation of the *Encyclopedia*'s structure, and there is a more concrete account, although equally fragmentary, in the concluding remarks of the SL, which indicates an interesting *practical* motivation for what Hegel had called the "expansion" (*Erweiterung*) of the *Logic* into these further domains. It is exactly the purity, the strict apriority of the domain of logic that calls for such an expansion as an impulse or *Trieb*:

> Because the pure idea of cognition is to this extent shut up within subjectivity, it is the impulse to sublate it, and pure truth becomes as final result also the beginning of another sphere and science.

> Weil die reine Idee des Erkennens insofern in die Subjectivität eingeschlossen ist, ist sie Trieb, diese aufzuheben, und die reine Wahrheit wird als letztes Resultat auch der Anfang einer andern Sphäre und Wissenschaft. (12.253)

That is, it is precisely the absolute self-sufficiency of the realm of logic (that thinking and only thinking can determine the *Denkbestimmungen* of knowing and the knowable) and not any deficiency that propels thinking to raise for itself the question of its shape in the domain understood abstractly as the pure other of thinking, the non-thinking, nature. Hence his claim that there is no real transition here. He describes what would have been a transition as:

> What is to be grasped, therefore, in the sense that the idea freely discharges itself, absolutely certain of itself and internally at rest.

> ... ist also hier vielmehr so zu fassen, daß die Idee sich selbst frey entläßt, ihrer absolut sicher und in sich ruhend. (12.253)

He closes the book with a sweeping account of the completion of the *Encyclopedia*, one that returns us to his early characterization of the ground of a presuppositionless logic as a resolve:

> But what is posited by this first resolve of the pure idea to determine itself as external idea is only the mediation out of which the concept, as free concrete

existence that from externality has come to itself, raises itself up, completes this self-liberation in the science of spirit, and in the science of logic finds the highest concept of itself, the pure concept conceptually comprehending itself.

Dieser nächste Entschluß der reinen Idee sich als äusserliche Idee zu bestimmen, setzt sich aber damit nur die Vermittlung, aus welcher sich der Begriff als freye aus der Äusserlichkeit in sich gegangene Existenz emporhebt, in der Wissenschaft des Geistes seine Befreyung durch sich vollendet, und den höchsten Begriff seiner selbst in der logischen Wissenschaft, als dem sich begreifenden reinen Begriffe, findet. (12.253)

We will not be able to understand the role of such notions as resolution and releasing or discharging itself without understand the penultimate conclusion of the SL in the unity of the theoretical and practical idea, but the idea is one Hegel shares with Kant, that reason is not a mere tool for making inferences, but, as they both say, a purposeful activity (*zweckmäßiges Tun*), that reason is a living activity dedicated to a final end, the unconditioned in Kant, and Absolute knowledge in Hegel. That impulse has other dimensions too, as we have just seen. But our task now is to examine in closing whether these rather fragmentary remarks in the SL have prepared us for the different treatment of life in the philosophy of nature.

One aspect of it we can discuss economically, I hope. That is Hegel's claim that the root of all logical movement is contradiction. In this case the practical and conative language is not metaphorical, because what Hegel is referring to is always *an essentially practical contradiction*, an *activity's* contradiction of its own end, something clearer, I hope, if we recall Kant's account of the inherent purposiveness of reflective judgment and the hypothetical use of reason. Take, for example, the kind of things he says about the necessity of any development, that of the empirical sciences for example. He will often say things that seem outrageous philosophically: that philosophy gives the form of necessity to what would otherwise appear merely contingent (EL, §12A). This can sound as if Hegel wants to say that the actual course of that development, philosophy can prove, could not have happened otherwise, as if, in science as well as philosophy (logic), there is a development over time that could not have been otherwise. If this sort of claim is supported by a claim about a self-transforming, underlying metaphysical entity, "cosmic spirit," or "God," developing according to some necessary law of internal teleology, then the claim seems hopeless. At a more modest level, though (and this is very much how I think he wants to be understood), he could mean that a significant transition in art history, or political history, or religious history, a shift in collective ethical commitments, or a development in a speculative logic (that the content of some determinate concept cannot be fixed without reliance on a successor, more comprehensive concept) can all be rendered intelligible by a philosophical account. This account is based on a form of practical contradiction that introduces a more familiar form of necessity and one different from logical necessity or material necessity, the form appropriate to "he who wills the end *must* will, or necessarily wills, the means" (otherwise we have evidence that he has not willed the end). If a collective attempt to accomplish some goal can be said to learn collectively that commitment to that end is impossible without commitment to, let us say, a broader and more comprehensive end, then it must pursue such a new end or give up the enterprise. Or, if it develops that the means chosen actually make achieving the end impossible, then the means *must* be altered. They are not arbitrarily altered. They *must* be altered, on pain of practical incoherence. A philosophical account, assuming the rationality of such a teleological enterprise, can show this. It can give the form of (practical) necessity to what would otherwise seem contingent alterations. (So if reason can be said to have an end indispensible to its possible realization, any means indispensible to that end are likewise indispensible, necessary in that sense. This sort of argument plays out at the highest level of conceptual abstraction for Hegel.)

1.7   The Theological Version

The most important result from the above account is that there is no "transition" in the logical sense from the *Logic* to the PN. (This is also why any model of application or imposition of the *Logic*, or it being "filled in" by empirical details, is impossible.) This means that there is no logical or conceptual incompleteness in the SL. It remains wholly self-determining, autonomous and complete in itself, a perfect identity of logic and metaphysics. There is rather some sort of existential – I don't think there is any other word for it – dissatisfaction with a conceptual order "shut in on itself," and a resolve to examine nature as it is treated by the individual sciences in all its manifold forms. This resolve is to understand what Hegel calls, in the Introduction of the PN, the "self-determination" of the concept (*in seiner eigenen, immanenten Notwendigkeit nach der Selbstbestimmung des Begriffs*) (PN §246) in the "thinking" relation to nature, first of all in physics. And his descriptions of this relation are systematically rather imprecise. He says:

> Physics must therefore work together with philosophy so that the universalized understanding which it provides may be translated into the concept by

showing how this universal, as an intrinsically necessary whole, proceeds out of the Concept.

> ... die Physik muß so der Philosophie in die Hände arbeiten, damit diese das ihr überlieferte verständige Allgemeine in den Begriff übersetze, indem sie zeigt, wie es als ein in sich selbst notwendiges Ganzes aus dem Begriff hervorgeht. (§246A)

And,

> The determination and the purpose of the philosophy of nature is therefore that spirit should find its own essence, its counterpart, i.e. the Concept, within nature. The study of nature is therefore the liberation of what belongs to spirit within nature, for spirit is in nature in so far as it relates itself not to another, but to itself. This is likewise the liberation of nature, which in itself is reason; it is only through spirit, however, that reason as such comes forth from nature into existence.

> Dies ist nun die Bestimmung und der Zweck der Naturphilosophie, daß der Geist sein eigenes Wesen, d. i. den Begriff in der Natur, sein Gegenbild in ihr finde. So ist das Naturstudium die Befreiung seiner in ihr; denn er wird darin, insofern er nicht auf ein Anderes sich bezieht, sondern auf sich selbst. Es ist dies ebenso die Befreiung der Natur; sie ist an sich die Vernunft, aber erst durch den Geist tritt diese als solche an ihr heraus in die Existenz. (§246A)

Nature then is the idea in pure otherness, and what Hegel calls the metaphysics of nature is the concept of the idea in its otherness. The impulse to sublate this otherness by recognizing the structure of the Idea in such otherness is largely treated by Hegel as a practical impulse. Those of you who know paragraph §247 in the PN will know that to make clear what he means, Hegel indulges in something like a riot of theological metaphors. (This had begun in §246 where Hegel has called Nature the bride of spirit and compared its relation to spirit with Adam telling Eve that she was flesh of his flesh.)

All of this means that there is no general discussion in the *Philosophy of Nature* of life as such. Life as such is a topic for the *Logic*, not the PN, which treats only the variety of living beings, having assumed life as such. Rather, such a logical structure is assumed, again as absolutely self-determining and self-sufficient of the intelligibility of nature and Geist, and all the attention is devoted to the empirical content of the sciences of Hegel's day, "interpreted," we might say, or as he said, "translated," in such logical terms. We try to understand first the model of explanation provided by mathematical mechanics, until we reach astronomy, and then shift attention to metereology and topics that begin to indicate the central conceptual move of chemism, as Hegel explores phenomena that in his day suggested the role of non-mechanical explanations, magnetism, galvanism, fire, and then, rather suddenly, plants and finally animals. But the conceptual relations among these moments of what the *Logic* had called Objectivity are assumed rather than demonstrated. Hegel wants only, as it were, to exfoliate what he simply calls "*wie in jeder Stufe der Natur selbst die Idee vorhanden ist.*" This manner of treatment preserves and realizes the way Hegel had introduced the project by means of those theological images mentioned earlier. None of his characterizations suggests that anything about the metaphysical sufficiency of the concept as the truth of all actuality requires such a demonstration, however.

That is, Hegel always keeps faith with the idea that the Concept, *der Begriff*, is, on this account,

> the true Idea, the divine idea of the universe, the sole actuality.

> ... ist sogleich die wahrhafte Idee, die göttliche Idee des Universums, die allein das Wirkliche ist. (PN §246)

He makes clear that it is this, this philosophical point, that Plato expressed by saying that God alone is truth. (Of course, Plato, not a Christian monotheist, never said any such thing. Hegel means to refer imagistically to the doctrine of ideas, and in the *Republic*, to the Idea of the Good.) But it is this theological language that allows him to repeat in one final form the question of the transition out of the *Logic* that we have been raising. Namely, with the concept understood as the self-sufficient truth, that is God, why create the other of God, nature? And he uses yet another word to discuss this dissatisfaction with such self-sufficiency.

> If God is all sufficient and lacks nothing, how does He come to release Himself into something so clearly unequal to Him? The divine Idea is just this self-release, the expulsion of this other out of itself, and the acceptance of it again, in order to constitute subjectivity and spirit.

> Ist Gott das Allgenügende, Unbedürftige, wie kommt er dazu, sich zu einem schlechthin Ungleichen zu entschließen? Die göttliche Idee ist eben dies, sich zu entschließen, dieses Andere aus sich herauszusetzen und wieder in sich zurückzunehmen, um Subjektivität und Geist zu sein.

In the *Phenomenology* the term had been Luther's for *kenosis*, *Entäusserung*, and in the *Logic* it had been *entlassen*.

What I am suggesting is that this question, "why would God create the natural world?," is quite an unusual, figurative way to understand the question "why would a wholly autonomous self-determining thought turn to a consideration of its bearing on nature and spirit?" What is the significance of such a set of topics? The theological interpretation usually turns on some image of the overflow of God's love to explain his "emptying himself out into the world," and Hegel makes use of this image in his own way in the introductory material of the *Concept Logic*. But the explanations we have seen in the PN all rather suggest that there is something practically unsatisfying, painful – one is tempted to say, philosophically lonely – in being shut up, *eingeschlossen*, in the *Reich der Schatten* or in *einem trüben nördlichen Nebel*.

CHAPTER 2

Hegel's Encyclopedia *as the Science of Freedom*

Sally Sedgwick

In the Introduction to his 1817 (Heidelberg) *Encyclopedia*, Hegel describes philosophy as "the science of freedom [*Freiheit*]" (§5).[1] The remark is curious for a variety of reasons. For one thing, Hegel's *Encyclopedia* includes among its three divisions the science of nature; and nature, on his description, is a realm of *un*freedom.[2] For another, the science of logic is a division of the *Encyclopedia* as well, and once again, it is hard to see why Hegel would suggest that logic is a science of freedom. Hegel's *Science of Logic* is concerned with thought's "determinations and laws" rather than with action (HE §12). At least if we consider the science of freedom to take as its object features of human action, it is not clear why the *Logic* should belong within its purview. Moreover, if all of Hegel's system is "the science of freedom," as he asserts, the implication would seem to be that freedom – or the science that has freedom as its object (namely the science of spirit [*Geist*]) – must be more fundamental, somehow, than the other two sciences. But Hegel presents the three divisions of his *Encyclopedia* as equal parts or determinations of the whole; he doesn't arrange the divisions hierarchically, at least not in any obvious way (HE §§11, 37).[3]

---

[1] Hegel (1968–: vol. 13). Hereafter I refer to this work as ("HE"). I sometimes consult and alter the English translation, Hegel (1990a). Where necessary, and in my references to all of Hegel's texts, I give page or section numbers first of the German edition and then of the English translation. When I quote from Hegel's Additions (*Zusätze*), I rely on the *Theorie-Werkausgabe* edition of his works, Hegel (1970–1).

[2] Although Hegel is committed to the view that all organic nature possesses powers of self-motion, he argues that only humans have the capacity of freedom. See §381 of his *Enzyklopädie der philosophischen Wissenschaften im Grundrisse, Zweiter Theil: Philosophie des Geistes (1830)*, in Hegel (1968–: vol. 20) (hereafter "EG").

Even highly complex non-human animals lack the capacity for thought; they cannot bring any content or object "to consciousness [*zum Bewußtsein bringen*]." See Hegel's *Enzyklopädie der philosophischen Wissenschaften im Grundrisse, Erster Theil: Die Wissenschaft der Logik (1830)*, in Hegel (1968–: vol. 20, §2) (hereafter "EL").

[3] Hegel explicitly notes that each part of the philosophical system is equally part of the whole also in EL §15.

In describing philosophy as "the science of freedom," Hegel is very likely not forgetting the aims and objects proper to his sciences of nature and of logic. He seems to want to privilege freedom in *some* way, and perhaps what he has in mind is the following: he designates each of his three sciences as "philosophical," and he describes philosophy as the "thinking about thinking [*Denken des Denkens*]" (HE §12).[4] Thinking, on his account, is an activity only creatures possessing freedom can perform.[5] Perhaps the message Hegel wishes to convey when he describes his system as "the science of freedom," then, is simply that thinking in general, and therefore also philosophy in each of its three divisions, is an act and expression of freedom.[6]

This interpretation is plausible, but it risks trivializing Hegel's thesis. Interpreted in this way, the thesis that philosophy is "the science of freedom" reduces to the claim that since philosophy is an activity that can be pursued only by thinking and therefore free [*geistig*] natures, each division of the encyclopedic system is an instance of the science of freedom.

My task in this chapter is to argue that Hegel's thesis is not trivial, and that we can discover evidence of this already in the introductory paragraphs of the 1817 edition of the *Encyclopedia*. In explaining why philosophy is a "science of freedom," Hegel makes the following remark: philosophy is a science of freedom, he says, "because in philosophy the heterogeneity of topics and with it the finitude of consciousness disappear" (HE §5). Hegel gives us little help deciphering this remark in these pages, but we can venture some guesses about what he has in mind. He presumably means to compare philosophy – in each of its three divisions – to a form of consciousness or subjectivity, one that is "free," presumably, because it somehow overcomes finitude.[7] Less obvious is the connection Hegel draws between freedom and the disappearance, in philosophy, of a "heterogeneity of topics." Very likely, his point is that a heterogeneity of parts 'disappears' in philosophy, because philosophy on his conception is a systematic unity rather than an aggregate of heterogeneous or contingently related parts. Although he does not say so explicitly here, Hegel models the whole of

---

[4] In philosophy, thought itself is made the "object of thought [*Gegenstande des Denkens*]" (EL §17).
[5] Thinking is "my activity [*Tätigkeit*]," the "*product of my spirit*" – of my "*freedom*" (EL §23).
[6] In beginning our philosophy, he says in EL, all we have is the "free act of thinking ... *producing its own object for itself* ... and *giving it to itself*" (EL §17).
[7] Finite consciousness, for Hegel, is excessively "subjective" and "contingent"; it lacks awareness of its universal character. A finite or unfree consciousness is infected with bad "idealism," he furthermore suggests, in that it "sees itself as something particular in contrast to objects" (HE §5). By contrast, the version of idealism Hegel prefers is one in which the "contingency" and "necessity of nature" "fall away" (HE §5). It is a system that doesn't consider the thought-determinations of its science as mere representations, and hence as one-sidedly subjective, but as objective in some way.

philosophy on the idea of an organic totality.[8] In an organism, as he understands it, the arrangement of parts is internally generated rather than imposed from without. An organic totality is both cause and effect of itself; it is similar to a *free* nature in this respect.

My purpose in reviewing these passages is simply to provide textual support for my suggestion that that there is more to Hegel's remark that philosophy is "the science of freedom" than we might initially suppose. Superficially, his message is that philosophy is an activity in which only thinking and therefore free natures can engage. His deeper point, I believe, is that we can discover in each of the three divisions of his system properties that mirror the nature of free subjectivity.

In this chapter, I confine my attention to just one division of the *Encyclopedia*, namely the *Science of Logic*, and explore what Hegel might mean by implying that it is a science of freedom. How can Hegelian freedom illuminate features of the *Logic*, such as its structure, aims, and presuppositions? Hegel describes freedom as an "achievement" that results from a progressive development, and in his works on the philosophy of right and of history, for instance, he has a complicated story to tell about the factors that move the process along.[9] He gives us a progressive developmental account in the *Logic* as well – not of freedom but of what he refers to as the "Concept [*Begriff*]." I want to explore how Hegel's treatment of development in the idea of freedom can help us understand the progression, in the *Logic*, of the particular determinations or specifications of the Concept. How and out of what do the determinations get generated? Why is the direction of the progression, in both cases, from more to less abstract; and what connection is there, if any, between the progressive development and human freedom?

2.1   Features of Hegelian Freedom

Hegel is persuaded that there has been progress, in human history, in the implications we associate with the idea of freedom and in our conception

---

[8] As he writes in ¶2 of his Preface to the *Phenomenology*, the whole of philosophy is an "organic unity," where "each [form or part] is as necessary as the other, and the necessity of each alone constitutes the life of the whole." The parts of philosophy are not simply derived from or deduced out of the idea of the whole (HE §8). Instead, the whole of philosophy depends upon its parts for its very possibility. The idea of philosophy makes possible its parts or divisions; their content may be "justified" only as "a moment of the whole" (HE §7). (See also EL §237A.)

[9] In his *Lectures on the Philosophy of History* (Hegel 1988a) (hereafter "PH"), for example, Hegel asserts that freedom "does not exist as an original and natural state." It must be "achieved and won through an endless process involving the discipline of knowledge and will" (PH 73/43). The general trajectory of the history of the idea of freedom, he says, is from "imperfect to the more perfect" (PH 92f./6of.).

of ourselves as free; there has been progress as well in the kinds of demands we make in the interest of sustaining and satisfying our self-conception.[10] The concept "progress" implies development versus mere change – that is, it implies necessary versus accidental connection. Only because we can discover necessary connection in the history of the idea of freedom is it possible for us to give an account of how the 'higher' versions of the idea emerge in response to deficiencies in the 'lower' ones. Our commitment to the thesis of necessary connection is what allows us to explain, for example, how Rousseau's treatment of the nature and demands of freedom was both a response to and an improvement upon that of Hobbes.

The interpreter of this Hegelian progressivist story faces the special challenge of identifying the factors that move the transitions along. What conditions must be in place to generate the advances from lower to higher levels? Does the fact that the advances are necessary mean, for Hegel, that they are fated or pre-determined? Is there no place for contingency in this developmental story? I am going to suggest the general shape of Hegel's answers to these questions by considering his description of transitions in the earliest developmental stages of the idea of freedom. I will be emphasizing respects in which both the idea and the experience of freedom are for Hegel initially empty and abstract. In addition, I will try to clarify his reasons for asserting that the movement forward is in the direction of a richer, more perfect conception of freedom. Although Hegel represents the movement as a development and therefore as necessary, I will argue that he nonetheless grants that it depends on contingent factors.

Just *how* is the idea of freedom with which Hegel's developmental story begins initially empty and abstract? Freedom first appears on the scene as an object of awareness in what he describes as a natural condition, a condition prior to the formation of a state. Freedom is an object of awareness only for creatures like us, creatures capable of thought and therefore also of self-consciousness. But creatures like us do not just think; we seek to give our thoughts existence. We possess, in addition, a will.[11]

---

[10] The progress is tied to the way in which human subjectivity has gradually had success in overcoming finitude and subjectivity in order to achieve a place where reason is "altogether by itself [*durchaus bei sich selbst*]" (HE §5).

[11] The will is "a particular way of thinking – thinking . . . as the drive to give itself existence." The will is indeed "thought translating itself into existence [*das Denken als sich übersetzend ins Dasein*]" (Hegel 1968–: 14:1, §4A) (hereafter "PR"). See also PR §§11, 57.

The freedom of which we are aware and which we exercise at this initial
stage is empty and abstract in a number of respects. In the state of nature,
the particular will is a psychological egoist, motivated above all by the
desire to satisfy its own physical and psychological needs. It becomes aware
of itself as free only when it encounters a certain kind of obstacle, only
when conditions of scarcity force it to compete for goods with creatures
significantly like itself. Confronted with other thinking animals, it discovers the need to signal what it becomes aware of as its right to put its will
into things and appropriate them as its own. It becomes conscious of itself
as a bearer of right, that is, as a "person."[12]

The idea of freedom at this stage is empty and abstract, Hegel argues,
because it refers to nothing more than the particular will's right to make things
its own in pursuit of its private purposes. At this stage, the particular will's
freedom is essentially a freedom from the interference of other persons. The
particular will in the natural condition knows that it must sometimes compete
with creatures like itself, but it isn't yet aware that its right to things is based on
a feature of itself that it *shares* with other thinking natures. Because it so far
ignores what Hegel refers to as the "universal" aspect of itself, it does not
recognize or care about the rightful claims of other wills. The particular will of
abstract right does not yet "will the universal as such" (PR §103).[13]

The freedom experienced in the state of nature is abstract and empty for
the further reason that the natural condition, as Hegel describes it, is not
truly a state of freedom at all. Following Hobbes, Hegel portrays the state
of nature as a system of right that is more coercive than free (PR §94); it is
a state "governed by force [*Zustand der Gewalt*]" (PR §93). In a situation in
which particular wills are relatively equal physically and psychologically,
and in which there is no law and order (because there is no all-powerful
sovereign to keep the peace, and no system of impartial and effectively
enforced laws), what remains is a condition in which each will seeks the
satisfaction of its own ends and by any means. The result is a condition of
perpetual insecurity and fear, a Hobbesian "war of all against all." As Hegel
puts it in the Heidelberg *Encyclopedia*, the natural condition is one of
"violence and injustice, of which nothing truer may be said than that one
ought to depart from it" (HE §415).

Hegel's story of development in the idea of freedom thus begins with
creatures in a state of nature, creatures endowed with the special capacity of

---

[12] "Personality contains in general the capacity for right" (PR §36).
[13] From the particular will's point of view, *it* is the bearer of right, and "*someone else* has the
corresponding duty" (PR §155; my emphasis).

thought as well as the drive to make thought existent. The idea of freedom – more precisely, the thinking animal's awareness of its right to put its will into things – is first awakened when a particular will is forced to compete with other creatures similarly capable of expressing their will. At this stage, the particular will doesn't recognize those other beings as significantly similar to itself and therefore as likewise bearers of right. The particular will is blind, too, to the extent to which the nature of some of its needs and desires is intimately tied to its relations to others. Nor does it yet appreciate that it can most effectively express and realize its freedom in a system governed by impartial judges and laws, a system that promotes and defends the freedom of all versus only some. The poverty or emptiness of this initial idea of freedom is evident in the failure of this system of abstract right to sustain itself, for on Hegel's analysis, the state of nature is in effect a state governed by force.

So much for the empty and abstract nature of our initial idea of freedom. How does *contingency* enter this Hegelian story? It does so in at least two respects. First, the way in which we tell the story depends on our particular vantage point. From the vantage point of Hobbes, the story begins with a depiction of the state of nature and ends with what he takes to be the best remedy for the inconveniences of such a state. The Hobbesian story ends with subjects transferring their natural right to judge and punish (that is, their right to a system of private justice) to an absolute sovereign. From a different vantage point, however, the story has a different plot and follows a different trajectory. For Rousseau and Kant, for example, it begins with the conflicts they take to result from the Hobbesian conception of sovereignty. Their plot is largely driven by the perception that these conflicts must be resolved, and that what is needed is a form of state power that is not absolute in the Hobbesian sense and thus not experienced by subjects as external or coercive. Their story ends with the emergence of a new idea of what counts as a legitimate source of practical law. The new idea proposed by Rousseau and Kant is that law will be experienced by a subject as legitimately authoritative and therefore as non-coercive only if the subject is able to discover the source of law not in some external or alien power, but in itself.

The point most deserving emphasis here is that our tale of the unfolding of the idea of freedom is shaped by our particular vantage point. The Hobbesian, the Rousseauian, the Kantian, and even the Hegelian conceive of the overall trajectory of history – including its beginning and its end – differently. Indeed, one of the larger messages of Hegel's history of human freedom is that it is a history composed of evolving conceptions of the

conditions and nature of freedom and right, as well as of evolving conceptions of who we are as free natures. Hegel wants us to appreciate that in any
historical narrative, the problems we single out as demanding a solution, as
well as the tools we have available for solving them, reflect our place in
history, a place that is not a product of choice.

The second respect in which contingency shows up in the history of
human freedom is this: not all features of the various stages in the history
are expressions of choice. Although any developmental story must for
Hegel be pieced together from connections he considers necessary, this
doesn't imply that he must be committed to the thesis that accidents play
no role whatsoever in the historical narrative. Hegel doesn't, for example,
hold that, in a state of nature, the situation of scarcity is one we choose.
Nor does he suggest that we ever had the option of being fashioned more as
altruists than as egoists. Although he of course defends a thesis of human
freedom, he does not hold that our freedom is wholly unlimited. Not only
do we have to contend with situations that are not of our own making, but
such situations also have the potential to shape the form our freedom takes.
The story of our freedom would surely have followed a different course, for
instance, were our natural condition a situation of plenty rather than of
scarcity.

If we take these contingencies seriously, we have to accept the implication that, on Hegel's account, the history of human freedom could have
unfolded differently. Admittedly, he sometimes conveys the impression
that he thinks otherwise. He writes in a passage from his *Lectures on the
Philosophy of History*, for example, that what drives the advances in freedom
from the "imperfect to the more perfect" is the "internal impulse of
spiritual life, the drive to break through its own shell of naturalness,
sensuality, and self-estrangement" (PH 92f./60f.). The reference to the
"internal impulse of spiritual life" in this remark might tempt us to suppose
that Hegel takes the idea of freedom to be fully formed or determinate
from the start, and to rely on contingent factors merely for its awakening or
activation. But if our foregoing discussion is on target, development in the
idea of freedom is shaped by thought's engagement with situations that are
by no means entirely within its control. When Hegel writes of the "internal
impulse" of spiritual life, what he arguably has in mind is not a pre-given
and fully determinate idea, but rather thought's drive to give itself existence. Just *how* thought gives itself existence isn't entirely left up to thought
itself. Nor does thought generate entirely out of its own resources the story
we tell about its unfolding. Hegel looks back at the course of history and
discovers that spirit has left its "shell of naturalness" behind and now

experiences itself as less self-estranged. He doesn't generate his historical narrative *ex nihilo*. His narrative reflects his unique place in history.[14]

2.2   Features of Hegel's Logic

What do the features of freedom I just outlined reveal about the aims, structure, and argumentative strategy of Hegel's *Science of Logic*? In particular, how do they illuminate Hegel's suggestion that the *Logic*, along with the two other divisions of his system, is "the science of freedom"? As we've seen, Hegel is committed to the view that there is development in the idea of freedom. He likewise holds that there is development in the concepts of the *Logic*. The idea of freedom on his account progresses from abstract to concrete; the same is the case regarding the progressions in the *Logic*. The idea of freedom is initially maximally empty, and this is likewise true of the first concept of the *Logic*. In common with the history of freedom, the *Logic* begins with a bare capacity, namely our capacity for thought.[15] The logical progression follows a path of ever greater concreteness, from thoughts that are initially empty and abstract, to thoughts that are increasingly rich and determinate, and as such increasingly adequate categories of being and vehicles of knowledge. As developmental, the story moreover connects concepts "not in an accidental but in a necessary way" (HE §39/§40).

Hegel describes his *Logic* as the "science of thinking [*Wissenschaft des Denkens*]" and as the "thinking about thinking" (HE §12).[16] Its proper object is not some specific object or class of objects (such as God or nature) but thought itself, or more precisely, thought's "determinations and laws" (HE §12). The *Logic* concerns thoughts of concrete objects only and solely *as* thoughts; in this respect, its objects are "pure abstractions" (HE §12).[17]

---

[14] Philosophy is "*its own time considered in thoughts*" (PR 15/21). See similar remarks in PH: "each individual is the child of his people, and likewise . . . the child of his time . . . No one is left behind his time, nor can he overstep it" (PH 87/55). For a recent and very different (and far more Kantian) account of Hegelian freedom, see McDowell (2017).

[15] Hegel writes that "science presupposes nothing except that it is pure thought" (HE §36). This is a point about science in general, including the *Logic*. Consider again his remark in EL §17: in beginning our philosophy, all we have is the "free act of thinking . . . *producing its own object for itself* . . . and *giving it to itself*."

[16] In EL, Hegel describes the content of the *Logic* as "nothing other than its own thinking" (EL §19; see also §24A2).

[17] See also Hegel (1968–: 21:13/34) (hereafter "SL"). In EL §24A2, Hegel remarks that, in the context of the logic, thoughts are considered in this way: "they have no other content than that which belongs to thought itself and which is generated by thought." The objects of the *Logic* are the pure thought forms considered in abstraction from their application to any particular kind of object, whether an object of nature (of empirical intuition) or an object of geometry (of pure intuition).

I want to explore the idea that there is a parallel between the beginning
of the *Logic* and the beginning of the history of freedom. In my review of
the freedom case, I suggested that the story does *not* begin with a pre-
given and fully formed idea. It begins with a capacity that, in combination with contingent situational factors, results in the production of
specific concepts or ideas. I will argue in this section that the same is true
for the *Logic*. To make good on this claim, I need to show that the
concept with which the *Logic* begins is initially empty and accrues
determination only once the progression gets under way. I must also
meet the greater challenge of showing that – as in the freedom case –
accruing determination depends on factors that are contingent. I will
suggest that Hegel awards contingency a role to play, even though he
describes the progressive generation of concepts in the *Logic* not just as
"necessary" but as produced by "logical deduction [*logische Ausführung*]"
(HE §39/§40).

I turn, first, to address the following question. In what respect is the
beginning of the *Logic* empty? Its initial concept is that of "pure being,"
which Hegel describes as "pure thought [*reiner Gedanke*]" and "simple
immediacy [*einfache Unmittelbare*]" (HE §38/§39). The fact that the
concept "pure being" is a "simple immediacy," he says, implies that it
"can neither be mediated nor further determined" (HE §38/§39). Hegel's
point seems to be that the concept "pure being" possesses no mark or
attribute by means of which we can say anything more about it than that it
is "both pure thought and simple immediacy."

It is worth considering Hegel's reasons for beginning the *Logic* in this
way. In the first section of his Introduction to the Heidelberg *Encyclopedia*,
he notes that other sciences *fail* in their efforts to begin from a standpoint
of immediacy. Other sciences, he says, typically take some object or
"doctrine" or "classification" as an "immediately given" "representation
[*Vorstellung*]" (HE §1). They do so, because they seek to rest their science
on solid ground – on some premise or assumption that is beyond doubt
and that can serve as a foundation for further concepts and laws. These
sciences "fail" in this endeavor, on Hegel's account, because they are
insufficiently self-critical. They take themselves to begin with immediacy
and hence with certainty (HE §1), but they do so without warrant. Even
Kant, who insisted upon the necessity of a criticism or meta-critique
supposed to occur outside the actual practice of science, failed to subject
his presuppositions to sufficient critical scrutiny. As Hegel puts it, the
"demand made fashionable by Kantian philosophy, that prior to actual
cognition the faculty of cognition should be investigated critically" at first

seems "plausible," but Kant seems not to have appreciated that "this investigation is itself cognitive" (HE §36; see also EL §41A1).

It is tempting to suppose that, in starting with "pure being," Hegel's aim is to convince us that *his* effort to begin with immediacy succeeds where others fail. According to this line of interpretation, Hegel is committed to the thesis that the *Science of Logic* improves upon the efforts of other sciences to start from scratch. For precisely this reason, it is suggested, the *Logic* begins with a concept that is defined as wholly indeterminate, as not question-begging, and as something of which we can be absolutely certain (HE 38/§39). But on a different (and I believe more accurate) reading, the point of Hegel's discussion is to persuade us that any effort to begin with simple immediacy is a false start; it is "untrue [*nicht wahrhaft*]," as he sometimes says (HE §38/§39).[18]

"Pure being" is a false start, because "pure being" on Hegel's description is an "empty abstraction [*leere Abstraktion*]"; it is indeed "something unsayable" (HE §39/§40).[19] The fact that pure being is unsayable becomes evident when we reflect on what it means for a concept to stand for or represent "pure thought and simple immediacy." There is nothing obviously unsayable about the definition of pure being as simple immediacy. The definition conforms to the norms of intelligibility; it is grammatical, and we know what the words composing it mean. But problems become apparent when we consider the definition's implications. As simple immediacy, the concept of pure being can in Hegel's words "neither be mediated nor further determined" (HE §38/§39). Lacking all determination, "pure being" effectively stands for nothing and can be equally well expressed as the concept "nothing" (HE §39/§40).

This implication is paradoxical enough, but Hegel draws our attention to further problems.[20] If "pure being" is wholly indeterminate, then it gives us grounds for asserting neither its identity nor its difference from the concept "nothing." For if we are to be entitled to assert that identity or difference, we must be able to discover in "pure being" some attribute or determination that warrants us in doing so (HE §39/§40). We cannot discover determination,

---

[18] Truth is demonstrated not at the beginning, but only as the "result of philosophical knowledge" (HE 6/46). Hegel makes this point again in his PR where he writes that all thinking must begin "from a point not demonstrated." Our starting point is "immediately relative" and later recognized to be a "result" (PR §2).

[19] "On the basis of pure immediacy, [pure being] is nothingness – something unsayable" (HE §30/§40). Pure immediacy or pure being *"cannot be said"* (EL §87). Because it in fact already contains mediation, pure being is not "truly [*wahrhaft*]" the first (EL §86).

[20] In EL §88, Hegel writes of the 'apparently' "paradoxical [*paradoxer*]" nature of the proposition "Being and Nothing are the same."

however, in a concept that we define as simple immediacy and that, as such, *lacks* all determination. In at least these respects, the concept of pure being is unsayable. When we consider the concept's implications, we discover its instability and internal contradictions.

Hegel's aim in these first paragraphs of Part One of the *Logic* is therefore not to try to improve upon other efforts to begin from a standpoint of immediacy. Instead, he seeks to convince us that such efforts are ill-fated. He explicitly alerts us to the fact that he begins his *Logic* with a concept that, on his own estimation, is "untrue."[21] If our starting point is simple immediacy, we effectively begin with what cannot be said. We give ourselves no way to move forward – no means of grounding our science or generating further concepts.[22]

The way forward, then, requires us to *negate* our initial concept – or, as Hegel puts the point more positively, it requires us to give our initial concept "more precise specification and truer definition" (HE §39/§40).[23] We move forward by acknowledging that if we are to say anything meaningful about "being" at all – even just that it is either identical to or different from nothing – we have to assign it some determination. Doing so doesn't require us to wholly dispense with the concept but rather to understand it in a new way, in particular, as no longer "pure" being or "simple immediacy."[24] Attributing to the concept "being" some determination is precisely what allows us to advance to the less abstract and therefore truer concepts of "becoming," "determinate being," and so forth.[25]

The message I especially want to extract from this tale of the transition from "pure being" to the 'higher' or 'truer' concepts is a message about how

---

[21] We initially 'take' pure being as our beginning; that is, we think we can start with pure immediacy. But we learn that, in fact, pure being "contains a mediation" (HE §38/§39). We learn that the "truth" of being and nothing is their "unity" (HE §40/§41). As Hegel notes in PR, philosophy "must begin somewhere"; it must begin "from a point not demonstrated." But the starting point is "immediately relative" and shows up later as a "result" (PR §2).

[22] For a different account of the beginning of the *Logic*, one that persuasively emphasizes its metaphysical implications, see Houlgate (2018).

[23] The basis of all determination, for Hegel (following Spinoza), is negation (EL §91A).

[24] Hegel notes that the only thing *really* "immediate" about the concept of pure being with which we began is that it serves as our initial starting point (HE §3, EL §238).

[25] For the sake of brevity, I have skipped any discussion of the role of the concept of "becoming" which Hegel describes as exhibiting attributes both of being and of its opposite, namely "nothingness" (HE §40M/§41B). "Becoming" is the unity of being and nothingness. It is "inward unrest" in that it is "pure being," recognized as unstable, as containing mediation or negativity ("pure being" passing over to or becoming "determinate being" (see also EL §§88, 238)).

For a fine recent discussion of the way in which the concepts of Hegel's *Logic* come to be as the result of a "genetic" developmental process, see especially §3.2 of Heidemann (2019). Heidemann argues that, in this and other respects, Hegel distinguishes himself from the rationalists of the seventeenth and eighteenth centuries.

the latter concepts come to be, on Hegel's account. In the *freedom* case, we begin with a capacity, namely with the will (that is, with thought's drive to give itself existence). A will is triggered into action in response to conflict, and conflicts result from a constellation of various factors, some of which are not products of choice. In the *logic* case, we likewise begin with a capacity – the capacity of thought seeking to express itself in the form of concepts and judgments.

It is tempting to suppose, however, that the analogy ends here for at least two reasons. First, in the *Logic*, we're in the realm of pure thought and our objects are abstractions; they lack spatial as well as temporal dimension.[26] It is not obvious, then, that we can discover in the *Logic* anything analogous to the contingent situational factors that partially constrain the development of our idea of freedom. I will address this worry in my final section, but I first want to turn my attention to a second apparent disanalogy. Hegel writes that, in the *Logic*, the way forward requires us to appreciate that our initial concept, "pure being," contains an "implicit" content or determination; our initial concept implicitly contains the concepts "nothing," "becoming," "determinate being," and so forth (HE §40/§41).[27] We might take Hegel's reference to "implicit" determination to imply that the concept "pure being" is fully formed from the start; it possesses *pre-given* marks or subordinate concepts. The concept's marks are "implicit" in that they are not yet known by us; they become explicit once we subject it to analysis. On this reading, the story of the development of concepts in the *Logic* is significantly *unlike* Hegel's treatment of development in the idea of freedom, as I just presented it.

But this interpretation leaves a great deal unaccounted for. Hegel doesn't argue that the transitions in the *Logic* come to be thanks simply to thought's proficiency in dividing complex concepts into their constituent parts. That is, the transitions don't just result from our quest for clarity – from our efforts to make explicit the various marks of a complex concept. To put the point differently, the transitions don't derive merely from what Hegel describes as "the drive to find a fixed significance [*der Trieb ... eine feste Bedeutung zu finden*]" (HE §39/§40; see also EL §87). Hegel identifies as the "moving soul [*bewegende Seele*]" of development not analysis but rather "dialectic" (HE §15).[28] Dialectic is the moving soul of

---

[26] Concepts are not "sensible representations"; they have neither spatial nor temporal extension (EL §20).

[27] Hegel describes a dialectical process as one of "*development [Entwicklung]*," "through which only that is posited which is already implicitly present" (EL §161A).

[28] Every moment in the progression is *both* analytic and synthetic (EL §238A).

"all life," he says, as well as of all "scientific progression" (EL §§81, 81A; see also PR §31). Dialectic directs our attention to concepts we take to have fixed significance and 'negates' them. Its negation is not a mere discovery of what is already there; it is instead an *alteration* or *transformation* of what is already there.[29] As a transformative and productive force, dialectic on Hegel's account *generates* "determinate content" (HE §16; EL §81).

Again, my aim is to challenge a certain interpretation of what Hegel has in mind in referring to the "implicit" determination of a concept. On that interpretation, he holds that the concept with which the *Logic* begins, the concept he characterizes as the most abstract, is fully determinate at the start. The concept is abstract and empty only insofar as its determination is initially unknown to us. The position I am defending, in contrast, is that conceptual determination or form is *not* given at the start but instead gets *generated* out of a process that requires dialectic as well as analysis. Dialectic, in Hegel's view, produces determinations that are "implicit" in a concept not because they are pre-given, but simply because they are logically possible.

An Addition (*Zusatz*) from the 1830 *Encyclopedia* supports my reading of what Hegel has in mind by "implicit" determination:

> [A] plant develops from its germ: the germ already contains the whole plant within itself, but in an ideal way, so that we must not envisage its development as if the various parts of the plant . . . were already present in the germ *realiter*, though only in very minute form. This is the so-called Chinese box hypothesis [*Einschachtelungshypothese*], the defect of which is that what is present initially only in an ideal way is regarded as already existent. What is correct in this course of its process, however, is just that the Concept [*Begriff*] remains at home with itself in the course of its process, and that the process does not posit anything new as regards content [*Inhalt*], but only brings forth an alteration of form [*Formveränderung*]. This nature of the Concept, which shows itself in its process to be a development of itself, is what people have in view when they speak of the ideas that are innate in man, or when they say, as Plato himself did, that all learning is merely reminiscence [*Erinnerung*]; but, all the same, *'reminiscence' should not be understood to mean that whatever constitutes the content of a mind that is educated by instruction was already present in that mind previously in its determinate unfolding.* (EL §161A; my emphasis)

The main lesson I believe we should draw from this passage is that Hegel rejects a certain version of the innate ideas hypothesis. We are warranted in

---

[29] By means of "reflection [*Nachdenken*]" on what is given in "sensation, intuition, or representation," "something changes [etwas *verändert*]" (EL §22).

asserting that the germ of a plant "already contains the whole plant" only if we do *not* take this to imply that all the stages and shapes of the plant's development are present in the plant at the start, like a plan or blueprint. Whether in a plant or in the idea of freedom or in the "Concept," development describes necessarily connected stages or moments of or in a single thing. What alters, on Hegel's account, is "form." Crucially, however, we are not to suppose that new or 'higher' forms are "already present" in 'lower' forms. That is, we are not to consider the appearance of a new form on analogy with the recollection of a previously existing one.[30]

In another passage in the same text, Hegel describes the movement of thought in the *Logic* as "the self-developing totality of its own peculiar determinations and laws, that it *does not already have and find given within itself, but which it gives to itself* [*die es sich selbst gibt, nicht schon hat und in sich vorfindet*]" (EL §19; my emphasis). Thought performs its function not just by analyzing what is already there; thought can also bring into being determinations that, as Hegel says here, it "does not already have and find" in itself. There is a lesson to be learned, from this remark, not just about what Hegel means by the implicit determination of a concept, but also about his claim that his *Encyclopedia of Philosophical Sciences* – including his *Logic* – is "the science of freedom." Thought can be a genuinely creative or productive power; it can generate new concepts and not just analyze already given concepts. Likewise, a truly free subject does not on Hegel's account merely respond to forces that are already there; she is capable of taking what is already there and producing something new from it.[31]

2.3   Freedom and Temporality in the *Logic*

A moment ago, I called attention to a further apparent disanalogy between the freedom and logic cases. This disanalogy concerns the role that contingent factors play in the two sciences. In section 2.1, I suggested that Hegel grants that contingent situational factors actually *shape* the development of the idea of freedom, that is, they contribute to the idea's determination or

---

[30] For further critical remarks on the innate ideas hypothesis, see also EL §67.

[31] In an intriguing passage in his *Lectures on the Philosophy of History*, Hegel notes that in the case of free natures, there can be a gap between their concept or "inner determination" and its realization – between what he refers to as "the implicitly determinate nature of the seed and the adaptation of its existence thereto" (PH 89f./58). In virtue of their "inner determination," free natures participate in their self-production and are thereby capable of creating themselves. In the case of a non-human organism, by contrast, "nothing can come between the concept and its realization." Presumably, Hegel means to imply that in the case of a human organism it *is* possible for something to "come between" its "concept and its realization." It is possible, precisely because human organisms are capable of freedom.

form. I went on to ask how there could be anything similar to this in the *Logic* case. The *Logic* is the "science of thinking," and its objects are "pure abstractions" (HE §12).[32] How could contingent situational factors have a bearing, then, on the nature and development of the concepts of the *Logic*? Needless to say, the answer to this question very much depends on how we understand Hegel's characterization of thoughts as "pure abstractions." It could after all be the case that the thoughts or concepts of the *Logic* are abstract in some respects but not others.

Hegel suggests that the concepts of the *Logic* are most obviously abstract in that they are significantly different in nature from sense impressions. Thoughts, on his account, are not "sensible representations"; they are neither sense impressions nor empirical objects. They are unlike both, because they are universals rather than singular representations (EL §20).[33]

Thoughts or concepts are in addition abstract in that they lack spatial and temporal extension. Thoughts lack spatial extension because they are not the kind of thing that fills space, nor do we locate one thought or concept to the left or right of another. The *non-temporal* nature of thoughts or concepts, however, is less obvious. After all, we do sometimes say (as Hegel does) that a certain idea came into existence at a certain time and sparked a series of subsequent ideas. Hegel is nonetheless committed to the thesis that the concepts of the *Logic* lack temporality in some way. He tells us that their "content [*Inhalt*]" "is not affected [*behaften*] by time"; their content does not pass away or change (EL §20). Hegel surely cannot mean by this that the thoughts or concepts of the *Logic* undergo no change whatsoever. As we saw, the concept we initially understand as "pure being" passes over into the concepts "nothing," "becoming," and so forth. The entire *Science of Logic* is an exploration of conceptual development; and the dialectical method that moves the progressions along is meant to reveal what he refers to as the 'plasticity' of concepts.[34] When Hegel claims that

---

[32] In the context of the *Logic*, thoughts are considered in this way: "they [have] no other content than that which belongs to thinking itself and which is brought into being by means of thinking" (EL §24A2). So, the objects of the *Logic* are the pure thought forms considered in abstraction from their application to any particular kind of object. Compared with the *Logic*, the other two divisions "appear as applied logic." The concern of these other two sciences "is only to [re]cognize the logical forms in the shapes of nature and spirit, shapes that are only a particular mode of expression of the forms of pure thinking" (EL §24A2).

[33] Logic belongs to the "spiritual" or "supernatural [*Übernatürliche*]" world, not to nature or the realm of the physical (SL 10/31f.). See Mure (1940: 108) on how space and time for Hegel belong to the sphere of nature and not to the *Logic*.

[34] See, e.g., the final paragraphs of Hegel's Preface to the second edition of that work where he refers to concepts as "*plastisch*." What alters or develops, according to Hegel, is a concept's "form" (he writes here of "*Formveränderung*") (EL §161A).

the "content" of ideas or concepts is fixed, he simply means to highlight a necessary condition of our identifying development in anything at all. Development is development *of* or *in* something – *of* or *in* some "content" we take to be fixed. When we take some content to be fixed, we award that content no temporal dimension in that respect.

The *Logic* is furthermore abstract, for Hegel, in that it does not set out to provide a record of the chronological appearance of concepts. The *Logic* does not, in other words, concern itself with mere temporal sequence. For precisely this reason, Hegel insists that his *Logic* is not an instance of what he calls "external" history. External history, in his words, "gives the form of a contingent succession to the stages of the Idea's development" (EL §13).[35] The *Logic*, however, concerns itself with *necessary* conceptual connections rather than with "contingent succession" or mere change.[36]

In at least these respects, then, the concepts of the *Science of Logic* are abstract and have neither spatial nor temporal extension. Crucially, however, none of this implies that the concepts of the *Logic* have no temporal dimension whatsoever. It could be that the concepts of the *Logic* as well as their development are in some way indebted to temporally locatable historical conditions. It could be the case, too, that the freedom of thought that moves the dialectic forward originates in a temporal domain, in nature and/or history. The view I am proposing is that the plot and trajectory of the *Logic*, as well as Hegel's choices about how the story begins and ends, reflect his own unique place in history. In my remaining final paragraphs, I say a few things to motivate this interpretation.

We can appreciate the point that there is a temporal or historical dimension to the *Logic* if we consider why the development, as Hegel portrays it, takes the particular shape that it does, and why he chooses to begin and end the science just as he does. In my discussion of the freedom case, I asserted that the shape of our historical narrative rests on the vantage point from which we tell it. The trajectory of freedom's course appears one way to the Hobbesian and another way to the Kantian; each assigns the story a different beginning and a different plot. The same is true, I am now suggesting, in the case of the *Logic*. For Hegel, but not for Parmenides, the

---

[35] Although Hegel grants that the "same development of thinking that is presented in the history of philosophy is presented in philosophy itself," that development is in philosophy "free [*befreit*]" of any historical "externality [*Äußerlichkeit*]"; in philosophy, we are "purely in the element of thought" (EL §14).

[36] For a good discussion of the respect in which logical development in Hegel is not temporal, see Petry (1970: 25). Petry challenges efforts of Darwinians to "present Hegel as the philosopher of evolution" and argues that we should instead understand development in the context of Hegel's *Logic* not as evolution over a period of time but rather as development from what is simple to what is complex.

story introduces a Heraclitean perspective into our understanding of the
nature of concepts – a perspective that takes their sense or "form" to be in
flux rather than fixed. Likewise, for Hegel but not for Locke or Kant, the
story includes a chapter that lays out a radically new way of thinking about
the relation of the concept "appearance" to that of "essence," a way of
thinking that purportedly harmonizes what the earlier philosophers took to
be a rigid opposition.[37]

In effect, what I am proposing is that Hegel's *Logic*, like his history of
human freedom, is a story told from a point of view, one that reflects not
just the work he has already completed in the *Phenomenology* but also the
spirit of his age. His choice to begin the *Logic* as he does (with "pure
being") isn't arbitrary. He has an agenda; he sets out with a purpose in
mind. In undertaking to attack the thesis of simple immediacy, he is
guided by his idea of where the story must end up. His own philosophical
system, no less than other philosophical systems, is not a product of pure
spontaneity; it is, as he says, a "result [*Resultat*]" of previous philosophical
systems (EL §13).

No doubt, some will grant that the beginning of Hegel's *Logic* is not
arbitrary but nonetheless insist that it is not historically conditioned either.
These critics will tell us that the beginning of Hegel's story, and the shape
of its unfolding, is (on Hegel's own account) conditioned not by his
contingent place in history but rather by the nature of thought itself.
They will remind us that the *Logic* deals with pure abstractions that, as
such, have no temporal dimension. They will quote passages in which
Hegel remarks that philosophical development is "free [*befreit*]" of "historical externality [*geschichtlichen Äußerlichkeit*]" (EL §14) and in which he
asserts that his science "presupposes nothing except that it is pure thought"
(HE §36). But what position is really being attributed to Hegel, here, and
in precisely what respect does his science presuppose nothing? The idea is
supposed to be that although Hegel repeatedly chastises *other* thinkers for
failing to make good on their claims to begin without presuppositions, *he* is
remarkably able to succeed. *His* starting point is *truly* self-evident and as
such worthy of immediate and universal assent.

I suspect that this kind of response rests on a confusion about the message
Hegel means to convey when he insists that his science "presupposes nothing

---

[37] "The logical is to be sought in a system of thought-determinations in which the opposition
[*Gegensatz*] between the subjective and the objective (in its common meaning) falls away
[*hinwegfällt*]" (EL §24A1). Told through the eyes of Kant, in contrast, the story of conceptual
development does *not* consist in an attack on the "fixed determinations" of the logic of the
understanding.

except that it is pure thought." When Hegel contrasts his science with other purported sciences, his point is not that the latter begin with presuppositions and his does not. His point is rather that his science self-consciously takes its beginning to be, as he says, "awkward [*Unbequeme*]"; his beginning is in other words a problem that derives from the fact that its object, as he puts it, "immediately and necessarily provokes doubt and controversy [*zugleich dem Zweifel und Streite notwendig unterworfen is*t]" (HE §2). All thinking has to begin somewhere, but every beginning, Hegel says, is initially "ungrounded [*unbegründetes*]" and "anticipatory [*anticipirtes*]" (HE §§4, 11). Truth cannot be taken for granted at the start; it must be established or demonstrated (HE §3). The demonstration is possible only as the "result of philosophical knowledge" (HE 6/47).

When Hegel writes, then, that a true science "presupposes nothing except that it is pure thought," his point is that a true science is self-critical in a way that less true sciences are not. He does not commit himself to the assumption that his starting point is self-justifying or self-evident.[38] He does not assume that his thinking possesses the special power to start its reflections from nowhere and to thus abstract all contingency away. After all, were Hegel attributing to himself this kind of abstractive power, he would in effect be awarding himself a form of freedom he believes none of us possess – a freedom to transcend [*überspringe*] our time in thought (PR 15/21). In effect, he would be awarding himself the power to start from a standpoint of simple immediacy, a standpoint he believes philosophy in his time has revealed to be "untrue."

In what respect is Hegel's *Science of Logic* "the science of freedom"? I've argued that, in common with the other two branches of his encyclopedic system, the *Logic* shares features Hegel associates with the nature of free subjectivity. The concepts of the *Logic* originate in our capacity for thought, a capacity that seeks to express itself. Thought for Hegel is a genuinely creative power; it expresses itself not just by analyzing what is already there but also by transforming what is already there. Thought's "implicit" form isn't given as determinate at the start. Thought generates its determinate form, and it does so in response to factors that are not wholly within its control.

---

[38] When Hegel says in the 1830 *Encyclopedia* that all presuppositions "must ... be given up when we enter into the science," his point is likewise that none of our presuppositions should be simply taken for granted. As he puts it, "all determinations ... must first be investigated" (EL §78).

CHAPTER 3

Essence in Hegel's Encyclopedia and Science of Logic

The Problem of Form

Stephen Houlgate

Hegel concedes that his *Encyclopedia* contains an abbreviated version of his philosophy.[1] His *Encyclopedia Logic* (EL) does not, therefore, present the detailed analysis of categories we find in the *Science of Logic* (SL), and some categories derived in SL are omitted from EL altogether.[2] In one part of Hegel's logic – the doctrine of essence – there is a further significant difference between EL and SL: the categories of *form*, *matter* and *content* are considered at different places in the two texts. In SL they are examined in the chapter on *ground* (see SL 389–97). In EL, however, form and matter are not introduced until the categories of *existence* and *thing* have been derived from that of ground, and form and content are considered together with the category of *appearance* (see EL §§127–34).[3]

This "relocation" of form, matter and content leads David Kolb to argue that in EL Hegel presents a different logical sequence from the one in SL and that this challenges one common understanding of his logic. Kolb notes that, for many commentators, Hegel's logic is meant to be "unique and self-determining" (Kolb 2010: 42).[4] He also maintains, however, that the two versions of the logic of essence both make "good points" and this makes it difficult to recognize which sets out the true derivation of the categories (Kolb 2010: 45–6). Indeed, it suggests that "there is not necessarily one best version"

---

[1] Hegel (2010a: 5, 8, 43 [§16]) (henceforth EL). Reference is made in this chapter to the 1830 edition of Hegel's *Encyclopedia*, unless otherwise indicated.

[2] Omissions include various forms of measure and the different forms of reflexion. See Burbidge (2006: 110). Note that page references to SL are to di Giovanni's translation of the *Science of Logic* (Hegel 2010b). Note, too, that I have occasionally altered the translations of both EL and SL.

[3] Note, too, that the category of *condition*, considered in the ground chapter in SL, is moved in EL to the section on actuality (see EL §§146–8).

[4] Kolb has several commentators in mind, including Richard Winfield and William Maker, but he cites my views (Houlgate 2006) "as representative" of the interpretation he wishes to challenge (Kolb 2010: 41).

(Kolb 2010: 50). This in turn undermines the idea that Hegel's logic is "unique and self-determining".

There is also another problem to be considered. Kolb maintains that form, matter and content are conceived in the same way in EL and SL, even though they are located in different logical contexts. In "a unique self-development of pure thought", however, categories should "find their identity through their location in the sequence", and "when they are moved they should change their nature and meaning". The fact (as Kolb sees it) that Hegel treats form, matter and content as "relocatable fragments", which preserve their meaning wherever they are inserted, suggests again, therefore, that Hegel's logic is not the "unique and self-determining" logic that (on many interpretations) he claims it to be (Kolb 2010: 53).

In this chapter I will respond to Kolb's challenge by examining the differences between EL and SL to which he draws attention, and I will endeavour to show that, *pace* Kolb, they do not undermine the idea that Hegel's logic is "unique and self-determining".

3.1   Essence and Reflexion in SL

In SL essence is initially conceived not as substrate or possibility, but as "absolute negativity" (SL 342). Such negativity can be understood, in contrast to the immediacy of being, as sheer *non*-immediacy.[5] In the sphere of being, Hegel maintains, categories and things are inextricably connected to other categories and things, but they nonetheless have their own immediacy. Something, for example, is always other than, and related to, something else, but it is also immediately itself, something of its own (see SL 89–93). In the sphere of essence, by contrast, categories and things are never simply what they are. Essence is thus the sphere of non-immediacy or "negativity", in which things always negate themselves in some way.

Yet what precisely does it mean to say that essence is *negativity*? Hegel clarifies this idea in SL by drawing out its necessary consequences. First, since essence is sheer negativity or non-immediacy, there is *in essence* no immediacy. Accordingly, the immediacy of being is in essence an *illusion* (*Schein*). Essence, therefore, does not occur on its own but is inseparable from the illusion to which it reduces immediate being (see SL 342–5).[6]

---

[5]   See Rohs (1982: 57): "Nicht-Unmittelbarkeit".
[6]   See Hegel (1968–: 11:246–9). Di Giovanni translates *Schein* as "*shine*" (Hegel 2010b: 341), as do Brinkmann and Dahlstrom (Hegel 2010a: 173 [§112]).

Second, since essence is sheer negativity, not only must it be the thorough negation of itself, but even the "self" it negates must be negative. Essence, therefore, must be the process of *not*-just-being-*negative*, or the negation of negation. In the sphere of being, being is negated by being limited or coming to an end (see SL 98–103); in essence, by contrast, it is not being that is negated, but the negative. Essence is thus described by Hegel as the "negation of a nothing [*Nichts*]", or "the *movement from nothing to nothing and thereby back to itself*" (SL 346) – the movement he calls "reflexion" (*Reflexion*).[7]

Third, if essence is pure reflexion, or *not*-just-*negative*, then it must be entangled with the non-negative or *immediacy*. Such immediacy is not just the illusion to which essence reduces being, but is produced or "posited" *by* reflexion itself: it is the being there is because there is not just the negative or, alternatively, *because there is not just nothing*. Hegel calls such being "*positedness*" (*Gesetztseyn*) (SL 347).[8] This positedness – which is important throughout the logic of essence – is the product of negativity and so is a mediated, dependent immediacy. It is thus not free-standing immediacy, but is inseparable from the negativity through which it is posited.

Fourth, however, reflexion also constitutes free-standing immediacy. It does so because in being sheer negativity, and so negating *itself*, it relates solely to itself and thereby constitutes *self-relating* being. Such being or immediacy is not merely dependent on reflexion, but is identical to the latter: it is reflexion *as* "simple equality with itself or immediacy" and for that reason is free-standing (SL 346). Such immediacy is certainly *posited* by reflexion; yet it differs from the "positedness" mentioned above by being co-extensive with, rather than just the product of, reflexion. It is the immediacy exhibited by reflexion as it relates to itself in its negativity or is "reflected" into itself – into being "itself" – and so it is what Hegel calls "reflexion into itself" (SL 352). When reflexion is conceived explicitly and solely as reflexion into itself, it is conceived as *identity* – identity that contains the reflexion or negativity by which it is constituted immanent within itself (see SL 356–8).

3.2   Identity and Opposition in EL

We still do not understand fully what "essence" or "absolute negativity" is, but we see that it is connected to a series of other concepts: *Schein,*

---

[7] Hegel (1968–: 11:250). I have spelt "reflexion" with an "x" (rather than "ct") to indicate that Hegel has in mind a logical-ontological category, rather than "reflection" as an activity of understanding (see SL 350).

[8] Hegel (1968–: 11:251).

reflexion, positedness, reflexion into itself, and identity. My account of these concepts is highly truncated, but in EL Hegel, too, provides a truncated account of them.[9]

In EL (§112) Hegel gives the following definition of essence. Essence, he states, is "being that mediates itself with itself in virtue of its negativity" and as such is "relation to itself only insofar as it is relation to an other that is, however, not immediately a being, but something *posited* [*Gesetztes*] and *mediated*".[10] Hegel does not state that this other is posited by essence, but insofar as it is, then essence is conceived here, as in SL, as negativity that both posits something – a "positedness" – and relates to, or is reflected into, itself. Hegel then notes that, while essence constitutes "being" through relating to itself, it also reduces immediate being – quality and quantity – to "something merely negative, to an *illusion* [*Schein*]".[11] Furthermore, in the remark to §112 he names the negativity of essence "*reflexion*". In these respects, therefore, Hegel's account of essence in EL, though truncated, is consistent with the account in SL.[12]

In §113 Hegel then notes that essence, conceived simply as "*reflexion-into -itself*", is *identity*. In EL as in SL, therefore, identity is not just being or immediacy, but being that is constituted by reflexion, by negativity. Indeed, it is just "negativity that relates itself to itself" – negativity as *self-relating* being (EL §116).[13] When such negativity is conceived explicitly as *negative* – as negating itself, and so *not* being itself, and so "repelling" itself from itself – it is conceived as difference (EL §116).[14] Difference is thus not something utterly distinct from identity but is intrinsic to the latter. It is the movement of *not*-just-being-negative *through which* there is identity.[15]

In EL and SL Hegel argues that such difference develops logically into diversity, in which two items differ simply by having separate identities. It then turns into opposition, in which each side is "for itself", or independent, in being the explicit negation of the other. One side of the opposition, the positive, is "the identical relation to itself in such a way that it is *not* the negative", and the other side, the negative, is "the differentiated for itself in such a way that it is *not* the positive" (EL §119). The one is thus not just independent of the other, but each includes its negation of, and difference from, the other within its independence: each *within itself* is not-the-other

---

[9] For a more extensive examination of these categories, see Houlgate (2011).
[10] Hegel (1970–1: 8:231).   [11] Hegel (1970–1: 8:231).
[12] Note, too, that in EL §114 Hegel contrasts "the *inessential*" with essence as what is "*essential*". In SL these categories are the first to be discussed in the doctrine of essence (see SL 341–2).
[13] See also SL 356: "equal to itself in its absolute negativity".   [14] See also SL 357, 361.
[15] On the difference between true and abstract identity, see Harris (1983: 161–2).

and so is internally opposed to the other. That other, therefore, does not just fall outside its counterpart, but belongs *to* the latter such that each is "the other's *own* other". Note, however, the ambiguity implicit in this structure of opposition: for each is included *in* the other as *not* that other and so as excluded *from* the latter. Each, within its own separate identity, is thus bound, through negation and exclusion, to the other that lies outside it.

Note, too, that in opposition essence becomes explicitly what it is at the start. Essence, for Hegel, is at first pure negativity or the negative of a negative. In opposition, by contrast, each side has a separate, affirmative identity. Yet each is separate and independent only through explicitly negating its negation, that is, only as explicit *negativity*. Opposition is thus simply essence or reflexion in a more developed form.[16] Yet that is not the end of the story, for opposition proves to be contradictory.

3.3   Contradiction and Ground in EL

Hegel highlights the contradiction in opposition in EL §120. The positive, he argues, is "that *diverse* [*jenes* Verschiedene] that is supposed to be for itself", or independent, and indifferent to the negative. Yet it is "*not* indifferent to its relation *to its other*", since it is positive only in excluding, and so being the negation of, its other. The positive is thus independent in being *bound*, by negation, to its other, and so is contradictory. The negative, Hegel continues, is supposed to be "equally independent" (*ebenso selbständig*), but as explicitly *negative* it, too, is itself only in being bound by negation to its other – or, as Hegel puts it, it has "its relation to itself, its positive [aspect], only in the other".[17] The negative is thus also independent in not being independent, and so is contradictory. Note that Hegel does not use the word "exclude" in §120 itself. In the first addition to §119, however, we read that each side of opposition "is only to the extent that it excludes [*ausschließt*] the other from itself and, precisely by this means, relates itself to the other".[18] It is, therefore, the *relation* to the other, built into the *exclusion* of the latter, that makes each side contradictory in its independence.

Insofar as the positive and negative are both contradictory, they are the same, though only "*in themselves*" (*an sich*) or *implicitly*. This is because they remain essentially distinct from one another. Hegel claims, however,

---

[16] See Kang (1999: 192).   [17] Hegel (1970–1: 8:247).
[18] Hegel (1970–1: 8:246). Hegel is talking here about inorganic and organic nature, but his point applies generally to the sides of an opposition.

that they are also the same *"for themselves"* (*für sich*) or *explicitly*, insofar as each negates or "sublates" the other and itself, and both are thus under-mined or fall "to the *ground"* (*zu* Grunde) (EL §120).[19] Yet Hegel does not explain in §120 precisely how the positive and negative thereby prove to be explicitly *the same*. An explanation is, however, suggested by lines from his lectures on EL in which he states that the positive and negative sublate themselves by turning themselves *into one another*. So the positive is positive, not negative, but precisely by *not* being negative it turns itself into the *negative* and so is the "opposite [*Gegenteil*] of itself'. Conversely, the negative is utterly negative, not positive, but by simply being itself, it exhibits its own "identity" and so proves to be *positive* after all.[20] The positive and negative are thus not just implicitly, but explicitly, the same, because each, in being *itself*, proves to be *the other* and each thereby proves to be the same unity of both.[21]

Essence is negativity or "reflexion" and as such is never simply what it is. Indeed, it proves to be not just self-negation, but self-relating being or identity. Identity then proves to be not just itself, but difference, and difference in turn proves to be not just difference or diversity but oppos-ition. Now we see that opposition is not just itself either, but also entails the explicit *sameness* or *identity* of its moments. This explicit identity is not initially present in opposition. It emerges, however, when the positive and negative turn themselves into one another: for at that point both prove to be the same unity of the two. Note that the difference or opposition between positive and negative proves to be their identity as each *side* of that opposition proves to be the unity of both of them. In Hegel's words, *"as self-relating*, difference is likewise already declared to be *identical with itself*, and the *opposed"* – the positive or negative – "is in general what contains *the one* and *its other*, *itself* and *its opposite*, in itself [*in sich selbst*]" (EL §120).[22] By contradicting and sublating themselves, therefore, the positive and negative give rise to a new logical structure: one in which they remain distinguished *as* positive and negative, but each is also the same unity *of* the positive and negative.

When this logical structure is considered in its own right as a new category, it is called the *"ground"* (*Grund*), though it is more precisely the relation between the ground and the grounded: "it is ground only insofar as it is ground of something, of an other" (EL §121 remark).[23] In

---

[19] Hegel (1970–1: 8:247).   [20] Hegel (2008a: 139–40). See also Hegel (2001: 144).

[21] For this reason, the opposition, or "essential difference" between the positive and negative, is "only the difference of itself from itself and hence contains the identical" (EL §120).

[22] Hegel (1970–1: 8:247).   [23] See Hegel (1970–1: 8:247) and Lakebrink (1979: 246–7).

sublating themselves and falling "to the ground", therefore, the positive and negative also give rise to the ground relation. To put it another way, when *contradiction* is developed logically, *it turns into the ground relation*. This is not to say that the newly emerged ground must now be understood, in retrospect, to be the ground *of* all contradiction. The ground relation is, rather, contradiction itself in a more developed form.[24]

In contrast to mere contradiction, however, the ground relation contains two different moments that are explicitly identical *from the start*. The ground and grounded are, indeed, distinguished as positive and negative: the ground is positively itself, whereas the grounded is posited by the ground and dependent on the latter, and so is *not* simply itself, and so in that sense is the negation of the ground. Yet the ground and grounded are also *identical* in their difference. As we read in the addition to EL §121, they are the same in having "one and the same content", and "the difference between the two is the mere difference of form" between the ground and the "state of being posited". Accordingly, when "we ask for the grounds of things", what we want is to see "the matter" or thing "as it were, doubled, first in its immediacy and second in its ground".[25]

As Hegel states in §121 itself, therefore, "the *ground* is the unity of identity and difference". Hegel also conceives of the ground as "the reflexion-into-itself that is just as much reflexion-into-another and vice versa", and a further significant idea is implied by this expression: since the ground – and thus correspondingly the grounded – is "reflexion-into-itself", each must have its *own* identity. This identity, however, is inseparable from "reflexion-into-another", that is, from the relation to the other, and this relation, as we have seen, is itself one of difference and identity. The ground and grounded thus exhibit identity in two senses: they are identical to one another, but each also has a separate identity of its own.

Why, though, must the ground *ground* the grounded? This is not fully explained in §121, but we learn more in the accompanying addition when Hegel notes that the ground is "the repelling [*Abstoßen*] of itself from itself".[26] The ground grounds the grounded, therefore, because it sets itself *outside itself*. This self-repulsion in turn explains why "what has emerged from the ground is itself" and why, therefore, the ground and the grounded are identical to one another (despite their difference in form). What is missing from the addition (and also from §§120–1), however, is a detailed

---

[24] See EL §121 addition: "a new contradiction".

[25] The true, rational ground of a thing will not just duplicate the latter, but will have its own determinate content, namely the "concept" of the thing.

[26] Hegel (1970–1: 8:248).

account of *contradiction* that explains that (and how) it, too, entails self-repulsion or self-exclusion. Self-exclusion is implicit in the idea that the positive and negative "sublate" themselves (§120), for in so doing each proves to be the other and so excludes *itself* from itself. In EL, however, Hegel does not locate the contradiction in the positive and negative explicitly in their self-exclusion. He does that only in SL.

Hegel's account of contradiction and ground in EL is also marked by other, more striking, omissions in comparison with the account in SL, even though it coincides in broad outline with the latter. There is no analysis of form in relation to essence, matter and content, and the transition to existence is not made via condition and the unconditioned but proceeds directly from the ground.[27] Form and matter are introduced in the subsequent discussion of the "thing" (§§127–30), and form and content arise in "appearance" (§133), but these categories do not belong to the official logic of the ground. As we have just seen, form and content are mentioned in the addition to §121 on ground, but the main paragraphs and remarks on ground (§§121–2) contain no examination of form, essence, matter and content to match that found in SL.[28]

This difference between EL and SL prompts Kolb to ask how we can know which version of the logic is correct, and at first the question seems well-founded. Closer inspection reveals, however, that priority must be given to the account in SL. This is because Hegel explains in painstaking and persuasive detail in SL *why* contradiction must give rise not just to the ground relation in general (as in EL), but to the specific distinction between form and essence, and later to that between form and content. When this explanation is set next to the account of contradiction and ground in EL, it becomes clear that the latter is not an alternative to that in SL, which leaves us wondering which account is correct, but merely a more general account that abstracts from the details presented in SL. Our task now, therefore, is to examine the transition from contradiction to ground in SL.

3.4   Contradiction in SL

In EL the positive and negative are "the posited contradiction" because each asserts its independence by negating, and so binding itself to, the

<hr />

[27] See EL §122 and Lakebrink (1979: 247–53).
[28] In the remark to EL §122 Hegel describes the "*determinate* ground" as "something formal", but this does not amount to a detailed discussion of form (or the formal ground).

other (§120). In SL Hegel highlights the same contradiction, but he also examines an aspect of contradiction that is not given prominence in EL, namely *self-exclusion* (see SL 374–6).

Hegel argues in SL that opposed determinations necessarily exclude one another, for being opposed consists not just in not being one another, but, in so doing, in setting oneself apart from, and thereby *shutting out*, the other (see SL 370).[29] Through such exclusion the positive and negative establish their utterly opposed, independent identities. The contradiction in the positive, however, is that "as the positing of self-identity by the *excluding* of the negative, it makes itself into a *negative*, hence into the other which it excludes from itself". This negative in turn excludes the positive, so by excluding the negative the positive turns itself into "its other which excludes it". In both these respects, therefore, the positive *excludes itself* (SL 375).[30] Hegel's failure in EL to make explicit this aspect of the contradiction in the positive (and negative) constitutes, in my view, a deficiency of that text.

According to SL, the positive excludes itself by turning into the negative, and the negative excludes itself by turning into the positive.[31] Neither, therefore, has a stable identity, but each proves to be "the passing over [*Uebergehen*], or rather the self-transposition [*sich Uebersetzen*] of itself into its opposite". Furthermore, Hegel maintains, their "ceaseless vanishing" into one another undermines the difference between them and establishes their "*first unity*" – a unity that is itself neither positive, nor negative and so is a mere "*null*" (SL 376).[32] As in EL §120, therefore, the positive and negative undermine themselves or fall "to the *ground*".

In both SL and EL Hegel then argues that the self-sublation of the positive and negative has a positive as well as a negative result: the result is "not only the null" (SL 376). This positive result, in SL as in EL, is the *ground*. In SL, however, the ground does not immediately give rise to existence (as it does in EL), but takes a series of different forms, including

---

[29] See Kang (1999: 196).

[30] The positive and negative also exclude themselves in another sense: each includes the other within its own independence, so insofar as it excludes the other, it excludes what makes it itself and thus excludes itself (see SL 374).

[31] Hegel notes, however, that the negative is more explicitly contradictory than the positive (SL 375–6). This is because the negative *immediately negates itself*. It negates the negative that it is, and so is "*identical with itself*" and turns itself into the positive; yet *qua negative* it also negates the positive that it is. The positive, by contrast, negates itself only insofar as it is the negative *of its other*, of the negative, for only in that way does it turn itself into the *negative* that it negates. See Iber (1990: 460–3).

[32] Hegel (1968–: ii:280).

the relations between form itself and essence, matter and content. As Hegel demonstrates in SL, these relations are made necessary by the nature of *contradiction*. To see why, we need to look more closely at the latter.

Hegel emphasises in SL that the positive and negative are both "*positedness*" (SL 376). To be "posited" is to owe one's identity, and so to be related, to an other, but also to differ from the latter and so to be "the negative of an other". It is thus to be dependent on an other that is in some respect one's negation. The positive and negative are "positedness", therefore, because each is itself *through not being* the other.

Yet these two moments are also "reflected" into themselves and so independent of one another: each has its *own* separate identity.[33] Moreover, each establishes its separate identity by *excluding* the other; that is to say, "their excluding reflexion sublates this [their] positedness" and "turns them into independent beings existing for themselves [*fürsichseyenden Selbstständigen*]" (SL 376).[34] Paradoxically, however, such exclusion also cancels their independence because it renders the latter *dependent* on the negation of another – exclusion being a negation – and so turns the positive and negative once again into mere positedness. By excluding one another, therefore, the positive and negative undermine their separate, exclusive identities and in that sense "*they destroy themselves*" (*sie richten sich zu Grunde*) (SL 376). In other words, by excluding the other, each excludes its own exclusive *self*.[35]

Yet this is not the end of the story: for the positive and negative prove again to be posited determinations, dependent on negation, *only because they exclude one another*. Their positedness does not, therefore, put an end to their mutual exclusion, because they exhibit it only *in* excluding one another – exclusion that must continue to be given its due. As "excluding reflexion", however, each sets itself apart from, and negates its dependence on, the other and so "sublates" its positedness. As mutually *exclusive*, therefore, they must also sublate the positedness to which they reduce themselves *by* excluding one another.

---

[33] See SL 368, 376. Note that this independence is inherited by the sides of opposition from diversity; see EL §120: "The *positive* is that *diverse* [...]."

[34] Hegel (1968–: 11:281).

[35] Hegel (1968–: 11:281). Di Giovanni (Hegel 2010b) has "*they fate themselves to founder*". Note that the contradiction set out in this paragraph is essentially the same as the one Hegel highlights in EL §120: each side of the opposition negates its own independence by turning itself into a *posited*, dependent determination (see this chapter, p. 50). There are, however, other ways of conceiving of such contradiction (or other forms of it). (1) The positive and negative turn themselves into their opposites and thereby form a "*unity*" with one another that is neither positive nor negative, and so is a mere "*null*" (SL 376; see also this chapter, pp. 50–1, 54). (2) Each side also excludes itself by excluding the other that belongs to its *own* independent identity (see this chapter, note 30).

This is the deeper contradiction that besets the positive and negative: each excludes the other and in so doing disavows, so to speak, any connection to that other; yet, in excluding the other, each binds itself to the other as *not*-that-other and so turns itself into a dependent, posited being, or "positedness"; and yet each is bound to the other precisely by *excluding* the other, so each disavows the connection between them that is built into exclusion itself: each sublates the positedness to which it reduces itself by excluding the other. As Hegel puts it, "the excluding reflexion of independence [*Selbstständigkeit*]" – positive or negative – "makes itself a positedness but is just as much the sublation of its positedness" (SL 376–7).[36]

To repeat: the positive and negative are opposed, and thus are the negation of one another, and thus are positedness – one-sided determinations that are posited by negating one another. At the same time, they negate, or sublate, their mere positedness, and give themselves separate, independent identities, through *excluding* one another. Yet, precisely through such mutual exclusion, they turn themselves once again into mere positedness, into determinations whose identity is established, or posited, through negating the other. Yet, insofar as they are mutually *exclusive*, they sublate this positedness too – the positedness they exhibit by excluding one another – and so set themselves apart from one another after all.

Yet does this not simply repeat the problem? Do not the positive and negative once again bind themselves to one another through their mutual exclusion and so prove to be mere *positedness*? Hegel says no, because they now exhibit a new logical structure we have not encountered before. At first, the positive and negative, in excluding one another, simply sublate the positedness, or moment of not-being-one-another, that belongs to being opposed determinations. Now, by contrast, each, in excluding the other, also sublates the positedness to which it reduces itself *by* excluding the other; that is, each, as "excluding reflexion", sublates the positedness and the negative *that it itself proves to be*. In Hegel's words, "the *exclusive determination* is *itself that other* of itself of which it is the negation" (SL 377). Accordingly, the "exclusive determination" – positive or negative – does not simply become positedness once again, but proves to be self-sublating or self-negating, and thus *self-relating*, being. It negates its *own* positedness and so *relates to itself* in negating the latter, and so, as Hegel puts it, "goes together with itself" (*ist das Zusammengehen mit sich selbst*).[37]

[36] Hegel (1968–: II:281).
[37] Hegel (1968–: II:281). Di Giovanni (Hegel 2010b) has "is self-withdrawal".

It proves to be wholly self-relating being, therefore – or the "positive unity with itself" – in *negating* the positedness, or negative, that it itself is.

Indeed, this is the only way an "exclusive determination" – positive or negative – can be *itself* and enjoy its own identity. It cannot enjoy such an identity purely by excluding the other because that turns it into something posited. It can do so, however, by excluding the other *and also* negating the positedness, or dependence, to which it reduces *itself* through such exclusion: for in negating itself in this way, it relates solely to itself and, as sheer self-relation, proves to be nothing but *itself*. In Hegel's words, therefore, the exclusive determination "turns back into itself by virtue of *its own* negation, for it turns into itself through the negation of *its* positedness". It is "identical with itself through the negation not of an other, but of itself" (SL 377).

This is a hard idea to grasp, but it becomes clearer if we focus on the positive in particular, rather than "excluding reflexion" as such. The positive secures its independent identity by excluding the negative; through such exclusion, however, it turns itself into that which is *not-the-negative* and thus into a *negative* that itself excludes the positive. By being exclusively positive, therefore, the positive turns itself into that which excludes it, and thereby excludes itself. Yet the positive turns itself into its opposite *through excluding the negative*. It must, therefore, exclude and negate the negative that *it* proves to be in excluding the negative. In so doing it negates *itself*, and so relates solely to itself, and so proves to be self-relating *positive* being. The positive is positive, therefore, by being not just positive but also negative, yet by not just being negative either but relating to itself, and so being *itself*, in negating the negative that *it* proves to be. In other words, the positive is – or becomes – positive by *turning back into itself* in negating the negative that it has become.[38]

The positive thus undergoes a double development when it proves to be self-contradictory. On the one hand, it undermines itself by turning into its opposite through simply being itself, and so proves to be neither just itself, nor just its negation. On the other hand, it turns back into itself in negating the negative that it itself is, and so proves to be *both* positive *and* negative together (as well as the explicit movement of negativity or reflexion).

In EL Hegel comes to a similar understanding of the positive (and negative). He concludes, for example, that "the *opposed* is in general what

[38] Similarly, the negative, in negating the one-sided negative (or positedness) that *it* is, proves to be explicitly (and positively) *negative*.

contains *the one* and *its other*, *itself* and *its opposite*, in itself" (EL §120). What is missing from EL, however, is an account of self-exclusion in contradiction, as well as a consideration of a crucial ambiguity in contradiction (that belongs to the ground too). The ambiguity is the following (again taking the positive as our example).

On the one hand, the positive is *not* the negative, and so is in fact negative, but *this* negative is simply what the positive itself proves to be (in excluding the negative): it is the positive *as negative*. Furthermore, the positive relates to itself, and so is *itself*, rather than just this negative, only in *negating* the latter. In these respects, therefore, the positive is positive only *in being negative*, in being positive-*as-negative*.

On the other hand, the positive is *not* the negative, and so is itself negative, but – as *positive* – it is *not* this negative either. So it secures its independence – an identity that sets it *apart from* the negative – by excluding from itself, and so negating, both the negative over against it and the negative that it itself is. In this respect, the positive proves to be genuinely positive and self-identical through the thoroughgoing exclusion of the negative from itself.[39]

These two conceptions of the positive are at odds with one another, but they are also inseparable because they express the ambiguity in the very nature of the positive: the latter is positive through not being negative *at all*, and therefore precisely through being *negative* itself.[40] The positive thus enjoys its own exclusive identity, quite apart from the negative, only insofar as it negates the negative that it itself is and so *relates to itself in being negative*.

Note that this moment of self-relation distinguishes the logical structure we are now considering from simple contradiction. In SL a determination is contradictory because it excludes itself by proving to be its opposite, and thereby undermines itself and its independence. Now, by contrast, the positive and negative *relate to themselves* in excluding themselves and in that sense do not just undermine themselves, but preserve, or establish, their own identities through self-exclusion and self-negation. This new logical structure also characterizes the ground: because the ground, too, enjoys its identity, *apart* from the grounded, only insofar as it excludes itself from itself, and so turns itself into the grounded, but relates to itself *in* the latter (see SL 378).

---

[39] See Iber (1990: 476): "it thereby lets *its own being-negative fall outside it*" (my translation).
[40] Similarly, the negative, as utterly *negative*, is *positively* itself.

3.5   Ground in SL

The ground is what emerges when the identity or unity that results from contradiction is rendered fully explicit. As we have seen, each side of opposition proves to be "identical with itself" by excluding its own one-sidedness or "positedness" (SL 377); that is to say, each proves to be *positively* itself by *negating* its negation of the other. In this respect, both prove to be the same unity of the positive and negative, and when this unity is conceived explicitly as a *single* identity that is constituted through the movement of self-exclusion and self-negation, it is conceived as "ground".[41] The ground is thus the identity that remains *positively* itself in excluding itself and so being the *negative* of itself (namely, the grounded). Accordingly, it remains contradictory, since the positive still turns into the negative (and vice versa); but it also resolves the contradiction, since the positive and negative preserve their identities (as ground and grounded) and also form a settled unity with one another. As Hegel puts it, "in ground, therefore, opposition and its contradiction are just as much sublated [*aufgehoben*] as preserved" (SL 378).[42]

The concept of "ground" is one with which we are all familiar, but we do not usually think of it as contradictory. Hegel, however, conceives of the ground as a more developed form of contradiction, because he locates its logical core in *self-exclusion*. "As ground", Hegel writes, "essence excludes *itself* from itself" and in so doing "posits *itself*" (SL 377); furthermore, he adds, essence thereby also "*determines itself*" (SL 386). It is important to see the close connection between these ideas. The ground excludes itself by setting itself outside itself as the grounded; this grounded, as that which has been excluded, and so posited, by the ground is thus characterized by explicit positedness, in contrast to the ground itself which is the moment that posits. The grounded, however, is not just different from the ground, but is the ground itself *as* positedness, *as* that which it has posited itself to be. It is also the ground, insofar as the latter has given itself *determinate* form: the form of being something determined, posited and excluded by itself.[43] As such, of course, it is dependent on the ground and is also the negative of the latter: for it is precisely the grounded, *not* the ground itself.

The ground itself is characterized by self-identity, and so is positively itself, rather than negative. Indeed, it lacks all the characteristics of the grounded: it is neither something excluded, nor positedness, nor explicitly determinate or different-from-another. Accordingly, it is logically "*indeterminate*" or what

---

[41] See this chapter, pp. 51–2, and EL §120.   [42] Hegel (1968–: II:281).
[43] See Rohs (1982: 81): "The positedness that belongs to essence is the same as determinateness" (my translation).

Hegel calls "*non-positedness*" (SL 389). Yet, as the ground posits the grounded, it becomes positive *in contrast to the grounded*; that is to say, it becomes one side of a determinate difference, the other side of which is the grounded. The ground does not thereby just become the mirror image of its counterpart: it remains self-identical and positive, rather than posited and negative. Yet it is not simply indeterminate either, but it is "*determined* as *indeterminate* or as sublated positedness" in the same act of self-exclusion that generates the grounded; in other words, "the ground is essence *posited* as the non-posited *as against positedness*" (SL 389).

The "*determinateness* of essence" here is thus twofold: that "of the *ground* and of the *grounded*" (SL 389). Yet the ground remains positive, rather than explicitly determinate and negative, and so is "sublated determinate being" or "sublated positedness". It is distinct from and the negation of the grounded and so is itself posited being; but it equally negates, or sublates, its own positedness and negative character and thereby preserves its positive self-identity apart from the grounded. The ground is thus both posited (or negative) and non-posited (or positive) at the same time. Furthermore, the grounded is also both negative and positive: for it is that which has been excluded, and so posited, by the ground, and thus is the negation of the latter, yet it is also given its own positive identity by the ground, since it is, precisely, *excluded* by the latter as something of its own.

The ground and grounded are not, however, simply other than one another, but *the ground remains identical with itself in the grounded*, since the latter is just the ground once again: it is the ground, insofar as it has been excluded from itself. This is why, as Hegel notes in EL, when we ask for the ground of a thing, what we want is to see the thing "as it were, doubled, first in its immediacy and second in its ground" (EL §121 addition). The self-identical positive (the ground) and the self-identical negative (the grounded) are thus in fact the same thing in two different forms, or, as Hegel puts it, they are "*one and the same identity*" (SL 389).

This "identity" is, of course, simply the ground that relates to itself in the grounded. Yet, in another respect, it is *not* the ground as such: for, as we have seen, "the ground is essence *posited* as the non-posited *as against positedness*", whereas the identity that Hegel now brings to the fore is the "unity of this determinate identity (the ground) and of the negative identity (the grounded)". In order to distinguish this "simple identity" from the determinate identity of the ground, therefore, Hegel calls the former the "*essence as such*" (*Wesen überhaupt*) (SL 389).[44]

---

[44] Hegel (1968–: II:294).

This "essence as such" is thus the ground insofar as it has further sublated its determinate, posited, negative character and set itself apart not only from the grounded, but also from the determinate difference between ground and grounded. The grounded, we recall, is explicit *positedness* (and thus explicitly determinate and negative), since it is posited by the ground. The ground itself, by contrast, is *"posited as the non-posited"* and *"determined as indeterminate"* (SL 389). The identity that continues through both the ground and grounded, however, has cast off the last remnant of positedness and is *simple* identity.[45] It is the ground, insofar as it sublates and sets itself apart from *all* positedness, negation and difference, including the difference between the ground and grounded. It is the ground, therefore, insofar as it is not the *ground* as such, but rather the *"substrate"* (*Substrat*) or *"simple foundation"* (*einfache Grundlage*) that underlies the ground relation (SL 390–1).[46] Note that this identity is still constituted by negativity, and so is still a form of essence, since it is constituted by the sublation, or negation, of all negation; but it is the *radical* sublation of negation that excludes from itself even its own sublating of negation.

The space of difference and determinacy, from which this identity sets itself apart, Hegel calls "form". This form, however, includes the difference between not just ground and grounded, but also identity and difference, and positive and negative, since these are themselves components of the ground and grounded. Form thus comprises all the determinate differences that belong to essence (see SL 390). Such form, of course, does not consist just of difference, since the different "form determinations" have their own self-identity or "subsistence" (*Bestehen*); indeed, without such self-identity, there would be no "positive" opposed to a "negative", and no "ground" that posits a "grounded" (SL 389–90).[47] Nonetheless, what distinguishes form from the "simple identity" of the substrate is principally positedness, negation and difference. This in turn has a further logical consequence: for it means that form as a whole lacks a self-identity and "subsistence" of its own, and so finds its subsistence in the identity that constitutes its substrate (see SL 391). Form, therefore, cannot stand alone but is necessarily the form *of* its substrate. Indeed, this also follows from the nature of that substrate itself: for, although it sets itself apart from all essential differences, it is at the same time the identity *of* the ground and grounded, *of* the positive and

---

[45] See Rohs (1982: 139): "utterly indeterminate" (*schlechthin unbestimmt*).
[46] Hegel (1968–: II:295). Di Giovanni (2010b) translates both *Substrat* and *Grundlage* as "substrate".
[47] Hegel (1968–: II:294–5).

negative. It is *their* underlying identity that gives form as a whole the self-identity and subsistence that, as mere form, it lacks. Form, therefore, is necessarily the form *of* the substrate from which it differs (see SL 390–1).

As commentators have pointed out, this distinction between form and essence is central to Schelling's identity philosophy.[48] Yet Hegel examines this distinction in SL, not just because it is discussed by Schelling, but because it is made necessary *logically* by the nature of contradiction and ground (and ultimately essence itself). More specifically, it is made necessary by the fact that the ground is self-excluding identity. The ground first excludes the grounded as that which is posited by it, that is, as explicit positedness. In so doing, however, the ground turns itself into that which – in contrast to the grounded – is determined as *indeterminate* and posited as *non*-posited. It then performs a further act of exclusion, or sublation, and frees itself from any explicit contrast with the grounded. In other words, it sublates its *own* positedness – which consists in *not* being posited and *not* being determinate – and sets itself, as simple identity or "essence", quite apart from positedness, negation and difference, including the difference between ground and grounded.[49] At the same time it underlies and sustains all the "form determinations", which have no "subsistence" of their own without it.

The distinction between essence and form is thus logically necessary. Yet, as we have noted, it is omitted (together with other related distinctions) from the account of ground in EL. That account is certainly coherent and accords in general with the one in SL (since it proceeds from ground to existence). In comparison with the latter, however, it does not present a full account of ground and so is not a rival that would raise the question as to which account is correct. *Pace* Kolb, it is, rather, a truncated account that omits features of the ground that SL shows to be logically necessary.

3.6   Form, Matter and Content in EL and SL

In SL form and essence make necessary the further distinction between form and matter, and then that between form and content. There is not space here to consider this logical development in detail, but the argument, briefly, is as follows.

---

[48] See Rohs (1982: 122–9, 137, 155–6) and Schelling (1985: 2:52–4, 59 [*Darstellung meines Systems der Philosophie*, §15 addition 1, §18, §30 note]).

[49] See SL 390: "*their foundation* as an indeterminate which in its determination is indifferent to them".

Essence is simple identity in contrast to form, which comprises "everything *determinate*" (SL 390). Insofar as essence is distinct from form, however, it is itself determinate and so "*has* a form". Furthermore, essence is the foundation of form (which could not subsist without it) and so is, in an attenuated sense, the ground of form, and so is a "moment" *of* form (to which the ground-relation belongs) (SL 391). It turns out, therefore, that both essence and form are "*moments* of the simple form-relation [*Formbeziehung*] itself", and that form is "the completed whole" (SL 391–2).[50] When this thought is rendered explicit, essence is conceived as the "formless identity" set over against form *by form*; that is to say, it is conceived as *matter* (SL 392).

As "simple identity" matter is explicitly distinct from form and all the differences it encompasses (SL 392). By virtue of being explicitly *distinct*, however, "it contains form locked up inside it" and so is "an absolute receptivity for form", which is the *active* pole in relation to *passive* matter (SL 393). When matter has then been formed, and form rendered "material", both together constitute a *content* that is indifferent to the distinction between form and matter (SL 395–6). Such content, as a "formed identity" (*formirte Identität*), explicitly exhibits form, including the form of the ground-relation (SL 397).[51] The ground itself thus proves to be the "formal ground" in which "a determinate *content* is considered from *two sides*, once in so far as it is *ground*, then again in so far as it is *grounded*" (SL 397–8).[52]

All these categories are shown in SL to be logically necessary, but – together with the real ground, condition and the unconditioned – they are omitted from the official account of ground in EL, which proceeds directly from ground to existence.[53] Form, matter and content are considered by Hegel in later sections of EL. Yet, in Kolb's view, this apparent relocation of categories (compared with SL) is problematic, for it "disturbs the goal" – to which, for many commentators, Hegel is committed in his logic – "of purely internal self-development". If the logic is to be such a development, Kolb maintains, then categories "should find their identity through their location in the sequence", and so "Form/Matter or Form/Content should not be standardized mediation patterns that can be inserted" – unaltered – "in different locations" (Kolb 2010: 53). Kolb claims, however, that, in relocating these categories, Hegel treats them precisely as such standardized

---

[50] Hegel (1968–: 11:296–7).   [51] Hegel (1968–: 11:302).
[52] For helpful accounts of the development of form and its counterparts, see Rohs (1982: 122–95), Schmidt (1997: 83–104) and Okochi (2008: 212–22).
[53] The "formalism of the ground" is, however, mentioned briefly in the addition to EL §121 (Hegel 2010a: 187).

patterns or "relocatable fragments" and so undermines the "internal self-development" of his logic.

Yet Hegel in truth does no such thing. This is evident from the fact that form, matter and content, as they are set out in EL *after* the section on ground, match categories in the equivalent chapters of SL, and do not coincide exactly with form, matter and content in the ground chapter in SL, as they would have to do if they were treated by Hegel as "relocatable fragments".

Matter, in the ground chapter in SL, is conceived as "simple identity, void of distinction" (SL 392) in contrast to form, which, as we have seen, comprises the determinate differences that belong to reflexion: identity/difference, positive/negative and ground/grounded. In EL matter is also conceived as "identity", but the "form" with which it is contrasted does not just encompass the "determinations of reflexion" (as in SL). Form is the "external *relation*" (*äußerliche* Beziehung) between determinations that is found specifically in the *thing* (*Ding*) (EL §128).[54] The distinction between matter and form in EL thus coincides with that between matter and thing in SL: for, although the thing in SL is not explicitly equated with "form", it is conceived, as form is in EL, as an external relation, namely "an external collection of independent matters" (*eine äusserliche Sammlung selbstständiger Materien*) (SL 433; see EL §127).[55]

Note, too, that in SL form as such actively determines or *forms* matter, and thereby becomes "material, subsistent form", whereas the thing just "consists of independent matters indifferent to the relation [*Beziehung*] they have in the thing" (SL 395, 432).[56] In EL §130, however, the form in which matter is "determined" (by being "relegated to *properties*") is itself equated with the thing that consists of matters.

In the case of form and matter, therefore, it is clear that, *pace* Kolb, Hegel in EL does not simply relocate "fragments" from SL "that make more or less the same points wherever they are inserted" (Kolb 2010: 53). Rather, he highlights, through these categories, aspects of the *thing* that also belong to the thing in SL but that exceed what is said there about form and matter as such.

Hegel does something similar in the case of form and content. In SL content as such – in the ground chapter – is "formed matter" and so *unites* matter and form (SL 396). Content, however, is also distinct from form, insofar as the latter contains the *difference* between form and matter.

---

[54] Hegel (1970–1: 8:259).
[55] See Hegel (1968–: 11:336). The parallel between EL and SL can also be seen from these passages: EL §129: "The thing thus breaks down into *matter* and *form*", and SL 432: "the *matters* and *this thing*".
[56] Hegel (1968–: 11:300, 335).

A single content, therefore, has both a form and a matter, which differ from one another only formally.

The distinction between form and content then re-emerges in the "appearance" (*Erscheinung*) that the realm of existing things proves to be (see SL 441).[57] The content of appearance is contained in the *law* governing the latter, and appearance itself differs from this law principally through its form. More specifically, "the kingdom of laws is the *restful* content of appearance", whereas "the latter is this same content but displayed in restless flux [*unruhigen Wechsel*]" (SL 442). This "restless form" (*unruhige Form*), however, also confers an additional *content* on appearance, which is only "*externally bound up* with the law" (SL 441–2).[58]

In EL form and content are not examined in themselves, but are considered only in the context of appearance. In §133, as in the corresponding chapter in SL, content is thus contained in the law governing appearance, whereas what is "alterable" in the latter – or "restless", as Hegel puts it in SL – is assigned to its "indifferent *external form*" (though, in contrast to SL, Hegel makes no mention of any distinctive content to appearance beyond that contained in the law).[59] In the remark to §133, Hegel appears to consider form and content in abstraction from appearance, but appearance remains the context for these categories. This can be inferred from the fact that content is contrasted with "external existence [*Existenz*], indifferent to the content" – for, as Hegel states in §131, "existence is appearance".[60]

Hegel's account of form and content in EL coincides, therefore, with his remarks on these categories in the chapter on *appearance*, not in the *ground* chapter, in SL. This is evident not just from his equation of content with the "*law* of appearance", but also from the fact that he highlights something else that does not arise in the ground chapter in SL, namely the "conversion" (*Umschlagen*) of form and content into one another (EL §133 remark).[61]

Hegel makes no explicit mention of this conversion in the appearance chapter in SL either, so it might seem that there is no equivalent to it in SL. Yet the issue is not so simple. In EL Hegel notes that this conversion, which is implicit in appearance, is made explicit, or "*posited*", in the "*absolute relationship*" (which arises near the end of the logic of essence). It is made

[57] Hegel (1968–: 11:344–5). The distinction between content and form also appears briefly in the section on the thing, but there Hegel has in mind only the two aspects of "matters" (not the relation between such matters and the thing) (see SL 433). For longer discussions of the sections on the thing and appearance, see Schmidt (1997: 133–60) and Heidemann (2018: 335–73).

[58] Hegel (1968–: 11:345–6).

[59] The law containing the content of appearance also has "*form within itself*", so appearance in fact exhibits "a doubling of the form" (EL §133 remark). See Lakebrink (1979: 294–5).

[60] Hegel (1970–1: 8:262, 265).   [61] Hegel (1970–1: 8:265).

explicit, specifically, in the logical conversion into one another of the "form-activity" (*Formtätigkeit*), or "power", of substance – which *forms* its accidents by creating and destroying them – and the "*wealth of all content*" in the accidents themselves that is simply the "*manifestation*" of that form-activity (EL §§150–1).[62] The latter conversion is, however, indicated in SL too.[63] Hegel's remarks on form and content in EL thus not only match his remarks on appearance in SL, but also are compatible with his conception of the absolute relation in the latter.

It is again clear, therefore, that Hegel does not simply take "fragments" from the ground chapter in SL and reproduce them, without alteration, in a later context in EL. Rather, his remarks about form and content in EL match what he says about them in the corresponding contexts in SL – the accounts of appearance and the absolute relation. The differences between EL and SL to which Kolb draws attention do not, therefore, "disturb" the immanent development of Hegel's logic: for in each case form and its counterpart are conceived as they should be in the contexts in which they are considered.[64]

3.7   Conclusion

Faced with the differences between the accounts of essence in SL and EL, Kolb asks "how do you show which version is the one where Form/ Content is correctly derived?" (Kolb 2010: 46), and he suggests that, ultimately, we cannot know. Indeed, he claims that, since each version "offers significant insights", "there is not necessarily one best version" (Kolb 2010: 46, 50), so we do not actually need to decide between them. In this essay, however, I have argued that Kolb's suggestion is mistaken: SL and EL do not set out two alternative logics that are equally persuasive, but they present the *same* logic in different ways. Yet I have also argued that the SL version has clear priority over the EL version, because it explains in detail why form-and-essence and other determinations of ground, which

---

[62] Hegel (1970–1: 8:294–5).

[63] On SL 491 Hegel states that "*the flux of accidents*" is the "absolute *form-unity* of accidentality, substance as *absolute power*". In other words, in the coming-to-be and passing-away of accidents substance is at work changing their *form* (from possible to actual and from actual to possible). Yet "these form determinations" – "possible" and "actual" – "are equally determinations of content", so accidents with a new *content* are produced as substance changes their form. Indeed, the changing of their form by substance – which in EL Hegel calls its "*form-activity*" (§150) – just *is* the changing of their content (and vice versa), and in that sense in SL, as in EL, form and content "convert" themselves logically into one another in the absolute relation.

[64] This is not, of course, to deny that there is some overlap between what Hegel says about form, matter and content in the sections on the thing and appearance in EL and in the ground chapter of SL.

are absent from the section on ground in EL, are *logically necessary*. Accordingly, even though each edition of EL (1817, 1827 and 1830) was published after SL's logic of essence (1813), EL does not represent an improvement in logical terms on the latter, in the way the second edition of the logic of being in SL evidently improves on the first.[65]

In my judgement, therefore, the true derivation of the categories of essence is found in SL. Yet this does not mean that the account of essence in EL is incorrect. It is simply a condensed version of the logic set out in SL – one that omits form, matter and content from the account of ground, perhaps for ease of presentation, but then highlights them at later points in the argument at which they also occur, implicitly or explicitly, in SL. By focusing on the logic of essence, we thus learn an important lesson about EL. It often provides clear and helpful analyses that complement those found in SL (though it can also be more obscure, since it is so condensed).[66] It is, however, no substitute for SL: for, as Hegel reminds us in the *Phenomenology*, the "matter at hand" (*Sache*) is exhausted only in its "*elaboration*" (*Ausführung*) (Hegel 2018b: 6), and the concept of essence is fully elaborated only in SL.[67]

---

[65] For some brief remarks on the differences between the two editions, see Houlgate (2006: 320–1).

[66] See Hackenesch (2000: 132).

[67] See Hegel (1968–: 9: 10). Inwood translates *Sache* as "thing". Note that EL does not contain an altogether new version of the doctrine of essence, but in certain respects reverts to a version Hegel developed *before* he published Book Two of SL on essence. In the "Logic [for the Middle Class]" (1810–11), written for use in the school in which Hegel was teaching, the account of essence proceeds from identity, through diversity and opposition, to ground (though without mentioning contradiction), and then ground leads directly to the *thing* and *existence* (*Existenz*). The thing is understood to unite "matters", but the distinction between matter and form does not arise until we reach appearance, in which the distinction between content and form also emerges. Except for the later positioning of matter and form, therefore, the doctrine of essence from 1810–11 is similar in structure to that contained in the 1830 edition of EL (which has been the focus of this chapter); see Hegel (1986: 81–5 [§§33–53]). In 1813 Hegel published Book Two of SL in which, as we have seen, form, matter and content (and other categories) are included in the chapter on ground *before* existence and appearance are derived. Then in the first edition of the *Encyclopedia*, published in 1817, Hegel once again omits form, matter and content from the account of ground and proceeds directly from ground to existence. In this edition, however (as in the 1827 and 1830 editions), Hegel discusses matter and form in the context of the thing, not appearance. Indeed, he writes that "*form* and *matter*, the *thing in itself* and the *matters* [*Materien*] of which the thing consists, are one and the same antithesis of *inessential* and *essential* existence" (§79). Form and content, by contrast, play a role in the relation between force and expression (§85 remark); see Hegel (1968–: 13:57–60,1990b: 88–91). In the 1827 edition of EL the categories of essence are then in the order we find in the 1830 edition – with form and matter discussed in the context of the thing, and form and content considered in the context of appearance. Note that all these texts, apart from SL, were conceived as "outlines" for use in teaching or lecturing. It is likely, therefore, that their accounts of essence differ from that in SL (and from one another) for reasons of *presentation*, rather than logic. Indeed, in my view, the account of essence in SL has clear priority over the other versions in terms of *logic*, since it is so detailed and consistent in its argumentation. On the different versions of Hegel's doctrine of essence, see also Jaeschke (1999) and Okochi (2008).

CHAPTER 4

The Concept's Freedom

Jean-François Kervégan

Only the concept itself is free.

(Hegel 2010a: §214, 287)

In what follows, I investigate why Hegel could write that Logic is the "science of freedom" (Hegel 1968–: 13:§5, 18). This assertion can make sense only if we can understand exactly what "Logic" means (i.e., in my opinion, an "onto-logic"), and what Hegel asserts that the "concept" is, i.e. anything other than a "subjective" representation. Freedom is the predicate of the concept as it is its own subject, that is, as "idea" in which "forms of thought" and "forms of being" coincide.[1]

4.1 Encyclopedia: The Philosophical Discourse of Totality

The *Encyclopedia of Philosophical Sciences* is the realization of a programme phrased in the Preface of the *Phenomenology of Spirit* and justified thoroughly in the *Science of Logic*. Its aim is to set out a philosophical system expressing not a certain point of view (making it *a* system), but rather that of the Absolute (conceived as a dialectical process of its production of itself). The Introduction of the *Encyclopedia* describes this systematic science as follows.

> The science of [the absolute] is essentially a *system*, since the true insofar as it is *concrete* exists only through unfolding itself in itself, collecting and holding itself together in a unity, i.e. as a *totality*. Only by discerning and determining its distinctions can it be the necessity of them and the freedom of the whole.
>
> A philosophizing *without a system* can be nothing scientific. Apart from the fact that such philosophizing expresses by itself more of a subjective outlook, it is also random in terms of its content. A particular content is

---

[1] See Pippin (2019: 39ff.).

justified solely as a moment of the whole. When separated from it, it represents an unjustified presupposition or a subjective certainty. Many philosophical writings limit themselves to expressing in this way merely *attitudes* or *opinions*. – By a *system* one wrongly understands a philosophy built on a narrowly circumscribed *principle* distinct from other such principles; contrary to this, however, it is a principle of any genuine philosophy that it contains all particular principles within itself. (Hegel 2010a: §14, 43)

Three lessons can be drawn from this paragraph. (1) Science in the fullest sense of the word has to concern the totality of what is actual (*wirklich*). In turn, only philosophy can claim to be a science in the full sense of the word; such a philosophical science is not *a* philosophy concerning *a* particular principle, but the combination of these many principles into *the* unique system of philosophy. (2) Only such a philosophical science avoids the risk of abstraction inherent to all conceptual process. As fructuous as they may be, positive sciences are never sciences in the fuller sense. This is not because they are positive (which guarantees their fertility), but because they are organized around a regional viewpoint. This is even truer of the different philosophies organized by a "narrowly circumscribed principle": they are only views *on* the absolute, but not the knowledge *of* the absolute. (3) Systematicity concerns the knowledge stemming from a unique principle. It appears that there is *only one* philosophy of which each particular philosophy solely exposes an aspect. The *Lectures on the History of Philosophy* presents the "Unique Philosophy" (*die Eine Philosophie*) as the process of which the particular philosophies are the moments, both in the logical and in the chronological sense of the word. Systematicity is the mobile expression of the atemporal nature of the philosophical act. Hence the seemingly dazzling thesis of a homology between philosophy and the history of philosophy:

> I argue that the succession of philosophical systems in *history* is *the same* as the succession of the conceptual determinations of the idea in its logical development. (Hegel 1968–: 30–1:219)

That kind of assertion raises obvious questions: is Hegel asking us to identify his own system as this one and only, universal philosophy, of which the other philosophies are but moments? Is Hegel's philosophy *the* philosophy? Answering this key question is complex, even from Hegel's point of view. On the one hand, because of his understanding of the nature of a system, Hegel must understand his own philosophy as *the* science of the absolute (meaning, in turn, that it is not *his* philosophy). Indeed, the true meaning of systematicity is apparent only through the understanding of totality. On the other hand, such a vision of the Hegelian achievement of philosophy would arbitrarily interrupt the dynamic process of reason exposing itself in history. Hegel's dilemma then becomes only too apparent: Hegel cannot consider his philosophy as philosophy's final figure, but at the same time he has to do so.

Hegel's encyclopaedic system features an original structure, especially in comparison with the monism of Fichte's *Doctrine of Science* and with Schelling's methodological dualism (following Schelling, philosophy can be displayed either from the "subjective" viewpoint of the transcendental philosophy or from the "objective" perspective of the *Naturphilosophie*: Schelling (2005: 25; 2009: 109–10)). Since the achievement of the *Phenomenology of Spirit*, Hegel's system (the "philosophical science") consists of three parts, the Logic, the Philosophy of Nature, and the Philosophy of Spirit. Each part is "a philosophical whole, a circle coming to closure within itself", revealing the "philosophical Idea [...] in a particular determinacy or element" (Hegel 2010a: §15, 43): the Logic is "the science of the idea in and for itself", the philosophy of Nature is "the science of the idea in its otherness", and the philosophy of Spirit describes "the idea returning back to itself from its otherness" (Hegel 2010a: §18, 46). What does this original division mean, and, first of all, what is Hegel's understanding of Logic?

Hegel's conception of Logic is historically unprecedented. He sometimes said Logic "coincides" with traditional metaphysics as "the science of the being as being" (Hegel 1968–: 23-2:653–4); or, using Wolff's terminology, with ontology (or general metaphysics). But he said also that logic "takes the place" of "the former metaphysics", which means that it replaces it (Hegel 2010b: 42): "Logic" does not pretend to be an onto-logy (a discourse concerning a certain object, the being), but rather, an *onto-logic*, the very *logos* of being.[2] One could argue that Logic is the *reflection of being*. Reflection is to be understood in a non-psychological way, as the return on itself of a double process (that of the being *and* of thought), that gains its fundamental unity only due to this return: the process of the determinations of thought (concepts) *is* the process of the determinations of the being. In this sense of an onto-logic, Logic is by no means an "art of thinking" or an *organon* in the purpose of "thinking well". It rather presents in their systematic relationship all of the conditions (ontic as

---

[2] The relationship between Hegelian Logic and metaphysics is highly controversial, because Hegel's own position is ambivalent: see Fulda et al. (1980), Hartmann (1999), Kreines (2015) and Pippin (2019).

well as noetic) under which *a thought of the being* can exist. Thus, logic functions as an "objective thought" that is not defined in reference to subjective consciousness (Hegel 2010a: §§24–5, 58, 66).

Let's briefly focus on the two other parts of the system. The Philosophy of Nature is the doomed part of Hegel's system. Its discredit can be explained by general circumstances unfavourable to the very project of a philosophy of nature (in particular by the hazardous speculations and various aberrations of the romantic *Naturphilosophie*, from which Hegel distanced himself). Another factor is Hegel's various missteps in his doctoral dissertation *De orbitis planetarum*, in which he claims to correct Newton's mistakes by relying on Kepler; this blunder caused historians to largely disregard his work as a philosopher of the sciences. However, Hegel's view of the philosophy of nature is far from uninteresting. It is an attempt to escape from a conception of nature as a rhapsodic collection of levels of reality between which (despite the adage *in natura non datur saltus*) lay unbridgeable distances. Nature in its entirety is, according to Hegel, "the idea in its otherness" (Hegel 2010a: §18, 46); it proceeds from the "resolve" (*Entschluss*) by which the logical idea "*freely discharges* itself" (Hegel 2010b: 753). Most commentators perceived this "free resolve" as an attempt of Hegel's to escape from a trap he had set for himself by making the absolute idea the ultimate category of the first part of the system (the Logic) and not of the system as a whole. On the contrary, the claim can be made that the concept's free alienation (in a nature classically understood as a blend of necessity and contingency: see Hegel (1968–: 20:§248, 237)) is what allows one to understand nature not as a heterogeneous or incoherent ensemble of phenomena, but as a field open to the concept. Paradoxically, nature's radical otherness (*Anderssein*) is what allows the idea to find itself again inside of it. Nature is, in other words, a sign addressed to the spirit that, from the philosopher's point of view ("for us"), this kind of provocation allows to become itself.

There should be no mistake about the position of the spirit as the system's third moment: it does not mean that the spirit definitively "sublates" the previous spheres, in particular nature.[3] Rejecting any form of spiritualism, Hegel states that "*for us*, the spirit has its *presupposition* in *nature*" (Hegel 1968–: 20:§381, 381). The first section of the philosophy of

---

[3] It is impossible here to comment on and discuss the different English translations of the untranslatable word "aufheben", which has the value for Hegel of combining opposite meanings like "to preserve" and "to cease" (Hegel 2010b: 81–2; 2010a: Addition to §96, 153 [Hegel 1991b: 154]). The solution chosen by most recent translators is "to sublate" (Geraets–Suchting–Harris, di Giovanni, Brinkmann–Dahlstrom, Pinkard), but we also find "to cancel" (Wood–Nisbet), "to supersede", "to abolish" and/or "to nullify" (Knox–Houlgate).

the spirit ("Anthropology") describes the ways in which spirit emerges unconsciously from nature itself. The "soul" (that Hegel conceives in an Aristotelian way rather than in a modern one) is "the *sleep* of the spirit" (Hegel 1968–: 20:§389, 388): that from which the spirit awakens itself to consciousness and then to rationality. Hegel writes that the spirit is "the existing truth of matter" (Hegel 1968–: 20:§389, 389). This quasi-materialism appears to be required in order to avoid considering the spirit as a given thing. At the same time, according to the circular structure of knowledge explained in the *Phenomenology of Spirit*'s Preface, the spirit posits its natural presupposition.

Another peculiarity of Hegel's philosophy of spirit must be highlighted. Beyond its analysis of subjective spirit (gathering together the multiple levels of subjectivity, already analysed from another point of view in the *Phenomenology of Spirit*) and of the absolute spirit (that is the spirit's thinking of itself), the *Encyclopedia* gives a large place to the legal, social and political institutions that give freedom "the actuality of a world" (Hegel 1968–: 20:§484, 478). The historical incarnations of spirit in an "objective actual world" (Hegel 2018a: 254) were already the subject of the *Phenomenology of Spirit*'s sixth chapter. The introduction of the term "objective spirit" in the first edition of the *Encyclopedia* underlines the distance between Hegel's conception of spirit and any other understanding of it.

While keeping in mind that this division into three parts eludes the inner dynamism of the system, its implications must be considered: "The *representation* of the *division into parts* is thus incorrect insofar as it sets the particular parts or sciences alongside one another, as if they were merely static components with substantive distinctions, similar to *species*" (Hegel 2010a: §18, 46). In fact, each of the three spheres is both enclosed in itself (and may therefore be separately exposed, as is the doctrine of the objective spirit in the *Principles of the Philosophy of Right*) and a dependent moment of the united system of the (philosophical) science. The ultimate paragraphs of the *Encyclopedia* propose a solution to this paradox, through a presentation of the three syllogisms corresponding to different possible interpretations of the system's internal organization. Philosophy, as the point of completion of the doctrine of absolute spirit, that is, as "the idea *that thinks itself*" (Hegel 1968–: 20:§574, 569), presents itself as the logical sequence (the *system* in the etymological sense of the word) of three "syllogisms", where each of the three terms – Logic (L), Nature (N) and Spirit (S) – occupies in turn the median position. In the first syllogism (L–N–S), following the presentation order of the *Encyclopedia*, "the mediation of the concept has the external shape of a *transition*", in such a way that "it is only in one of the extremes [the spirit] that the concept's freedom is posited" (Hegel 1968–: 20:§575, 570). In the second syllogism (N–S–L), spirit is the median term that *"presupposes nature and ties it with logic"* (Hegel 1968–: 20:§576, 570); this second syllogism describes the process by which the subjectivity can comprehend its removal from natural necessity and its movement towards freedom. The third syllogism (S–L–N) has logic, "the *self-knowing reason*", as its middle term "that splits up into *spirit* and *nature*" (Hegel 1968–: 20:§577, 570). This syllogism, to the extent that it exposes the division of the logical idea into two poles – subjective (spirit) and objective (nature) – is both the presupposition *and* the result of the "self-judgment" (*Sich-Urteilen*) by which the idea, as a system, decomposes itself into two "phenomena" (*Erscheinungen*) corresponding to the two aforementioned syllogisms. Commentators are debating on the respective position and specific meaning of each of these syllogisms. In any case, by presenting "the idea of philosophy" as being potentially understandable in three different ways, each of them placed under the reason of one of the system's moments, Hegel strikingly illustrates the circularity of speculative knowledge. The system cannot be grasped from a single viewpoint, even from that of the whole: it is the coordinated genesis of each viewpoint through which "the nature of the matter (*Sache*), the concept [. . .] pursues its movement and develops itself" (Hegel 1968–: 20:§577, 571).

4.2 Logic as a "Science of Freedom"

This is a paradox, given common representations of systematicity as well as of liberty: the Hegelian *system* presents itself as the true expression of *freedom*. According to Hegel, only the systematic character of philosophy, that is, the fact that its arguments are organized and tied together by a chain of necessity, allows it to be defined as the "science of *freedom*" (Hegel 1968–: 13:§5, 18). This claim needs to be understood in its complexity. Since Hegel's system is not a "circle, which [is] enclosed within itself" (Hegel 2018a: 20), it must leave room for contingency in its apparent irreducibility to conceptual necessity. Nothing is falser than the myth of Hegel's "necessitarianism" that would exclude contingency or reduce it to being only the unconscious shadow of a blind necessity. There is in Hegel a real space for contingency: because it is rational, there must be some irrationality.

However, contingency is not freedom.[4] This is why the compatibility between necessity and freedom (and more specifically, the necessary link

---

[4] On Hegel's conception of contingency and its very relation to freedom, see Henrich (1971) and Mabille (1999).

between the two terms) needs to be justified. The *Logic* bears this justification in what is perceived as being "the hardest" transition to conceive
(Hegel 2010a: §159, 232), that is, the transition from the viewpoint of
"substance" (as the ultimate category of the "objective Logic") to that of
"concept", that is, to the "subjective Logic":

> Thus the concept is the *truth* of substance, and since *necessity* is the
> determining relational mode of substance, *freedom* reveals itself to be the
> *truth of necessity* and the *relational mode of the concept*. (Hegel 2010b: 509)

What this transition from substance to concept and from objective Logic
to subjective Logic corresponds to is the very emergence of freedom within
necessity itself, that is, what Hegel calls the *Beisichsein im Anderen*, the
being "near itself" or "in agreement with itself" of the concept even in
a non-conceptual background. Necessity is not abolished by this transition, but the free process of the concept reigns over it, to the extent that the
concept generates it by producing itself. However, if freedom is "the *truth
of necessity*" (Hegel 2010b: 509), and if necessity is the highest expression of
systematicity, then the system itself must be understood not as a finite
totality circumscribed by its "environment", but as a dynamic process.
Hegel's system itself is not an open system (if we understand by that an
indefinitely revisable one): there is but *one* system, although it is a mobile,
processual and plastic one. This is the reason why, in Hegel's system, the
synthetic moments of totalization are also moments of "*immediatization*".
The totality resulting from the process of spreading (through different
mediations) of an immediate term (or of a term seeming to be immediate)
constitutes itself as a secondary or "becoming" immediacy. This second
level of immediacy results from the process leading towards it and legitim-
ates it in return, so that the result (the second immediacy) becomes the very
ground of the mediating process it results from, and consequently of the
starting point of this process (the first immediacy). This complementarity
of what can be called (in reference to Plato) ascending and descending
dialectics is discernible in two strategic sections: (1) the transition from
Logic to Nature carried out at the end of the *Science of Logic*, and (2) the
return from absolute knowledge to sense certainty at the end of the
Phenomenology of Spirit.

(1) The circularity of systematic philosophical knowledge (justified in
the last chapter of both the *Science of Logic* and the *Phenomenology of Spirit*)
is the final, accomplished manifestation of its "freedom", that is to say, of
its capacity to generate its own presuppositions and its own "otherness".
This is why, at the end of the *Science of Logic*, the idea "*freely discharges* itself

(*sich selbst frei entlässt*)" to become an "external idea", i.e. nature (Hegel 2010b: 753). This linkage between freedom and otherness, logical idea and nature, is highlighted in the *Encyclopedia* (Hegel 2010a: §244, 303). In other words, it is only due to a radical alienation that the idea receives, or better, gives itself the proof of, its freedom. The concept, or its "adequate" form, the idea, demonstrates its power and creativity by exposing and recognizing itself in an environment of radical otherness. Such a process, however, can never completely end, and this is why the truth of the system, that means its ability to be an expression of the "absolute", manifests itself at each of its moments. Hegel's "absolute" is, etymologically, *utopian*: it doesn't have any *topos*; it resides nowhere. This is the reason why all the determinations of the logical process can be considered as "the definitions of the absolute", or as so many "*metaphysical definitions of God*" (Hegel 2010a: §85, 135).

(2) Immediacy is always becoming, it is in a sense paradoxically mediate: this final thesis of the *Science of Logic* (Hegel 2010b: 744) is what the "natural consciousness" blindly experienced as "sense certainty" in the *Phenomenology of Spirit* (Hegel 2018a: 60–8). The incapacity of this immediate consciousness to grasp (in a kind of pre-predicative experience) "this" in its absolute singularity means that it can be grasped only from the immediate consciousness's contrary: "absolute knowledge". This is, indeed, why sense certainty reappears at the end of the phenomenological development; it is then presented as the result of a dismissing that knowledge gives to itself:

> Science contains within itself this necessity to relinquish itself of the form of the pure concept and to make the transition from the concept into *consciousness*. For self-knowing spirit, just for the reason that it grasps its own concept, is an immediate equality with itself, which in its differences is the *certainty of the immediate*, or is *sensuous consciousness* – the beginning from which we started. (Hegel 2018a: 466)

This release even constitutes the "highest freedom" of "absolute" knowledge that spirit has acquired from itself as always already mediated. The use of the vocabulary of "release" (*Entlassung*) makes obvious the parallel between the phenomenological transition from absolute knowledge to sense consciousness and the logical transition from the absolute idea to natural otherness. In these strategic occurrences where the system seems to gather itself in a final concept, when we think we have reached a complete characterization of the absolute content of knowledge, circularity as an image of the system's freedom destroys the illusion of an endpoint or an ultimate truth. Furthermore, the absolute itself would only be an "an *intended* thought" (Hegel 2010a: §85, 135), once cut out of the process that the speculative process attempts to grasp; it would be merely an inchoate idea.

4.3   Logic as Explanation of the "Speculative" Mode of Thinking: Of the "Concept"

The *Logic* has a founding role within the "circle of circles" that is Hegel's system (Hegel 2010a: §15, 43, 2010b: 751).[5] Far from the usual understanding of this notion as an art of reasoning or as a "science of the rules of the understanding" (Kant 1969: A 52/B 76), logic in Hegel's sense is "the science of the *pure idea*, i.e. the idea in the abstract element of *thinking*" (Hegel 2010a: §19, 47). However, Hegel specifies in his lectures on logic that "one can have a very low and a very high opinion of thinking" (Hegel 2010a: §19, Addition: 49); according to him, those who consider logic as a formal discipline (including Kant) have a very low one! Hegel's logic is also formal, but in a very specific sense: by form one must understand, in an Aristotelian way, the immanent dynamism that sets into motion "a matter for which the form is nothing external, because this matter is rather pure thought and hence the absolute form itself" (Hegel 2010b: 29). Hegel's Logic therefore develops a non-formalist conception of form: logic is "of course the formal science, yet the science of *absolute form* which is a totality within itself" (Hegel 2010b: 523, modified). Logic reports the ("formal") movement of ("material") meanings, and thus sets out to be a *logic of truth*: logic means to make explicit the configuration of the being in its totality, and is therefore an onto-logic (but not an ontology).

This logic implements a kind of thinking that is "not just *mere* thought, but rather the highest and, properly viewed, the only manner in which it is possible to comprehend what is eternal and in and for itself" (Hegel 2010a: §19, Addition: 49). This mode of thinking, called *speculative*, must be distinguished from understanding knowledge and from non-speculative philosophy, both of which are acts of a "finite subjectivity" facing a world of given objects, whereas speculative thinking is driven by the "infinite subjectivity" of the concept constituting itself as its own object:

> If, by subjectivity, one understands merely the finite, immediate subjectivity with the contingent and arbitrary content of its particular inclinations and

---

[5] On Hegel's conception of Logic in general, see Hartmann (1999), Henrich (1986), Houlgate (2009), Koch and Schick (2002), Koch (2014a), Nuzzo (2018), Quante and Mooren (2018), Stekeler-Weithofer (1992), Theunissen (1980) and Wolff (2013).

interests, in general what one calls the 'person' in contrast to matter (*Sache*) in the emphatic sense of the word [. . .], then one cannot help but wonder at the Ancients' serene surrender to fate and recognize this attitude as the higher and more dignified one than that modern attitude that selfishly pursues its subjective purposes [. . .] the subjectivity is not merely the bad and finite subjectivity, standing opposite the matter; instead it is, in keeping with its truth, immanent to the matter and, accordingly as infinite subjectivity, is the truth of the matter itself. (Hegel 2010a: §147, Addition: 220, modified)

The Preface of the *Phenomenology of Spirit* distinguishes the knowledge *proprio sensu* (*Erkenntnis*) from the representation (*Vorstellung*) as an immediate relationship of the subject with a given, apparently self-constituted object. Representation provides at best a certain familiarity (*Bekanntschaft*) with the object, but not real knowledge of it; it follows that "What is familiar and well known (*bekannt*) as such is not really known (*erkannt*) for the very reason that it is *familiar and well known*" (Hegel 2018a: 20). True knowledge results from operations of discrimination and classification led by the understanding (*Verstand*), which learns to start "looking the negative in the face and lingering with it" (Hegel 2018a: 21). To avoid simplifications, one needs to bear in mind this vibrant praise of the "absolute power" of understanding.

However, understanding knowledge (which elevates representations to universality, but an abstract one) must be distinguished from "pure thinking", from speculative thought, that "set[s] fixed thoughts into fluid motion" and transforms them into *concepts* by following the movement of being (Hegel 2018a: 21).[6] Overcoming the external relationship that seems to exist only between the *onta* and the *logos* and elevating consciousness to a speculative viewpoint (by describing the experiences that make this elevation necessary): these are the primary goals of the *Phenomenology of Spirit*, that introduces us to the logical, purely speculative knowledge. But this presentation, as justified as it is from the propaedeutic status of the *Phenomenology*, inconveniently seems to convey speculative science as the result of a purifying process whose starting point is the sense-certainty of the given in its immediacy. Can we understand the speculative science (Logic) only as the retrospective key to our consciousness's missed experiences? Wouldn't it amount to removing the logical science from its *absolute* (autoreferential) position? To prevent this dubious interpretation, the

---

[6] On the relationship between representation, understanding and thinking, see Ferrarin (2019) and Pippin (2019).

"Preliminary conception" of the Logic in the *Encyclopedia* presents logical thinking as a generative structure that is presupposed both by the simple representation in which "the content [. . .] remains isolated" and by the intellectual acts that give this representation the form of universality by establishing "relations of necessity among the isolated determinations of representation" (Hegel 2010a: §20, 52).

Thinking (*das Denken*) must also be distinguished from the thoughts (*die Gedanken*) thought up by what Hegel names "thinking over" (*Nachdenken*), that is, the operation by which a finite subject revisits its own thoughts or acts as if it were observing things, introducing a relative exteriority between them and itself. The *thoughts* through which spirit attempts to register the truth of things are only instantaneous traces of the true movement of *thinking*. As *finite* thoughts, they remain tied to oppositions that congeal the flowing process of their shared generation: subject/object, finite/infinite, thought/being, etc. In general, every *dualist* thought structure falls under "the most ordinary metaphysics of the understanding" (Hegel 2010a: §95, 151). The speculative philosophy dissolves these oppositions that structure the ordinary representations of things as well as the reflexive return to them and the concepts of understanding that ensue from them, by revealing the dynamism that generates them. Speculative thought, as well as its condensed expression, the logical idea, is "essentially a *process*" (Hegel 2010a: §215, 286). And this process must be understood as that of the "concept" in a completely new meaning of the word, as we are about to understand.

The *Encyclopedia* expounds the tripartite division of the Logic as follows:

> The Logic falls into three parts: 1. The doctrine of being. 2. The doctrine of essence. 3. The doctrine of the concept and the idea.
>
> That is, into the doctrine of thought, 1. In its *immediacy* – the concept-in-itself, 2. In its *reflection* and *mediation* – the *being-for-itself* and the *shining [Schein]* of the concept, 3. In its *having returned back into itself* and in its developed being-with-itself – the concept *in-and-for-itself*. (Hegel 2010a: §83, 134)

Only through the viewpoint of the *concept*, of which being and essence can be seen as provisory, unaccomplished expressions, can Logic be thought of as a whole, and not as a juxtaposition of heterogeneous units. The "whole concept" can also be divided into the "*existent* concept" and the "*concept*" as such, or between the "concept *in itself*" and the "concept *that exists for itself*". Logic itself can be divided into a "logic of the *concept* as *being*" (or objective logic) and a "logic of the *concept as concept*" (or subjective logic)

(Hegel 2010b: 39). Thus, each of the logical categories (such as those of the "logic of being") is "only *implicitly* the concept" (Hegel 2010b: 531). They are *concepts* because they express the self-thinking of the being itself (the onto-logic); however, they are only partially *the* concept, because they are nothing but the particular traces of its self-producing movement. Consequently, the successive determinations of being and essence and the forms of process that generate them (the "passing over into otherness" and the "shining within itself": Hegel (2010a: §§84 and 112, 135, 173 [Hegel 1991b: 135, 175])) must be understood as partial "explanations" of the concept: "The diverse determinate concepts, rather than falling apart as they do when counted, are only *one* and the same concept" (Hegel 2010b: 541).

Thus, the whole Logic is in itself a logic of the concept. However, this is true only *in itself* ("for us", to use the words of the *Phenomenology of Spirit*) as long as it has not been confirmed by a re-reading of the whole logical process, taking the concept's viewpoint, and, more precisely, that of the idea, as "the unity of the concept and objectivity" (Hegel 2010a: §162, 235). But this systematic "second reading" of the Logic is made possible only by a "first reading" that closely follows the successive partial determinations of the being, essence and concept. The speculative insight avoids favouring one reading over another, or the perspective of process over the perspective of system. Rather, it seeks to consider them in their inseparability. In other words, *logic necessarily presupposes itself*: as system, it presupposes its process; as process, it makes sense only from the point of view of systematic totality. Ultimately, it is because logic is *one* (as the logic of a concept perceived "for itself" as an idea) that it can simultaneously be *double* (objective and subjective logic) and *triple* (logic of the being, essence and concept). Each one of these "points of view" is valuable only in its complementarity with the others.

4.4   The Concept's Freedom

What does Hegel precisely mean by the term "concept" (*Begriff*)? His understanding of this word undergoes one of the most profound semantic shifts he has made.[7] In accordance with its etymology (*con-cipere, be-greifen*: to grasp together), the concept traditionally derives from the unity of a consciousness: following Kant, a concept is "this unique consciousness

---

[7] On Hegel's conception of concept and thinking as an objective process, see Ferrarin (2019), Koch (2003, 2014a), Pippin (2019) and Stekeler-Weithofer (1992).

that brings together a manifold into one representation" (Kant 1969: A 104). On the contrary, Hegel radically separates consciousness and concept by turning the conceiving into the act by which thinking generates itself and thus produces its own subject as well as its object. The concept is not the product of a conceiving subject (of a "finite subjectivity"), it is the free thinking of being by itself or its "reflection" in an optical sense; that's why logic, also "subjective" logic, is an onto-logic. The concept is not a subject's good, because one doesn't own a concept as one would clothes: Hegel rejects the view that "I *have* concepts, and I *have* the concept, just as I also have a coat, complexion, and other external properties" (Hegel 2010b: 515). The concept is rather the subjectivity as such, much more than a simple "gram-matical subject" (Hegel 2010b: 525): the conceiving is the very dynamic of the self-generating of thinking as an impersonal process.

The concept is, so to speak, the arising subject of the objective thinking process. Therefore, it could not be considered as something abstract (in opposition to the concrete dimension of life and things). Even though it bears a moment of abstraction ("the abstract universal"), the concept is "what is concrete and, indeed, the absolutely concrete, the subject as such" (Hegel 2010a: §164, 239). Thus, the "subjective logic" deals much more with the *logical* subject (the concept) than with the *anthropological* subject, since the concept is "the subject" itself (Hegel 2010b: 511), that is to say, it is the immanent reason of its own develop-ment. Hegel strongly insists on what that kind of logical subjectivity implies in terms of spontaneity and creativity, of "*free* power" of think-ing the world (Hegel 2010b: 532).

Each of the three levels of the Logic has a specific type of process: passing over (*Übergehen)* for the logic of being; shining (*Scheinen*) for the logic of essence; and development (*Entwicklung*) for the logic of the concept (in the narrow sense). But, in contrast to the logic of being (in which each determination results from an external limitation) and to the logic of essence (in which each determination is relative to another, like the "essence" is to "shine", or the "inner" to the "outer"), the concept draws its own determinations from itself; that is, it "develops" them from itself. The concept displays from itself the negativity it incorporated by "assimi-lating" or integrating all the determinations of being and essence; in other words, it integrates the content of objective logic by "sublating" it. Organic life is an illustration of this kind of process: a living being (as we would say nowadays) assimilates the information transmitted by its environment and reformulates it according to its own code. Thus, the conceiving grows in a similar manner to a living being. However, it cannot be argued that

Hegel's theory of the concept is a kind of vitalism or organicism. Unlike many philosophers of the nineteenth century, Hegel does not believe that the concept is something alive; rather, life itself is conceptual. This is why he distinguishes "the logical life" (the life of the concept) from "natural life" (Hegel 2010b: 677).

Furthermore, the concept is not a pure asserting of identity; the "labor of the negative" (Hegel 2018a: 13) at work in the objective logic hasn't stopped operating in the subjective logic. However, in the sphere of the concept, negativity is never *given* or *presupposed*; it is the product of the very movement of the concept that brings to light "the *development* of the negativity which, implicitly, [the concept] already is" (Hegel 2010b: 559). I have already invoked a remarkable example of this free generating of negativity or otherness: it is the moment when the logical idea freely dismisses itself (*sich frei entlässt*) at the end of the *Logic*, turning itself into natural exteriority (Hegel 2010a: §244, 303, 2010b: 753). The concept's freedom consists in dissolving and resolving itself (*sich entschliessen*) to otherness:[8] it is precisely in this sense that we can attribute to the concept a "*creative power*" (Hegel 2010b: 533). The religious background behind this topic is clear, but it cannot be understood solely in a theological sense. Creation as seen by monotheism offers an illustration of the way in which the concept, by developing itself, "produces" determinacies such as universality, particularity or singularity, each of them being "as a free being of the whole concept" (Hegel 2010a: §161, 234); but this is only an illustration. The Logic of the concept is no more a theologism than it is a vitalism.

The third part of the *Logic* is divided into three sections. These respectively concern (conceptual, not finite) subjectivity, objectivity (understood as the kind of being devolved on the concept) and the (logical) idea understood not as a subjective representation, but as "the unity of the *concept* and *reality*" (Hegel 2010b: 673). There is obviously something paradoxical here: why would the logic of the concept (as a "subjective logic", though in a very specific sense) deal with objectivity, and not the objective logic (that is the theory of being and essence)? This paradox, in my opinion, can be explained by Hegel's radicalization of the transformation of the notions both of subjectivity and of objectivity undertaken by Fichte and Schelling in their discussion on the nature of philosophical

---

[8] The English verb "to resolve" does not accurately capture the diversity of meaning of the expression "sich entschliessen", used by Hegel in §244 of the *Encyclopedia* to designate the operation by which the concept "abandons itself" and "gives itself up" to the Otherness.

idealism.[9] Schelling establishes the terms of subjective and objective idealism in the *Philosophical Letters on Dogmatism and Criticism* (Schelling 1982:
9th Letter, 100); he applies them respectively to Fichte and himself
(Schelling 2009: 110–11). Fichte, in return, argues that idealism holds
meaning only as a subjectivism (Fichte 1971b: 197–8). I cannot enter into
the detail of this controversy; let's just say that it is an attempt at de-
substantializing subjectivity and at conceiving it not as a fact (*Tatsache*) but
as a "fact-action" (*Tathandlung*), as Fichte explains (Fichte 1971a: 459).
This allows us to understand that the logic of the concept in Hegel's
understanding is a *non-subjectivist theory of subjectivity*. This is carried out
through the programme formulated in the *Phenomenology*'s Preface:
"grasping and expressing the true not just as *substance* but just as much
as *subject*" (Hegel 2018a: 12).

The entire sphere of the concept is that of subjectivity, in the sense that
the concept is the subject emerging throughout the process of its explanation. In this perspective, the "subject" is indeed the "truth" (understood in
the Hegelian sense of that which exceeds something, while assuming it) of
the "substance" (as the ultimate category of objective logic), just as much as
freedom is the "truth" of necessity:

> Thus the concept is the *truth* of substance, and since *necessity* is the
> determining relational mode of substance, *freedom* reveals itself to be the
> *truth of necessity* and *the relational mode of the concept*. (Hegel 2010b: 509)

In a way, the concept is the substance conceived as being the production of
its attributes, its modes and its accidents; Hegel's doctrine of the concept is
the positive counterpart of his discussion of Spinozism (the most consistent
philosophy of substantiality) throughout the third part of *The Doctrine of
Essence*, "Actuality" (*Wirklichkeit*). The concept's transparency to itself in
each of its successive determinations (Hegel 2010b: 736) manifests itself
acutely when it transposes itself into objectivity, gaining "a *reality*" and "a
being" (Hegel 2010b: 624). But the meaning of "subjectivity" in the first
section of the *Doctrine of the Concept* has to be rendered more precisely in
order to correctly understand this passage.

Subjectivity is, generally speaking, the distinctive characteristic of the
concept as the "truth" (result and surpassing) of the objective logic. In
a narrower sense, subjectivity is still the attribute of the concept as opposed
to the objectivity facing it as "the *fact (Sache) itself as it exists in-and-for*

---

[9] On Hegel's approach to and redefinition of subjectivity, see Düsing (2016), Henrich (1986), Koch
(2003, 2014a), Ng (2019) and Schick (2018).

itself" (Hegel 2010b: 527). The subjective concept in this narrower sense –
or in the formal sense, as opposed to the material meaning – becomes
explicit through a series of forms that have been classified by scholastic
logic, following Aristotle's *Analytics*: the concept itself, including its different species (universality, particularity, singularity), and the different types
of judgements and syllogisms, be they conclusive or inconclusive. This
formal subjective concept appears as the "sphere of mere *understanding*"
(Hegel 2010b: 526) because it is – according to the post-Aristotelian
medieval school – only an "exterior form" applying itself to a passive
"matter". But Hegel decisively distances himself from the formalism of
medieval logic by restoring to the notion of *form* the dynamic meaning it
had for Aristotle himself[10] by understanding "form" as a power of information, and thus of generating reality.

> To be sure, the concept needs to be considered as form, but only as infinite,
> fecund form that encompasses the fullness of all content within itself and at
> the same time releases it from itself. (Hegel 2010a: §160, Addition: 233)

This rejection of formalism becomes especially apparent with regards to
Hegel's theory of the syllogism (*Schluss*). This theory may, at first glance,
appear to be a tedious continuation of the scholastic tradition, but in fact
that is not the case. In Hegel's sense, a syllogism is the act by which the
concept connects itself to itself (*schliesst sich mit sich zusammen*). The
syllogism is not a form of subjective reasoning (in the usual meaning). It
is rather a manifestation of the immanent dynamic of self-thinking that is
the logical "subject", the concept:

> The syllogism is what is *rational* and *everything* rational. [. . .] In a rational
> syllogism [. . .] the subject joins *itself together with itself* by means of this
> mediation. It is only a subject in this way, or the subject is only in itself the
> syllogism of reason. (Hegel 2010a: §§181–2, 253, 255)

In summary, Hegel's theory of the "subjective" concept is an attempt at
disentangling subjectivity from any and all psychological or even transcendental contexts and at breaking free from the "philosophy of subjectivity".
For Hegel, subjectivity refers to the self-engendering capacity of thinking.
The subject is the concept's self-movement: it is the rationality of self-acting
thinking, not the presumed origin of acts of such kinds. The subjective
concept can be said to be formal, but not in the traditional sense of a set of
forms that can be applied to an independent matter. The concept – as

---

[10] See *Metaphysics* H, 1042 a 24–1043 a 28, in Aristotle (1984) and Hegel's commentary (Hegel 1968–:
30–1:104 and 344).

a self-mediation – must inform reality, it must test itself as the very movement of the being; in that sense only can the concept be called "formal". Henceforth, subjectivity is but the conceptual mediation that constitutes objectivity as such.

Objectivity (*Objektivität*) is the ultimate expression of immediacy in the Logic, summarizing all of its previous displays: the being-there (*Dasein*),[11] the existence (*Existenz*) and the actuality (*Wirklichkeit*) (Hegel 2010b: 628). However, as with everything that seems immediate, objectivity is actually overloaded with (conceptual) mediations. In other words, it is because the concept is "subjective" that objectivity does not exist *for* a subject but *through* the mediation of subjectivity (even if mediation is seemingly abolished in its objective outcome). Objectivity – gathered within itself, having erased its constituting conceptual mediation – "has the meaning first of all of *the being in and for itself of the concept* that has sublated the *mediation* posited in its self-determination, raising it to *immediate* self-reference" (Hegel 2010b: 131). It is one of the remarkable peculiarities of the logic of the concept (in comparison with that of the being and essence): the mediation (of the subjective concept) *precedes* the immediate (the object), and the object can *only* be thought of as a becoming immediacy. The objective logic progressively revealed the essential mediation process at work in what appears immediate (the "given" being or being-there). In contrast, in the logic of the concept, the theory of objectivity allows the conceptual ("subjective") mediations to reveal themselves, even though the object seems to have "forgotten" them. Through mechanism, chemism and teleology, the theory of objectivity is an anamnesis (*Er-innerung*) of the conceptual mediation of all kinds of object: a recalling of the always mediated existence of the immediate objectivity.

As for subjectivity, Hegel distances himself from the common conception of what an object and objectivity are.[12] The object must be conceived as an object in and for itself; it does not exist first for and thanks to a subject. Even though *Gegen-stand* is a morphological equivalent to *objectum*, a conceptual distinction needs to be made between (so to speak) the

---

[11] This translation (Geraets–Harris) seems preferable to "existence" (Brinkmann, di Giovanni) just because Hegel explicitly distinguishes between *Dasein* (as a category of the sphere of being) and *Existenz* (as a category of the sphere of essence whose etymology implies a reflection): "The expression 'existence' (derived from *existere*) points to a having-gone-forth (*Hervorgegangensein*) and the concrete existence (*Existenz*) is the being that has gone forth from the ground, the being re-established through the sublation (*Aufhebung*) of the mediation" (Hegel 2010a: §123, Addition: 191 [Hegel 1991b: 193]). Moreover, the option of translating *Dasein* by "existence" requires 'overtranslating' *Existenz* by "concrete existence".

[12] See Brinkmann (2011).

ob-ject that "faces" a (finite) subject (*Gegenstand*) and the object "in itself" (*Objekt*). Only secondarily does the object (*Objekt*) become an ob-ject (*Gegenstand*) for a subject. In this respect, common sense is right in its opposition to the modern subjectivist philosophy.

> By 'object', however, one tends to understand not merely an abstract entity or concretely existing thing or something in general actual, but instead something concretely and *completely* self-sufficient in itself; this completeness is the *totality of the concept.* That the *object* is also something standing opposite [*Gegenstand*] and *external* to another, this will be determined subsequently insofar as it posits itself in *opposition* to *the subjective.* Here, as that into which *the* concept has passed over from its mediation, it is at first only an *immediate,* neutral object, just as the concept is determined to be the *subjective* only in the subsequent opposition. (Hegel 2010a: §193, 265)

Only during the presentation of teleology, when the object appears explicitly aimed towards subjective ends, does a "subjective" activity emerge again within objectivity; however, it does so as what must surpass itself in its realization: once realized, a subjective goal is no longer subjective, but rather "the *posited unity* of the subjective and the objective [dimensions]" (Hegel 2010a: §210, 281). Therefore, Hegel intends to surpass the opposition between internal and external purposiveness (*Zweckmässigkeit*): even if making this distinction is "one of Kant's greatest services to philosophy", it is necessary to go back to what constitutes the "essential element of the teleological": the "*form of purposiveness*", that is purely conceptual, and has therefore freedom as its ruling principle (Hegel 2010b: 157).

Objectivity is immediately conceptual, just because it results from an *Aufhebung* of the subjective concept: "objectivity is the *real concept* that *has emerged from its inwardness* and has passed over into the being-there" (Hegel 2010b: 527, modified). This explains Hegel's interest in the Anselmian or Cartesian ontological proof of the existence of God, despite the radical criticisms Kant left it with (Kant 1969, A 592/B 620). Beyond its theological content, Anselm's argument is a perfect example of the concept's transition from subjectivity to objectivity and of the processual identity of the being and concept: in both cases, "the concept posits itself as *something real,* a *being there*" (Hegel 2010b: 626, modified). Thus understood, the ontological proof is an illustration of the aim of the Hegelian Logic. This is why, in his 1829 lessons on the proofs of the existence of God, Hegel states that the *Logic* is the only proof of the veracity of religious representations: it is the "metaphysical theology" (Hegel 1968–: 17:419).

The complete revision of the concepts of subjectivity and objectivity in the Logic of the Concept serves a single purpose: to demonstrate that subjectivity is no separate form and that objectivity is no informal matter. When objectivity is not considered as inherently conceptual, the concept is doomed to be the veil of an empty subjectivity, separated from real things: "*in itself* concept, or also, if one prefers, subjectivity, and the object are *the same*" (Hegel 2010a: §193, 266).

The last section of the Doctrine deals with "the idea". Here again, the usual meaning of the term is completely changed. In Hegel's sense, the idea is not a subjective representation, a mental state. Rather, it is a process consisting in the dialectical explanation of the, until then, implicit identity of objectivity and subjectivity, of the being and concept, of actuality and rationality:

> The idea is instead its own result and, as such, just as much immediate as mediated. The stages considered so far, those of being and essence and equally of the concept and objectivity, are not something fixed and resting on themselves with regard to this difference among them. Instead they have been demonstrated to be dialectical and their truth is only that of being moments of the idea. (Hegel 2010a: §213, Addition: 284)

Thus, the idea is defined as a dynamic process, generating and abolishing all of the categories and oppositions that emerged from the Logic as the "Science of the *pure idea*" (Hegel 2010a: §19, 47). In Hegel's view, this conception of the idea is a shield against dualism. This is not only because it rejects the dualities that understanding considers ultimate, but, most importantly, because the idea serves as the immanent rule of construction and deconstruction of these dualities.

In the same way as the concept is not the product of a subject, but the subjectivity itself, the idea is not someone's idea *about* something. The idea is a "*subject-object*" (Hegel 2010b: 673) in the sense that it is an idea of self, an *act of self*: it is nothing more than the process by which thought and reality generate themselves simultaneously, the process that establishes the being as concept and the concept as being. Hence, the idea summarizes the Logic's purpose of being an onto-logic. Therefore, Hegel's philosophy is far from preaching what is commonly understood as "absolute" idealism; claiming that the idea is the only reality is different from pretending that the idea is the idea *of* reality. In this sense, if it is true that "every true philosophy is [. . .] *idealism*" (Hegel 2010a: §95, 152), then it must be added that it is an unprecedented idealism because it combines a radicalization both of idealism (nothing is real but the idea) and of realism (the idea is nothing if it *isn't*).

Thus, it is important not to misinterpret the "absolute idea" (the ending point of the *Logic*, but not of the system) in the same way as "absolute knowledge" (in the *Phenomenology of Spirit*) often is. The absolute idea is not the ultimate summary of all that was gathered throughout the logical process, because the result is nothing once cut off from the process leading up to it. The absolute idea has no other content than what can be found in each of the moments of the whole logical process, from the simplest categories ("pure being", "pure nothingness") to the most complex (like "syllogism" or "teleology"). However, it articulates this content (named "the very matter", *die Sache selbst*) around its processual nature:

> The absolute idea is comparable to the old man who says the same religious sentences as the child does, but for the old man they have the meaning of his entire life. Even if the child understands the religious content, what validity that content has for him is still of the sort that lies outside his entire life and world. (Hegel 2010a: §237, Addition: 300)

As the "old age" of thinking, the absolute idea summarizes its "life": this life is the work of freedom, that is of the very predicate of the concept.

CHAPTER 5

From Logic to Nature

Christian Martin

This chapter deals with a crucial juncture in Hegel's *Encyclopedia*, the transition from its first part, the 'science of logic', to its second part, the 'philosophy of nature', which is at the same time a transition to what Hegel calls "the real sciences of philosophy" (*die realen Wissenschaften der Philosophie*[1]).

After laying out, in Section 5.1, Hegel's conception of logic, I go on, in Section 5.2, to look at §244 of the *Encyclopedia*. This paragraph leads from logic to nature. Hegel's argument has been prominently criticized by Schelling as either question begging or involving a category mistake. I argue that Schelling's objections can be met, if one clearly distinguishes between the *transition* from the *logic* to the *philosophy of nature* and the *relation* between the *logical* and *nature*, which does not itself have the character of a *transition*. In Section 5.3 I engage with the very first steps of Hegel's philosophy of nature, arguing that we can know a priori that nature is an inhomogeneous material space-time continuum. Subsequently, in Section 5.4, I address the question of what it might mean to claim, as Hegel does, that 'the concept' is 'immanent' in nature. As I argue, it would be confused to assume that concepts or universals are somehow 'contained' in the material space-time continuum. We rather need to understand nature's 'peculiar logicality' in terms of recurrent, self-preserving configurations within the inhomogeneous continuum that allow to be articulated and known by means of the forms of discursive thinking. I conclude, in Section 5.5, with some remarks on what it means to know nature and on the difference in method between the 'science of logic' and the 'real sciences of philosophy'.

---

[1] *Science of Logic* (SL): 11, in the *Gesammelte Werke* (GW): 21:9 (Hegel 1968–).

5.1 The *Logic* as a Presuppositionless Investigation of Pure Thought

Hegel's *Logic* seeks to articulate the self-knowledge inherent to pure thought.[2] It does so by unfolding, without relying on any thematic presuppositions, the system of concepts that have their source in thinking alone, i.e. independently of anything that is *given* to it.[3] The *Logic* cannot, however, begin with thought as its *explicit* topic, for in that case it would have to proceed from a *preconceived* idea of what thought is. Instead, at its very beginning, it requires that all sorts of prejudices and contrasts in which thinking is usually seen as entangled be eliminated or bracketed.[4] Therefore it begins with the simplest concepts of all[5] – *being, nothing, becoming, being determinate, something* etc. The *Logic* is thus at the same time an investigation of what it means *to be*.[6] That the *Logic*, in passing through a series of conceptual determinations, deals with "nothing but one's own thinking"[7] is substantiated by the fact that each conceptual determination proves to be unintelligible *in isolation* and thus points beyond itself towards further concepts, only in connection with which can it be grasped undistortedly. The movement of thought carried out in the *Logic* thus consists in thought's procuring a system of pure concepts *all by itself*. Insofar as pure thought, by this very movement, provides what is needed to grasp itself in a fully articulate way, pure thinking becomes thematic as what it has proven itself to be all along, namely as unconditioned self-determination. Hegel's *Logic* thus concludes with the 'absolute idea', i.e. the concept of pure thought qua self-transparent self-determination that relates to the totality of pure concepts as its own manifestations[8].

Conceiving of logic as "the science of *pure* thinking"[9] presupposes a distinction between purity and impurity. This distinction does not coincide with that between the *a priori* and the *a posteriori*. For, in Hegel's encyclopedic system, even those disciplines which follow upon the *Logic* and do not treat of thinking purely as such aren't empirical in character, even though they have to relate their concepts to relevant findings of the empirical sciences. Hegel characterizes the distinction

---

[2] SL: 17 (GW 21:16), see also Pippin (2019: 101–39).
[3] Hegel (2010a (henceforth ENC): 1:125 (§78)). Reconstructions that take Hegel's claim to presuppositionlessness seriously can be found in Houlgate (2006), Martin (2012) and Koch (2014a).
[4] SL: 29 (GW 21:33).   [5] ENC 1:47 (§19).
[6] Houlgate (2006: 115–23) and Martin (2012: 1–13).   [7] ENC 1:47 (§19).
[8] ENC 1:299–300 (§§236–7), SL: 752 (GW 12:252–3). For an understanding of the absolute idea along these lines see Martin (2012: 571–607).
[9] SL: 38 (GW 21:45), see also ENC 1:125 (§78).

between purity and impurity by setting logic apart from what he calls "the
real sciences of philosophy", i.e. philosophy of nature and philosophy of
spirit:

> The logical is the general content of everything, but it also stands as what is
> general to what is specific. In this way, the Logic distinguishes itself from the
> real sciences of philosophy. In one of these, namely, the Philosophy of
> Nature, the idea is in the element of free self-externality and matter, in the
> other, the Philosophy of Spirit, it is in the element of being-in-and-for-itself,
> namely, knowledge. [...] Logic thus distinguishes itself from the real
> sciences, where 'real' means 'being determinate'.[10]

Provisionally, this distinction can be spelled out as follows: logic is *pure*
insofar as it is concerned only with concepts which have their source in
thinking alone, without invoking *spatio-temporal* determinacy *as such*.
Accordingly, the self-knowledge of thinking that the *Logic* articulates will
not exhibit thinking as an activity that requires spatio-temporal instantiation. The subject matters of the real sciences of philosophy, on the other
hand, are dealt with as involving a moment of spatio-temporal determinacy.

Pure thinking cannot, for methodological reasons, be dealt with *as
thinking* in the first part of the *Logic* but appears as fully absorbed in quasi-
objectual determinations, for which reason Hegel refers to that part as
"objective logic";[11] and the *explicit* self-knowledge of thinking that is
achieved in its second part, the "subjective logic", cannot yet be envisaged
as an activity that requires spatio-temporal instantiation. These peculiarities can easily give rise to confusions of which Hegel's own mode of
presentation is not entirely free. For, it might make it appear as if the
Logic treated of a *different kind of thinking* from ours, namely one that is (1)
completely absorbed in the quasi-objectual determinations it thinks and (2)
actual thinking *prior* to spatio-temporal instantiation and thus, as it were,
divine thinking before creation.[12]

The fact that Hegel sometimes expresses himself in this way should first
and foremost be understood as an attempt to bring a *methodological* trait of
his *Logic* into focus, namely that it abstracts from all real presuppositions. It
is not thereby claimed that pure thinking *exists* as divine activity prior to
spatio-temporal instantiation.[13] Rather, the *Logic* deals with the thinking of

---

[10] Hegel (1992 (henceforth V): 11:24) (my translation), see also SL: 11 (GW 21:9).
[11] For Hegel's distinction between "objective" and "subjective logic" see SL: 38–43 (GW 21:44–9).
[12] SL: 29 (GW 21:34) and V 11:91.
[13] Hegel stresses that "the knowing involved in the simple logical idea is just the concept of knowing as
     it is thought by us, but not knowing insofar as it exists for itself, – not actual spirit but only the
     possibility thereof" (Hegel 1970–1 (henceforth TW): 10:18 addition, translation modified).

us thinkers which requires spatial and temporal embodiment, but it does so in abstraction from such embodiment. Hegel expresses this point by stating that it is *spirit*, i.e. thinking *insofar as it is embodied in a real world shaped by its own activity*, which is engaged, in the *Logic*, to "think its own essence".[14] If it is true that "essence must appear",[15] then pure thinking as considered in the *Logic* cannot be attributed an independent existence prior to its real appearance in the workings of spirit, even while this appearance is bracketed throughout the *Logic*.

The abstraction from what is real extends only to the *content* of the *Logic*, i.e. to the pure concepts developed in it. That these are "determinations of thought"[16] (*Denkbestimmungen*) means precisely that their content does not involve any reference to spatio-temporal reality *as such*. However, as *a philosophical discipline* in which *spirit* undertakes to recognize its own logical essence, the *Logic* must avail itself of what is real. Its execution requires the use of *expressions* and must articulate itself in the form of propositions. This is so precisely because the *essence* of thinking is not itself *actual* thinking, but only amounts to the latter *insofar as it appears*.

That which is not itself a content of pure thought but a necessary prerequisite of its philosophical investigation is a topic for "external reflection".[17] External reflection considers relevant issues that do not, strictly speaking, belong to the subject matter of logic – at least not at a given place. What falls within the scope of external reflection, however, does not have to be an accidental feature of the self-knowledge of thinking achieved in logic. For thought's essence can only be articulated, *philosophically*, by availing oneself of real preconditions of thinking: spirit, when it undertakes to articulate its logical nature in abstraction from its real manifestation, remains spirit, i.e. requires real manifestation. The latter is thematically external to *logic's subject matter* (i.e. *the logical*) but is at the same time pragmatically internal to *logic*, i.e. an essential aspect of this kind of *philosophical activity*. In other words, the conditions of articulation of *pure* thought are essentially *impure* or *real*. Without the possibility, provided by language, to distinguish that which cannot be distinguished by recourse to *determinate characteristics* – e.g. 'being' and 'nothing', 'something' and 'other', etc. – and without recourse to propositional form, the *Logic* could not get under way.

[14] SL: 10 (GW 21:8), see also ENC 3:196 (§574).
[15] ENC 1:197 (§131) and SL: 418 (GW 11:323).
[16] SL: 13–14 (GW 21:12–13), SL: 30 (GW 21:35).   [17] See e.g. SL: 34 (GW 21:39).

One might expect that everything essentially involved in pure thinking that cannot be addressed at the beginning of the *Logic* or throughout its course and thus belongs to external reflection is eventually caught up with. For the *Logic* unfolds the concept of pure thinking, so that external reflection becomes internal insofar as its contents are integrated into the self-knowledge of pure thinking.[18] This is true as far as it goes. For instance, throughout the objective logic, concepts, judgements and inferences are merely *used* to articulate the conceptual determinations at issue; but they themselves become the subject of investigation in the subjective logic. The *Logic* thus culminates in the concept of pure thinking to which its own *modus operandi* is transparent.

However, even at the end of the *Logic*, the *concept* of thought's know-ledge of the totality of conceptual determinations as its own manifest-ations, i.e. the absolute idea, does not coincide with the *actual achievement* of such self-knowledge in a logic qua *philosophical discipline*. Neither is the distinction between purity and impurity a *purely logical* distinction nor can *philosophical* science, as an *actual* activity that presupposes *real* manifest-ation, be *sufficiently* characterized by means of *logical* concepts. Therefore, Hegel's final characterization of the absolute idea as the concept of the *science* of pure thinking[19] belongs to external reflection. Accordingly, the full-blown concept of logic *as a philosophical science* will be available only at the very end of the philosophy of spirit.[20]

Precisely because the *concept* of pure thought's self-knowledge in the totality of its determinations does not coincide with the concept of *philo-sophical* engagement with pure thinking, the transition from logic to the *real sciences of philosophy* has two categorically distinct dimensions that Hegel himself didn't distinguish sufficiently clearly. This makes this tran-sition somewhat nebulous and has shrouded it in mystery.[21] Thematically, the transition concerns the relationship between *the logical*[22] and *the real* (nature, spirit). As such, it raises the question of why there should be anything beyond the logical. Pragmatically, we are faced with a transition

---

[18] ENC 1:302–3 (§§242–3).
[19] According to Hegel, in the absolute idea "the *science of logic* has apprehended its own concept" (SL: 752 (GW 12:252)). "The science concludes in this way by grasping the concept of itself as the pure idea, for which the idea is" (ENC 1:303 (§243)). However, while the absolute idea indeed amounts to self-knowledge of the *way* in which *pure thinking* unfolds, namely its method, this does not yet amount to a full-blown conception of *philosophical science as such*.
[20] ENC 3:181–96 (§§572–4).
[21] According to Wandschneider (2004: 107) this transition is "one of the darkest passages in Hegel's œuvre".
[22] See e.g. ENC 1:125 (§79).

from one philosophical science (*logic*) to another (*the philosophy of nature*) and, thereby, to another *type* of philosophical science, namely, a *real science of philosophy*. Since the concept of philosophy cannot be grasped by means of logical concepts alone, the relevant transition between the two philosophical disciplines can only be a topic for external reflection at this point. Seen from this angle, it raises both the question of how the transition is motivated and that of what the crucial differences between the philosophical method before the transition and that after it are.

Unconsciously blending these two dimensions can easily give rise to the confused view that not only must the transition from logic to philosophy of nature be rationally motivated, but that there must also be a rationally motivated transition between *the logical* and *nature* – as if nature were something that owed its *existence* to pure thought. One may then find it a little awkward that the logical idea is supposed to ground nature or to turn itself into it, while it remains concealed that this way of speaking does not make sense. Disentangling the two dimensions of the transition at issue is what we now turn to.

5.2 The Externality of the Logical Idea *in* Nature versus the Transition from Logic *to* the Philosophy of Nature

The last sentence of the last paragraph of the *Encyclopedia Logic* which is supposed to justify the transition to the philosophy of nature reads as follows:

> [T]he absolute *freedom* of the idea is that it [. . .], in the absolute truth of itself, *resolves to release* freely *from itself* the moment of its particularity or the first determining and otherness, the *immediate idea*, as its *reflection*, itself as *nature*.[23]

A tenable reconstruction of the transition from logic to the philosophy of nature has to comply with the following adequacy requirement. Firstly, it must clearly distinguish between two dimensions of this crucial juncture of Hegel's encyclopedic system, namely the *thematic* relationship between *the logical* and *nature*, and the transition from one philosophical discipline, *logic*, to another, the *philosophy of nature*. Secondly, it must not only coherently characterize these dimensions on their own, but also do so in such a way that their internal connection becomes clear. It must be clarified why the philosophical investigation of nature (and of spirit) requires a method that is different from *logic* and thus amounts to a *real* science

---

[23] ENC 1:303 (§244).

of philosophy. Moreover, it needs to be shown that philosophical thinking does not *abruptly* turn to nature as a *new* topic, but that *thinking through* the logical makes it necessary to consider nature (and spirit).

Schelling notoriously objected to Hegel's talk of "resolve"[24] (*Entschluss*), "free self-release"[25] (*freies Sich-Entlassen*) and "externalization"[26] (*Entäußerung*) of the logical that the latter is thereby attributed personality.[27] This shows, according to Schelling, that Hegel subscribes to a view of pure thought as actually existing and, thus, implicitly, as already real.[28] As a critique of a dogmatic-metaphysical reading of the transition in terms of a production or a grounding of nature on the part of the logical idea this objection is valid. For the assumption of some such production indeed presupposes that the absolute idea – the self-referential totality of pure thought – enjoys independent existence on the basis of which it can then somehow give rise to nature. Since the *Logic* unfolds conceptual determinations that have their source in thinking alone, and since we *know* by external reflection that it is *spirit* which in the *Logic* recognizes its own essence and that essence must appear while not existing independently of and prior to its appearance, it would amount to a dubious metaphysical presupposition if we had to assume, at the very end of the *Logic*, that the absolute idea is an independently existing being that produces nature on its own initiative or somehow turns itself into it.

The most fundamental objection to such a dogmatic-metaphysical reading, however, is not that it is based on an external presupposition, but, rather, that it makes no sense. Hegel's talk of "resolution", "free self-release", "self-externalization" and even "creation"[29] at least suggests that he is referring to a *process* by which the logical generates nature or turns itself into it.[30] However, for there to be a process, there must be some respect in which its starting point and its result – what grounds and what is grounded – are continuous with each other. From this it follows that there can be no process that leads from the realm of pure thought to nature, for the two realms cannot be understood as continuous with each other.

---

[24] ENC 1:303 (§244).   [25] ENC 1:303 (§244), SL: 753 (GW 12:253).
[26] SL: 49 (GW 21:57), ENC 3:6 (§281).   [27] Schelling (1975: 135).   [28] Schelling (1975: 133).
[29] SL: 523 (GW 12:25).
[30] Various authors have stressed that Hegel's talk of "free resolve" should not be understood in the sense of a *voluntary decision* on the part of a *personal agent* (Houlgate 2005: 110; Wandschneider 2016: 64). According to Houlgate "the move to nature is in fact the impersonal, logical process, whereby the Idea determines itself to be nature" (Houlgate 2005: 110). Wandschneider talks of an "auto-differentiation" that ought to be understood as an eternal grounding relation between the logical idea and nature (Wandschneider 2004: 119–20). However, as I argue, the idea of a process that leads from the logical idea to nature or of a grounding relation that obtains between them does not make sense – irrespective of whether it is understood by recourse to a personal agent or not.

This can be seen as follows. Continuity is possible only between things that are at least in some respects similar, so that they may border onto each other. The logical and nature are opposed to each other insofar as thoughts have no spatial, temporal or material *properties*, whereas nature does; and nature does not in itself have logical properties such as validity or invalidity, whereas thoughts do.[31] The realm of pure thoughts and that of nature cannot therefore hang together *immediately amongst each other*, but can only be integrated *within* an *overarching* unity, namely in *spirit* qua *actual* thinking that is *manifest* in a *world*.

For the logical idea to produce nature or to turn itself into it both would have to interpenetrate each other, i.e. that which is not a thought would also 'somehow' have to be a thought, and that which is a thought would also 'somewhere' have to not be a thought. It is absurd, however, to assume that nature begins 'somewhere at the border of the logical'.

The relation of the logical to nature cannot therefore be understood as a process by means of which one grounds the other, but needs rather to be understood by analogy to the relation between soul and body, as a complementarity of form and matter which belong to each other, originally.

The embarrassment to which the dogmatic-metaphysical reading leads cannot be bypassed by interpreting the transition from logic to philosophy of nature purely epistemologically.[32] According to a purely epistemological reading, this transition simply amounts to a *return* to the real – to the wealth of our everyday and scientific knowledge of nature and spirit – which had been *bracketed* at the beginning of the *Logic*. On this interpretation, once the logical categories have been systematically unfolded and thereby cleansed of dogmatic-metaphysical distortions, the real can and must be philosophically addressed by means of them. This is necessary because all cognition of nature and spirit is already in itself, albeit latently and confusedly, shaped by these categories.

Against such a reading, Schelling argued that mere recourse to a presupposition from which the *Logic* had initially abstracted nevertheless remains *recourse* to a *presupposition* that has not been philosophically

---

[31] Denying that the logical has real *properties* does not imply a Cartesian conception of thought. On Hegel's account, thought, far from enjoying *independent* existence, *presupposes real manifestation*. This, however, does not impart to thought *properties* of the sort that pertain to that in which it is manifest, see note 37.

[32] According to Plevrakis §244 treats of the relation between two *philosophical disciplines* – logic and *philosophy of nature* – rather than between the *logical idea* and *nature* (Plevrakis 2018: 116–17). Plevrakis does not, however, coherently stick to this reading, but falls back into talk about the "origination" (*Zustandekommen*) of nature (Plevrakis 2018: 121) and about the *idea* of knowing as providing "matter" (*Stoff*) (Plevrakis 2018: 123).

vindicated. Contrary to Hegel's assertion, the step beyond logic would thus be motivated only by our *recollection* of the real insofar as we are acquainted with it prior to the investigation of pure thinking and by a desire to find a way back from the logical 'realm of shadows' to the plenitude of what really exists.[33]

However, Hegel's own procedure deviates from the position justly criticized by Schelling. This deviation is apparent from the fact that the real sciences of philosophy do not, according to Hegel, content themselves with a logical articulation of material provided by the non-philosophical sciences. They *continue* the philosophical development of pure concepts by coming up with peculiar *non-logical* concepts, even while these must indeed be put into correlation with such material[34] – a task which Hegel mainly pursues in his lecture courses rather than in the *Encyclopedia* itself. The transition from the *Logic* to the real sciences of philosophy cannot be understood *purely* epistemologically as a transition to a kind of philosophizing that seeks to unlock the fabric of experience by means of logical categories, because this task, if it is to understand itself, requires an understanding of the difference and connection between the *logical* and *the real*, i.e. *nature and spirit*. Such an understanding cannot be available, *pre-philosophically*, for the logical *as such* is brought into view only by logic; its difference from and connection with the real can therefore only be clarified *subsequently* and thus needs to be addressed at the very juncture between *logic* and the *real sciences of philosophy*.

The *epistemological* transition from logic to philosophy of nature can thus be rendered clear only if the *metaphysical* connection between the logical and the real is brought into view as well, though not in the dogmatic-metaphysical fashion discussed above. I have argued elsewhere that insight into the complementarity between the logical and the real can be gained by showing that *logical form*, i.e. the kind of unity that belongs to thought as such, requires expression and thus presupposes the real as a sphere from which expressions can be drawn.[35] According to this line of argumentation, by thinking through the notion of logical form we can recognize that what the *Logic* is about, namely pure thoughts, cannot exist prior to and independent of expressive activity. Accordingly, the activity of thinking requires the guise of the real. Thoughts cannot, therefore, exist independently of expressive activity, even while they cannot be identified with such activity or sets of expressions either, for embodied activity in

[33] Schelling (1975: 115) and Schick (2012).   [34] ENC 2.1:197 (§246).
[35] Martin (2017a: 152–67, 2020: chapter 2).

space and time can bring thoughts into play only to the extent that its own particularity is made irrelevant.[36] The relationship between the logical and the real is therefore a paradoxical one: the logical presupposes the real insofar as it depends upon the active articulation, repercussion and *disappearance* of something real, namely expressions.[37] The logical thus exists independently of the real, albeit not as something that is prior to it, but as something emancipated from it.

While Hegel himself addresses this paradoxical tie between thought and expression in his *philosophy of spirit*[38] – and most clearly in his Jena writings[39] – he mentions it only in passing in connection with the 'self-externalization' of the absolute idea at the end of the *Logic*, echoing the incarnation of the word from the prologue of St. John's gospel.[40] It seems to me, however, that an argument along the lines indicated here, according to which logical form essentially presupposes real manifestation, is the only way to philosophically understand the metaphysical connection between the logical and the real without falling into nonsense. An argument of this type thus meets Hegel's demand that one must not merely assume the existence of nature quasi-empirically, but 'prove' philosophically that there must be nature.[41]

5.3   The Concept of Nature

As I shall now argue, a philosophical conception of nature can be achieved by spelling out the insight that logical form essentially presupposes a realm that does not itself consist of thoughts but is not simply alien to thought, either. Rather, this realm must be tied back to the logical and, as it were, belong to it as its other side.

As indicated, Hegel himself does not provide a detailed characterization of the real in contrast to the logical.[42] But he introduces nature as the "idea

---

[36] Martin (2020: chapter 4).

[37] In the *Phenomenology of Spirit* Hegel characterizes the relation between a particular utterance and the thought expressed by it as follows: "The 'I' that utters itself is heard or perceived. [. . .] That it is perceived or heard means that its real existence dies away; this its otherness has been taken back into itself; and its real existence is just this: that as a self-conscious Now, as a real existence, it is not a real existence, and through this vanishing it is a real existence. This vanishing is thus itself at once its abiding" (PS: 309 (§508)).

[38] ENC 3:75–84 (§§457–60).   [39] GW 8:188–201.   [40] V 11:226, SL: 736 (GW 12:237).

[41] At the beginning of the *Philosophy of Nature* Hegel refers back to §244 of the *Encyclopedia* as containing a "proof that there necessarily is a nature" (ENC 2.1:192, addition).

[42] See the references in note 9. Hegel uses the terms 'real' and 'reality' mostly in the *logical* sense of an immediate positive determination or quality, e.g. SL: 84–8 (GW 21:98–102). It cannot, however, be just this logical understanding which is at issue in his distinction between 'logic' and the 'real sciences of philosophy'.

in the form of otherness" (*Idee in der Form des Andersseins*)[43] and spirit as
the "return" of the idea from this otherness.[44] This allows us to gain insight
into his conception of the real, i.e. that which nature and spirit have in
common in contrast to the logical. What they have in common does not
amount to a genus that might equally well be grasped independently of its
two species, nature and spirit. What is common to nature and spirit is what
Hegel calls the "being-other" (*Anderssein*) or the "self-externality"
(*Außersichsein*) of the logical idea. With respect to *nature*, this amounts
to a *global* characterization of this sphere of the real, while also amounting
to a *subordinate* trait of *spirit*, namely as that from which the latter is said to
'return'. Our primary concern in what follows will be to understand
Hegel's conception of nature as the idea in the form of otherness.

That nature is said to be the logical idea that is posited in a certain *form*
means that nature exhibits a kind of unity that is different from the unity
pertaining to logical determinations *as such*. Given that form and content
are not external to each other, the assertion that nature is the logical idea in
another form cannot be understood as if nature amounted to another
'configuration' *of thoughts*. Rather, in nature, the concept – the universal,
the thought – is "immersed", "lost" and "vanished", as Hegel puts it.[45] The
fact that nature is nevertheless said to be a guise of the logical idea, namely
its own otherness or externality, means the following: while nature does not
consist of thoughts, it is nevertheless essentially intelligible. That a realm
that doesn't *consist of* thoughts must nevertheless be intelligible is an insight
that had already been vindicated in the *Logic* itself, in the course of the
transition from subjectivity to the object.[46]

Intelligibility is only the first, not particularly surprising, trait of nature
that results from its characterization as the idea in the form of otherness. It
needs to be added that the peculiar kind of unity that pertains to nature is
otherness or *externality*. This indicates that nature is a sphere that does not
consist of *distinct* constituents that are *internally related* (as pure concepts
indeed are) and so make up a system whose moments do not have separate
existence independently of each other. Rather, the constituents of nature
can indeed relate to each other *as other*, namely as *external*.[47] According to
Hegel, the externality or otherness characteristic of nature manifests itself
both as contingency, i.e. as *real independence*, and as necessity,[48] i.e. such
that something is not *as such* inscribed *into the other* (as pure concepts

[43] ENC 2.1:205 (§247).   [44] ENC 3:6 (§381).   [45] Hegel (2002b: 22–3; ENC 1:276 (§203)).
[46] ENC 1:265–70 (§§193–4), SL: 624–30 (12:126–32) and Martin (2012: 340–70).
[47] ENC 2.1:208 (§248).   [48] ENC 2.1:208 (§248).

indeed are), while bringing about the *subsequent* existence of something else. Items that are *necessarily coupled* in this way are thus at the same time external to each other.

The fact that the realm of nature is both essentially intelligible and such that entities that fall within it can be external to each other does not, however, amount to a self-sufficient conception of nature. For *intelligibility* designates only the *possibility* of being known. We thus need to ask for the *actual* constitution of nature in which its intelligibility is grounded, i.e. for the peculiar *logicality of nature* (*Logizität der Natur*) in contrast to the logical *as such*. At first sight, however, it is hard to see how to assign a sense to the apparently contradictory phrase "peculiar logicality of nature".

So far, the peculiar form of nature, its otherness, has only been explained *locally*, namely as the possibility that entities that *belong to* nature can be external to each other. Hegel's phrase "idea in the form of otherness", however, primarily serves the purpose of bringing the *global* outlook of nature into view. By unpacking this phrase and by thus articulating the global outlook of nature we will put ourselves in a position to answer the question regarding its peculiar logicality.

That *otherness* or *externality* is the basic *global* trait of nature means not only that entities that *fall within* the realm of nature can behave towards each other as external, but that *the whole* of nature must be characterized by otherness or externality. While the constituents of nature are subject to *relative* otherness, nature on the whole is characterized by *absolute* otherness, that is, by otherness-in-*itself* or "*self*-externality" (*Außersichsein*).[49] That the first, inchoate trait of nature is *self*-externality means that it is a manifold that does not leave to what it comprises any determination *for itself*. What is thus comprised is accordingly such that by being what it is it already points beyond itself. Accordingly, it lacks a *proper* determinacy *of its own* in distinction to its surroundings. By being what it is, it is at the same time already beyond itself, i.e. it is *pure* transience into an environment. The most elementary *global* trait of nature is, accordingly, that it is a continuum, namely a manifold that does not consist of a *definite number* of *distinct actual* parts that have an *independent determinacy of their own*. However, *as a manifold*, it must at least *allow the possibility* of an *arbitrary number* of *virtual* parts being singled out.[50]

Even if nature *qua continuum* does not consist of distinct components and is thus a whole without parts – albeit of a certain extension – it can be distinguished from what is *absolutely simple* only by recourse to *virtual* parts.

---

[49] ENC 2.1:215 (§250), 221 (§253, addition), 223 (§254).   [50] ENC 2.1:223 (§254).

Accordingly, we had to introduce the continuum by alluding to something contained in it – points – and by thus assuming a distinction between these points and their environment, in order to then take this distinction back by declaring it to be virtual, stressing that what had just been distinguished has no self-sufficient standing of its own but is pure transiency into an environment.[51] To get hold of the continuum, one cannot do without distinguishing something within it that is thereby posited as *relatively* independent, while one must immediately add that what is thus distinguished is not *by itself* distinct and is thus *absolutely* dependent. To the extent that this characterization is appropriate to its topic, nature qua continuum is thus *in itself* determined in a contradictory manner.[52]

Insofar as the continuum of nature involves a real contradiction, and insofar as a real contradiction binds together what *cannot* peacefully coexist, the continuum of nature must come along with a dimension in which the consequence of its essential instability or 'decrepitude' manifests itself. The real manifestation of instability is decay – a passing away – and *global* passing-away is nothing other than time.[53]

Accordingly, by thinking through Hegel's characterization of nature as self-externality and, hence, as a continuum, a difference has arisen, namely between the continuum *insofar* as it is merely instable and the continuum *insofar* as it manifests the real consequence of its instability, i.e. as global passing-away. The continuum of nature thus essentially involves two dimensions or modes of occurrence: a *static* one corresponding to *mere* self-externality – space – and an *ephemeral* one in which its essential instability becomes manifest – time. Time is thus not merely a further dimension of the real *besides* space, but is, so to speak, nothing but the real manifestation of the essential instability of space.

Since it is essential to nature that its determinations can appear as external to each other, the impression that space and time are independent, juxtaposed dimensions does not arise by mere chance. However, the otherness or independence of global features of nature can only be a relative one; that is, it can obtain only against the background of a further trait of nature in which these features concretely hang together.

---

[51] "Although the heres are also differentiated, their being different is identical with their lack of difference, and the difference is therefore abstract. Space is therefore punctiformity without points, or complete continuity" (ENC 2.1:224 (§254, addition)).

[52] "Space is this contradiction, to involve negation, but in such a way that this negation disintegrates into indifferent subsistence" (ENC 2.1:229 (§257, addition)).

[53] "As space is merely this inner negation of itself, its truth is the self-transcendence of its moments. It is precisely the existence of this perpetual self-transcendence which constitutes time. In time therefore the point has actuality" (ENC 2.1:229 (§257, addition)).

The trait of nature that counteracts the apparent independence of space and time in the shape of their concrete unity is motion qua change of place with time.[54] Since there can only be movement in contrast to something which is at rest, the space-time continuum must be inhomogeneous within itself. For only on this condition does it allow contrasts between movement and rest. Insofar as matter is that which moves in space, nature must hence be *globally* characterized as an inhomogeneous material space-time continuum.

Inhomogeneity as such by no means implies *actual discretion*, since inhomogeneity requires only that the continuum's manner of continuous coherence varies discontinuously in places. *Actual* discretion requires logical activity which singles out re-identifiable sections of the continuum, positing them *as objects* of a certain type.[55] Accordingly, nature is an inhomogeneous continuum that does not on its own involve *actual* discreteness, but merely *allows* for *non-arbitrary* logical acts which provide for *actual* discreteness by singling out distinct natural objects of various sorts.[56]

5.4 The Intelligibility of Nature and the 'Internality' of 'the Concept' in Nature

We have expanded Hegel's *inchoate* characterization of nature as self-externality (*Außersichsein*) into the insight that nature must be understood as an inhomogeneous material space-time continuum that is essentially in motion. We can now tackle the question of the *peculiar* logicality of nature. That is, we can now ask how one should understand the *actual* constitution of nature in which its *intelligibility* pursuant to the forms of discursive thinking is rooted. Hegel characterizes the peculiar logicality of nature by remarking that "the concept" occurs in nature only as "internal"[57] (*Inneres*, *Innerliches*) or as "in itself"[58] (*an sich*). He thus distinguishes between an inner and an outer of nature. He characterizes the latter as perceptual content or appearance, whereas he refers to the former as the "universal" in nature, which is said to be accessible to thinking only.

His claim that "the concept" occurs in nature only as "internal" or "in itself" is meaningless as long as one has not resolved the apparent contradiction that

---

[54] ENC 2.1:237–41 (§261).
[55] For a systematic elaboration of this idea see Martin (2020: chapter 3).
[56] For an articulation and defence of this view as a reading of Hegel's logical concept of the 'world' or 'the object' see Martin (2012: 354–70, 2014: 230–3).
[57] ENC 2.1:208 (§248), 212 (§249); Hegel (2002b: 7–8, 10, 22–3).   [58] ENC 2.1:207 (§247).

what Hegel calls "the concept", i.e. *self-referential self-determination*,[59] is essentially *for itself*. Therefore, it is not immediately clear what it might mean to say that the concept as it occurs in nature is "merely in itself". It is further unclear how the logical might count as "the inner" of nature insofar as it has no real spatio-temporal properties, while that whose "interior" it is supposed to be is a *material* space-time continuum. As long as one merely adds to the *logical* understanding of the concept the alleged further property of being somehow 'contained in nature' rather than taking the pains of articulating a *modified, non-logical* understanding of the concept that allows one to concretely grasp it as "internal in" it, nature's peculiar logicality remains a mystery.

Hegel himself indicates that a *modification* of the *logical* understanding of the concept is needed in order to understand its immanence in nature by saying that the concept is "lost" in nature or has "disappeared" in it. Readings that take his recourse to "objective thoughts",[60] "thought in the world"[61] and the "interiority of the concept in nature" directly at face value, instead of recognizing the task indicated by the latent contradiction in such phrases, namely the need to work one's way towards a concrete understanding of the peculiar logicality of nature and spirit, content themselves with a mere potpourri of the logical and the real. Unwittingly, they thus fall back behind Hegel (*and Kant*) onto a form of rationalist metaphysics that imagines logical determinations that have their source in thinking alone as somehow equally existent on the part of the world, making it appear as if it were a contingent fact, on Hegel's account, that any actual thinking is going on.[62] This applies, for instance, to the reading put forward by James Kreines, who claims:

> Hegel's *Begriffe*, including natural kinds governed by universal laws, are not mind-dependent in the sense we would expect given the term 'concept': the reality and the real effective impact of laws governing natural kinds does not depend on their being represented by us. They are not mind-dependent, but they are accessible only to thought.[63]

---

[59] ENC 1:236 (§163). For a systematic elucidation of 'the concept' in terms of self-referential self-determination see Martin (2012: 222–52, 2014: 224–30).

[60] ENC 1:66 (§24).   [61] SL: 29 (GW 21:34).

[62] As Fulda has shown, such a reading of Hegel is both exegetically as well as systematically futile: "Nowhere does Hegel in his *Logic* attempt to prove that the objective thoughts and conceptual determinations it examines are thoughts and determinations of something that exists independently of being thought. [. . .] Only insofar as it engages with its determinations in this way, rather than as determinations of a substrate which is simply there, can *Logic* be first philosophy. With such a substrate, its pretension to be scientific cognition would fall prey to its own inherent scepticism" (Fulda 1999: 474, my translation).

[63] Kreines (2007: 325).

Kreines attributes the following 'concept thesis' to Hegel:

> The reasons that explain why things are as they are and do what they do are always found in immanent 'concepts', akin to immanent universals or kinds.[64]

Just like the philosophical stance that Hegel calls "former metaphysics"[65] (*vormalige Metaphysik*), Kreines's unquestioned subscription to the 'immanence' of the universal – of concepts, kinds, rules and laws – in the world or in nature whose existence qua substratum he simply takes for granted, is "unconscious of its opposition".[66] It is marked by a lack of insight into the fact that *logical* determinations *as such* which have their source in thinking alone, i.e. concepts, rules and laws, cannot *as well* be *contained* 'in' nature. This is so, because the logical and the real are determined in a completely different way: one is a totality of *distinct* internally related thoughts that have their source in the self-determination of thinking, whereas the other is an *inhomogeneous* material space-time continuum that does not *in itself* involve any *distinctions*. Dwelling on their categorical difference does *not* amount to subscribing to the view that nature is unintelligible but rather to stressing that the *actual* ground of its intelligibility can be understood only if one does not simply stipulate that logical determinations do not have their only place in thinking but are also 'contained' in nature independently of any actual thinking, which is at best a somewhat misleading way of claiming that nature is intelligible and at worst sheer nonsense.

Dogmatic-rationalist readings thus project logical determinations which have their only source in thought and are thus essentially tied back to actual thinking onto that which does not depend on being conceived, i.e. nature, instead of tackling the task of articulating the peculiar logicality of nature by virtue of which it can indeed be recognized through the logical forms of thinking.

One might retort that Hegel himself emphasizes time and again that 'the concept', or 'the universal', is the 'inner' of nature which is said to be concealed by its 'exterior' – i.e. by its appearance in intuition and perception.[67] However, Hegel does not confine himself to remarks of this sort which need to be *expanded* into a coherent understanding of the

---

[64] Kreines (2015: 22). Kreines's book is an example of a deplorable tendency in current anglophone literature on Hegel, namely to largely ignore decades of profound Hegel research in other languages than English. Had Kreines consulted the works of Cramer, Fulda, Henrich, Falk, Koch, Schick and others, he might have avoided reading Hegel's *Logic* in terms of a dogmatic rationalism, to the overcoming of which that work in fact contributes.

[65] ENC 1:91 (§47), SL: 42 (GW 21:48). For accounts of Hegel's critique of dogmatic-rationalist metaphysics see Cramer (1999), Fulda (1999) and Martin (2019).

[66] ENC 1:67 (§§26–7).   [67] Hegel (2002b: 7–9).

logicality of nature instead of being *iterated*. In any event, his position cannot be read as if the cognition of nature were concerned with those conceptual determinations which had already been at issue in the *Logic* and which, once the veil of appearances has been lifted, can be recognized as equally extant 'in' nature prior to any actual thinking. Such an assumption would be nonsensical for the following reason. If the concept or the universal which according to Hegel constitutes the inner kernel of nature were simply the logical concept or, as the case may be, a mere specification of it, then it would remain unintelligible how the 'interior' of nature can come along with an 'exterior' that appears to the senses, while the logical as such cannot affect them. Moreover, cognition of that interior would either not yield knowledge *of nature* at all, if that interior were taken as identical to the logical, or it would be engaged with an aggregate of the logical and the real whose concrete unity remains aporetic.

The task of arriving at a coherent understanding of the *actual* outlook of nature in which its intelligibility is rooted instead of merely projecting logical determinations which have their only source and place in thought onto it and thereby taking too literally Hegel's dictum of the 'interiority' of the concept in nature can be fulfilled by recognizing an *analogue* of the logical concept in the *actual* constitution of nature qua inhomogeneous material space-time continuum. In Hegel's own words, this continuum is to be recognized as the "element"[68] to which the concept, insofar as it is found in nature, is 'adapted'. Within nature the concept exhibits a peculiar 'state of aggregation', so to speak, which is different from that of the *logical* concept in the "element of thinking"[69] (*Element des Denkens*).

The *logical* concept is self-referential self-determination which is the source of universality that can hold together a manifold of specific determinations in such a way that their unity makes up particulars whose internal development is essentially the object of an articulation by means of concepts, judgements and inferences.[70] An analogue of the logical concept in the 'element' of the material space-time continuum will consist precisely in the fact that the latter involves subsections whose specific traits are held together into a unity that sets itself apart from its environment as *relatively* independent by holding sway and preserving itself throughout

---

[68] In each part of philosophy the idea "exists in a particular determinacy or element" (ENC 1:43 (§15)) according to Hegel. He refers to nature or externality as such an element of "the concept" in various places, e.g. ENC 2.1:209 (§248, addition); V 17:17–18, 23, 46; see also SL 581 (GW 12:83).

[69] Hegel characterizes logic as the "science of the pure idea, i.e. the idea in the abstract element of thinking" (ENC 1:47 (§19)), see also V 11:3, 19; SL: 738 (GW 12:239).

[70] For a comprehensive overview of the logical concept see Schick (2018).

changes of the continuum and its inhomogeneous constellations. The real counterpart of the logical concept on the part of nature will thus consist in self-preserving configurations of the continuum, i.e. in the formation and preservation of inhomogeneous units within it. A paradigmatic example would be the solar system. There, bodies revolve around a centre in such a way that the whole forms a self-sustaining unity that is specifically organized within itself and whose repetitive movements amount to a *real* way in which the universal is actual in the element of nature.[71] The peculiar logicality of nature thus consists, paradigmatically, in actual recurrent processes by means of which specific configurations or subsections of the continuum hold sway and preserve themselves, thereby establishing a contrast to their surroundings. It does not, on the other hand, consist in the supposed fact that the laws by means of which we truthfully think and predict such processes are somehow extant on the part of nature itself and are, as it were, "inscribed in the sky".[72]

Accordingly, in cognizing nature by articulating natural laws we do not simply repeat something that is *as such – in that very form –* already extant 'in' nature, but rather this articulation is, as Hegel puts it in a lecture course, a 'translation' of the peculiar logicality of nature into the element of thinking.[73] This means that nature can indeed be *pursuant to* the laws in form of which our knowledge of nature is articulated, but this compliance with them cannot be understood as an *identity* between *laws that are thought* and *unthought laws* 'inherent' in nature itself.

If no real definition of truth is possible that would allow one to explain that notion in terms that do not themselves presuppose it – this being a Kantian insight which Hegel, on my reading, subscribes to[74] – and if propositional truth, accordingly, cannot be broken down into an external relation between two independent factors, one on the part of the thinking subject and one on the part of the world, it follows that laws of nature, and, more generally, that which is thought when nature is known, have their only place in what is *irreducibly* cognition of nature. Cognition of nature involves an aspect that doesn't have its source in thinking while being articulated according to logical forms that have their only source in thinking and are not as such somehow 'contained' in nature, even while the latter is essentially *intelligible* by means of them.[75]

---

[71] ENC 2:260–81 (§§269–70), see also SL: 640–4 (GW 12:143–7).   [72] ENC 1:56 (§21, addition).
[73] Hegel speaks of "the concept which I am; I am the activity which translates nature into the concept" (V 17, 21, my translation). Accordingly, the *logical* concept does not *as such* exist in nature: "The concept as concept exists only within spirit, which is its own element" (V 11:214, my translation).
[74] Martin (2017b: 197–200).   [75] Martin (2012: 191–201, 366–70).

Hegel expresses the fact that knowledge of nature is articulation by means of conceptual determinations that have their only source in thinking while providing the form of cognition of that which is not itself a thought by referring to Hamann's dictum that nature is like a Hebrew word: written in consonants only, to which the intellect must add vowels.[76] Discursive cognition of nature is thus not simply a *repetition* or *mirroring* but is rather an *articulation* which can only do justice to what is to be articulated by incorporating it into its own form and thus giving it a new way of unity by virtue of which it can be pronounced, while being silent and inarticulate in itself.[77] Putting things like this in no way implies that the logical form of knowing is *arbitrary* or *alien to nature*. Insofar as that form can be unfolded in *presuppositionless* thinking it is thereby exhibited as without alternative; and insofar as the *Logic*, according to its starting point, investigates what it means *to be*, there cannot be *something* that would not be *intelligible* by means of precisely those forms which are arrived at by thinking through what it means *to be*. That what is *essentially intelligible* by means of logical forms of thinking does not, however, imply that it would need to 'consist' of these forms or to somehow 'contain' them.

Knowledge of nature involves, accordingly, recourse to something that cannot *itself* be *given* by thinking even while it can be *thought of* truly and while its *concept* can be arrived at by *pure* thinking insofar as it is recognized as the necessary complement of pure thought, namely the material space-time continuum. *Empirical* knowledge of nature even involves *conceptual* determinations which we cannot rationally arrive at by means of thinking alone, but can think only on condition of sensory affection.

5.5   On the Difference between Logic and the 'Real Sciences of Philosophy'

Insofar as cognition of nature is essentially articulation-of-nature, knowledge of nature cannot be adequate to its subject matter by 'mirroring' thoughts that lay ready in its 'interior', but can become so only by 'translating' the peculiar, unarticulated logicality of self-sustaining configurations within the inhomogeneous material space-time continuum into its own element – thinking. Nature thus comes to full bloom, so to speak, by being known, i.e. cognition of nature is an articulation-and-expansion of the material space-time continuum. Non-arbitrary subsections of the

---

[76] ENC 2.1:201 (§246, addition).
[77] By virtue of being thought, nature and its appearance receive a new form, see V 17:12.

continuum of nature come *into their own* by being *singled out as distinct objects* according to the forms of thinking – their objectivity is, as Hegel puts it, following Kant in this respect, the unity of the self-consciousness of thought into which they are incorporated.[78]

Insofar as thinking makes the muteness of nature speak by translating the peculiar logicality of the continuum into its own form, cognition of nature does not *simply* engage with nature-*in-itself*. The topic of philosophy of nature is thus not *just* nature *per se*, about which nothing further is to be said, but nature *as cognized in the forms of thinking* – the universality and necessity of thought insofar as it proves its own strength by engagement with what is not itself a thought but actual and real.

Since thinking requires real embodiment, our first mode of thinking is not *logical* thought *as such*, but thinking that is engaged with phenomena and, as it were, immersed in them. Accordingly, *empirical* cognition of nature is a necessary precondition of its non-empirical cognition in philosophy, even while philosophy of nature does not as such *primarily* deal with nature *as experienced* but unfolds the *pure non-logical* concept of nature as an inhomogeneous material space-time continuum. However, since nature, qua real, does not consist of thoughts, pure concepts of traits of nature need to be put into correspondence with aspects of nature that are dealt with in empirical cognition. This requirement does not amount to a conflation of philosophy of nature with the empirical sciences of nature, but it amounts to a corroboration and concretization of the former in the face of results achieved by the latter.

The real sciences of philosophy can now be distinguished from logic as follows. It is logic which deals, in the element of pure thinking, with just those concepts that have their source in thinking alone while their content is exhausted by what thinking itself 'gives' on its own initiative.[79] The *real sciences of philosophy*, for their part, equally unfold in the 'element of thinking', independently of experience. However, while their concepts have their source in thinking alone, they refer to what is not itself a thought and thus cannot *itself* be *given* and *exhausted* by thinking alone, being situated in (or supervening on) the inhomogeneous material space-time continuum. Envisaging the real as the necessary complement of

---

[78] "The object has its objectivity in the concept, and the latter is the unity of self-consciousness into which it has been incorporated; its objectivity or its concept is thus nothing but the nature of self-consciousness" (SL: 516 (GW 12:18–19), translation modified).

[79] Evidently, the fact that these forms have their source in thinking alone does not mean that they would have merely subjective value, for it is part and parcel of logic to show that *what is* is as such intelligible through these forms, see Martin (2012: 1–17, 196–201).

logical form is what renders non-empirical philosophical insight into the real possible, at all.

Insofar as the real, notwithstanding its intelligibility, does not consist of thoughts and can therefore appear to the senses, the *real sciences of philosophy* have to correlate their a priori concepts of aspects of the real to what is empirically known of the latter in order thereby to prove their worth. Accordingly, they differ from logic in that it is part and parcel of them to confront their non-empirical concepts with experience.[80] Both the philosophy of nature and that of spirit do not *exclusively* engage with the real as it is *in itself*, but rather engage with it *insofar as it is thought*, while not thereby running the risk of missing any of it. It is for this reason that they presuppose the pure forms of thinking and can be transparently pursued only subsequently to the *Logic*.

While philosophical cognition of nature articulates solely the material space-time continuum and its inhomogeneous configurations, the philosophy of the spirit forms concepts of the real insofar as it is already shaped by accomplishments of thinking living beings and is thus transformed into a world that supervenes on the material space-time continuum. Spirit, as a concrete unity of the logical and the real, is actual thinking that manifests itself in what is real and proves its power by transforming it. Insofar as the act of thinking relates to its own real preconditions as that which makes them irrelevant, the philosophy of spirit is the real-philosophical science of the sublation of the real.[81] It therefore culminates in the concept of that activity which pursues the return from the exteriority of the nature to the interiority of actual thinking most radically – philosophy.

---

[80] ENC 2.1:197 (§246), see Fulda (2003: 133–55).   [81] ENC 3:6 (§381).

CHAPTER 6

Hegel's Philosophy of Nature
The Expansion of Particularity as the Filling of Space and Time

Ralph M. Kaufmann, Ansgar Lyssy, and Christopher Yeomans

Of the three main parts of Hegel's *Encyclopedia*, the *Philosophy of Nature* is probably the most difficult to approach. It initially presents itself as a grab bag of now-outdated details cited from early-nineteenth-century natural science sprinkled with the occasional, seemingly arbitrary logical phrase to act as a binding agent. However the text is remarkably structured – but that this structure would be difficult to see is nothing less than one would expect from Hegel's initial definition of nature as essentially external: natural phenomena are external not only to logic, but also to each other (§247).[1] Such phenomena do not express abstract ideas "*abbildungstreu*," i.e., as perfect illustrations, because they contain not just the merely abstractly universal elements but also the diverse particularities by which those elements can find an individual manifestation. Nature represents the complete expansion of particularity into the world, and thus a kind of limit case for rational understanding of that world (§244).

Luckily, there is a thread to follow through the details: Hegel's *Philosophy of Nature* proceeds by exploring the different forms of filling space and time that provide the latter with their metrics and orientations. Since those metrics and orientations are required by the Euclidean[2] space and time that are, in turn, required for the physics to which mechanist philosophies of nature have wanted to reduce the rest of nature, Hegel offers a transcendental argument against reductionism which threads its way through the whole *Philosophy of Nature*.

---

[1] Citations from Hegel's *Philosophy of Nature* are first by section number (with 'R' indicating the Remark or *Anmerkung* and 'Z' the *Zusatz* or Addition). Here our reference has been Hegel (1970–1: vol. 9). For lecture notes we have cited not only the *Zusatz* but also the notes themselves in Hegel (1968–: vol. 24). For English translations we have followed Hegel (2015), with some modifications.

[2] Here and throughout the chapter 'Euclidean' is used in the contemporary mathematical sense as referring to a measurable and orientable space rather than in the historical sense as referring to Euclid's own constructions. Its primary contrast is 'affine' space rather than 'non-Euclidean' space.

In Section 6.1, we offer a very brief overview of the development of modern natural science up to Hegel's time. In Sections 6.2 and 6.3, we go more deeply into the structure of space and time themselves, and in Section 6.4, we treat the first form of filled space and time, namely mechanics. In Section 6.5, we briefly sketch the remainder of the argument of the *Philosophy of Nature*.

But one final caveat before we begin: though there is this essential relation of dependence of Euclidean space on its filling, there is an equally important relation of dependence of filled space on abstract (not-yet-Euclidean) space as set out in the early sections of the *Philosophy of Nature*. The exact analysis of space and time as a lower level is essential for the development of the higher levels. One must first understand space in its abstractness before one grasps it as filled with material, even though one must be clear what one is grasping when one understands abstract space. The primary interpretive mistake with respect to Hegel's initial discussion of space and time is to commit what Whitehead called the fallacy of misplaced concreteness (Whitehead 1997: 51), i.e., mistaking abstract concepts for concrete entities.

6.1 Historical Introduction

Modern conceptions of nature were informed and motivated by the great successes of early modern science. The latter is profoundly shaped by a core belief that was developed by Descartes and Galileo, and renewed by Newton: that science could reduce nature to certain irreducible *quantities* (such as size, mass, shape, directional velocity), ignoring all intrinsic *qualities*. This was a breakthrough of unprecedented significance, as it allowed reducing some seemingly basic and inexplicable phenomenal qualities such as heat, weight, color, etc. to mere quantities. Philosophers hoped that thereby they would be able to understand nature by means of mathematics, *especially geometry*, independent of tedious debates concerning the nature of substances. This rather optimistic reductionist approach was also conceived as a solid foundation both for the essential uniformity of nature as well as for the applicability of mathematics to nature. Newton's groundbreaking expansion of Galileo's laws of falling bodies and their successful application to celestial bodies established the fundamental homogeneity of the entire universe, big and small, near and far. Within a relatively short time frame – between roughly 1650 and 1770 – a great diversity of previously inexplicable phenomena became explicable: from falling bodies over celestial epicycles to rainbows and even basic sensations – *everything* seemed to be explicable through nothing more than the mathematics of simple, moving bodies and their interaction.

But then things got more complicated. This belief in a comprehensive reduction of qualities onto quantities was profoundly shaken with the emergence of new sciences and phenomena, especially the rise of chemistry. Lavoisier introduced chemical elements to science, a new version of the alchemical substances, enabling explanations of bodies and their interaction by irreducible qualities or by their respective chemical nature. Physics cannot explain why and how iron turns into rust, since the core physical concepts of mass, speed etc. are of little importance here. Suddenly the particular identity of bodies in terms of their elemental composure *did* matter again. The same holds for phenomena such as electricity and magnetism: certain types of matter are more conductive to electricity and more receptive to magnetism than others. Surprising discoveries made it clear that the nature of physical bodies had not even been remotely understood, and yet was of clear importance: Faraday had shown that electricity can generate a magnetic field, and Galvani had surprised everyone with the discovery that electricity apparently had something to do with the specific nature of organic tissue, since dead frog legs started twitching when struck by an electrical spark. Finally, even within physics itself, phenomena such as the three-body problem, the principle of least action, and the problem of vibrating strings could not easily be integrated into established mechanics (or required more advanced mathematics). Thus it had become clear that even within physics, the mechanist reductionist approach of Galileo, Descartes, and, to a lesser degree, Newton, finally had to be discarded.

It was clear that the diverging concepts and methods of science could no longer be derived from a few core principles. But one cannot simply abandon the belief in the unity of nature, as this serves as a foundation for the applicability of general concepts. Galileo's and Newton's *physics* had abandoned all conceptions of teleology and all elemental differences in matter. But it had long become clear that *biology* was not possible without teleological concepts, as *functionality* was needed to conceive of ontogenesis, organs, or the adaptive relation of animals to their environment. *Chemistry*, then again, had reintroduced elements, and it seemed as if bodies were, in fact, interacting with each other without movement and external causes, just by virtue of being 'opposed' or 'aligned' elements. Kant, in his *Metaphysical Foundations of Natural Science*, could still attempt to ground natural science, broadly construed, in what amounts to essentially Newtonian and Leibnizian terms. For Hegel, writing roughly thirty years after Kant's seminal work on the philosophy of science, this was no longer possible. Instead, Hegel faced a heap of natural sciences that had fallen apart into separate spheres.

One major aim of Hegel's philosophy of nature is thus *to put science back together*.[3] He strives to show that many of the conceptual problems arising from the attempt to hold science together while accommodating its new results can be solved by carefully attending to the different concepts involved and their relations. He suggests that nature, in the broadest sense, can be understood as a system of different 'levels' (§249), i.e., different concepts that can be used to explain certain phenomena and which also serve as the foundation for other concepts that deal with a different set of phenomena or explanations. While some conceptual problems may arise on one more abstract level, adopting the stance of a higher, more concrete level can resolve these problems by adding the requisite complexity. The special sciences and their paradigmatic phenomena must then be placed together in a hierarchical system rather than side-by-side in a mosaic. As the hierarchy is built in steps, this system at the same time affords the possibility of interaction via lower levels, as these are an integral part of any higher level.

If the task is putting science back together, what is the nature of the argument that does so? Hegel initially focuses on the specific problem of accounting for precisely those basic geometrical properties that are central to the reductionist approach. More specifically, Hegel takes up two properties of space and time which are necessary conditions for the above-mentioned reductionistic approach to natural science and which are furthermore central to the contemporary mathematical concept of Euclidean space: *metric* and *orientation*. These are the two properties needed for the parallelogram of forces in physics, for example, where they are represented as a magnitude and direction.[4] But in Euclidean geometry itself, and the reductionist approach to science it makes possible, these specific properties of space are more or less presupposed without justification. The mapping of the number line onto the time line to generate its Euclidean properties is similarly unmotivated, and its connection to the direction of physical transformation is equally tenuous.

At least *philosophically*, neither geometry nor arithmetic is a self-sufficient account of the structure of space or time, nor is reductionism

---

[3] Cf. Pinkard (2013: 21).

[4] It behooves us to stress here that Hegel, in contrast to Newton, is against the idea of the parallelogram of forces as an ontological principle (see Section 6.4).

well founded in the absence of an account of these Euclidean properties. It will turn out that what *is* required to ground these two properties is a much more complex set of phenomena and concepts (reflected in different types of explanations of the natural world) than the reductionist approach is willing to admit. This is the sense in which Hegel's *Philosophy of Nature* offers us a transcendental argument against reductionism: *that more complex set of phenomena and concepts is the necessary condition for the metric and orientation which are themselves necessary conditions for the science that motivates reductionism.*

Of course, the necessity of these two properties is itself conceptually grounded – one can find the corresponding argument in Hegel's discussions of quantity and measure in the *Science of Logic* (Kaufmann and Yeomans 2017). But such *logical* properties are only loosely related to the proximate function of space and time to present the basic form of nature. After all, these logical properties have to be instantiated by anything that is in any sense, including abstract objects such as numbers and concrete but non-spatiotemporal objects such as historical institutions. How space and time present the form of nature and how they provide the features necessary for the scientific successes that motivate the reductionist approach cannot be explained through either logic or mathematics alone.

The concrete spatial and temporal forms of metric and orientation which are valid for natural objects can neither be derived from the *concepts* of space and time nor be grasped as *forms* of sensible or receptive intuition as Kant would have it. Hegel argues that they can be derived only from filled spatiotemporal location (a place [*Ort*]), i.e., from the natural phenomena themselves. In geometry, we can assign every body a certain place by referring it to a system of coordinates, and those are assumed to be fundamentally external both to the body and to the observer. But Hegel argues that the simple forms of temporal and spatial intuition are insufficient to generate this coordinate system, and in nature no such coordinates exist independently of the natural phenomena that are referred to them. Intuitively, we find ourselves drawn toward the abstract idea that any two places would be equal if they were equally empty – but such a consideration has no place in our experience or conception of nature. On the contrary, different places are fundamentally unequal: we have a conception of a system of gravitationally interdependent bodies, such as a solar system, and a different conception of an ecological system, in which plants and animals are adapted to climate and geology. While we may start out with a generic mathematical conception of geometrical relations that are supposed to represent spatiotemporal relations, we can arrive at a complete understanding of nature only after we can describe how these relations are developed through a hierarchy of natural phenomena which define specific places in nature precisely by giving them metric and orientation.[5] The 'filling' of space does not consist in putting pre-conceived bodies *into* pre-conceived, abstract, and uniform places, as if space were a mere container, but rather in understanding spatiotemporal relations *by means of* the specific nature of the objects of this relation.

This basic project is, of course, part of the long argument for Hegel's idealism.[6] Before he gets to the *Philosophy of Nature*, Hegel already takes himself to have shown that anything that could be living, true, or good (i.e., anything at all) must be perspectival. In the preceding and foundational *Science of Logic* he develops both the argument for that claim and a specific structure of fundamental perspectives which he calls the concept (*der Begriff*) (Yeomans 2019).

Here we use 'perspective' to gloss Hegel's term 'subjectivity.' The key to interpreting 'subjectivity' is to find a way to characterize Hegel's use of it that does justice *both* to its opposition to 'objectivity' *and* to the fact that Hegel frequently uses it in circumstances in which consciousness, perception, and mentality are not involved. Even if 'subjectivity' is *paradigmatically* self-consciousness, it is nonetheless the case that Hegel thinks that there is a subjective logic (of the concept) and that there are forms of subjectivity manifested by natural phenomena which clearly neither possess consciousness nor have mental states (e.g., the solar system (§269)).[7] This progressive search for a natural perspective is registered in the different extent to which subjectivity is present or existent. For example, the solar system only manifests "subjectivity as appearing being" (§269) whereas "The organic individual exists as *subjectivity*" (§350). A fuller exploration of this theme would map the development of spatiotemporal perspective to these levels of subjectivity, but that is beyond the scope of this chapter.[8]

The development of the metric and orientation of space and time is the search for a natural *perspective*, and that means a search for a form of

[5] This 'filling' of space by dispositional powers is still a theme in recent philosophy, e.g., Blackburn (1990).

[6] In fact, in some respects longer than Kant. The structural connection between logic, geometry, and filled space is crucial for Hegel to provide an alternative to Kant's transcendental idealism, since Kant takes our ability to do geometry as something best explained by the supposition of space as a form of intuition (cf. §262R). On long and short arguments see Ameriks (1990).

[7] For a more detailed discussion of this notion of perspective, see Yeomans (2019). On the way in which Hegel takes animals to be subjects but not mental, see Pinkard (2013: 23–7).

[8] The authors would like to thank Anton Friedrich Koch for pushing them to make this point clearer.

subjectivity within the natural world. Though not a developmental account in the genetic or temporal sense, it is supposed to be about how "*ideality* comes to *existence*"; all translations are our own). This gives Hegel a lens through which to interpret natural phenomena, but does not either generate or entail any specific phenomenon: "Here as everywhere, that which is immanently philosophical is the inherent necessity of *conceptual determination*, which then has to be illustrated by *some* natural existence or *other*" (§276R; see also GW 24:1522 (§353Z)).[9]

But one more feature of the argument is essential to understanding it: Hegel also describes nature in contrast to logic as allowing the *free release of particularity* (§244). Particularity is a logical determination – i.e., there is nothing necessarily sensible or spatiotemporal about it – but natural, spatiotemporal phenomena exhibit a uniquely wide range and diversity of particular characteristics. In keeping with the way that this existence is an expansion of particularity, part of what happens is that the three basic perspectives of the *Logic* (the universal, the particular, and the individual) ramify into first four and then ultimately five different perspectives. The key to this movement is actually relatively simple: in this free release of particularity, we have at least two particulars. (Of course, we normally have more than two; but two is enough for Hegel's argument.) With two particulars we first double the relation of the particular to the universal, and then we double the relation of the particular to the individual. This first doubling gets us to four perspectives (e.g., the elements as Hegel understands them); the second doubling gets us to five perspectives (e.g., the five senses possessed by animals). The five perspectives then give us enough to find the metric and orientation required for natural science, as we briefly indicate in our final section.

6.2   Space

Hegel begins with a claim about space and time, namely that these are forms of intuition (*Anschauung*) (EN §258R). It can be puzzling to make

---

[9] This is why we reject aprioristic interpretations of Hegel's philosophy of nature according to which there is some sort of direct derivation of natural phenomena from logical bases. For a more dedicated argument to this purpose, see Rand (2007). Though perhaps not entirely aprioristic in the derivational sense, Alison Stone's interpretation nonetheless centers on the resolution of purely rational tensions between the concepts relating to nature. In our view, something much more physical and particular is at issue (Stone 2018b: chapter 7).

out what he means by this, though the explicit reference is obviously to Kant's thought, wherein these abstract forms enable us to conceive or perceive any other particular spatiotemporal relation. Hegel calls the idea of an abstract, uniform, 'container-like' space an "abstraction" (§254), which means that we reach this idea only by ignoring all concrete spatio-temporal relations, i.e., the 'filled' space that we encounter in the sciences. But this passage is puzzling also because Hegel explicitly denies that the intuitive nature of space and time primarily involves a subjective con-sciousness confronting an object, or any particular receptive faculty or route by which information about the world comes to us (e.g., as the shape of the channel of that information). The usual interpretations of Kant's doctrine of intuition are thus ruled out as interpretations of Hegel on this point. But *Anschauung* can sometimes be properly translated as 'perspective,'[10] and that is the sense in which Hegel takes space and time to be forms of *Anschauung*. Within the *Philosophy of Nature*, they are thus the names for the basic form of perspective in the empirical world.

Nonetheless, Hegel's reference to Kant has the significance of announ-cing an intervention by Hegel into the debate for which Kant took his own doctrine of space to be a resolution, namely, the debate between Newtonian absolute theories of space and Leibnizian relational theories of space. Hegel argues that that the essential aspects of Euclidean space that are supposed to be validated by these theories – its metric and orientation – cannot be so validated. To do so, we need to relate the 'abstract' conception of space back to the relations between bodies from which it is abstracted. This involves three recursive steps: (1) beginning with a simple conception of space and time and showing that it does not yet have the full Euclidean features simply so considered; (2) advancing to the relations between bodies and places that do display some of those features to some degree; and then (1′) working with space and time as having those newly displayed features (and yet still not the full Euclidean features).

Hegel begins his discussion of space and time with ideas that recall Book I of Euclid's *Elements*, but he quickly argues that neither the three dimen-sions nor the distinction between points, lines, and planes can give you the orientation required for Euclidean space in the contemporary sense (Step 1). In its abstract form, space is homogeneous and thus no metric or preferred orientation is possible within it.

We should clarify that here and throughout the chapter, 'orientation' is that of vectors and, more generally, fixing a choice of coordinate system

---

[10] Cf. Heiddeger's interpretation of Schelling's use of the term in Heidegger (1985: 17–18).

without regarding helicity. At the level of space as such (§§254–6), no particular orientation is privileged as everything is homogeneous. The realization of a particular orientation and coordinate happens at the later, higher levels. A concrete example of this lack of spatial orientation is given by crystal growth. The more advanced the sphere of nature, the more orientation is exhibited.

But to return to Step 2 of the initial discussion of space and time, one can get the orientation one needs by giving the spatial point a temporal interpretation, i.e., as the "now" which is privileged in time. But precisely because the "now" is privileged, one cannot get a metric. A metric would require identifying two points on the time line and taking the difference between them, but this eliminates the privilege of the now that made it the orientation point and returns us to the indifference of space (its *Gleichgültigkeit* – literally 'equal validity' (of all points)). This is the first example of the difficulty of getting metric and orientation at the same time. The subsequent category, place (*Ort*) is a placeholder for the solution to this problem (i.e., the beginnings of Step 1'), which Hegel suggests will ultimately be filled by subjectivity (§262R).

Let us unpack the argument regarding space. In §255 Hegel had argued that there must be three basic perspectives in space if it is to represent the expansion of the logical idea. But in the remark that leads into §256, Hegel argues that the three dimensions of space that might be thought to model these perspectives cannot yet do so because they cannot yet be distinguished from each other in any principled way – they are all equally intersubstitutable. (They do reappear later – and their relationships will be explored in some detail – in more sophisticated forms of nature that provide bases for distinguishing between them.)

In §256 Hegel proposes that the basic geometrical elements might play this role: points, lines, and planes. It is clear that they cannot be substituted for one another, and we have three that seem conceptually basic. But Hegel immediately points out that there is an ambiguity concerning the different way that the generation of a line out of a point can be understood.[11] On the one hand, that generation could be understood as Kant and Euclid did, namely by the following construction: given a point, I posit a second point and then draw a line through the two points. On the other hand, that generation could be understood as contemporary mathematicians do, namely through the notion of the point as the *germ* of a line: the point itself contains within it the potential to be moved in any direction, and

---

[11] The authors would like to thank Luca Illeterati for helping us to make this point more clearly.

such a choice of direction will be fixed in a natural process of interaction. The first understanding makes visible the way in which a metric is presented by the line, and the second an orientation.

There is an analogous ambiguity in the relation between the line and the plane. On one understanding, one could take a line and a point outside of it, then generate lines through the point that intersect the first line. The set of lines that so intersects generates the plane (*Fläche überhaupt*). On a second understanding, that first line itself could be moved relative to the point, thus giving a family of planes that can be used to define an enclosing surface (*umschließende Oberfläche*).[12]

We can then go to a third level of detail in unpacking this argument. The proper composition of space is completed in three strands. The first produces the hierarchy point–line–area (*Fläche*), and the second point–line–surface–space. The last two of the latter group (i.e., surface (*Oberfläche*) and space) provide then a phoenix figure (see the last paragraph of this section), insofar as an enclosing surface can be transformed into a closed space. The closed space is, as closed, *finite*, and so can be put as the second element of the figure $(\infty, \neg\infty)^\infty$. (We mean by the general schematic mode of presentation: $(A, B)^C$ to indicate that a trinity arises through the supersession (*Aufheben*) of an opposition generated by a diremption. What this example shows is that the three elements A, B, and C can coincide. That is, the three elements can be functionally distinct without being numerically distinct.) On the other hand, as space, even closed space is infinite and demonstrates thereby how something finite (like a human being) can possess an infinite spirit, which is indispensable for Hegel's philosophy of nature. The third strand is first of all a bifurcation and then brings us to time.

First space (R) enters as the infinite in the formula $(\infty, \neg\infty)$, where if $\neg\infty$ is grasped as the point P (as "differenceless self-externality") it generates the formula (R, P). From Hegel's perspective this is a natural formula to posit, since space already has this externality within itself as different from it; an explanation is, no doubt, in order. Space is characterized by Hegel as essentially homogeneous. Since 'homogeneity' means 'of the same kind,' it presupposes the concept of a plurality of the same, which are differentiated as a plurality (external to each other) but are in all other aspects the same. And, in fact, all the points in space are both similar and diverse in exactly this sense. Hegel's development of space in §256 proceeds from the

---

[12] In order to avoid misunderstanding, let us stress that the line is not *composed* of points nor the surface of lines – they are rather *constructed* by points (as germs), from which they *result*.

identification of the negation of space as the point ($\neg R = P$). If one takes 'self-externality' (*Außersichseins*) in a spatial sense as in Hegel's usage, then one refers to the existence of at least two points, P_1 and P_2. Their opposition supersedes itself into the line (L), which is defined by reference to them: $(P_1, P_2)^L$. The next step is a bifurcation which produces either a plane (*Fläche*) (F) or an enclosing surface (*umschließende Oberfläche*) (O). Then, in the first inference the relationship of L to its own moments is considered. Since, however, the points are homogeneous, this is at first just the relationship (L, P). This opposition then supersedes itself as the plane: $(L, P)^F$. If one accepts that L has already arisen from the previous inference $(P_1, P_2)^L$, then these can be combined to generate an additional figure: $((P_1, P_2)^L, P)^O$. This enclosing surface then represents the space that is enclosed by it (§256). One can also grasp this inference symbolically insofar as one makes the reverse substitution of $P = \neg R$, which generates $((\neg R_1, \neg R_2)^L, \neg R)^O$. The last determinacy is that the O which is so derived defines a closed space °, which at the same time can be substituted as the finite $\neg R$ in $(R, °)^R$. Thus it can serve as a unity, but also as the entire space. (This duality of the delimited finite is also that which underlies spirit.)

Furthermore we should also bear in mind the following: in both inferences ($(L, P)^F$ and $(P_1, P_2)^L$) there is first a logical process in three steps which takes us from zero to three dimensions by taking us from points to space. These three steps involve four elements ($(0, 1, 2, 3)$ or (P, L, F, R)). When the first two arguments are put together, one generates five elements $((P_1, P_2)^L, P)^O$, which hangs on the way that R itself is superseded in its generality when it is taken to arise from the specific nature of the point. These three steps move in different directions, as it were, or are logically grounded in different aspects of space: ". . . space may be considered as that which is positive, the plane as the first negation of space, and the line as the second negation, which, because it is the second, is in truth the self-relating negation of the point. The necessity of this transition is the same as it was in the first case" (§256R).

For Hegel these three steps moving in different directions manifest three dimensions: "As a second negation, the plane has two dimensions; for two belongs just as much to the second as to [the number] *two*" (GW 24:1200 (§256Z)). But these three dimensions take on a more complex form in the progression to surface (*Oberfläche*), where the more complex logical inference generates the very important self-contained subspace. The spatial unfolding P, L, F, R as well as the higher logical level of O is to be found in many of the detailed analysis of the later discussions of the *Philosophy of Nature*. In particular, the difference between plane (*Fläche*) and surface

(*Oberfläche*) plays a role in the complexity and liveliness of certain forms of nature, particularly the organic (e.g., GW 24: 1312 (§310Z)). A hybrid between plane and surface is presented by cylindrical structures, which are linear in one dimension but closed in the other two. This makes its appearance in Hegel's treatment of the structure of bones in §354, for example.

To step back again, this development of space is one example of a general feature of Hegel's argument which we can briefly mention here, which is a sort of mathematical expansion that fills out the dimensions of space and time. This expansion is intimately tied to the numbers 1, 2, 3, 4, and 5, which are first introduced in an early discussion of polarity in the lectures (GW 24:1191 (§248Z)) and also extensively discussed later on in the long analysis of harmonies and their relation to judgment (GW 24: 1292–1300 (§301Z)). This expansion takes place according to a few basic processes. The first process is diremption. It produces 2, of course, and is often used as the first step. This takes place through the multiplication of the particular, discussed above. The paradigmatic physical case of this is electricity and magnetism: the former gives actual point particles a polarity that drives them apart and generates actual lines of varying direction and magnitude (§312 and *Nürnberger Propadeutik* §118), while the latter is the inherent capacity of points to move apart, manifesting itself as polarity. In a second process, the trinity arises through the supersession of the opposition generated by the diremption. This is expressed in the following schematic mode of presentation: $(A, B)^C$. Because, as noted above, these elements can play multiple functional roles within the process, we can get a completion, capstone, or phoenix figure: the figure $(A, B)^A$, where A recurs in two different functional roles. This is the hallmark of the infinite, as this figure appears when A is the infinite and B the finite, as the negation of the infinite. The unity of both is infinity itself: $(\infty, \neg\infty)^\infty$. For the philosophy of nature, spirit (G) is the infinite and nature (N) the finite, which then in a capstone step from and in spirit is grasped as a unity $(G, N)^G$. The infinity of spirit is akin to the infinity of enclosed space as it is at the same time infinite and finite as a part of nature.

6.3   Time

Now let us say just a bit about time and how it is initially presented. There is somewhat less to say here, since on Hegel's own account the three dimensions of natural time are less developed than are the three dimensions of space. In the mathematical sense of the term, the dimensions of natural time are *degenerate*, by which is meant the following: they are colinear and symmetric, and thus not distinguished in the way that the dimensions of natural space are. Nonetheless, there is a development.

Step 1: Time (T) undergoes a similar bifurcation as space, but one which is introduced one logical step earlier. It arises through an inference in the form $(A, A)^B$ or more exactly as $(\neg R, \neg R)^T$. The pluralism of homogeneity and the inherent negativity of space ($\neg R$) are grasped as self-externality (*Außersichsein*) and then time as "the negative unity of self-externality." The supersession into T is the supersession of the common negativity, the $\neg$ itself. (This figure is then equated to the "I = I of pure self-consciousness," at least insofar as its form is concerned.) A further consequence of this derivation of time is the beginning of a dynamic which is the condition for processes, whose understanding forms the foundation of the knowledge of nature. Hegel emphasizes the "unrest (*Unruhe*)" of these processes (e.g., GW 24: 1202 (§257Z) and §258R). Formally speaking, these processes can by understood as the oscillation between two of the same moments (A, A), which are superseded in the process. This temporal unrest stems from a logical imbalance which drives the processes. The supersession of the unrest is "*intuited* becoming (angeschaute[s] *Werden*)" (§258). This is the distinctively Hegelian sense in which time (and space) are forms of intuition (*Anschauung*).

Just as there are three dimensions of space, three dimensions of time can be derived through logical inference structures. These are then understood as the moments of becoming. Becoming oscillates between being and nothing (§258). At first only one such moment is in view: ($\neg R$, T). But the two moments in becoming must be differentiated through being and nothing (or non-being). This is the quintessence of opposition. A priori, however, there is nothing to determine which of the two sides correspond to being and non-being – this is precisely Hegel's point at the beginning of the *Logic*. At this point in the argument of the *Philosophy of Nature*, time does not yet have any directionality, despite the fact that past and future are understood as the transition from being to non-being and from non-being to being. The middle term of these two moments is the present (*das Jetzt*) (J), in which they supersede themselves. Formally, we can put this in a way quite analogous to the formula for surface as $(\neg R, (\neg R, \neg R)^T)^J$. The analog to enclosed space is the now as the finite present or point in time, which delimits itself as the affirmative concrete unity of the past and the future (Step 2). This determination as finite point in time is a making-discrete of the previously continuous time (§258R) and produces the transition to arithmetic ("This dead unit, which is thought's highest externality, is external combination;

these are the figures of *arithmetic* [...]." (§259R)). The temporal point is discrete, but it is not a unit in the sense of an extended interval. So it gives the figure of a granular number line but without the measurable intervals that would be analogous to enclosed space.

When one opposes space and time to each other then there arises the place (*der Ort*) (Step 1'). One can say that through the existence of the now there is a possibility of individual points, first in time, to be made concrete. That would be impossible in the case of complete homogeneity.

6.4   The First Filled Space-Time: Mechanics

The filling of space-time is a core concept of Kant's *Metaphysical Foundations*, as he there tries to define the concepts of body, matter, motion, and force by reference to filling space (4:496; but cf. 2:287, 4:520, and 4:535). He even argues that space is divisible (and infinitesimal calculus is applicable to space) precisely because matter fills it. If the approach developed in this chapter is plausible, Hegel's natural philosophy can be understood as an answer to Kant's *Metaphysical Foundations*.

In Hegel's view, the most basic filling for space and time that will give them a metric and orientation is ordinary mechanics. Put very schematically, he investigates the idea that matter (*Materie*) could provide the metric, and motion (*Bewegung*) could provide the orientation (§261). Mechanics is then conceptually reconstructed as providing the details of this solution. Bodies become the real metrics (units) (§263), and impact (*Stoß*) makes the metric (weight) and the orientation (velocity) commensurable (§265). There is still a difficulty in determining the fundamental orientation – one gets it with falling objects, but then weight falls out of the equation and thus the metric is lost (§268). Hegel's diagnosis for this inability to obtain the metric and orientation together is that the case of a falling object treats both space and time too ideally. It develops space merely to the level of a line (the path taken by a falling object), and it treats the mechanics of the falling body as a two-place relation (between the falling object and the center of the earth). But the two places are not truly two bodies, since under this abstract perspective the earth as a concrete body drops out and becomes merely a point. We have something we know to be a two-body system that we treat abstractly as slightly less than two bodies. To get the metric back, Hegel thinks we have to move to laws of the solar system (a multi-body system) that treat the motions involved abstractly as involving fundamentally two bodies. These are Kepler's laws, which in the ellipse has the sun in one focus, with the planet orbiting. We then get a real metric,

Hegel thinks, in Kepler's third law, in the form of the relation of the semi-major axis (the distance from the planet to the sun) to the orbital period.

The relevant background here is this: Kepler's three laws of planetary motion can explain the elliptical form of planetary orbits around the sun by simple mathematical formulas that include nothing else but spatial and temporal relations that are defined by their proportionality and powers. Newton then democratized the two bodies by postulating two basic forces, an inertial force related to the mass of a body (*vis insita*, often also called centrifugal force) and a force acting over distance and related to the mass and distance apart of two bodies (*vis impressa*, often called centrifugal force). One scientifically important consequence of this (and an advantage of Newton over Kepler) is that one can add other two-body interactions as perturbations to explain the apsidal precession, that is, the observed deviation from the elliptical orbits.

As Hegel sees it, however, the problem lies in Newton's conception of these forces as fundamental (§269R) over their *systematic* arrangement. In the movement of celestial bodies, forces stand in an 'oscillating equilibrium' to each other. Within the elliptical trajectory, the relation of the two forces involved will change between aphelion and perihelion, i.e., the points farthest from or closest to the center: As the body moves toward the perihelion, the (gravitational) centripetal force is greater than the centrifugal force (derived from the body's inertia), but it is weaker on the direction toward the aphelion. Hegel insists that this oscillating relation between the two forces cannot be inferred from the nature of the forces, as they are developed by Newton (§270R). Newton has falsely postulated a force dualism as fundamental, as he has falsely abstracted them from what he wanted to explain in the first place, namely bodies moving on a roughly elliptical path; the ellipsis explains the oscillation of forces rather than the other way around.

Only if we integrate space and time as diverging determinations into the picture, as Kepler did, can we make sense of trajectories. Because the proportion of the distance to the sun and the time each body takes to traverse one section of the ellipse is constant, Kepler's third law can "easily and immediately present the *reason of the matter* (einfach und unmittelbar die *Vernunft der Sache* darstellt)" (§270R). Kepler's third law holds that the square of the orbital period (time) of a planet is directly proportional to the cube of the semi-major axis (space) of its orbit. Here the mathematical proportion of the powers of space and time exhibits the reciprocal determination of the bodies in relation to each other, and thus gives us a metric. This is what Hegel seems to intend to say when he complains that some scientists (i.e., Newton) try to analyze the entity at stake instead of its concept (GW 24: 1237–8 (§270Z)).

This is not only a discussion of scientific methods. It is Hegel's way to emphasize the importance of proportions and proportionality over speculations concerning forces. This proportionality is called *form* (§271), and it relates ideal (and idealized) determinations of space, time, and motion to each other. In this determining *form* we understand not only that matter has its own internal or immanent center (its own mass point), but also that it is related to an external center, which serves as the center of the system of interacting bodies (i.e., the gravitational center of the solar system). Thus, Hegel turns to a three-body system, exemplified by the sun–earth–moon system in which all the possible configurations of centers are possible. The sun has an internal center which is the external center of earth. Earth's internal center is the external center of the moon. Here every position is privileged, with the earth having both an external center and an internal center that is the external center for another body. This complexity is the one needed to support the logical perspectives. In contrast to Newton, this three-body system does not merely result in perturbations, but adds a new complexity and thus a step up in the ladder.

As these two centers are conceptually interrelated by means of the concept of *form*, Hegel transitions from *mechanics* as the science of matter as it is in itself (determined only by its own center) to the next level, *physics*. In physics, the mass point center of the system of bodies is understood as a *sun*, its material identity is *light*. In accord with eighteenth-century usage, Hegel conceives of physics as the science of *qualified* bodies, i.e., not simply mass points, but bodies with physical qualities derived from their systematic relations with each other (Bonsiepen 1997: 27–9). This marks a transition to a dynamical system. Technically Hegel does this by doubling the role of the moon into two principles, the lunar and the cometary. This transition to four perspectives is possible in and only in nature.

6.5   The General Argument

We have thus far done two things. First, we characterized the general argument of the *Philosophy of Nature*: it is a regress on the conditions for the Euclidean features of space and time – their metric and orientation – that are essential for space and time to play the functional role of providing the basic structure for nature. Not only the measurements constitutive of natural science, but also the perspectival experience of natural phenomena, require these features. Second, we reconstructed the first step in this argument through space, time, and mechanics. In concluding, we sketch the workings of the argument in the remainder of the text, focusing on the development of time.

Hegel's treatment of nature is divided into three large divisions: Mechanics, Physics, and Organic Physics. Each is built upon the preceding one with the foundations of space and time at the base. The conceptual development of time doesn't map onto those divisions as neatly as one might like, but one can distinguish at each of the three levels between the kinds of *processes* that are paradigmatic of that level.

At the level of Mechanics, there are *oscillatory* processes with no inherent direction. They seem to take place *in time*, but they presuppose some other process that can give time the filling it needs to have a direction (the 'arrow of time'). These oscillatory processes are entirely reversible, and in this respect they model the inferential structures of the *Logic*. If the two end-points can be adequately distinguished, however, such processes at least provide a metric for time.

At the level of Physics – and particularly once we get to chemistry – we have *directional* processes. That is, we have systems in which heat loss generates an objective difference between a low-entropy past and a high-entropy future, and which are reversible but only with the external input of energy. The paradigmatic case here is that of a battery which can be recharged finitely many times. This time of physics thus first provides the orientation to time that was required. Chemism responds to mechanism as the breakdown of objects into their parts is dependent on the object's own substantial nature, even though these objects can be divided according to external principles and may stand externally to one another. Here, the external relation of different types of bodies is mediated by the spatiotemporal orientation provided by mechanics: the mechanical part–whole relation, in which the parts maintain their identity, is thereby transformed into the processual nature of chemical composition, in which the independent identity of these parts is dissolved to give rise to something else, namely, the chemical compound.

Finally, in Organic Physics we find processes which are *cyclical*. Life recharges itself, but also only finitely many times. Living processes have a direction (orientation); deciduous trees first grow leaves in the spring and then lose them in the fall and then grow them again the following spring. And because they have a circuit, living processes also have a temporal metric, which is the temporal distance between sequential occupations of the same stations in the circuit (in addition to the spatial metric of, e.g., their size). In the realm of biology, mechanical and chemical explanations are incomplete insofar as they do not understand the object within its specific horizon of possible purposes. A proper understanding of objects would transcend mechanical and chemical reasoning and lead to an explanation of things by invoking either internal or external purposes. These purposes are conceived by relying on the oriented framework of space and time filled out by mechanical and chemical objects: the wings of a bird are *for* flying, which is a mechanical process; the animal eats some fruit for the purpose of *chemically* digesting it. In the species-process (*Gattungsprozess*) one gets even further a relation between organisms – which is simultaneously a relation to their kind and its purposes – that binds together the individual cycles to a directed process. When these relational processes become transparent to themselves, nature gives rise to consciousness or *spirit*.[13]

---

[13] For their many helpful questions and corrections, the authors would like to thank the editors of this volume and audiences in Heidelberg, San Diego, Parma, and Padua.

CHAPTER 7

Hegel's Anthropology
Transforming the Body

Jane Dryden

The trajectory of the "Anthropology" section of Hegel's *Encyclopedia* brings us from the uncultivated, natural soul which humans share with non-human animals to its development into an individual subject, ready to become the conscious "I" of the "Phenomenology." Much of this entails the transformation of the body from something purely determined by nature to being a home for spirit as it freely relates itself to the world. The "Anthropology" thus dwells on the theme of liberation from nature. Especially in the *Zusätze* and in the 1827/8 *Lectures on the Philosophy of Spirit*, Hegel notes that that cultivation is associated with minimizing the effects of natural determinations on one's body.[1] Insofar as nature is associated with particularity and reason with universality, it may seem as though idiosyncratic embodiments are incompatible with the kind of mastery of the body Hegel envisions. At the same time, given that the focus of the "Anthropology" is on the development of the soul rather than the matter of the body itself, there may be a range of compatible bodily possibilities. This raises the question of how much the body and its comportment ought to correspond to an ideal, and what the implications may be for those humans whose embodiment marks them out (in Hegel's system) as closer to nature.

One way to make sense of this is to distinguish between the imperative to *overcome* nature in our development and an invitation to come to *own* our natural determinations by taking them up and turning them into expressions of our freedom. *Owning* our natural determinations and *overcoming* nature are related, for Hegel, insofar as both involve the spirit's development and mastery of the body. Both involve an ensouled body becoming ready to

---

[1] Much of the interesting discussion in the "Anthropology" is in the *Zusätze* of the *Encyclopedia*, which is supported in many instances by the text of the 1827/8 lectures. These lectures are a transcript of Hegel's entire course, by his student Johann Eduard Erdman with supplemental text by Ferdinand Walter, provided in footnotes in Williams (2007). I will refer to them in the text as the 1827/8 *Lectures*.

participate in the moral, social, cultural, and political world. Both are certainly implied in Hegel's text, and the difference between them is largely one of focus; this focus, however, matters when we are considering the use of Hegel's account for us today. A focus on overcoming natural determinations suggests that those perceived as closer to nature are ranked below those who are further from nature, and thus may risk reinforcing social inequality linked with a hierarchy of development. A focus on owning our natural determinations, on the other hand, may allow a broader range of determinations to be taken up and made over by spirit, not merely those which are markers for a greater distance from nature.

Carefully examining the body in the "Anthropology" raises the question of whether there are limitations to the embodiments that may be appropriated and claimed as our own. In addition, when considering bodily changes over a lifetime, we realize that mastering our bodies is an ongoing process, not something we have completed once we are adults. Despite the location of the "Anthropology" early in the *Philosophy of Subjective Spirit*, the relationship it depicts between soul and body remains a project for us long after we have reached maturity. After providing a brief overview of the "Anthropology," I will explore the implications of interpretations focusing on owning or ownership, within the context of Hegel's criticisms of excessive particularity and idiosyncrasy, his discussion of the ages of life, and the situation of bodies marked by race, gender, and disability. Overall, an ownership focus allows us to propose a more inclusive interpretation of Hegel, but even this is limited by the association of nature and unfreedom.

7.1 Overview of the Anthropology

The "Anthropology" opens after the conclusion of the Philosophy of Nature, where still-slumbering spirit had begun to be individualized in and through the encountering of opposition.[2] With the "Anthropology," Hegel is focused on human formation. At this stage, this developing humanity is still deeply embedded in the natural world,[3] a world of contingency (LPS 58) and without freedom (PM §381Z, 10).[4] As Hegel writes, we begin

---

[2] "The subjectivity of the animal contains a contradiction and the urge to preserve itself by sublating this contradiction; this self-preservation is the privilege of the living being and, in a still greater degree, of mind" (PM §381Z, 11).

[3] "Anthropology as such considers spirit in its natural life, when spirit is still immersed in nature, and appears as spirit in conflict and in relation to corporeality" (LPS 57).

[4] Abbreviations used: EL, Hegel (1991b); LPS, Hegel (2007b); PN, Hegel (1970); and PR, Hegel (1991a).

"with mind still in the grip of nature, related to its bodiliness, mind that is not as yet together with itself, not yet free" (PM §387Z, 27).[5] Humanity's development involves the imposition of order as well as the capacity to not be limited by the determinations of nature. While the progression of the "Anthropology" involves a kind of liberation from nature, this should not be taken to be a *denial* of our situatedness as natural beings; "spirit's liberation *from* nature is more precisely its liberation *within* (and *with*) nature" (Nuzzo 2013: 1). The story of our liberation is a complex and ambiguous one. As is consistent in Hegel's methodology, the stages of the development of the mind are just moments which need to be reconstructed in order to be understood; as we discuss lower ones, the higher ones are already anticipated (PM §380; PM §396Z, 61–2).[6]

Hegel begins with a discussion of the soul, which is described as still abstract, and "only the *sleep* of mind – the passive νοῦς of Aristotle, which is *potentially* all things" (PM §389, 30). It is "the organizational structure of the body that endures in its dynamism beyond any replacement of the body's matter" (Testa 2013: 26). The soul will be the foundation of the particular individual we are to become, as it is shaped by various determinations and moves away from abstraction and possibility and into actuality.

In its least developed form, "in its immediate *natural determinacy*" (PM §390), the soul is the natural soul. It is shaped by natural qualities, natural alterations, and sensation. Natural qualities include climate and the seasons, geography (which leads to an account of different races and ethnicities, discussed below), predisposition, temperament, and character. Each of these plays a role in forming the soul, giving its eventual subjectivity some natural foundation, but none of them is depicted as entirely determining on its own; upbringing and education are intended to mitigate these particular determinations.

The natural alterations discussed by Hegel are the ages of life (from childhood to old age), the opposition experienced in the sex relationship, and the alternation of sleep and waking. As Murray Greene notes, this seems to be an unexpected and disconnected triad (Greene 1972: 80). What they have in common, however, is the presence of an ongoing subjectivity throughout changes and oppositions (PM §396), thus anticipating the soul's individuation.

[5] As I am using the Wallace, Miller, and Inwood translation of the *Philosophie des Geistes*, I will follow their translation of *Geist* as spirit; and similarly will follow the usage of other sources when I quote them. My own usage will depend on context.
[6] This point is helpfully made clear by Murray Greene (1972: 70).

The final stage of the natural soul is sensation; Hegel discusses bodily determinations such as the senses as well as determinations originating in the mind (such as cheerfulness or grief) (PM §401R, 72). Sensation is not yet the detailed and contextualized experience of a self-aware subjectivity, and sensations themselves are individual, contingent, and transitory. At this stage, we are still at the mercy of the outside world, not yet capable of deciding for ourselves how to respond; as Hegel writes, "This *natural* subjectivity is not yet a self-determining subjectivity following its own law and acting in a necessary manner, but a subjectivity determined from outside, tied to *this* space and to *this* time, dependent on contingent circumstances" (PM §400, 71). We are thus neither overcoming these external forces nor making them our own, but rather are merely buffeted by them.

Hegel next discusses the feeling soul, in which "the soul is no longer merely a natural, but an inward, individuality" (PM §403, 87). As Greene notes, this is "the state where opposition is pre-eminent" (Greene 1972: 104). Our response to the buffeting of external forces is to turn in on ourselves; this turns us away from the world but is also a step toward our ability to distinguish ourselves from our surroundings; we begin to feel ourselves as a totality.

The experiences that are part of the feeling soul "in its immediacy" (PM §405) are dreaming, those of the child in the womb, and our relationship to our inner life. In dreaming, the soul passively experiences a sense of itself as a totality (PM §405Z, 92–4). The child in the womb and the mother represent a duality between a passive individuality, which is not yet self-reflective, and another individuality determining it. With the relationship to our inner life, which Hegel calls genius ("the *particularity* of the individual, which in all situations and relationships decides its conduct and fate"), the duality is made one again, in that I am now a "*twofold* entity within myself," experiencing my life circumstances and my own inward sense of particular destiny (PM §405Z, 94).

This state becomes a "disease" when it "becomes a *form*, a *state*, of the self-conscious, educated, sober human being" (PM §406). This involves "a surrender of his existence as mental self-possession," to what is conveyed through a "haze of feeling," such as in clairvoyance (PM §406R, 95). Through passivity, the subject also risks becoming susceptible to coming under the power of someone or something else, as in the phenomenon of animal magnetism (PM §406Z, 108).[7]

---

[7] The full discussion of clairvoyance, animal magnetism, and divination can be found at PM §406R and Z, 95–114, and LPS 130–9. As Robert R. Williams notes in his introduction to the 1827/8 lectures, "Hegel does not believe that animal magnetism and hypnotism provide access to a superior epistemic

The next stage is self-feeling, in which the subject "is immersed in this *particularity* of sensations, and at the same time, through the ideality of the particular, in them it joins together with itself as a subjective unit" (PM §407, 114). On the one hand, this continues the subject's individuation; on the other, it runs the risk of the subject being bound up with itself to the exclusion of the external world. Here Hegel discusses various forms of "derangement" (*Verrücktheit*),[8] in which reason has closed itself off from the outside; these are extreme forms of self-feeling in which the soul is "*divided against itself*" (PM §402Z, 87). Hegel does not suggest that every subject must experience a period of "derangement" in order to progress, but, "because the soul appears here at the standpoint of its rupture with itself, we have to consider it in its *diseased* state" (PM §402Z, 84).

Habit is the way in which we come to move on from being caught up in our own feeling and sensations; it involves a hardening to immediate sensation, the dulling of urges to satisfy desires, and bodily dexterity (PM §410R, 132). Regular and repeated sensation and activity become second nature, thus freeing the soul from being consumed by attention to them (PM §409). Hegel describes it as "the most essential feature of the *existence* of all mental life in the individual subject, enabling the subject to be *concrete* immediacy" (PM §410R, 133). A habituated body operates at the behest of the soul, rather than being determined by its impulses, instincts, and bodily reflexes. As McCumber writes, "when my feelings are reduced to habits, they continue to be *mine*; what they cease to be is *me*" (McCumber 1990: 158).

With the development of habit, the soul pervades the body, making it its own, even though "something of bodiliness remains . . . purely organic and consequently removed from the power of the soul" (PM §412Z, 140). At this point, the body is not merely something experienced by the soul, or housing the soul, but the sign of the soul's activity and expression: "As this identity of the inner with the outer, the outer being subjugated to the inner, the soul is *actual*; in its bodiliness it has its free shape, in which it feels *itself* and makes *itself* felt, and which, as the soul's work of art, has *human*, pathognomic and physiognomic, expression" (PM §411, 136).

The last stage of the "Anthropology" is the actual soul. Here Hegel describes "the soul's higher awakening to the I" (PM §412, 140), which is

position, much less reveal 'higher truths.' Rather such phenomena are evidence that spirit can fall below its level and regress into quasi-natural immediacy and dependence" (Williams 2007: 15).

[8] Williams translates this as "dementia" in LPS; it is translated as "madness" by Berthold-Bond, who provides an extensive discussion of the relation of Hegel's theory to nineteenth-century science (Berthold-Bond 1995: 9–35).

"*for itself* and *freed* from *bodiliness*" (PM §412Z, 141).[9] It will now be able to interact as an individuated subject with the external world, and can begin to move into the forms of life described in the "Phenomenology," such as perception, encountering others, and coming to recognize and be recognized.

7.2 Ownership and Overcoming

What might it mean to be "freed from bodiliness," for an embodied subject? Freedom from bodiliness does not imply a metaphysical separation where "bodiliness is a materiality outside the soul and with its parts external to each other" (PM §403Z, 88). Following Hegel's logic, we can consider the double meaning of sublation, or *Aufhebung*, as both "canceling" and "preserving" (EL §96Z, 154). In one sense, we can think of the actual soul as having canceled out the effects of the external determinations of nature and bodily limitations, through the cultivation of habit and the awakening of its self-conscious agency. In another, we can think of it having accepted these determinations as its own, "at home with itself [in its externality]" (LPS 159). Both senses are present, as we would expect from Hegel. However, interpretations which focus on one or the other can suggest different possibilities for the lessons we might draw from Hegel today.

I will refer to the first – canceling – as the "overcoming interpretation." Insofar as our bodies are the part of us most associated with nature, being able to determine ourselves consciously and rationally involves freedom from the limitations of the body and the immediacy of bodiliness. This is sometimes described as overcoming:

> Even in the most perfect form to which nature raises itself, in animal life, the concept does not attain to an actuality resembling its soulful essence, to the complete overcoming of the externality and finitude of its embodied reality. This first happens in the *mind*, which, precisely by this overcoming accomplished in it, distinguishes itself from nature, so that this distinguishing is not merely the doing of an external reflection on the essence of mind. (PM §381Z, 12)

In the Introduction to the *Philosophy of Spirit*, Hegel writes "But the freedom of mind is not merely an independence of the Other won outside

---

[9] "So the soul is subject existing for itself; it is substance whose corporeity is no longer due to being, but rather corporeity is only a moment in the soul ... This [corporeal] externality is only a sign of the soul, only represents the soul" (LPS 159).

the other, but won within the Other; it attains actuality not by fleeing from the Other but by overcoming it" (PM §382Z, 16). A similar attitude is expressed in Hegel's characterization of the outcome of the "Anthropology" as "the triumph of the soul over its bodiliness" (PM §387Z, 27). In this focus, our natural determinations are something to be canceled, such that our bodies can be brought into line with universal expectations; this is most overt in Hegel's criticisms of idiosyncrasies and excessive particularity. This interpretation also accords with Hegel's Philosophy of History, where the movement away from nature is unambiguously presented as a mark of greater civilization and freedom (Stone 2020: 16–18).

The interpretation connected with "preserving" will be referred to as the "ownership interpretation," insofar as it depicts the soul gradually taking ownership of the body, in line with Hegel's description of the actual soul as "when its bodiliness has been thoroughly trained and made its own" (PM §411). Drawing on the work of Helmuth Plessner, Karen Ng describes the ambiguity of both "*being* a body" and "*having* a body"; with the latter, "I can relate to my body as an instrument or means, exerting control over my embodiment, eventually directing it to self-conscious ends" (Ng 2016: 36). This focus on "having" or owning a body suggests a somewhat different relationship to my natural determinations than the overcoming focus. Simon Lumsden describes habit as "the way in which human beings can be at home with nature," specifying that, through habit, "the natural is transformed into a second nature, but in so doing it does not leave the natural behind" (Lumsden 2013: 134). As Lydia Moland writes, the "Anthropology" "chronicles the slow process of earning and finally owning what one has inherited; it narrates how the agent turns passively received traits into characteristics that express her freedom" (Moland 2003: 141). While Moland does not discuss the body specifically, her account makes the shape of the ownership interpretation clear:

> Although I begin with a vicious temper, I can come to own that temper by transforming it into something that reflects my will. Indeed, in describing the results of this process, Hegel often uses language of ownership, describing the agent as "self-possessed," coming into a character that is "his own." Clearly, this ownership is crucial to the idea of agency at all. If humans were nothing but their inherited determinations, there would be no freedom, no responsibility, no agency. Inherited traits that are earned and converted into owned characteristics, however, bear the stamp of self-determination that converts them from determined to free components of agency. (Moland 2003: 141)

This conversion means that while we are liberated from them as *determinations*, we nonetheless preserve them as aspects of our selves, that make us the particular individuals that we are. David Ciavatta presents a similar account of the way we come to own our bodies in the *Philosophy of Right*, noting that it allows a positive experience of an agent's particularity as "a constitutive feature of her very self-identity and freedom" (Ciavatta 2005: 15).

7.3   The Stakes of Ownership and Overcoming: Our Particularities

On the trajectory of the "Anthropology," development toward the universal is associated with greater cultivation and freedom, and development away from the contingent and particular is associated with greater distance from nature. Therefore, while it is our particular determinations that make us who we are as individuals (PM §406Z, 102), Hegel cautions against excess; these cautions are found in the *Zusätze* and 1827/8 lectures. We are not supposed to be *too* particular. However, the forms of particularity that are acceptable may depend on the interpretation we follow. On an ownership interpretation, a particular determination can come to express my freedom once I have made it my own. An overcoming interpretation, on the other hand, means minimizing determinations that tie me to nature.

An example of such a caution is in his discussion of the effects of predisposition, temperament, character, and "so-called *idiosyncrasies*" (PM §395Z, 52). Hegel states:

> Now first of all we must remark that it is in the individual soul that the sphere of the contingent begins, for only the universal is the necessary. Individual souls are distinguished from each other by an infinite number of contingent modifications. But this infinity belongs to the bad kind of infinite.[10] One should not therefore rate the peculiarity of people too highly. . . . The more cultivated a man is, the less his behaviour exhibits anything peculiar only to him, anything therefore contingent. (PM §395Z, 50)[11]

He specifies that "In times of greater cultivation, the various contingent mannerisms of conduct and action disappear, and with them the varieties of temperament" (PM §395Z, 51; also LPS 94). Meanwhile, in the 1827/8 lectures, he glosses cultivation as "conduct according to a universal norm" (LPS 95). While we are individuated by particular determinations, a core part of our development involves minimizing or remoulding them. This is

---

[10] For a discussion of the meaning of the "bad infinite," refer to EL §§94–5, 149–52.
[11] Compare this with PR §187R, 226.

true even of those differences that are connected to our particular communities; as Hegel notes in the 1827/8 lectures, "Cultivated men raise themselves above these [regional] differences, and it is difficult to recognize any
national character in them, because the distinguishing feature of educated
human beings consists in acting, existing, and being actual in accordance
with universal modes of thought" (LPS 94 n. 58).

This also applies to our bodily expression. The cultivation of our
character can be discerned in our way of holding ourselves: "above all
things, gait must be cultivated; in it the soul must betray its mastery over
the physical body" (PM §411Z, 139). In a *Zusatz* to §400, Hegel describes
various "embodiments of the mental," through which our soul is exterior-
ized in ways that can be evident to others; these include weeping and
laughter (PM §400Z, 81). Noting the variety of forms laughter can take
("from the vulgar peals of side-splitting guffaw of someone empty or coarse
to the gentle smile of the noble soul, smiling through tears"), Hegel argues
that

> the various modes of laughter indicate, therefore, the cultural level of
> individuals in a very characteristic manner. A man of reflection never, or
> only rarely, abandons himself to peals of laughter ... Excessive laughter is
> rightly held to be evidence of dullness, of a foolish mentality that is insensi-
> tive to all great, genuinely substantial interests and regards them as external
> and alien to it. (PM §401Z, 82)

The minimization of particularity includes things that might aid in com-
munication and seem to have no intrinsic harm; Hegel notes approvingly
that "the cultivated man has a less animated play of looks and gestures than
the uncultivated" (PM §411Z, 139). This downplaying of expression is
connected to the valorization of articulate speech (and reason): "The
cultured individual does not need to be lavish with looks and gestures;
he possesses in *talk* the worthiest and most suitable means of expressing
himself; for *speech* is able immediately to receive and reproduce every
modification of representation" (PM §411Z, 139).

These examples lend themselves strongly to an overcoming interpretation, in which the point is to move beyond the determinations of nature.
However, Hegel does not instruct us to eliminate all of our particular
determinations; after all, these make us who we are. Following his instruc-
tion to cultivate one's gait, he notes that both vices and virtues such as
"orderliness, modesty, good sense, candour etc., ... express themselves in
the peculiar style of walking; so that it is easy to distinguish people from
one another by their gait" (PM §411Z, 139). We are individuated by these

differences. The key thing is that we not be at the mercy of our natural urges and inclinations.

Habit plays an important role in allowing us a more reflective stance toward them. Lydia Moland writes, "Habit has ... brought forth the individual as a budding universal, a thinking self at home with itself instead of a self ruled solely by its natural determinations" (Moland 2003: 150). Hegel's discussion of habit suggests an interpretation more focused on ownership, in which what matters is less the universalized appearance of the body, and more the soul's relationship to that body. As he writes, the soul "must make its identity with its body into an identity *posited* or mediated by the mind, take *possession* of its body, form it into a *pliant* and *skillful instrument* of its activity" (PM §410Z, 135). Dexterity is a sign of this achievement:

> If the activities of the body to be performed in the service of mind are often *repeated*, they acquire an ever higher degree of adequacy, for the soul gains an ever greater familiarity with all the circumstances to be considered, hence becomes more and more *at home* in its *expressions* and consequently achieves a continually growing capacity for immediately embodying its inner deter-minations and accordingly transforms the body more and more into its own property, into its serviceable instrument; there thus arises a *magical*[12] rela-tionship, an immediate operation of mind on body. (PM §410Z, 136)

If this is what matters most, then a wide range of embodiments might be included. Consider the virtuosity of many disabled dancers, such as Alice Sheppard, which demonstrates the dexterity possible for bodies still marked by particularity.[13] As Moland writes, "habit gives us an idea of how determinations can be appropriated into the subject's freedom with-out becoming negated. The subject need not reject her melancholy dispos-ition but she can control and own it" (Moland 2003: 155). With this appropriation, our determinations cease to be contingent and can acquire rational significance in terms of our own purposes and self-understanding.

The two approaches to interpretation – overcoming and ownership – thus have different implications for which forms of embodiment can be intended in the spirit's transformation of the body. The narrative of the "Anthropology" can be further complicated through a closer examination of the ages of life.

---

[12] For Hegel, magic refers to interactions which appear unmediated: "A magical force is one whose effect is not determined by the interconnection, the conditions and mediations of objective relationships" (PM §405Z, 91). Merleau-Ponty uses magic in a similar way: "In movement, the relations between my decision and my body are magical ones" (Merleau-Ponty 2012: 97).

[13] Watch, for example, her video at Sheppard (2014).

7.4 The Ages of Life and Coping with the Changing Body

Hegel's discussion of the ages of life (PM §396Z, 54–61; LPS 96–100) portrays the mastery of the body as an achievement of childhood. The narrative of the baby in the womb, birth, and the initial development of the child regularly refers to the body, including the growth of teeth, learning to speak, and the development of an upright gait (PM §396Z, 55–6). Learning to speak is identified with the ability to pronounce "the I" (PM §396Z, 57) and the ability to distinguish one's self from one's environment. Hegel notes that "mind . . . reveals its independence of its bodiliness in the fact that it can develop earlier than the body" (PM §396Z, 54).

After boyhood, other than a brief mention of hypochondria as weakness (PM §396Z, 60), Hegel discusses education, cultivation, and choosing a vocation with no reference to the body or any embodied constraints.[14] The description of old age focuses on the mental, even while briefly acknowledging a physical dimension: "Thus by the habit of mental life, as well as by the dulling of the activity of his physical organism, the man becomes an *old man*" (PM §396Z, 61). The old man is characterized primarily by his abandoning of hope, living in recollection of the past, and wisdom and knowledge of the universal (PM §396Z, 61). The path to death similarly foregrounds the mental: "But this wisdom, this lifeless, complete coincidence of subjective activity with its world, leads back to oppositionless childhood, in the same way that the growth of the activity of his physical organism into a static habit leads on to the abstract negation of the living individuality, to *death*" (PM §396Z, 61).[15]

This fits the macro level narrative of the *Philosophy of Spirit*, in which, once the soul pervades the body at the end of the "Anthropology," it does not re-emerge as a significant philosophical concern for us. At the level of individual human development, it suggests that adults have largely mastered their bodies. Of course, the trajectory of the "Anthropology" is not necessarily chronological, but rather is logical. Most of the examples that Hegel gives of various stages of soul are drawn from mature adult experience, and a more advanced form is often anticipated in the discussion of an

---

[14] This is in contrast to the *Philosophy of Right*, where Hegel notes that some individuals are poor because of "contingent physical factors" (PR §241) and "differences in the development of natural physical and mental [*geistigen*] aptitudes" (PR §200).
[15] The *Philosophy of Nature* presents much the same account: "its activity has become deadened and ossified and the process of life has become the inertia of *habit*; it is in this way that the animal brings about its own destruction" (PN §375).

earlier one.[16] However, the discussion of the ages of life warrants a closer examination, given the vulnerability of our bodies. As Wes Furlotte notes, nature continues to pose a problem for us, and "the unruliness of nature itself . . . operates as a necessary precondition, yet problem, for the life of the concept and spirit" (Furlotte 2018: 246).

The *Philosophy of Nature* points out that disease is an inevitable part of the life of organisms (PN §371Z, 429, §375Z, 441), and so the mastery of our bodies must be limited. Diseases present challenges to our usual habits and routines; they do not merely affect the biological processes but impact our sense of self-control, as well as social, economic, and political systems and expectations.[17]

The body undergoes many developments in middle and old age that challenge our sense of control over it, such as changes in metabolism, changes in sensitivity to foods and digestion, and menopause. In response to these, the formation of new habits might be required, such as new diets or new fitness regimes. New mental habits may also be formed, such as a greater acceptance of one's vulnerability and the need for help from others. Adapting from a life lived in one's home to institutional life in a hospital or retirement home may require the formation of new social habits and expectations. Inwood comments that certain tasks such as "playing chess, teaching philosophy, and possibly political activity are not easily mastered or exhausted in a single lifetime" (Inwood 2010: 345), but the aging body itself presents a far from "oppositionless" existence.

This suggests that the soul's achievement, described at the end of the "Anthropology," is not a singular event, but an ongoing process that might ebb and flow over a lifetime. This echoes Hegel's acknowledgment in his discussion of derangement that "the cultivated, intellectual consciousness" is "at the same time the *natural* self of *self-feeling*" (PM §408R, 115). The development of our minds out of the enclosed state of the feeling soul is not a singular achievement for those who later experience mental illness. In that case it is treated as a disease that some, but not all, people will experience. The embodied vicissitudes of middle and old age, however, are close to inevitable for all humans who live long enough, even though not everyone experiences the same changes in the same way.

For an "overcoming" interpretation, this means that liberation from the body is something to be achieved more than once; this complicates the

---

[16] For example, "In considering derangement we must likewise anticipate the cultivated, intellectual consciousness, the subject which is at the same time the *natural* self of *self-feeling*" (PM §408R, 115).

[17] For example, we might consider how the phenomenon of sick leave complicates Hegel's account of the system of needs in Objective Spirit.

story of cultivation as smoothing out idiosyncrasy, as even a highly educated individual may yet be taken by surprise by new pains or bodily weaknesses. For an "ownership" interpretation, it means that there is an ongoing process of appropriating our determinations; there may be challenges in doing this for those acquired later in life. In both cases, the process of aging involves a complex and dynamic interaction between nature and spirit, persisting into maturity. To further pick out the significance of each interpretation, it is useful to consider their effects on bodies marked by difference from a universalized norm.

7.5 Race, Gender, Disability in the Anthropology

As we have seen, Hegel's philosophy largely expects that, as agents become more cultivated, their demeanor and gait will more closely come to resemble the universal, rather than the particular. But what does this universal involve? Nicholas Mowad argues that, despite some of Hegel's comments, overall his argument challenges the dominance of any particular type of person. Insofar as Hegel conceives of both gender and race as limitations that prevent a broader perspective, and everyone ought to establish distance from their natural determinations, both masculinity and whiteness are traits that ought to be stripped of their status as default or normative (Mowad 2019: 91, 118). Mowad argues that we can interpret insights of the "Anthropology" while rejecting the idea of a "hierarchy of peoples" (Mowad 2019: 92).

Mowad's interpretation, in which something taken to be an abstract and unquestioned universal is in fact itself a particular, fits with Hegel's philosophy in general. The pattern of Hegel's description of cultivated norms and expectations, however, suggests that there is a dominant image of a human at work. Comments throughout the "Anthropology" and the corresponding section in the 1827/8 lectures center a European,[18] non-disabled, heterosexual man. This is apparent in how Hegel uses the term "us," as in the example "Orientals cover the lower half of the face with beards; with us one can view the varied outlooks and musculature" (LPS 161). Hegel's accounts of the senses, gait, and use of other bodily features seem to presuppose a non-disabled subject. The sex relationship specifies

---

[18] This includes "Europeans" living in the Americas and their descendants: "As far as the more precise spiritual differences among races are concerned, America is a highly interesting continent, but only by virtue of the fact that Europeans have settled there. The ones who have drawn attention to themselves through the fact that they have made themselves independent and have given themselves rational laws, are not the native Americans as such, but the Creoles" (LPS 90).

relating to "an individual of the opposite sex" (PM §398Z 63–4).[19] The overview of the ages of life names the young man who will enter civil society, not the young woman, whose "highest vocation is to be the mother of the family" (LPS 102).

On an overcoming interpretation, this implies an advantage to those who – by virtue of their natural determinations – are already perceived as closer to the dominant image of the universal, and farther from the contingent particularity of nature. Since, as I will discuss below, some kinds of bodies are more closely associated with nature, the focus on distancing oneself from nature can create a hierarchy.

An ownership interpretation may facilitate valuing a wider range of bodily determinations once they have been appropriated by the subject and made over by spirit. Even on this interpretation, however, the association of nature and unfreedom suggests limitations for how agents may be perceived when they preserve particular traits linked with nature. To explore this, I will discuss race, gender, and disability in turn.

There has been a fair amount of discussion of Hegel's accounts of race, drawing on his *Philosophy of History* and other texts.[20] Commentators on Hegel's "Anthropology" generally condemn the descriptions Hegel gives of different races and ethnicities. For example, Andreja Novakovic describes the section in PM §412 as "notorious, because in it (or, more accurately, in the additions) Hegel voices many cultural and racial prejudices of his age" (Novakovic 2017: 412). She concludes: "What all of these reflections are meant to illustrate is more generally that climate and other environmental factors affect our personalities" (Novakovic 2017: 412). Similarly, Moland states that the stereotypes are "unacceptable," but that "we can salvage the point that our ethnic identities sometimes figure in our understanding of our own and others' actions" (Moland 2003: 143).

For Mowad, the salvageable message from this section is that whiteness is not taken as default, but is marked through Hegel's discussion of the "peculiarities of Europeans" (Mowad 2019: 91), and that members of all races and ethnicities ought to develop beyond the particularities of their contingent, particular origins in order to identify with the human species more broadly. Not all particularities are portrayed equally, however. Germans are particularized in Hegel's descriptions of various European peoples; he notes their inward-turning minds, their slowness to act, and

---

[19] Kirk Pillow provides a helpful overview of the insistence on heterosexuality in Hegel's system (Pillow 2002).

[20] For example, De Laurentiis (2014), Bernasconi (1998, 2000), Parekh (2009), and Buchwalter (2009).

"inordinate desire" for official posts and titles (PM §394Z, 49). None of these are in significant tension with the traits assigned to highly cultivated people, unlike those of the Italians, whom Hegel considers to have "the closest tie to nature" (Moland 2003: 142), and who accordingly are described in terms of their "uninhibitedness" (PM §394Z, 46–7).[21]

Non-European races are explicitly described in terms of their lack of development. Referring to Africans, Hegel writes that they "are to be regarded as a nation of children," and that so long as they remain in Africa, "they do not attain to the feeling of man's personality, – their mind is entirely dormant, it remains sunk within itself, it makes no progress" (PM §393Z, 41).[22] For "the Asiatic race," mind is "beginning to awake, to separate itself from naturalness," and yet "in this identity of mind with nature true freedom is impossible" (PM §393Z, 41). Contrast this with "the Caucasian race," where "for the first time mind enters into complete opposition to naturalness" (PM §393Z, 42).

While Hegel may particularize European ethnicities in one section, European standards are employed as default and universal throughout the rest of the text. For example, in the ages of life section, after Hegel notes that "the child" learns the alphabet as "the most abstract thing that the child's mind can grasp" (PM §396Z, 58), he immediately claims that "This presupposes an abstraction to which entire races, for example, even the Chinese, have not attained" (PM §396Z, 58). This implies that the supposedly universal narrative of the ages of man is one which refers only to specific groups – that is, those which use an alphabet.

Later on, Hegel states that Europeans bow only with the upper part of their body "since in doing it we do not wish to surrender our independence," whereas "Orientals, by contrast, express reverence for their master by throwing themselves on the ground before him; they may not look him in the eye, for by doing so they would be asserting their being-for-self, and only the master has the right freely to survey the servant and the slave" (PM §411Z, 138). What could simply have been a note about different bodily habits acquires a normative significance when we recall that the entire progression of the "Anthropology" is toward bodily independence and "the

---

[21] Compare this with the 1828/9 lectures, where he notes: "More education and less use of gestures go together. The Italians have many antics" (LPS 161).

[22] In the 1828/9 lectures, Hegel states: "The Africans retain a pure inwardness that never progresses to development. The Africans are now as they have been for the last thousand years. They have never gone out of themselves, but always remain within themselves in a childlike manner. They have remained in the condition of [raw] particularity, of individuality, of desire, and have not developed the oppositions of the understanding, of [universal] law and particular instances" (LPS 91).

soul's higher awakening to the I" (PM §412). This example marks Europeans as independent, and "Orientals" as slavish.

Given the pattern of Hegel's comments, achieving distance from nature implies behaving more similarly to "the Caucasian race." On an overcoming interpretation, the use of European standards as universal norms for what cultivation entails creates a hierarchy in which others rank lower so long as they preserve any lingering markers of their origins.

An ownership interpretation allows ethnic and racial determinations to be taken up into our developed sense of ourselves, as meaningful aspects of our identity. However, whether we have deliberately taken them up is not necessarily visible to others. Given that Hegel's conception of cultivation is entwined with a hierarchical distancing from nature, appropriating racialized traits can still cause someone to appear undeveloped, insofar as those traits are associated with nature. The ownership interpretation does not free us from worries about hierarchy, as long as closeness to nature is read as less free, and non-Europeans are read as closer to nature.

Gender[23] can likewise lead to hierarchy. There has been extensive discussion of gender in Hegel's thought, primarily based on the *Phenomenology of Spirit* and the *Philosophy of Right*.[24] The "Anthropology" contains a one-paragraph discussion of the sexual relationship that invokes a distinction between a sex focused primarily on sentiment and love and the other focused on "universal purposes" (PM §397); in a *Zusatz*, Hegel contrasts "a subjectivity remaining in immediate unity with its substance and a subjectivity entering into opposition to this substance" (PM §398Z, 64). The corresponding section of the 1827/8 lectures provides more detail, emphasizing women's lack of development. There, Hegel notes that: "In order to make the universal one's end, to will the universal, the rupture [of universal and particular] is necessary, as is deep self-absorption and the activity of labor. It is a matter of bringing forth the unity of universal and particular. – Woman remains in this non-disrupted unity of the heart" (LPS 101).

Echoing his argument concerning race, Mowad argues that "gender, as Hegel understands it, is an original limitation in the individual human, whose presence is ineradicable, and whose influence is powerful" (Mowad 2019: 109). He argues that when the "Anthropology" is read alongside the

[23] The contemporary distinction between sex and gender does not have much traction for Hegel, as the social and ethical conception of women as a gender is entirely founded on their natural determinacy as a sex (PR §165, LPS 102). I will use both terms depending on context. For a helpful discussion of sexual difference in Hegel, refer to Stone (2018a). Similarly, while we now acknowledge more than two genders, in order to discuss Hegel's account I will follow his usage.
[24] For example, the essays in Mills (1996) and Hutchings and Pulkinnen (2010).

Phenomenology, a theory of gender emerges in which masculinity is marked as one-sided, and showing that the "ever-present danger in gender identity is that the feminine is devalued, ignored, and taken for granted" (Mowad 2019: 118). Mowad notes that Hegel criticizes the masculine perspective in the *Phenomenology*, where "abstract masculinity brings about madness" (Mowad 2019: 118).

This is a rich and provocative reading of gender in Hegel, inviting both sides to surpass their original limitation. This might be read into an "overcoming" interpretation. However, this overcoming is intended only for men. The one-sidedness of masculinity is the means by which men progress, whereas women are consistently described in terms of a lack of development. As Hegel says:

> In her development into objective existence, woman remains in the form of subjectivity. In her being woman exhibits a development, but this occurs in a beautiful inner peace, concord, and stability. The woman is not subject to the one-sided extremes that man is. Through feeling she senses what is fitting and proper. (LPS 102 n. 79)

While Hegel's description of women here may sound positive, within the framework of the "Anthropology" it describes a limitation to her possibility for development. For Hegel, the development of our minds requires precisely "the negative, contradiction, rupture" (PM §382Z, 16) which is denied of women.

Meanwhile, the anthropology section of the 1827/8 lectures states, in its description of sexual difference: "The matters of the understanding are the domain of men, who thus experience alienation, whereas women enjoy plant-like unity and harmony" (LPS 102, n. 79).[25] This positions women closest to the feeling soul, rather than the achievement of the actual soul. There is a similar passage in the ages of life section of the "Anthropology": "The life of the unborn child resembles the life of a plant ... When the child is brought into the world out of this vegetative state in which it resides in the womb, it passes into the animal mode of life" (PM §396Z, 56). Comparison of the two passages suggests that a plantlike existence is an undeveloped one, but note that unlike that of the child in the womb, women's plantlike status is not described as a phase, but as their whole existence.

---

[25] Compare this with the notorious *Zusatz* in the *Philosophy of Right*, which states that "the difference between man and woman is the difference between animal and plant; the animal is closer in character to man, the plant to woman, for the latter is a more peaceful [process of] unfolding whose principle is the more indeterminate unity of feeling [*Empfindung*]" (PR §166Z, 207).

Women are situated closer to nature than men, and thus are described as more susceptible to natural disturbances and animal magnetism (PM §406Z, 109) – a feature earlier ascribed to animals (PM §405Z, 91). They are more likely to be "crazy" when living in small towns and "comfortable in this parochialism of theirs" (PM §408Z, 124). Pregnancy and "the *onset of puberty* in young *women*" are not framed as part of the normal human trajectory, but particularized and named as illnesses (PM §406Z, 99).

On an overcoming interpretation, women are thus clearly limited. Even when learned, they do not experience the kind of rupture and opposition required for full liberation from nature. An ownership interpretation is more likely to encourage both genders to gain a reflective perspective on their gender identity, though it remains problematic as long as women's activity in the home is still perceived as closer to nature, and nature is associated with unfreedom. A fuller exploration of an ownership account of gender in Hegel might require rethinking that activity, and acknowledging that care work done within the family does not, in fact, come immediately but with practice, skill, and habituation.[26]

Less has been written on disability in Hegel's thought than on gender or race.[27] Contemporary disability theory and activism note that non-disabled people often assume disability is a limitation to be suffered, fixed, or cured, rather than a bodily difference which can be acknowledged and incorporated into one's identity.[28] The distinction between an overcoming interpretation and an ownership interpretation is thus especially salient here.

Hegel's discussion of human development centers a non-disabled body. Hegel's descriptions of the cultivated body suggest normative expectations for the way that this body will present itself; consider Hegel's comment that "man's *absolute* gesture is his *upright position*; only *man* shows himself capable of this, whereas even the orang-outang can stand upright only with a stick" (PM §411Z, 138). In the ages of life, he associates the development of an upright gait and the skill of walking with a "freer relationship to the external world" (PM §396Z, 57), and does not consider the movements possible for other kinds of bodies. As mentioned above, however, disabled

---

[26] For a discussion of the connection between feminist ethics of care and Hegel's philosophy, which argues that care can be broadened out beyond its gendered associations, refer to Molas (2019). If care is conceived of in this context, it becomes easier to perceive it as something that must be practiced and cultivated.

[27] For more general discussions of disability in Hegel, refer to Dryden (2013) and Wendte (2012).

[28] For a recent exploration of this theme, which is common across Disability Studies, refer to Clare (2017).

people can develop their own forms of embodied habits and dexterity.[29] Focusing on overcoming the determinations of nature will obscure these possibilities, failing to acknowledge the important ways in which disabled people respond and adapt to their environments.

An ownership interpretation opens up possibilities for understanding the embodied particularity of disability as part of our agency. Hegel notes that "When a person is blind he knows that he cannot see, but he has no consciousness of defect. In this diseased condition the human being is in a rational dream – he is still outwardly directed, but in such a way that an obstruction has arisen" (LPS 129). He assumes here that blindness must be construed as a defect or disease which necessarily limits someone's relation to the world, rather than something which can present a valuable perspective on the world in its own right.[30] This stands in contrast with his observation that "Blind people are particularly attentive to the symbolism of the human voice" (PM §401Z, 78). Expanding on this might have opened an opportunity for Hegel to consider blindness as amongst the natural determinations which can be appropriated by us.

While an ownership interpretation seems to offer up useful possibilities for thinking through disability in Hegel, it will not necessarily address his discussion of *Blödsinnigkeit*. This is generally translated as "imbecility," but also sometimes as "idiocy" (PM §408Z, 123, LPS 145).[31] Berthold-Bond summarizes Hegel's description of it as "a more or less complete separation from reality and depletion of the capacities of rationality and volition" (Berthold-Bond 1995: 20). Hegel dismisses this condition entirely: "It is the merely vegetative existence without interest. This condition is wretched and incurable" (LPS 145). Commentators describe it as "analogous to modern diagnostic classifications of organic brain syndromes" (Berthold-Bond 1995: 20) and "incurable because it stems from physiological causes" (Mowad 2019: 276 n. 41).[32]

In other words, Hegel assumes that since this condition is "organic" or "physiological" it is incurable. The condition is so closely associated with

---

[29] In addition to the example of Alice Sheppard, above, we can also consider the habits and bodily dexterity involved in navigating chronic illness (Dryden 2016: 13–17).

[30] For example, in the work of Rod Michalko, such as Michalko (1999). Tobin Siebers argues for a theory of complex embodiment that understands disability as "a body of knowledge" (Siebers 2019: 47).

[31] It corresponds to Pinel's "idiotisme," and Hegel refers to Pinel both in the main text (PM §408R) and in his lectures (PM §408Z, 123, LPS 145).

[32] Both Berthold-Bond and Mowad refer to *Blödsinnigkeit* as equivalent to "mental retardation." This is no longer the appropriate term, but rather either "intellectual disability" or "intellectual developmental disorder."

nature that no emergence seems possible.[33] Insofar as it seems to prevent any human development, it is hard to conceive of how it can be overcome or owned. Given Hegel's insistence on the importance of human community, however, it seems a failure of imagination to discard people. Recently a number of philosophers have explored ways to integrate people with intellectual and developmental disabilities into our moral communities.[34] Carlson (2009) challenges the frequent philosophical assumption that intellectual disability is static and homogeneous, as well as its association with animality. Both of these seem to underlie Hegel's assessment. It would be worthwhile to explore whether, learning from this recent work, there may be more nuanced possibilities for intellectual disability within the scope of Hegelian thought, in which proximity to nature is not a disqualification from community, and in which no one's existence is "without interest."

In general, examining the treatment of race, gender, and disability within the "Anthropology" shows that an interpretation which focuses on overcoming natural limitations will largely tend to preserve hierarchy. An interpretation that focuses on ownership has some advantages, but also encounters the problem of the link between nature and unfreedom.[35] Within Hegel's philosophy, qualities that distinguish people from the presumed European, male, non-disabled norm tend to be associated with nature and a lack of cultivation. Coming to claim them as one's own, then, risks reinforcing this association, unless we try to widen Hegel's conception of the kinds of embodiment compatible with the development of spirit.

7.6   The Anthropology Today

Regardless of our focus on overcoming or ownership, the underlying framework of a hierarchy of development away from nature determines what Hegel recognizes as free embodiment. Bringing the strains of overcoming and ownership back together draws our attention to this hierarchy.

Alison Stone notes the same underlying hierarchy in the *Philosophy of History* and encourages us to "think carefully and critically about how far to take these inherited ideas forward and how we might do so differently"

---

[33] This is somewhat ironic, since the main example Hegel invokes is cretinism (PM §408Z/122, LPS 145), which we now understand to be caused by an iodine deficiency, and thus in fact curable.

[34] For example, in Carlson and Kittay (2010), Kittay (1999), and Wong (2002).

[35] There are also limitations of the language of ownership, where it comes to our relationship to our bodies, if our primary model is property. With respect to Hegel's discussion of the body in the *Philosophy of Right*, Ciavatta discusses models of ownership that need not be modeled on property rights (Ciavatta 2005: 17–18). For a more general discussion of the body as property in European philosophy, refer also to McWhorter (1999: 141–4).

(Stone 2020: 19). As Stone writes, "through his understanding of freedom as involving spirit extricating itself from nature, that account has sustained links with his Eurocentrism and so his pro-colonialism" (Stone 2020: 19). A way to theorize the development of freedom for all the world's peoples might be "by saying that they have several conceptions of freedom where freedom can, but does not have to, include self-liberation from nature" (Stone 2020: 19).

This suggestion can be applied to the "Anthropology." It is useful to remember that the "Anthropology," while coming at the beginning of the *Philosophy of Spirit*, continually assumes later developments. Hegel notes that "we must not regard the distinction between subjective and objective mind as a rigid distinction" (PM §387, 26). Andreja Novakovic writes, "As I read this reminder, Hegel is noting that human beings become conscious subjects, not in the midst of brute nature, but in a social world that allows them to make the most of what nature has given them" (Novakovic 2017: 409). If we pursue a conception of freedom that allows different kinds of relation to nature, this can be reflected in our social world. If we expand our social imaginary around what a "cultivated" body might do, how it might behave, and what relation to nature it might have, we can open up possibilities for a fuller account of the embodiments that free expressions of spirit can include.

A birds-eye view of the "Anthropology" might take it to be a linear path by which the soul gradually transforms the body, leading from the sleep of spirit in the *Philosophy of Nature* to its self-conscious self-awareness in the "Phenomenology" section of the *Philosophy of Spirit*. The details of this trajectory, however, tell a more complicated story which can be prone to reversals. The narrative of cultivating the body toward minimal particularity and a universalized vision of maturity is complicated by the consideration of race, disability, gender, and the ages of life. Given Hegel's insistence on the importance of the concrete rather than the merely abstract, this should not come as a surprise. However, it is important for us, in our interpretation of the text, to make sure that we are doing justice to this complexity. This allows us to read the "Anthropology" not as leaving nature behind, but as giving us a framework for understanding how we bring nature with us as we develop in freedom.

CHAPTER 8

Hegel's Critique of Materialism

Joshua I. Wretzel

There are more things in heaven and earth, Horatio,
Than are dreamt of in your philosophy.

Shakespeare, *Hamlet* (1.5.167–8)

8.1 Introduction

Under the entry on Hegel in his *A History of Western Philosophy*, Bertrand Russell writes

> From his early interest in mysticism [Hegel] retained a belief in the unreality of separateness: the world, in his view, was not a collection of hard units, whether atoms or souls, each completely self-subsistent. The apparent self-subsistence of finite things appeared to him to be an illusion; nothing, he held, is ultimately and completely real except the whole. But he differed from Parmenides and Spinoza in conceiving the whole, not as simple substance, but as a complex system, of the sort that we should call an organism. The apparently separate things of which the world seems to be composed are not simply an illusion; each has a greater or lesser degree of reality, and its reality consists in an aspect of the whole, which is what it is seen to be when viewed truly. (Russell 1945: 701–2)[1]

With this view in mind, Russell joined Moore at the vanguard of a century-long movement, in Western philosophy, against idealist metaphysics. Central to that movement was the notion that idealists relegated material reality to a subordinate metaphysical status, that the realm of matter was somehow "less real" than the immaterial realm of thought. Until recently, Hegelians had combatted such claims by arguing that Hegel was less interested in metaphysics and more interested in epistemology: Hegel's claims about mindedness had less to do with the metaphysical status of

---

[1] For an alternative interpretation of this passage, see Stern (2009).

148

objects and more to do with their being susceptible of cognition by intellects like ours.[2] But in the past few years, a number of major works in Hegel scholarship have contributed to the notion that Hegel actually held fairly robust metaphysical commitments.[3]

These works, insightful and impactful as they have been, have yet to address the metaphysics of matter in Hegel. They leave unanswered questions about how to respond to the charge that Hegel is an immaterialist – and whatever Russell gets wrong about Hegel, he is right about that – and whether his immaterialism confirms all the worst about his metaphysics. My aim in this chapter is to address these worries. I clarify the terms of Hegel's argument in order to show that his immaterialist metaphysics provides a viable alternative to those who may be dissatisfied with a "disenchanted" materialist outlook. I incorporate a three-pronged approach in order to do so. First, I introduce and defend what I call a "minimalist critique of materialism." I show that what Hegel criticizes in materialism is not the *reality* of matter, but only its *ultimate* reality. That is, Hegel thinks that there are elements of reality that are explicable in materialist terms, but that the greatest desideratum of metaphysics – the so-called "absolute" – is not. As we shall see, Hegel's way of putting this is quite Kantian: he undertakes, in several places, an examination of the scope and bounds of the materialist outlook. He shows that certain phenomena – for instance, those in chemistry – fit quite nicely within the materialist framework, while the phenomena of organic nature, say, fall outside of it. His ultimate claim about materialism is thus not that matter is unreal, but that it only constitutes an aspect of reality as a whole.

We must thus accept, I argue, that Hegel thinks there are immaterial phenomena. In order to show how Hegel addresses such matters, I introduce and defend, as my second "prong," what I call a "minimalist conception of immateriality" in Hegel. I argue that Hegel operates with a very specific notion of matter: it refers, as we shall see, to mutually independent entities that are formed by means of external activities upon them. So when Hegel makes mention of the *immaterial*, he is only referring to entities that *are not material*, i.e., that are not mutually interrelated and/or are formed by means of their internal activity upon themselves.

But once we admit a conception of immateriality into our metaphysics, Hegel thinks this changes the way we look at the way things are generally. For Hegel thought that, once we grasped the nature of the immaterial, we

---

[2] See Findlay (1962), Hartmann (1972), Pinkard (1996), and Pippin (1989).
[3] See, e.g., Bowman (2013), Kreines (2015), and Yeomans (2012).

would start to see immaterial processes at work in all things. Hegel thus starts to speak in rather extravagant terms about how all things strive toward some ultimate immateriality. This represents the third element of Hegel's critique of materialism, what I shall call the "transformational conception of immateriality." This, I recognize, is a feature of Hegel's thought that is more difficult to take on. But as I shall argue, Hegel's extravagances are just his uniquely bold way of incorporating an expansive, "re-enchanted" conception of nature, one that allows material reality to exist alongside immaterial entities as Hegel conceives them.

This chapter shall proceed as follows. After a brief overview of Hegel's take on materialism in Section 8.2, I examine Hegel's minimalist critique of materialism in Sections 8.3–8.5. Specifically, I shall address the three central sites of Hegel's critique of materialism in the *Encyclopedia Logic*: they occur in his treatments of empiricism (Section 8.3), pure quantity (Section 8.4), and the "thing" (Section 8.5). I show how Hegel puts his critique in Kantian terms: he speaks, at times explicitly, of the "right" to employ materialist terminology when we do, as if he were answering a question *quid juris* about materialism.

I then turn, in Sections 8.6 and 8.7, to Hegel's minimalist and transformational conceptions of immateriality. Analyzing a key passage, §389 of the *Encyclopedia Philosophy of Mind*, I show how Hegel unfolds a conception of the *soul* as a facet of immaterial reality. As we shall see, Hegel's conception of the soul has very little to do with human immortality, and much more to do with unconscious processes of the developing mind. Hegel describes these processes in immaterialist terms, again, according to our minimalist conception: it is a self-developmental entity that contains its form within itself. Bringing the self-determining structure of the soul into focus, however, allows us to see processes of self-determination alive within all of nature: it awakens us to the aesthetic, purposive unity of nature at work in Kant and the post-Kantian tradition. This is, again, the "transformational conception of immateriality" we spoke of above.

Taken together, then, the minimalist critique of materialism, the minimalist conception of immateriality, and the transformational conception of immateriality all tend toward Hegel's demonstration of a nature alive with beauty and purpose, a philosophical version of the kind of nature spoken of in the aesthetics of Kant and other post-Kantians.

8.2 Materialism According to Hegel

For Hegel, materialism characterizes the position that "matter as such counts as the truly objective," or that matter constitutes the ultimate reality of all things (Hegel 2010a: §38Z, 81/8:111[4]). Matter itself he characterizes according to three features.

1. *Determination by form.* In Hegel's view of materialism, objects are what they are by means of a synthesis of form and matter. Specifically, forms *shape* matter, give it its determinacy. According to this view, everything is "formed matter."

2. For Hegel, materialists characterize these *forms as "external" to matter*: the features of an object that give it its determinacy do not emanate from any of its intrinsic features, but must come from without. So, for instance, one needs the form of *threeness* to be added to a surface from without in order to make it into a triangle. The threeness is not "contained" within the surface.[5]

3. Hegel's materialists also believe in the *mutual indifference* of matters (a) *to one another*, (b) *of matter to form*, and (c) *of parts to the whole* of the material object. This is to say that the interaction of different determinate objects does not alter the objects themselves: hydrogen remains hydrogen whether or not it is, say, in a water molecule. Similarly, the determination of matter by form does not fundamentally alter either the form or the matter: the surface remains essentially a surface, whether or not it is delimited by threeness. And threeness remains essentially threeness, whether it is delimiting a surface or not.

Hegel will ultimately disagree with all three of these central tenets of materialism. But it bears emphasizing that this is a disagreement in qualified form: there is a certain context, certain circumstances of application, in which it makes perfect sense to think of things in accordance with these tenets. Hegel's point, as we shall see, is that we run into trouble when we try to universalize them or mistake them for determinations of the absolute.

8.3 Materialism, Empiricism, and Unfreedom

In the *Vorbegriff* to the *Logic*, Hegel contends that materialism characterizes the underlying, metaphysical presupposition of all empiricist philosophy. He also conjoins materialism with *unfreedom*, insofar as he thinks any

---

[4] All references to the German cite volume and page number from Hegel (1970–1).

[5] In this sense, there is an analogy between the external form of determination in Hegel and analyticity in Kant: try though I might, I will never find the concept of "threeness" within the concept of "surface."

materialistic metaphysics is incompatible with a metaphysics of freedom. Concerning the former, here is a characteristic passage:

> The fundamental delusion in scientific empiricism is always that it uses the metaphysical categories of matter, force (not to mention those of the one, the many, universality, and infinity, etc.), and proceeds to make *inferences* guided by such categories, all the while presupposing and applying the forms of syllogistic inference, ignorant that in so doing it itself contains and pursues metaphysics and that it uses those categories and their relationships in a completely uncritical and unconscious fashion. (Hegel 2010a: §38 Anm., 79/8:108–9)

Empiricism, he claims, fails to address the issues with the metaphysical categories that it nevertheless employs. As a philosophical approach, empiricism has not yet attained the level of a science because it has not subjected these metaphysical claims to rigorous critique, has not yet examined the scope and bounds of their applicability. So there is a *quid juris* question about materialism that empiricism needs to answer and yet has not.

Therefore, by relying on an unjustified materialism, empiricism smuggles in a problematic approach to its study of experience. This is due to a principal feature of Hegel's empiricist's conception of matter, that wholes can be divided into any number of primordially unrelated or mutually independent parts (feature 3(c) of materialism, in the list above). This empiricist formulates his theory of experience by applying this already unjustified presupposition about objectivity to a theory of perception. On this view, the objects of perceptual experience are wholes constituted of pre-perceptual bits. Our various perceptual apparatuses then synthesize, somehow, those bits into the whole object. The thought is that one may get at those pre-perceptual bits by analyzing the whole as product into its pre-perceptual, antecedent parts. Hegel says:

> In order to have experiences, empiricism principally utilizes the form of *analysis*. In perception, one possesses something concrete in multiple ways whose determinations one is supposed to take apart like peeling away the layers of an onion. This process of splitting them up is therefore intended to dissolve the determinations that have grown together … Analysis is, however, the progression from the immediacy of perception to thought, insofar as the determinations, which the object analyzed contains amalgamated within itself, receive the form of universality by being separated. Because empiricism analyzes objects, it is in error if it believes that it leaves them as they are, since it in fact transforms the concrete into something abstract. (Hegel 2010a: §38Z, 80/8:109)

For the empiricist, there is some correspondence between the metaphysical view that the objects of a specifically *material* reality are made up of concatenated parts and the epistemological view that perceptual wholes are made up of concatenated, pre-perceptual bits. Of course, the parts concatenated in each case are different – chemical elements, say, versus various perceptual qualities – but the underlying assumption remains the same both on the objective side and on the subjective side: that the whole object is somehow less "real" than the constituent parts, which come to light only by means of analysis.

Hegel also frequently associates materialism with a particular kind of "unfreedom." Thus he writes, just below the claim about analysis, that

> ... the abstraction called matter is supposed to be the foundation of everything sensory, i.e., the sensory as such, the absolute individuation in itself, and thus what are outside one another. Now, insofar as this sensory component is and remains a given for empiricism, *it is a doctrine of unfreedom* [my emphasis], for freedom consists precisely in having no absolutely other over against me, but depending instead only on a content that I am myself. (Hegel 2010a: §38Z, 81/8:111)

In this passage, we see Hegel defending, in part, the views on epistemic agency that Pippin, McDowell, and others have attributed to him. On this view, one's epistemic holdings are the result of one's own epistemic activity, i.e. the result of a thorough, rational investigation of all candidate claims to know. But empiricists, first, think claims to know depend solely on the direct delivery of sensory contents, and second, think those contents are fundamentally irrational; thus, according to empiricism, one finds oneself holding claims that one both has not and cannot affirm for oneself. The subject, in this case, thus has no agency over its epistemic holdings, it is just a matter of rote cause and effect.

8.4 Materialism and Quantity

Hegel's critique of materialism also overlaps with his various criticisms of the natural sciences. There, the claim will be that the natural sciences all depend upon underlying metaphysical claims of one sort or another, and that the former are ultimately limited by the latter. In Kantian fashion, Hegel's critique involves an examination of where those metaphysical limitations lie. Hegel begins such investigations by introducing the relevant metaphysical framework and then seeking to discover whether that framework is absolute, or can explain matters of ultimate reality.[6]

---

[6] I am indebted to Kreines's work, here as elsewhere. Where Hegel differs from Kant is in what follows when we find the explanatory framework wanting. Kant's critique of the faculty of reason culminates

We find Hegel undertaking a relevant form of this critique in his discussion of Pure Quantity (Hegel 2010a: §§99–100). There, Hegel investigates the possibility that "the absolute is pure quantity," or that the way things are ultimately exhibits a quantitative structure. He holds that "the standpoint [of pure quantity] ultimately coincides with determining the absolute as *matter* in which the form is indeed on hand, but as an indifferent determination." Again, for Hegel, discussions of "matter" always involve the external determination of matter by form. In this instance, the claim is that all form is a quantitative determination or magnitude shaping matter from without.

The paradigmatic expression of quantitative classification is found, of course, in mathematics. According to the broad terms in which Hegel couches mathematical expression, it treats these determining forms as so-called "quantitative magnitudes": it categorizes, according to some number, the amount of some property present within a form, e.g., mass according to kilograms, velocity according to kilometers per second. It then employs these quantitative measurements in equations or formulas which allow the construction of certain laws of relation between the various magnitudes, as, e.g., the law of falling bodies posits a relation between mass and velocity. Hegel does not wish to deny that there is a certain "correctness" that is "immediately obvious to representational consciousness" (Hegel 2010a: §99Z, 158/8:210). But terms like "correctness," "immediacy," and "representational consciousness" all possess a negative connotation in Hegelian language and refer to various modes of *limitation* or distance from the absolute. Again, the limitation typically denotes a range of applicability of some category, mode of expression, or explanatory framework, where one may not employ these outside of that realm without also expressing something untrue.

In this instance, perhaps the most apt indication of Hegel's thoughts on mathematics is his use of the word "correct." Generally, for Hegel, "correctness" refers to some merely conditioned concordance between propositions and states of affairs. Here, Hegel is speaking of the "correctness" of specifically mathematical formulas: that he assigns them mere "correctness" means that they apply only in certain circumstances. Just as Kant thinks that the categories of quantity (unity, plurality,

in a kind of "humility" (see Ameriks (2000)), a need to remain within the boundaries of that framework. Hegel, by contrast, sees a need to transcend those boundaries, to leave them behind. If this cannot be done, typically this is demonstrated by an examination of a transitional moment, where the explanatory framework reaches the limits of its explanatory efficacy and what happens when one tries to transcend that limitation.

totality) only obtain within the realm of appearance, so does Hegel hold that quantitative claims obtain only for so-called "representational consciousness." He is thus expressing agreement with Kant about the fact that quantitative claims are not properly applicable to matters concerning the highest aims of metaphysics, and thus agreement that it is problematic to employ quantitative claims without knowledge of the proper limits of their applicability. This is why Hegel says that, "when quantity is taken up directly from representation without being mediated by thinking, it easily happens that quantity is overestimated with respect to its scope and even raised to an absolute category" (Hegel 2010a: §99Z, 158/8:210).

However, Kant and Hegel disagree about the implications of this limitation. For one, Kant thinks this implies something about the limitations of intellects like ours, while Hegel sees this merely as a limitation of an explanatory framework, the fact that matters of ultimate reality cannot be known *in this way*. For another, Hegel's worry is that the Kantian kind of limitation, to say that things can be known only insofar as they conform to a quantitative determination, and are unknowable otherwise, leads to an unacceptable subjectivism about matters of ultimate reality. He writes:

> Our knowing would indeed be in bad shape, if, renouncing exact knowledge, we generally had to be satisfied merely with a vague representation of such objects as freedom, law, the ethical life, even God himself, merely because they cannot be measured and calculated or expressed in a mathematical formula; and if, when it comes to the more specific or particular details of those matters, it would be left to each individual's whim to make of it what they want. (Hegel 2010a: §99Z, 158/8:210)

But despite the overlap with Kant and the reference to the subjectivism of this view, Hegel ultimately identifies this view on the quantitative determination of reality with materialism, specifically with the *philosophes* of the French Enlightenment:

> Looked at more closely, the exclusively mathematical standpoint mentioned here (for which *quantity*, this specific stage of the logical idea, becomes identical with the idea itself) is none other than *materialism*. Indeed, this is fully confirmed in the history of scientific consciousness, notably in France since the middle of the last century. The abstractness of matter is precisely this: that the form is indeed on hand in it, but merely as an indifferent and external determination. (Hegel 2010a: §99Z, 158/8:211)

This is feature 2 of materialism that we mentioned, in the list above. For the materialist, form represents an external determination of matter: form shapes matter from without. Hegel's claim is that, where it is the case that forms stand in relation to matter in this way, quantitative materialism is a perfectly adequate framework. This is, again, what Hegel means by "correct": quantitative materialism is explanatorily applicable within these bounds. But when we turn to matters of ultimate reality, materialism loses its efficacy. That is not because these matters are unknowable – i.e., because there is no explanatory system that is adequate to them – nor is it because he thinks such matters do not exist. Rather, it is because, for Hegel, matters of ultimate reality cannot be couched in materialist terms. To see what Hegel means, let us consider the case of freedom, one of the main desiderata of the metaphysics of his time. According to Hegel, an entity counts as free only insofar as it is self-determining, i.e., becomes what it is by means of its own activity. This means that its form must, in a sense, be *internal* to it: the free entity must be able to *shape itself* by means of itself. But according to materialism, all formation is the activity of an external form impinging upon matter. It thus rules out, a priori, any possibility of admitting the reality of freedom.

Still, Hegel does not believe that quantitative modes of explanation are without any explanatory import at all: there are bounds within which this form of explanation is perfectly legitimate. Again, this is just what Hegel means when he speaks of the "correctness" of pure quantity. And he admits that quantity plays *some* role even in the determination of the absolute: he refers, as an example, to the explanation of the divine as a *trinity*. But he also hastens to add that "it is immediately obvious that when we contemplate God as a trinity the number *three* has a much more subordinate significance than if we were to contemplate the three dimensions of space, not to mention the three sides of a triangle" (Hegel 2010a: §99Z, 158–9/8:211–12). So the issue with quantity concerns the context of its application: the phenomena under consideration and what it is we wish to say about them.

8.5 Materialism and Quality

Hegel's next engagement with materialism occurs in his discussion of "the thing" (Hegel 2010a: §§125–30). He defines the thing as an "identity" or a singular entity containing many constitutive properties.[7] He claims that, while other classifications of what is *identify* the singular entity with its properties, "the thing" has an independent existence over and above them, so that

---

[7] Cf. in the *Phenomenology of Spirit*: "Perception, or *the thing* and deception" (Hegel 2018a).

> ... the thing, while also existing concretely only insofar as it has properties, is nevertheless not bound to this or that determinate property and thus can even lose that very property without ceasing for that reason to be what it is. (Hegel 2010a: §125Z, 193/8:256)

And Hegel adds that

> ... the properties are just as much identical with themselves, *self-standing*, and freed from their being bound to the thing. However, because they are the thing's determinacies, *different from one another* as reflected-in-themselves, they are not themselves things which are concrete, but instead concrete existences, reflected in themselves as abstract determinacies, *sorts of matter* [*Materien*]. (Hegel 2010a: §126, 193–4/8:257)

In other words, the relationship that obtains, both between the thing and its properties, and of the various properties with one another, is that of *mutual indifference*, feature 3(c) of materiality we spoke of, in the list above. In this case, the thing and its various constituent properties gain their determinacy, are what they are, by virtue of their not-being other things or properties.

Conceiving of the underlying properties in terms of matters allows a certain dependence relation between a thing and its constituent properties to come into focus. In this case, the thing becomes identified not with any one of its matters, but with the concatenation of them. One finds the paradigm case of such a "thing" in chemical compounds: water is what it is not merely because it contains hydrogen or merely because it contains oxygen, but because it contains the concatenation of them. Hegel thus says that this form of materialism finds its proper expression in sciences like chemistry and geology:

> This analysis into self-standing stuff has its proper place only in inorganic nature and it is the chemist's right to analyze cooking salts or gypsum, for example, into the stuff they consist of and then to say that the former consists of hydrochloric acid and sodium bicarbonate and the latter of sulfuric acid and calcium. Similarly, it is with right that the geologist may regard granite to be composed of quartz, feldspar, and mica. (Hegel 2010a: §126Z, 194/8:257–8)

The key word, here, is "right" or "*Recht*." It is not that the chemist or geologist *is* right to conduct their analyses in the fashion they do, but rather that they *possess* the right to do so. Hegel is answering a question *quid juris* about the term "matter": he is showing *with what right* one might apply the term "matter" to an explanation of what is. And, according to Hegel's minimalist critique, it is appropriate when applied to chemicals, rock formations, or similar elements of inorganic nature. But one *lacks* the right to apply this term more generally, as if *all things* were explicable by means of a reduction to material components: this would be to transcend the limits of the explanatory range of the term. Thus, to take a favorite example of Hegel's, the material form of explanation transcends its range of applicability if it is applied to an explanation of *organic* nature:

> Even within nature, in the case of organic life, this category proves to be insufficient. One says, indeed, that this animal consists of bones, muscles, nerves, and so forth, but it is immediately apparent that the context here is different from the piece of granite consisting of the aforementioned sorts of matter. The sorts of matter behave in a manner utterly indifferent to their unification and can just as well subsist without the latter. By contrast, the diverse parts of the organic body subsist only in their unification and, separate from one another, they cease to exist concretely as such. (Hegel 2010a: §126Z, 194/8:258)

As we said above, the parts of a compound are *indifferent* to the whole: hydrogen, sulfur, and oxygen remain what they are, even outside their relationship to sulfuric acid. There is thus a certain *contingency* to their formation: they don't need to belong to sulfuric acid in order to be what they are. And while Hegel admits that one may certainly find the same contingency in organic matter, one fails to achieve the same kind of explanatory sufficiency that one attains in chemical nature. Treating, say, a lion as matter would not help to explain what a lion is or how it differs from other species of animal. Reducing the lion to "bones, muscles, nerves, and so forth" does not get at the "lion-ness" of the lion; these constituents are only fully what they are in relation to the whole (here, the lion). In this case, then, the parts bear a *necessary* relation to the whole: the nerves can only be nerves – i.e., do what nerves do – when they are inside a living organism. Thus one lacks the right to explain organic entities in this way because the parts lack the contingent relationship to the whole present in other parts of nature. Organic entities are, therefore, not fully material according to Hegel's understanding of the term.

8.6 Materialism and Mind

Hegel addresses materialist accounts of mind in §389 of the *Encyclopedia*, at the beginning of the "Anthropology" section of the *Philosophy of Mind*. To be sure, he distinguishes mind from soul, which Hegel understands as something like an animating force alive within all organic nature. Here, he's speaking particularly of the *human* soul, which he considers to be the basis from which *Geist* springs, as an acorn to an oak. But even at this embryonic stage of the mind's development, what is distinctive about it, for Hegel, is its *immateriality*. He writes: "the soul is not only immaterial for itself. It is the universal immateriality of nature, its simple ideal life" (Hegel 2007c: §389, 29/10:43). There is some initial unclarity at work, here, in the relationship between immateriality and ideality. It is at least understandable how one might construe this in terms of a commitment to *esse est percipi* idealism. To make matters worse, he follows up with the assertion that

> Soul is the *substance*, the absolute foundation, of all the particularizing and individualizing of mind, so that it is in the soul that *mind* finds all the stuff of its determination, and the soul remains the pervading, identical ideality of this determination. (Hegel 2007c)

It is, of course, easy to be overwhelmed by the metaphysical heft of passages like this, and it is difficult to see how one might navigate the equation between soul, substance, and immateriality without committing Hegel either to a substance dualism or to a problematic idealism. For their part, non-metaphysical Hegelians have tended to interpret passages like these in largely epistemological terms, and so to think that, by calling the soul "substance," he is referring to it as the object of investigation for some observing subject. But especially here in §389, Hegel spends too much time speaking in explicitly metaphysical terms for an epistemological interpretation to do full justice to it. Hegel is concerned not only with the immateriality of the soul, as in the above passage, but also with attempts materialists make to treat the mind as a material entity, not to mention concerns with the formulation and materialist solution to the mind–body problem. There is, in other words, too much metaphysics in this passage for one to treat it with a simply epistemological reading.

But again, this does not mean that we need to treat Hegel as an *esse est percipi* idealist, either: just because Hegel has a metaphysics, it doesn't mean he has *that* kind of metaphysics. Rather, we would do well to keep in mind the conception of materiality at work in Hegel: matter consists of mutually independent entities that are formed by means of external activities impinging upon them. When Hegel calls the mind "immaterial," he is only saying that it cannot be described in those terms. Instead, mind must be the (determinate) negation of those things: it consists of mutually interrelated parts and determines itself by means of its own activity. This is what I called, at the outset, the minimalist conception of immateriality. Thus, when Hegel calls the soul "the substance . . . of mind," he means that mind is not to be conceived of as a material formed by the impingement of external forces upon it, but as an organic, embryonic, self-developing structure that contains its form within it. Indeed, in the soul, the distinction between matter and form breaks down completely, so that Hegel will say "it is in the soul that mind finds all the stuff" – i.e., neither form nor matter – "of its determination."

On the other hand, even if we accept the minimalist conception of immateriality, it is hard to see how that allows Hegel to *escape* the problem of substance dualism. And of course, Hegel was no dualist. In fact, when Hegel turns his attention to materialist accounts of mind, it is in order to praise them for their "enthusiastic endeavor" to overcome substance dualism. It is just that, as he sees it, the monism of materialism moves in the wrong direction. For, as he says,

> ... there is nothing more unsatisfactory than the discussions conducted in materialistic writings of the various relationships and combinations by which a result such as thinking is to be produced. Such discussions entirely overlook the fact that, just as the cause is sublated in the effect, and the means in the accomplished ends, so too that from which thinking is supposed to result is conversely sublated in thinking, and that mind as such is not produced by an Other, but raises itself from its being-in-itself to its being-for-itself, from its concept to actuality, and makes that by which mind is supposed to be posited into something posited by mind. (Hegel 2007c: §389Z, 33/10:49)

In order for materialism to account for thinking, it must be capable of showing how something that determines itself arises from out of matter, which is always determined by another. But this is not possible. Thus either we need to rest content with a dissatisfying substance dualism, or we need to reconsider the place of matter in metaphysics. Hegel considers the latter option to be the one worth pursuing. This introduces what we called, at the outset, the "transformational conception of immateriality": once we recognize that thinking must result from immateriality, it shifts the way we think about materiality as well. This is because, again, Hegel thinks there is no way for immateriality to arise from materiality. So we must conceive of what is in terms of its immateriality. Hegel makes several claims in this section to this effect. For instance,

> Since, then, everything material is sublated by the mind that is in itself and at work within nature, and this sublation is consummated in the substance of *soul*, the soul emerges as the ideality of *everything* material, as *all* immateriality, so that everything called matter, however much it simulates independence to representation, is known to have no independence in the face of mind. (Hegel 2007c: S389Z, 32/10:47)

Or, when speaking of the attempt to construct a dualistic opposition between mind and body, that

> ... this way of posing it ... must be recognized as inadmissible; for in truth the immaterial is not related to the material as a particular is to a particular, but as the genuine universal which overarches particularity is related to a particular; the material in its particularizations has no truth, no independence in the face of the material. Consequently ... the separation of the material and the immaterial can be explained only on the basis of the original unity of both. (Hegel 2007c: S389Z, 33/10:48)

These are strong claims that Hegel is making, and they seem to confirm all the worst suppositions about Hegel's idealism. But there are at least two ways to understand them that do not seem so objectionable. For one, these claims may be read as lending credence to the metaphysical/ epistemological claims about the knowability of a merely material nature. What one grasps in thought is not a substance existing *partes extra partes*, but a conceptual whole. This belongs to the class of what have come to be known as "conceptual realist" interpretations of Hegel's thought.

For another, in the *Encyclopedia*, this discussion of the transformational conception of immateriality follows on the heels of the *Philosophy of Nature*, which Hegel describes in terms of another kind of transformational experience. As Martin (unpublished) has recently written, Hegel opens that text by showing how our ordinary attitudes toward nature are underwritten by and presuppose an aesthetic attitude, which views it as a purposive unity. One may well understand the transformational conception of immateriality in these terms: there is simply no way to understand the fit between mind and nature without also fundamentally changing the way we understand nature.

This means that, even in those moments where Hegel seems to think that matter belongs in nature, i.e., when discussing matter in its qualitative or quantitative context, the *mere* adequacy or *mere* correctness of materialism comes from its ultimate failure to grasp how these phenomena are part of larger, purposive activities at work within them. He says:

> The philosophy of nature teaches us how nature sublates its externality by stages, how matter already refutes the independence of the individual, of the many, by *gravity*, and how this refutation begun by gravity, and still more by simple, indivisible *light*, is completed by animal life, by the sentient creature, since this reveals to us the omnipresence of the one soul at every point of its bodiliness, and so the sublatedness of the asunderness of matter. (Hegel 2007c: S389Z, 32/10:47)

According to the minimalist critique of immateriality, again, Hegel does not want to deny the reality of matter or processes explained in materialistic terms. But materialism fails to see these processes as part of a larger process, unfolding in a way that eludes materialistic explanation. In order to grasp such things as self-causation or, as he says here, a whole that precedes and is present in each of the parts, we need to alter our conception of what nature is and what is contained within it.

8.7   The Transformational Conception and the Immaterial Mind

These points about the transformational conception of immateriality are not ones that we might expect to move the materialist skeptic, but they do unite Hegel with the re-enchanted conceptions of nature alive within Kant and the post-Kantian tradition. Kant agreed that materialist explanations of nature are applicable only within the realm of appearance and also thought that this conception of nature could not accommodate the existence of self-causing entities.[8] But Kant thought that immaterialist elements of nature, such as self-causing entities, were completely unknowable by intellects like ours. Thus, *Kant's* minimalist critique of materialism consists of his saying that we have the capacity to grasp materialist elements of nature, but that they are the only elements of nature we have the capacity to grasp. Hegel moves beyond Kant by developing the means to grasp immaterial nature as well.

But there remains a question about what sort of thing an immaterial mind is: how it functions, what it does. Hegel's view presents an intensification of other figures in the classical German tradition: following Fichte, Hegel sees a fundamental connection between the conception of the self one adopts and the conception of the not-self. In this case, there is such a connection between the manifoldness of the self and the manifoldness of the not-self. In its initial, pre-reflective stages, then, there is a manifoldness of the not-self corresponding to the manifoldness of the self. And, to be sure, what separates Hegel from Fichte is the belief that the positing of the self does not *create* the not-self as product: the strongest claim we could make in this direction is to say that the positing of the self places limits on what aspects of the not-self are open to it. Thus, if one posits oneself as manifold, this limits one to a view of the not-self as (merely) manifold. For, as Kant himself says, the unified object is only for a subject that is capable of unifying it, and only a self that is constituted *as* a unity is capable of

---

[8] Kant (2000: §63, 239/1968: 5:366–7 and ff.).

unifying it. Thus when speaking of *sensation* in the *Anthropology*, Hegel says:

> The *subjectivity* of sensation must . . . be sought . . . in the fact that he posits something in his *natural* [my emphasis], immediate, individual subjectivity, not in his free, spiritual, universal subjectivity. This *natural* subjectivity is not yet a self-determining subjectivity following its own law and acting in a necessary manner but a subjectivity determined from outside, tied to *this* space and *this* time, dependent on contingent circumstances. (Hegel 2007c: §400Z, 71/10:100)

The key word in this passage is "natural," which Hegel always associates with varying kinds of *externality*. The externality of nature is most present in its *mechanistic* form and becomes increasingly internalized as it develops. But even in its most sophisticated, "organic" form, nature remains external to itself. Even though the organism consists of an internal, self-developmental process, it remains *unaware* of itself as an organism. And that lacuna in nature is what occasions the transition from *Natur* to *Geist*.[9] Thus, in this part of the text, Hegel is describing a subject still mainly immersed in nature, still mostly unaware of itself. The description of a subject thus tied merely to "*this* space and to *this* time" is a description of a subject with only discrete, independent moments of self-awareness, with those moments standing in no connection to each other: *this* I in *this* spatiotemporal location bears no relation to *this* I in now *this* spatiotemporal location. The subject does not yet see that both of those moments belong to it, that it is the *same* I in both spatiotemporal locations. Since, according to the Kantian notion of apperception, the self cannot unify the object unless it is, *itself*, unified, a subject that remains external to itself can only see the world as similarly disjointed. That is why the standpoint of sensation has the structure it does.

This is an argumentative gambit that appears throughout Hegel's work, but also at three different points in the *Philosophy of Spirit*: the "Anthropology," the "Phenomenology of Spirit," and the "Psychology." This is, itself, indicative of a process of internalization occurring at a *higher* level, a process of increasing self-awareness of the process of internalization: the argument remains the same, but the context in which it appears changes in each case. In the "Anthropology," we read of the human as a biological kind: thus, there is a kind of externality present here in the sense that the object of study – the human organism – remains external to/from the internalizing/synthetic capacities of the one undertaking the investigation. In the "Phenomenology of

---

[9] See Wretzel (2020).

Spirit," we read of the I as an *abstraction*: one grasps the I as *subject*, but only as a theoretical construct: one does not yet see oneself reflected in the object of investigation. That only happens, initially, in the "Psychology." For as Hegel there says, each stage of the process of internalization reflects on the previous stage: thus,

> as consciousness [in the "Phenomenology of Spirit"] has as its object the preceeding stage, the natural soul [i.e., "Anthropology"], so mind [i.e., "Psychology"] has consciousness as its object or rather makes it its object, i.e. whereas consciousness is only in itself the identity of the I with its other (§415), the mind posits this identity for itself, so that mind is now aware of it, of this *concrete* unity. (Hegel 2007c: §443, 169/10:236)

Because it is only in psychology that the self begins a fully explicit reflection on oneself, it is only in the "Psychology" that the mind becomes fully internal. Thus, what we see in each case of this progression is an increasingly *immaterial* process according to the terms we laid out above. The "Anthropology" considers a mind largely unaware of itself and so largely *external*. The subject of study in the "Anthropology" thus represents the subject in its most material state. By contrast, a subject that learns about itself by means of reflection on its own conscious activity is engaged in a form of internal determination, and so exhibits the kind of immateriality we spoke of above.

8.8   Conclusion

This chapter has sought to reconfigure the way Hegelians ought to respond to the materialist skepticism of early analytic philosophy. It used to be that Hegelians did so by denying that Hegel had any robust metaphysical commitments; but with the advent of more recent, metaphysical interpretations of Hegel, there arises, also, the need to revisit Hegel's metaphysical language and see how it squares with these early analytic critiques. We now need to take seriously, once again, that Hegel rejected metaphysical positions like materialism with the aim of establishing his own immaterialism in their stead. What I hope to have shown, here, is that Hegel had good reason for doing so, that his shift to immaterialism is not the reckless abstraction of a dogmatic idealist, but a sober attempt to realize the highest aims of metaphysics. His position against materialism is, for one, quite nuanced: it is, as I have argued, a *minimalist* critique of materiality that rejects only the notion that *all* things possess the various forms of externality present in material things. This Hegel pairs with what I called his "minimalist conception of immateriality," the notion that some things exhibit an "internal" structure that cannot be accounted for in materialist terms.

Thus, the real "extravagance" of Hegel's metaphysics concerns his "transformational conception of immateriality," the notion that, once we realize the processes of immateriality at work within the mind, we realize them at work within all things. But even this is not so extravagant as it may seem at first glance; for all Hegel means by this is that there is more to things than what appears to us at first glance, that there is, as Kreines (2015) expresses it, "reason in the world." This is what I hope to have shown.

CHAPTER 9

Hegel's Psychology
The Unity of Theoretical and Practical Mind

Dean Moyar

The "Psychology" section of the *Encyclopedia* is situated between
"Phenomenology" and "Objective Spirit," the two parts of the *Philosophy
of Spirit* that Hegel published in expanded form as the Jena *Phenomenology
of Spirit* and the *Philosophy of Right* (PR).[1] The "Psychology" has long been
overshadowed by its neighbors and neglected by scholars, and while the
text has recently received some much overdue attention,[2] the account is
still often read as an addendum to the *Phenomenology* or a precursor to the
Philosophy of Right. The first main interpretive challenge is to provide
a clear account of why Hegel's *distinctive* understanding of the structure
of self-consciousness, the Concept, enables him to develop a unified
account of the theoretical and practical capacities. Without such an
account, Hegel's compressed treatment of intuition, representation, the
drives, etc., will seem like so much repackaging of familiar themes from
Kant and Fichte. In this short chapter I cannot provide a full reconstruction of Hegel's view, or a full comparison with his predecessors. I will chart
the main stages of the account and the *unity* of the "Psychology" with
specific attention to the role of the Concept, Hegel's signature structure of
self-referring negativity and *self-particularizing universality*.[3] The goal of
Hegel's account is the theory of *free mind* in which the theoretical capacities (intuition, representation, thinking) are united with the practical

---

[1] The translation of *Geist* as spirit is especially unfortunate in the case of the subject matter of the
"Psychology," since here, if anywhere, we have Hegel's treatment of what philosophers refer to in
English as philosophy of mind. For that reason I follow Inwood's translation in Hegel (2007c) and
Herrmann-Sinai and Zigliogli (2016) in using "mind" in my title and in the passages from the text.
I leave "spirit" for titles of Hegel's works and elsewhere.
[2] See the essays in Herrmann-Sinai and Zigliogli (2016). Herrmann-Sinai (2016) and Ikäheimo (2017)
are exemplary efforts to capture the unity of "Psychology" in a single essay. On "Theoretical Mind,"
I have been guided by DeVries (1988) and Halbig (2002).
[3] The Concept is not only a structure of universality, particularity, and individuality, but also the
activity of unification of those three moments. For a discussion of why the Concept should be
equated with self-referring negativity, see Bowman (2013).

166

capacities (choice, drive, happiness). I argue that free mind should be conceived as the capacity to make *valid practical inferences*, where those inferences have the form of the purpose that is the key to Hegelian rationality.

The second interpretive challenge is to bring the distinctive Hegelian method to bear in a way that makes sense of well-known phenomena and solves well-known problems. In this chapter I read the "Psychology" through the classic question of whether knowing the good is sufficient for acting on the good. I call this the *internalism question* because it concerns the issue of whether motivation to act on the good is internal to knowledge of the good. The affirmative answer, usually dubbed "intellectualist" and attributed to Plato, is that if one knows the good one will act on it.[4] The negative answer to the question often focuses on the issue of weakness of will and other such *counternormative* phenomena in which one acts contrary to one's knowledge and judgment of the good. Hegel's views on this question have been hard to pin down, and most of the discussions have been focused on the theory of "Objective Spirit" laid out in the *Philosophy of Right*. But the structure of the "Psychology" makes it the more obvious place to look for Hegel's answer, for his "free mind" just is the unity of the judging (and inferring) capacities of the intellect with the volitional capacities of the will. I argue that while the free mind, as the structure of the *practical inference*, does to a great extent identify the will with practical reason, Hegel is also able through the Concept to make room for the counternormative within the normative. Showing how the derivation of free mind gives us a new way to think about familiar capacities and the internalism question also provides an indirect proof of Hegel's Concept itself.

9.1 The Internalism Question

Hegel's unification of thinking and willing can seem to make him an *intellectualist* who holds that one does not really will if one fails to do what one knows to be right. Robert Pippin thus writes, "Hegel's notion of the will is simply practical reason, and so his position is more Socratic – there is no weakness of the will. There is only ignorance, self-deceit and self-discovery."[5] Pippin is denying that on Hegel's picture one can genuinely will and then fail in one's specific willing to live up to that original willing. One's will, as united with thinking, just is practical reason, so if

---

[4] For Plato's classic statement, see *Protagoras* 358b–c.   [5] Pippin (2008: 165).

you fail to act on what you claim is your purpose, that just means that you *never really willed* that purpose. If you had genuinely willed the purpose, rather than deceiving yourself that you had willed it, you would have taken the specific means to bring it about. Though Hegel does indeed bring the will and reason quite close, there are also grounds for thinking that Hegel would admit counternormative action into the picture, for he discusses as commonplace many cases in which knowing the good and willing the good come apart.[6] In his discussion of evil in PR §139, for instance, Hegel seems to think that the self-conscious agent can very easily will an action in which her particular motives are preferred over what she knows to be the universal (I return to this passage at the end of the essay). I argue in this chapter that a main attraction of Hegel's view in the "Psychology" is that alongside making a case for the unity of thinking and willing, and thereby arguing for internalism, he lays out stages of theoretical and practical activity that help explain, and thus render intelligible, cases of counternormative agency.

The internalism question turns on the issue of how closely to identify the judgment of what action is good and the actual acting (or willing) on that judgment. The intellectualist or Socratic position is that if one truly judges, and thus *truly* knows the good, one cannot then fail to act on it. Failure to act would instead be evidence that one did not truly judge or truly know in the first place. Weakness of will seems to be a problem for the *intellectualist internalist* because cases in which one's will does not follow judgment indicate that knowing and acting can easily come apart. It seems more natural to say with the *voluntarist* that you really did in fact will the good and then subsequently failed to live up to your willing. The intellectualist internalist says that you never really did will the good, but only *deceived yourself* into thinking you did. You *discover* (Pippin's "self-discovery") that what you thought was a genuine act of willing (a commitment) was in fact a semblance of willing – your heart was not really in it, as we like to say. The internalist holds that a genuine act of willing just is a robust commitment to what one has judged to be good (willing *is* practical reason), so we should not countenance as genuine a judgment of the good that does not motivate or a willing of the good that turns out to be too weak for the agent to actually follow through.

The voluntarist position typically goes together with a certain judgment *externalism* and the acceptance of weakness of will. On this view, it is perfectly normal to think of willing something and then failing to live up to that, without thereby saying "oh, I guess I never really did will that after

---

[6] See Alznauer (2015: 101–2) on this point.

all." One can simply judge the good, and even adopt its pursuit as one's intention, and yet not thereby be sufficiently motivated to follow through with action on the good. It happens all the time. The voluntarist does not see the point in reserving "willing" for "truly willing," i.e., for the judgments of the good that one succeeds in following through on. Similarly, the voluntarist thinks that one can make valid judgments of what one is supposed to do without thereby being motivated to action.

The best response to this voluntarist challenge is to emphasize that our understanding of rational agency breaks down if we allow the will to come too far apart from rational assessment (judgment). The situation that the externalist asks us to take seriously is one in which I judge that "X is the right (rational) thing for me to do," thereby declaring that it ought to govern my willing, and then I choose to do something else. In order to make the choice against one's judgment seem intuitive, the externalist voluntarist relies on the lack of motivational efficacy of the judgment. But the internalist can say that such a judgment is supposed to be *practical* in a sense that *already* involves commitment. As Gary Watson writes, "In weakness of will, properly so-called, one goes against the grain of one's own commitments, and this is an appropriate description only if practical judgement constitutes a commitment *to act*. On the externalist view, however, going against reasons must always come down to a choice among possible commitments" (Watson 2004, 134). Being a rational agent means governing one's volition through one's judgment. To think of volition as a power of choice standing over against one's judgment is to threaten the very idea of rational agency. Yet internalists do have to find a way to account for choice against the good. When I act against my rational assessment, it cannot be that I thereby cease to be an agent at all, as if I was simply taken over by desire. Counternormative agency has to be preserved as intelligible within the overall account of rational agency.

The internalism question is typically thought to be a central question in moral psychology and theories of practical reason. It can seem that debates over the right answer inevitably end in a standoff over which cases – those of the virtuous or those of the wayward – we take to be central. One way to prevent such a standoff is by building up an account of the virtuous agent from more basic human capacities of representing and choosing. The strength of the internalist case very much turns on the link of representation and judgment, on the one hand, to the conative capacities associated with motivation and the will, on the other. The internalist aims to demonstrate a close connection of the cognitive and conative in the virtuous agent, but the internalist need not allow herself to be blindsided by tales of the wayward. She can demonstrate the willing within knowing, and the knowing within willing, at every less than complete stage of agency, and also show that those stages are incomplete forms of the full agency that develops out of them. By preemptively accounting for the powers that disrupt the link of knowing and acting, and by showing how those should be conceived as stemming from limited but still essential capacities of the normal agent, the internalist can defend a normative account as more than simply a stipulation that good agency is real agency.

Hegel is in a good position to answer the internalism question because of his interpretation of the form of conceptuality as self-referring negativity and self-particularizing universality. Hegel's Concept is many things, and it makes an official appearance in "Psychology" only in the section on "thinking," but as the core of Hegel's concept of mind and his method-ology the Concept is pervasive. The derivation of content from self-consciousness that Hegel takes over from Fichte is so much more fruitful in Hegel's hands because of his conception of a three-fold Concept that internally differentiates its universality and restores that unity in a concrete whole of "moments." In terms of internalism, we can appreciate Hegel's innovation through his ability not only to derive the universality of the capacities and norms, but also to unpack the opposition of particularity within that universality. Every universal is tied to the particular, so every universal norm is bound to particular modes of specification and realiza-tion. With a picture of mind as fundamentally a power of unification, uniting both a manifold of representation and a manifold of drives, Hegel's internalist account develops a harmony of knowing and acting at a very deep level. The way to deal with the counternormative is not to disqualify it as a non-entity but rather to identify its source and show its suspension (*Aufhebung*) in the next stages. In contrast to Fichte, who endorses a representationalist internalism that rules out counternormative agency,[7] Hegel holds that the universal is not simply a blank positive under which individuals are subsumed. The universal itself is determinate, and thus always related to the particular.[8] Hegel thinks of the universal as reaching its true form in the form of a purpose or end that contains the particular means to its realization and re-unites with itself in the end's

---

[7] Fichte writes in his "System of Ethics," "It is absolutely impossible and contradictory that anyone with a clear consciousness of his duty at the moment he acts could, with good consciousness, *decide not to do his duty*, that he should rebel against the law, refusing to obey it and making it his maxim not to do his duty, because it is his duty" (Fichte 1971c (henceforth SW): IV:191–2, 1988 (henceforth *SE*): 181–2).

[8] See PR §6, where Hegel explicitly notes this point of contrast with Fichte.

realization. In the end Hegel incorporates a voluntarist element within his overall internalism and can thereby defend the claim that to know the good is to be in a good position to will it even while acknowledging a genuine power of the will to act against one's knowledge.

9.2 Theoretical Mind

The starting point of "Psychology" is the standpoint of *reason* that has been achieved by the previous "Phenomenology" section. In the "Phenomenology" the opposition of subject and object is overcome in the "universal self-consciousness," the basis of the *idealism* that is evident in his formulations of *reason* as an identity of mind and world. Though there is a real advance in "Phenomenology," in approaching the "Psychology" text we must not think of Hegel's procedure as purely *linear*, a view that would lead us to think that *all* the progress of the "Phenomenology" is already contained in the first level of "Psychology." Rather, as Heikki Ikäheimo (2017) has shown, we have instead a largely *parallel* structure in which the three moments of both consciousness and self-consciousness parallel the three moments of theoretical mind and practical mind.[9] This parallel structure allows Hegel to consider different levels of the subject–object relation in isolation while simultaneously building them into a picture of the whole. It is owing to this structure that practical activity can be mentioned already within the theoretical shapes. Thus, while you might think that his method bars him from referring in the theoretical section to practical shapes that he has not yet introduced, these inter-dependencies are a feature, not a bug, of the approach. They highlight the unity presupposed at the outset of "Psychology" and achieved in explicit form at the conclusion of the text.

In the beginning the material of knowledge is *given*, but it is already (by virtue of the standpoint of *psychology*) given *to mind*, and the deficiency of the standpoint is that the mind has not fully appropriated the material for itself. Hegel writes, "Thus, when in its initial stages the mind is *determined*, this determinacy is twofold, a determinacy *of what is* and a determinacy of *what is its own*; by the former, the mind finds within itself something that *is*, by the latter it posits it only as *its own*" (§443). The difference between these two moments is the mind's finitude. Each of the three main stages – intuition,

---

[9] This is closely related to the distinction made by Corti (2016) between "descriptivist" and "reconstructivist" readings of the "Psychology." In my view the reconstructivist reading is in a better position to capture the non-linearity of the account.

representation, thinking – itself has three moments that follow Hegel's usual progression of immediacy, mediation, and a return to immediacy on the basis of rational relations. There is an initial inarticulate unity of what is and what is my own, followed by a breaking apart of the two moments through the activity of the subject, and then a restoration of the unity. My argument focuses on the three "middle" stages – attention, imagination, and judgment – for it is in these capacities that we find the negative activity that both prepares the content for full normative unity and leads the subject to go astray in counternormative cases. The immediate unity is broken up in order to be re-articulated, and herein lies the dissolving and binding power of the mind. But in *failures of attention, arbitrary imagining*, and *judgment* that *favors particularity over universality* we also have some of the basic cognitive sources of counternormative action.

In the initial account of "Intuition" the two moments – "what is" and "what is *its own*" – are immediately identical. Hegel identifies "feeling" as the first moment of intuition, a form of "contingent particularity" (*Encyclopedia* [E] §447) that reappears at the outset of practical mind as well (where he is more positive about it, as we shall see in Section 9.3). In the second moment of "Intuition," *attention*, the identity of mind and world involves both a taking in and a casting out. The taking in is "the moment of *its own*, but as the still *formal* self-determination of the intelligence" (E §448).[10] Hegel unites this with the positing of externality through his conception of self-referring negativity:

> The other moment is thus: contrary to its own inwardness, the intelligence posits the determinacy of feeling as a *being*, but as a *negative*, as the abstract otherness of its own self. Intelligence hereby determines the content of sensation as a *being* that is *outside itself*, casts it out *into space and time*, which are the *forms* in which intelligence is intuitive. According to consciousness the material is only an object of consciousness, a relative other; from mind it receives the rational determination of being the *other of itself*. (E §448)

There is a lot going on in this passage, touching as it does on issues central to Kant's transcendental aesthetic and Hegel's differentiation of "consciousness" and "intelligence."[11] The crucial point is Hegel's distinctive

---

[10] References to the *Encyclopedia* provide the section number of the 1830 edition. Translations are from Hegel (2007c), with some emendations.

[11] There is a complicated story about Hegel's relation to Kant's transcendental idealism. See DeVries (1988: 111ff.), for a good account of Hegel's treatment of space and time here. The short version of the story is that Hegel aims to avoid Kant's "subjective idealism" by claiming that space and time are real determinations, while also holding that the mind *takes* sensation to be in space and time and thus realizes what they already were in themselves. See also DeVries (2016).

conception of the negativity of self-conscious intelligence, which allows Hegel to think of the external "as the abstract otherness of its own self" and as "being the *other of itself*." The negation is what determines the object as an other (a Fichtean not-I); in its simultaneous *self-reference* intelligence also identifies the object as its own. This move is an instance of Hegel overcoming a dualism of subject (I) and object (not-I) by treating the self- and object-reference as one and the same act. The relevance of this move to our issue of counternormativity is not immediately apparent, but as a first gloss we can say that the activity that generates norms is not simply and solely universal (as Fichte's I is abstractly universal), but rather is always a unity of abstract universality and particularity. The normative must *include* particularity, the source of the counternormative, rather than exclude particularity by stipulation as the intellectualist is tempted to do.

The full (normative) form of intuition shows already how Hegel thinks of the discipline of the mind in the process of moving from feeling to thinking. While attention is an act of will as choice (*Willkür*), and thus something potentially arbitrary, Hegel also takes pains in the lectures to tie it to education and the full objectivity of developed intuition. In the lectures we find Hegel claiming "that attention is something dependent on my *choice* [Willkür], therefore, that I am only attentive when I *will* to be so" (E §448Z). Yet he also writes that attention "involves the *negation of one's own self-assertion* and *devoting oneself* to the *subject-matter* [Sache]" (E §448Z). As an example of the link of education and attention he cites the expert botanist who "notices incomparably more in a plant" (E §448Z) as the result of study. Intuition does not get left behind in such cognition, but is rather enriched and expanded as the result of thinking. These references to expert intuition are a prime example of the "top down" reading of the stages from the endpoint of developed knowledge and properly functioning practical reason. As Ikäheimo has emphasized, this complements the "bottom up" approach that deduces the stages from a more basic conception of our animal nature (Ikäheimo 2017). The stages on the way up must be *compatible* with the full normative picture achieved at the end, a point I emphasize in my discussion of "Practical Mind" below.

In the second phase of theoretical mind, "Representation," the moment of "my own" comes to the fore, as the power of intelligence over "what is" expands by further internalizing the material and by developing the capacity for re-externalization. The first main move of representation is to isolate the external singular intuition from its merely external connections by taking it up as an *image*, and thereby placing the content in the space and time of intelligence, in "the universality of the I in general" (E §452).

The images are stored in the "universal pit" (E §455) of intelligence, waiting to be called up by the reproductive imagination in what is usually called the association of ideas. In the lectures we get a better sense of how Hegel conceives the activity of binding the ideas together in association:

> What concerns us here is only the bond, the connection between the objects. In this connection the intelligence singles out, emphasizes, and lays hold of one particular aspect. The intelligence is attentive to the images that are present before it, but since it is the subject of this content, the content itself is no longer internally connected; rather, the intelligence itself holds it together, and can equally allow it to fall apart. The intelligence can pull apart the concrete image, and since it thus dissolves the concrete images, it has particular determinations before itself, and so one particular representation is singled out for emphasis, which the intelligence makes into the connection with another representation. (Hegel 1994 (henceforth VPG): 204, 2007b (henceforth LPS): 220–1)

This activity is itself a form of attention, but here intelligence "is the subject of this content," indicating the way that the content has been more fully internalized. The intelligence can hold the intuition together, now with itself as the unifying factor, or break it up into component particulars that it can recombine at will. Hegel aligns this *dissolving* ability of intelligence with the ability to break up the concrete material of intuition into particulars. There remains at this level a certain arbitrariness in the subjection of the images to self-consciousness.

The completion of imagination is already a move to the normative or "substantial." In fantasy or productive imagination the mind is able to *generate* signs, language, and thus to re-externalize the content that it had previously (in an immediate form) internalized. "The substantial [act of] connection is productive imagination, which can be symbolizing, allegorizing, or poetic" (VPG 205, LPS 221). Spirit is united with the world not simply by conforming to what is, but by making that *its own* and gaining mastery over the content by drawing out its objectivity. Here we have a clear sense in which the *taking to be true* has as its completion, or realization, a *making true* in the objectification of representation through language. In the final phase of representation, *memory* takes up the linguistic sign into a new process of reproduction and solidification of meaning.[12]

Hegel holds that the final level of theoretical mind, *thinking* proper, is from the beginning fundamentally normative. We thus find, at the opening of his lectures on thinking, "Everything that is untrue in the world consists in the

---

[12] For an excellent account of how language emerges as a requirement for actions, see Herrmann-Sinai (2016).

fact that the objectivity does not correspond to the concept. A bad man can exist, but what exists in the world does not correspond to its concept, and this non-coincidence is its finitude" (VPG 228, LPS 240). In its first phase, thinking is only the abstraction of the understanding. This level is nonetheless quite important, as Hegel illustrates with the idea of acting on an essential purpose. "Now if it separates off the *contingent* from the *essential* it is entirely within its rights and appears as what in truth it ought to be. Therefore, someone who pursues an essential purpose is called a man of understanding" (E §467Z). The ability to remain focused on a purpose, to not be distracted from the essential by contingent factors, is a mark of the understanding. Then again, this very fixity can become "one-sided," and thereby "become the opposite of *sound common sense*" (§467Z). Think, for example, of the obsessive quest of some parents to get their children into a top university.

Judgment, the second stage of thinking, is characterized by the power to separate out the different aspects of a concrete whole and then to re-unite those different aspects in a conclusive or normative judgment (what Hegel calls the *judgment of the concept*). In contrast to the simple universality of the first stage, this second stage does not refer everything to a single universal, but rather breaks up the substantial universal into separate predicates through which an object can be related to other objects (e.g., both a soccer ball and a car tire are round). In the practical domain we say that it takes judgment, rather than the mere universality of the understanding, to know how to adjust one's actions to the various circumstances of a given case. In Hegel's speculative terms, it can seem that judgment most fully captures thought as "self-explicating, self-determining, self-specifying, positing the particularity, judging and coinciding with itself" (VPG 229, LPS 241). But Hegel worries about the reliance on judgment as a reliance on the *particularity* or contingent *insight* of the judging subject. His identification of formal conscience with judgment and his critique of its formality is a good indication of this deficiency (PR §137–8).

With the *inference*, thinking finally achieves the *truth* that theoretical mind has been aiming for all along. This truth turns out to be a truth of action, of something the mind *does*, and does in a free manner because all givenness, or immediacy, has been overcome. In the Logic Hegel criticizes the formal inferences (Aristotelian syllogisms) and gives six non-formal types of inference, but the full form of the inference comes only with the *teleological* or *practical inference*.[13] In other words, thinking as inferring has

---

[13] See Moyar (2018). The "inferences of necessity" come close, but they are not the inferences of the Concept, which Hegel clearly identifies with the purpose.

a *purposive structure.* Hegel comes close to identifying inference with practical inference when in the lectures he takes the end or purpose as the typical form and content of the inference: "The inference is the activity of the rational in general. In ordinary life one designates as rational that which is in and for itself, something firm; a self-standing essential end, an end existing in and for itself, that which expresses an essential end. When something is firm and secure, it is so because it is not abstract, one-sided, but something that stands the test" (VPG 236, LPS 246). The essential end or purpose is what remains in the process of its realization or particularizing activity. This is the basic conception of the *normative* that Hegel calls the Idea, the unity of Concept and existence, for the purpose both identifies the good and accomplishes something in the world that is adequate to that good.

In the relation of universal and particular in the teleological inference we find the key to Hegel's account of internalism and a clear way to think of how the counternormative can appear within the normative. The internalism is secured when one's universal commitments and the specific actions that fulfill them are closely connected in intersubjectively recognized practices. What distinguishes the substantive inference from the formal inference is a "negative element," of which Hegel writes, "it posits its modification as its own, so that it remains at home with itself in its modification, and thus has joined and integrated with itself in its modification" (VPG 237, LPS 246). The main point is a variant on the point about the self-referring negativity of the Concept: in this case, the universal negates its abstract purity, posits some particular alteration of the world, and then relates that particular back to itself as belonging to the universal. The practical inference thereby suspends the difference between the given and the activity of cognition, rendering the given something posited through the Concept. The key is the status of the minor premise, the judgment that identifies the particular as an instance of or means to the universal. As we shall see, willing goes awry when that power of negativity of the individual agent comes apart from the knowledge of universality (the major premise) that is supposed to control it.

9.3 Practical Mind

When we ask the internalist question of whether or not agency in the full-blown sense rules out counternormativity, we are asking whether the *form* of agency is fully adequate to the *content* of the good. That is, we are asking whether fulfilling the formal characteristics of agency is incompatible with acting contrary to known ethical content. I have argued that an internalist should not just stipulate the conditions of agency or willing (so as to rule out counternormativity), but rather should give an account of why acting for reasons is genuine action that includes an explanation of counternormativity as significant. Hegel's development of practical mind is especially illuminating because he does not assume a fixed model of full-blown agency and then conceive of activity inadequate to norms as mere non-agency. Rather, he aims to *develop* agency from the failures and insufficiencies of the previous stages. For this account to work, the earlier stages – even in their failures – do have to be significant, intelligible, as genuine activities of the subject.

In this section I exhibit the first two stages of practical spirit as stages in which Hegel works through the basic forms of the conative. I identify in each stage three steps that secure a *limited role* for the stage in the ultimate account.

Step 1: State the identity of form and content while noting the limitation of the form to secure universal content.

Step 2: Show that this as yet inadequate particular form is *compatible* with true universal content, thereby securing its place in the overall account. The lesson of this step is that the particularizing activity of the subject is itself one side of the self-referring negativity that is essential to all action.

Step 3: Show how the limitation of this shape becomes a contradiction by showing how the universal self-reference implicit in the subject's thinking contradicts the particular realizations. Show that this is a productive contradiction insofar as it leads to a more developed self-consciousness and a richer universality in the subject's return to itself in the subsequent shape.

In Hegel's view, the account of practical mind has to begin in the form of immediacy, or the form of feeling. What this means is that feeling, conceived as a felt affirmation of a purpose, is what guides action, both motivating the subject and justifying the action (to the subject). Hegel's overall point in criticizing feeling's immediacy is that while one can certainly feel the correct content of duty (and religion), there is nothing in the form of feeling itself to guarantee that one will in fact act on the right content. Step 1 in the account should say what is good about this form while also highlighting its limitations. On its own, feeling is a standard of agreement between a self-determining *ought* of simple identity, on the one hand, and my individual subjective nature, on the other. This standard is no more than "the utterly subjective and superficial *feeling* of the *pleasant* or *unpleasant*" (E §472). Pleasure is clearly a part of any account of motivation, but in this first phase there is only a tenuous connection to the rationality of content.

In Step 2, the *compatibility* of feeling with correct content, Hegel emphasizes that even the best, truest content, can be felt. He aligns this shape with the appeal to the "*heart* in general," which "has (1) the correct sense that these determinations are the subject's *own, immanent* determinations, (2) and then that in so far as feeling is opposed to the *understanding*, feeling *can* be the *totality*, in contrast to the one-sided abstractions of the understanding" (E §471R). The compatibility comes into view on the parallel between practical feeling and "intuition." The fact that we have an intuition of a sensible object does not get in the way of representing and/or thinking that same object. We can also represent and think without being in the presence of the object, just as we can make ethical judgments without the immediate feeling (though in both cases one can say that intuition and feeling are necessary for the development and overall continued functioning of the human being). And just as the botanist has a developed intuition of the plant, so too the ethical agent has a developed set of ethical feelings (i.e., emotions) that she brings to bear on ethical situations.

In Step 3 Hegel writes of the limitation as a contradiction that is productive in spurring the development of a richer universality. The productive difference between subject and environment comes to the fore *in cases of failure*, of *evil*. He writes,

> In regard to contingent purposes, evil [*Übel*] is only the right that is imposed on the vanity and nullity of their devising [*Einbildung*]. They themselves are already what is evil. – The finitude of life and mind falls into their *judgment*, in which they have the Other that is separated from them at the same time within them as their negative, and thus they are the contradiction called evil. (E §472R)

The judgment is the mismatch between purpose and existence in the failure of a finite purpose. Life and spirit exhibit the structure of self-referring negativity in their ability to *be the contradiction* and thereby to *learn from their pain*. Such failures can be conceived as those of a merely living organism, but they are also what allow the subject to *emerge from life*. Hegel remarks, "In a dead thing there is no evil or pain, because in inorganic nature the concept does not confront its reality [*Dasein*] and does not in the distinction at the same time remain its subject. Already in life, and still more in mind, this immanent differentiation is present and thus an *ought* comes in; and this negativity, subjectivity, I, freedom are the principles of evil and pain" (E §472R). The counternormativity here is at first the simple failure to unite self and world in one's purpose. It is also the ability of the subject to act against mere life, to incur pain for the sake of freedom, and to develop reflective self-consciousness.

The successor to practical feeling is the *drive*, whose greater mediation and complexity parallels the advances made by *representation* over intuition. Just as representation had marked a transition from the immediate presence of singular objects to the capacity to recreate images from memory, so too the drive is a subjective capacity that relates to objectivity as something mediated by subjective activity. The drive is a clear advance over feeling insofar as its form is now *purposive*, including a negation and thereby determinate content within its very structure. The basic dynamics of negation and self-reference that I have stressed throughout are on display in this passage from the lectures:

> The drive is also an inner, a sense of a determination accompanied by a feeling of the non-conformity of my existence to the inner demand. The non-conformity is bound up with a defect, a lack, and the drive is the demand that this negative of the positive side of my nature be suspended. The non-conformity is necessary insofar as I am a spiritual and living nature. What I am is supposed to be something brought about by me. Spirit must know what it is, and it knows this only when it has posited itself as such. (VPG 251, LPS 256)

The principal negativity of the drive is the difference of my "inner demand" and my actual existence, but there is also a negativity in the specificity of the drive as against other drives. The unitary I, both spiritual and natural, is the activity through which the satisfaction of each drive, and of the drives in relation to each other, are bound together. The drives are individuated because they take a specific object domain through repeated satisfaction.[14] The drive "starts from the suspended opposition of the subjective and objective, and involves a *series* of satisfactions, and so is something *whole, universal*" (§473Z). Just as we learn to *perceive* the world (as representational intelligence) through repeated exposure and by *reproducing* the object in imagination, so too we learn to see the world practically as a function of our drives through repeated satisfaction of those drives

---

[14] Hegel's theory of the drives owes much to Fichte. In the *Lectures on the Vocation of the Scholar*, Fichte writes, "Every drive has to be *awakened* by experience before we can become conscious of it. Furthermore, in order for a drive to become an *inclination* and in order for its satisfaction to become a *need*, the drive in question has to be *developed* through frequently repeated experiences of the same type" (Fichte 1971d (henceforth SW VI): 313, 2005b (henceforth EPW): 162).

in purposes imagined and then carried out in the world.[15] But – and here is the limitation – satisfying a specific drive is a rational achievement only in the absence of other specific drives and their corresponding objects. Given the multiplicity of drives and a variegated environment, the *particularity* of the drives means that they cannot on their own settle the rationality of action.

In Step 2 Hegel once again stresses the *compatibility* of the drives, and the closely related passions and *interests*, with true ethical content. Hegel thinks that an *interest* must be in play whenever an individual pursues an end. "An action is both a purpose of the subject and also the subject's activity which carries out this purpose; it is only because the subject is in this way in even the most unselfish action, i.e. because of its interest, that there is an action at all" (E §475R). Every action is motivated action, where motivation expresses the identification of the subject with the content of the purpose. His view is that there is no way to transcend this, and no need to transcend it, for one can act on true ethical content even while acting with passion.[16] Once again, this is an instance of the particularity of the subject being compatible with, and even necessary for, the realization of true ethical (universal) content.

Step 3 of this stage is both an opposition of drives to each other and the emergence of a higher-order activity, choice (*Willkür*), that can adjudicate between them. I treat choice as part of a package with the drives (and not a stage of its own), for while it is an achievement in the development of practical subjectivity, in this argument its main role is to make explicit the contradictory character of the satisfaction of the drives. The drives are both multiple and indeterminate. As the solution to this multiplicity of the drives, the power of choice (*Willkür*) involves both a greater separation of the form (the subject) from the content and a greater role for thinking in practical activity. To determine an action the subject as a whole must stand above these drives, and the subject can do so because she is intelligence, thinking: "The will, as thinking and implicitly free, distinguishes itself from the *particularity* of the drives, and places itself as simple subjectivity of thinking above their manifold content. It is thus *reflecting* will" (E §476). The will as choice involves the subject's opposition to her own drives, and

---

[15] Herrmann-Sinai has helpfully contrasted drive with desire and related the drive to the linguistic capacities developed in "Representation": "Now we are in a position to express what we were not able to express at the level of the *Phenomenology*, namely the normativity of *repeatable* action types that bear a linguistic form which teleologically structures my activity and ultimately allows us to express that you and I are doing something of the same kind" (Herrmann-Sinai 2016, 139).

[16] I am in agreement with the argument by Wretzel (2020) that with the account of drives we have a key moment of organic nature's ineliminable role within ethical agency.

while it can seem to be the core activity of willing proper, Hegel insists that reflective choice is not the essence of free agency. Choice is certainly *compatible* with free agency, though Hegel does not think that one is free only when one can choose between alternatives. Hegel takes pains in his *Philosophy of Right* to mark out space for choice even while arguing that ethics and the rational state are based on the *rational* will as opposed to the will as choice (PR §§14–16). There is freedom in the elevation above the drives, and this elevation is at work in choosing (counternormatively) to act against one's judgment of the good. But the willing that follows thinking, that identifies with the practical inference, is rational agency proper.

The completion of Step 3, Hegel's transition from the drives and choice to happiness, operates by identifying a *contradiction* between the form and content (universality and particularity) of the power of choice. Even considered as a purpose realized in the actual world, the content is still tied to the subjectivity of the drive, and thus has not yet achieved the status of universality that the reflecting will has as intelligence. This means that there is still a mismatch between the form of the choosing will and the form of the realized content. The will as choice "is a *contradiction*: it actualizes itself in a particularity, which is at the same time a nullity for it, and has a satisfaction in the particularity which it has at the same time left behind" (E §478). As universal, the thinking will both identifies with chosen content and knows that such content is inadequate to it, for the content has not attained the status of universality that the thinking will possesses. This contradiction can be resolved if the satisfaction of the drive is not a mere particular, but rather a part of a whole of satisfaction, or happiness, which itself is the universal. With the power of choice as a capacity explicitly derived and subordinated on the way to the fully normative endpoint, we have secured a place for at least one main source of counternormativity within the normative.

9.4 Free Mind and Practical Inference

The first thing to say about the brief "Happiness" section is that it feels like a real missed opportunity, for happiness ought to be at the level of thinking, yet Hegel does virtually no work to show how happiness achieves the level of rationality achieved by judgment and inference in "Theoretical Mind."[17] Indeed, it seems that happiness does not fully emerge from the

---

[17] Ikäheimo comments on the failure of happiness to measure up to its γ-level status, "Here Hegel's architectonic breaks down somewhat as happiness is – analogically to the β-level in the theoretical side – a 'mixture of qualitative and quantitative determinations' (E §479)" (Ikäheimo 2017: 446).

middle level of representation (he calls it a "representation [Vorstellung]" that is "brought forth through reflective thought" (E §479)). It seems that only in the subsequent step, the free will itself, do we get a shape of willing that achieves the structure of the inference. This is especially odd in light of the obvious path available to unite happiness with thought. Hegel could have given a roughly Aristotelian account of practical reason here, and the Aristotelian practical syllogism could very well have served as the culmination of practical spirit. But instead of working through the inferences of happiness and their deficiency, Hegel in essence repeats his argument against the drives and will. He argues that the apparent satisfaction of happiness in action is in fact a particular that falls short of happiness, and the will thus remains mired in the bad infinity of an ongoing series. The will that chooses to take this or that path to happiness is formally free and universal, but this form finds no correspondingly universal content in the drives that constitute happiness. One searches for happiness but is never satisfied.

The move from happiness to the free will is a move to the willing of universality as such. Hegel thinks of this move as expressing agreement with Kant's claim that *freedom* rather than happiness is the proper end of the rational will. It can seem that Hegel's statement that free mind unites the theoretical and the practical is also Kantian, since we can take the theoretical to mean *the form of thinking* or *universality* or *lawfulness*. But Hegel disagrees with Kant on just this point because Hegel's view of the form of thought, as we have seen, is fundamentally inferential and purposive. Hegel's move here should be read not in terms of mere lawfulness, but rather in terms of the *practical inference*.[18] His unification of thinking and willing is a unity of will both with inferential form (the apex of thinking) and with the idea of truth conditions for that willing. Such truth conditions in the world are another way of giving the terms of the *validity* of practical inferences. Truth and validity are theoretical concepts that bear the *universality* that Hegel associates with the free will. The bite of this position is that the practical inference cannot be true just for me, or valid just for me, but must be true and valid for all.

One strand of Hegel's argument for the unity of the theoretical and practical is that the *object* of practical mind must be *found* just as much as it is *produced*. Freedom must be a *world* of freedom, an explicit *content* of freedom that can be willed as such by the individual. Hegel has in mind the

---

[18] See Schmidt am Busch (2010) for an examination of the 1805/6 account of the will in which Hegel explicitly treats it as a function of the inference.

world of *right*, the world of legal norms and social institutions. The norms and institutions constitute *objective* spirit, which Hegel thinks of as a world that is the *objectification of the free will*. To say that the free mind has itself as "content and purpose" (E §482) is just to say that the individual wills those norms that constitute right. The free will has the structure of universality–particularity–individuality, which enables Hegel to develop a variegated world of freedom in which the universal (which remains dominant) is enriched through particularity and the recombination of elements in the individual agent. So while Hegel does take the form of lawfulness as central to "Abstract Right," his argument for *property* and *contract rights* depends on a conception of the person as an *exclusive* individual. Hegel's conception of "Morality" is focused on the *particular* or *subjective* will, and includes a prominent place for individual welfare, a close cousin of happiness. At the level of right I do not simply will my happiness, but rather I will my welfare with the implicit requirement that I consider the welfare of all agents, and that I take into account the fact that my welfare depends on the welfare of others.

Another central aspect of the requirements of the free will is the mutual recognition that is built into Hegel's concept of right. Without thematizing the relation in "Psychology," Hegel has clearly carried over this intersubjective relation from the "Phenomenology," and it clearly does real work in the conception of a free will that wills itself. Mutual recognition is rather understated in the first two stages of objective spirit, but it comes to the fore in the move from "Morality" to "Ethical Life," which itself repeats the unification of the theoretical and practical, the true and the good, at a higher level.[19] His overall point is that the free will can be fulfilled only when it acts on the proper content, and that no formal requirement of rationality alone will suffice to secure the content. The complete conception of rational agency is attained only in the full-blown social world, a world that is itself rational because it has the form of a self-maintaining, living system.

What does the free will's reflexivity and the inseparability of form and content tell us, finally, about the significance of counternormative conduct? Recall that the internalist question raised the problem of how to think of cases in which all the formal requirements of agency are met, ethical knowledge is achieved, and yet the subject acts contrarily to the good. Many philosophers have been tempted to deny this possibility outright, namely to say that it is impossible to meet the formal requirements and yet not act on the good. Hegel's tight connection of reason and will would seem to align him with this

---

[19] See Moyar (2007).

camp (as in Pippin's view), yet he also holds that the formal standpoint from which the agent is conscious of an action as meeting the requirements of morality (conscience) is also the standpoint at which evil is a real possibility. You can consciously choose to will the bad (though he too does not believe in the diabolical will), and this makes just as much sense as willing the good in the absence of a stable set of socially sanctioned norms that specify what the good is. His claim is that "both morality and evil have their common root in that self-certainty which has being for itself and knows and resolves for itself" (PR §139R). When things go right, one wills "the universal in and for itself," whereas when things go wrong one wills "the *arbitrariness* of [one's] *own particularity*" (PR §139). We have now seen at length how the particularity is *compatible* with universality. The point is that one normally wills *as a particular agent* while giving the universal precedence, and this is just what the institutions of ethical life are designed to make actual. The inwardness whereby we become capable of free self-determination is destabilizing, and can result in our opting for the particular over the universal, but it is also essential to the freedom of the will to be able to break down and reconstitute the manifold of duties so that we are not beset by irresolvable moral conflict. The normative is captured by the interlocking inferences of ethical life, but in a complex moral landscape there is always the need for judgment, and always the possibility of going astray even when one knows the good.

The move away from the formal standpoint of "Morality" is also a move within metaethics away from thinking that we can solve intractable issues such as counternormative agency at the formal level of abstract rational requirements. Hegel's move to "Ethical Life" can seem puzzling because the account of agency there is not independent of a substantive account of the content of the good. Furthermore, he lowers the bar for the formal requirements of deliberation (one can act from habit rather than thinking each case through) while raising the bar for the social requirements (the norms must have legal validity). Once the subject is situated within a well-defined ethical environment, it is enough to be responsive to the reasons in play in that environment, without thinking that only if one clears a very high formal bar (e.g., self-legislation of norms as if for a kingdom of ends) can one act ethically. Hegel's point is that since no formal bar, however high, can guarantee right action, it is counterproductive to insist on formal conditions of rationality over the substantive ethical considerations. Satisfying the requirements of internalism depends, in the end, just as much on the health of our form of life as it does on the functioning of any individual's cognitive or conative capacities.

CHAPTER 10

Political Ontology and Rational Syllogistic in Hegel's Objective Spirit

Paul Redding

In the Preface to *The Philosophy of Right*, Hegel offers some brief suggestions meant to help orient the reader with what they are about to find in this outline written to accompany a course of lectures. He starts with noting that the work provides an enlarged, more systematic exposition of what is contained in the corresponding part of the *Encyclopaedia of the Philosophical Sciences*, but notes that it is important to recognize how the material one is about to encounter differs from what would normally be expected in an "ordinary compendium". Effectively, the difference lies, he points out, in the *method* employed in this work. A compendium is expected to present a comprehensive account in which a "content which has long been familiar and accepted" is laid out in a form "the rules and conventions [of] which have long been agreed", but philosophical outlines are "no longer expected to conform to this pattern" (Hegel 1991a: 9–10). That earlier philosophical form with its logic that appeals to rules of "definition, classification, and inference" had found itself out of step with the modern age. It's shortcomings for "speculative science" have been widely recognized – or, as he corrects himself, they have been "felt", rather than recognized (Hegel 1991a: 10). What seems implied is that had these *been* recognized one might expect some reasoned replacement of the older logic by a more adequate one, but in the present situation it has rather been simply cast off as some merely external constraint, unleashing "arbitrary pronouncements of the heart, of fantasy, and of contingent intuition" (Hegel 1991a: 10).

Hegel may lament the "shameful decline" into which the logic of speculative science has fallen, but it is clear that he is not advocating some simple return to the logic of yesteryear – effectively, Aristotle's syllogistic. The correctness of the modern *feeling* that the old logic is inadequate has to be acknowledged, but the proper attitude will be to find and give determinate form to the truth that is buried in the feelings of those who have spontaneously rejected it. That is, there are *reasons*, not just causes, behind the modern reader's dissatisfaction with the older logical method, and it is clearly

hinted that these reasons will concern its inadequacy as a source of convic-
tion for the modern intellect.

It is at this point that Hegel mentions his own "fully developed" treatise
on the nature of speculative knowledge in *The Science of Logic*, where
a complete account will be found of the principles that guide the presentation in this outline – a "manner of progressing from one topic to another
and of conducting a scientific proof – this entire speculative mode of
cognition [that] is essentially different from other modes of cognition"
(Hegel 1991a: 10). But the availability of *The Science of Logic* here serves as
little more than an excuse to pass over these important methodological
issues. Since he has already provided a systematic account *there*, Hegel
writes, "I have only occasionally added an explanatory comment on
procedure and method in the present outline" and have "omitted to
demonstrate and bring out the logical progression in each and every detail"
(Hegel 1991a: 10).

I suggest that Hegel has effectively left the reader in the wilderness as to
how to even start to make sense of these issues. The alternatives seem to be
either to rely on these occasional "explanatory comments" or immerse
oneself in *The Science of Logic*. But the former on their own can be of little
help, and as for the latter, I think it is fair to say that there is no guarantee
that, having invested the time and energy into working through that text,
the reader will be any less puzzled as to how the categories that unfold there
from "Being" to "The Idea" are meant to actually shed light on the
methodological issues found in Hegel's political theory as set out in *The
Philosophy of Right*.

Here I want to suggest another way of bringing these elements together
by examining them in relation to the way issues of logic and political
ontology had come together in Plato's thought, or at least as Hegel
understands it. In short, the inadequacy for the modern world of *Plato's*
recommendations in *The Republic* will effectively be shown to be grounded
in the same factors that make *the old logic* inadequate as philosophical
method for modern political thought. Moreover, this will also enable us to
get some bearing on how Hegel employs in his entirely *peculiar* way the
logical notion of a "syllogism" to model social relations and institutional
structures. The old logic that has come to be out of step with modern
thought was, of course, the syllogistic logic that Aristotle had constructed
on the basis of ideas taken from Plato. But, as we have glimpsed above, for
Hegel there were good reasons why the Aristotelian syllogistic had fallen
into disrepute, and this bears directly on the question of the shortcomings
of Plato's political ontology.

As becomes more obvious as the Preface of *The Philosophy of Right* progresses, the classical polis had not been able to tolerate the principle of "subjectivity", a principle that Hegel treats as a defining characteristic of the modern world. The old style of presentation had essentially been directed to giving some order to a set of publicly recognized truths accepted as unproblematic. "The truth concerning *right, ethics, and the state* is at any rate *as old as its exposition and promulgation* in *public laws and in public morality and religion*." But, as Hegel puts it, for the modern reader the contents presented must "appear justified to free thinking. For such thinking does not stop at what is *given* whether the latter is supported by the external positive authority of the state or of mutual agreement among human beings, or by the authority of inner feeling and the heart and by the testimony of the spirit which immediately concurs with this, but starts out from itself and thereby demands to know itself as united in its innermost being with the truth" (Hegel 1991a: 11). We might think of Descartes's methodological wielding of hyperbolic doubt as typifying this attitude.

In the concluding passages of Subjective Spirit leading up to the transition to Objective Spirit in the 1817 *Encyclopaedia* we see how such a free thinking has emerged as "actual free will", which is "the unity of theoretical and practical mind" – will which is "for itself, as free will ... *will* as free *intelligence*" (Hegel 1971: §481), mind "aware of itself as free" (Hegel 1971: §482). Hegel notes there that "whole continents ... have never had this idea, and are without it still", but what is especially significant for us is that "the Greeks and Romans, Plato and Aristotle, even the Stoics did not have it" (Hegel 1971: §482 remark (R)). However, the contrast between the ancient and modern worlds cannot be as simple as this and on Hegel's own criteria needs qualification. For example, in the *Lectures on the History of Philosophy* (Hegel 2006: 220) he notes that the principle of subjective freedom "did enter into the Greek world too, but as the principle that destroyed the Greek states and Greek life generally". What he is referring to here is, of course, the way that *Socrates* had embodied the principle of subjective freedom, and Socrates *qua* embodiment of subjective freedom was, after all, surely central to the development of Greek speculative thought – the thought of Plato and Aristotle.

As Hegel puts it in the Preface to *The Philosophy of Right*, Plato's *Republic* was "essentially the embodiment of nothing other than the nature of Greek *Sittlichkeit*" (Hegel 1991a: 20), instantiating the more general principle later expressed as philosophy being "*its own time comprehended in thoughts*" (Hegel 1991a: 21). The thoughts of Plato and Aristotle must be then understood as expressing this broader contradiction within the

Sittlichkeit of Greek life itself, both generating subjective freedom and refusing to accommodate it within its structures. It is against such a background that I want to look for the origins in Greek thought of Hegel's "syllogism", with its distinct inquiry-related or "inquisitorial" dimension as well as its more "ontological" dimension. This will enable us to get some sense of how the limits of Greek life and thought – its inability to tolerate the principle of subjective freedom – might be reflected in *both* these dimensions of syllogistic structure, and how Hegel might envisage his way of rescuing its rational core. After that we will briefly consider Hegel's portrayal of the relation of formal and ontological syllogisms in the Subjective Logic of *The Science of Logic*. Against this broad backdrop we might then be able to get a clearer picture of how the syllogisms of Hegel's own rejuvenated speculative logic are meant to guide our understanding of the political institutions of the modern state as set out in *The Philosophy of Right*.

10.1   The Syllogism of Plato's Speculative Dialectic

In the *Encyclopaedia Logic*, in the remark to the opening paragraph on the syllogism – *der Schluss* – Hegel says of the syllogism that it "is the *essential ground of everything true*; and *the definition of the absolute* is from now on that it is the syllogism [*dass es der Schluss ist*] or, articulated in the form of a sentence, it is the determinacy: '*everything is a syllogism*'" (Hegel 2010b: §181R). Given that *everything is a syllogism*, it is remarkable how seldom Hegel actually mentions syllogisms in *The Philosophy of Right*. As "the *essential ground of everything true*" and thereby surely the key to understanding political structure, the syllogism is essentially mentioned only *once* in the complete text – this is in relation to a discussion of "the Estates" in relation to the "mediating" role they play between the government and the people considered in their abstract individuality. Thus in the remark to §302, Hegel notes: "It is one of the most important insights of logic that a specific moment which, when it stands in opposition, has the position of an extreme, loses this quality and becomes an *organic* moment by being simultaneously a *mean*" (Hegel 1991a: §302R). This idea is expanded upon in §304. Considered in themselves, the estates are as just as capable of hostility to the monarch as they are of cooperation and this "abstract position becomes a rational relation (i.e., a syllogism [*zum Schlusse*] ...) only when its *mediation* comes into existence" (Hegel 1991a: §304). It would seem that it is the ubiquity of the syllogism here that leads to its invisibility, but why is what is generally known as an *inferential dynamic*

among judgements a model for *everything that exists?* Moreover, the syllogism of inquiry as presented in *The Science of Logic* is a formidably complex
structure. Surely more needs to be said.

There is no getting around the fact that Hegel's "logical" approach to
the achievement of a harmonious unity among the differing parts of
a political community is idiosyncratic. To the modern mind, the way
logic features in, say, Hobbes's approach to the role of reason in communal
life will be more familiar and immediately understandable. If creatures like
bees and ants, Hobbes asks rhetorically, can "live socially with another . . .
some man may perhaps desire to know why mankind cannot do the same"
(Hobbes 1994: Pt II, ch. xvii, 6). He answers that the agreement of social
non-human creatures is natural, whereas "that of men is by covenant only",
which, being artificial requires a "common power to keep them in awe, and
to direct their actions to the common benefit" (Hobbes 1994: Pt II, ch. xvii,
12). The group of humans must, therefore, erect a "Mortal God" who "hath
the use of so much power and strength conferred on him that by terror
thereof he is enabled to conform the wills of them all to peace at home and
mutual aid against their enemies abroad" (Hobbes 1994: Pt II, ch. xvii, 13).
The "logic" operative here is that which Hegel will denounce as a type of
instrumental use of the "mere understanding" (*der Verstand*). Each individual purported employs their capacity for reasoning to arrive at the
realization that a more preferable existence is to be achieved by the
surrender of their individual powers to an artificial external power capable
of controlling the disruptive effects of the passions driving human conduct.
Against this, Hegel appeals to something completely different when he
brings reason and logic into consideration. Reason cannot be reduced to
the *subjective* reasonings of individuals, nor is the state some external power
to be reckoned with in those reasonings. Rather, the structures and processes
that are conventionally interpreted as configurations among or movements
between subjective judgements in Aristotle's logic – "syllogisms" – are
treated as structures or processes at work within the world itself. This
thought has something of the way in which the Stoics, say, thought of
"nous" as coursing through the world, or the Neoplatonists conceived of
a world soul. It is in this ontological sense that they are meant to provide
the model upon which the institutional structure of the political community is to be conceived.[1] Exactly why Hegel has chosen not only the
general *language* of Aristotle's syllogistic but even details such as the

---

[1] Hobbes summed up his attitude to the use of Aristotelian syllogisms in verse: "I, tho' slowly Learn,
and then dispense / With them, and prove things after my own sense" (Hobbes 1994, lv).

"figures" and "modes" of such syllogisms can seem totally mysterious. In order to better understand Hegel's motivation here, I want to turn to what he has to say about this notion when reflecting on the achievements and limitations of the thought of Plato and Aristotle in the *Lectures on the History of Philosophy*.

In Hegel's discussion of Plato we find the inquisitional conception of logic or "dialectic" as a dynamic of inquiry discussed along with the stranger "objective" or "ontological" approach in Hegel's accounts of two distinctive Platonic texts: the first is the well-known discussion of the "Divided Line" in Plato's *Republic*, Book 6, and the second, the account of the forming of the cosmos in *Timaeus*. In the first Hegel identifies those rules of inquiry dealing with definition, classification and inference to which he had refered in the Preface of *The Philosophy of Right* in relation to the broader Platonic dialectic: "Plato embraced sensible consciousness and especially sensible representations, opinions and immediate knowing, under the term *dóxa* (opinion). Midway between *dóxa* (opinion) and science in and for itself there lies argumentative cognition, inferential reflection or reflective cognition which develops for itself universal categories or classes. But the highest [knowing] is *noesis*, thinking in and for itself" (Hegel 2006: 188). It is significant here that, as the translator of this edition notes, "Hegel's account of the Divided Line here reduces Plato's four modes of apprehension to three ... he combines the last two as *dóxa* (opinion), which he links with what, in discussing recent philosophy, he calls 'immediate knowing'" (Hegel 2006: 188 n. 35). This could be read simply as Hegel taking liberties with the text – a type of "creative misreading" designed to align Plato's views with his own dialectical triads in a style of which Hegel is sometimes accused. I believe that there may be something deeper at issue here, however, but before we can pursue this further we need to examine some of the details of Socrates' strange lesson of the Divided Line.

In this famous set piece that goes together with the discussions of the sun and the cave, Socrates asks Glaucon to imagine a line that is divided into two unequal parts representing the visible and intelligible realms, respectively. The text does not provide a diagram, but it has generally been represented by a vertical line with the smaller lower segment representing the visible realm and the upper larger segment the intelligible realm. Socrates then asks Glaucon to divide both segments "in the same ratio as the line". The four sections of the line will now be taken to represent different cognitive attitudes onto the world – two to the visible world, two to the intelligible – together with the distinct types of intentional objects that are correlated with those attitudes. Together with this, it is clear that the apparently increasing lengths of the segments from below upwards are meant to be understood as proportional to the relative degrees of *clarity* of those four forms of cognition. From below upwards, these segments represent (in the words of the Grube–Reeve translation) imagination (*eikasia*), belief (*pistis*), thought (*dianoia*) and understanding (*noesis*) (Plato 1997: *Republic VI*).[2] In *dianoia*, Socrates explains, the soul "using as images the things that were imitated before" that is, the objects of *pistis*, "is forced to investigate from hypotheses, proceeding not to a first principle but to a conclusion" (Plato 1997: *Republic VI*, 510b). In the following paragraph Plato makes it clear that the "hypothetical" reasoning of *dianoia* is mathematical – that is, geometry and arithmetic or "calculation" (Plato 1997: *Republic VI*, 510c). In contrast, *noesis* "makes its way to a first principle that is *not* a hypothesis, proceeding from a hypothesis but without the images used in the previous subsection, using forms themselves and making its investigation through them" (Plato 1997: *Republic VI*, 510b).

What may *not* be apparent to the modern reader of this passage is that when the diagram is actually constructed in the way in which Socrates instructs Glaucon, the sections representing *pistis* and *dianoia* turn out to be of equal length, confounding the idea that these attitudes are meant to be contrasted as of *increasing* clarity (Foley 2008). The fact of this, however, and its significance, would surely not have been lost on Plato's colleagues in the Academy as this type of geometric discussion of proportions was central to the activities in which members of the Academy were major figures. When four magnitudes (*a*, *b*, *c*, *d*) are arranged in a pair of equal proportions (*a*/*b* = *c*/*d*) such that the middle magnitudes turn out to be the same (*b* = *c*), the terms are said to be arranged in the "geometric mean" or "continued mean".[3] So, rather than being represented with *four* terms (*a*/*b* = *c*/*d*) the sequence can be represented with three, for example, *a*/*b* = *b*/*d*. Were the Divided Line to be understood as divided according to the geometric mean, then we can see why Hegel might indeed have reduced its fourfold structure to a threefold one. There is good evidence,

---

[2] A similar distinction is found in Aristotle in *Topics* (Aristotle 1984: *Topics* Bk 1, 17, 108a). Probably the best-known version of this structure in Aristotle is in relation to justice in *Nichomachean Ethics*, book V, 3.

[3] Archytas, the Pythagorean mathematician and friend of Plato, had distinguished the geometric mean from other means in a work on music (Heath 1921: 85). In relation to the treatment of justice in *Nichomachean Ethics*, Aristotle points out that the proportion involved there is *not* the geometric or "continued" mean (Aristotle 1984: *Nichomachean Ethics*, Book V, 3, 1131b).

I believe, that Hegel could easily have understood it in this way, and this
comes first from the second text to which we will refer, Plato's *Timaeus*, in
which we find Hegel's syllogism discussed in the *ontological* way.

Plato describes the dialogue *Timaeus* as actually taking place the day
after Socrates' speech on the nature of the rational state in the *Republic*, and
the two are connected in complex and important ways.[4] In fact, Timaeus'
story of the creation of the cosmos will form the backdrop to the dialogue
of the third day in which *Critias* will recount the *actual history* of ancient
Athens as he learnt it from Solon, who in turn had learnt of it from
Egyptian sources, and this sequence of abstractly normative political
theory, natural philosophy and history must surely have been significant
for Hegel. In fact, it seems to have been similarly significant for *Plato*, as in
the *Timaeus* he has Socrates expressing dissatisfaction with his story of the
previous day, that is, the account of the just state given in the *Republic*.[5]
"I'd like to go on now and tell you what I've come to feel about the political
structure we've described. My feelings are like those of a man who gazes
upon magnificent looking animals, whether they're animals in a painting
or even actually alive but standing still, and who then finds himself longing
to look at them in motion or engaged in some struggle or conflict that
seems to show off their distinctive physical qualities. I felt the same thing
about the city we've described. I'd love to see our city distinguish itself in
the way it goes to war and in the way it pursues the war; that it deals with
the other cities, one after another, in ways that reflect positively on its own
education and training, both in word and deed – that is, both in how it
behaves toward them and how it negotiates with them" (Plato 1997:
Timaeus 19b–c). Here Socrates seems to be *bringing into question* the radical
distinction between the visible and intelligible realms given two days
earlier. He wants to bring to bear an *empirically obtained* account of the
actual Athens, that is, one based in *pistis*, to test the conceptually generated
account of the good state he had delivered two days earlier. Conveniently,
Critias is able to help out with his historical account of Athens as it had
been (9,000 years earlier!) during its war against the then island state of
Atlantis, but all agree that before he speaks it would be good to hear from
Timaeus, a natural philosopher from the Italian city of Locri, who is an
"expert in astronomy and [who] has made it his main business to know the
nature of the universe". Timaeus will begin with "the origin of the

---

[4] It is widely recognized, however, that the *Timaeus* and *Critias* were written during a later period than
the *Republic*, and may reflect changes in Plato's earlier theory of the forms.
[5] This, of course, may reflect a change in Plato's views over the period between the writing of these
works.

universe" and end with "the nature of human beings" (Plato 1997: *Timaeus* 27b), and on the basis of this general account of human nature, Critias will *then* be able to show such human beings, now in the form as *actual Athenian citizens* (Plato 1997: *Timaeus* 27a–b).

In Timaeus' speech Hegel dwells on one particular episode in some detail, sometimes quoting, sometimes paraphrasing and sometimes commenting on it. Here it is worth quoting an entire paragraph from a modern English translation:

> Now that which comes to be must have bodily form, and be both visible and tangible, but nothing could ever become visible apart from fire, nor tangible without something solid, nor solid without earth. That is why, as he began to put the body of the universe together, the god came to make it out of fire and earth. But it isn't possible to combine two things well all by themselves, without a third; there has to be some bond between the two that unites them. Now the best bond is one that really and truly makes a unity of itself together with the things bonded by it, and this in the nature of things is best accomplished by proportion. For whenever of three numbers which are either solids or squares the middle term between any two of them is such that what the first term is to it, it is to the last, and, conversely, what the last term is to the middle, it is to the first, then, since the middle term turns out to be both first and last, and the last and the first likewise both turn out to be the middle terms, they will all of necessity turn out to have the same relationship to each other, and, given this, will all be unified. (Plato 1997, *Timaeus* 31b–32a)

Hegel makes some notable comments. After the description of "the best bond ... that really and truly makes a unity of itself together with the things bonded by it" he adds: "This is profound, since it contains the Concept, the Idea" (Hegel 1970–1: 19:89).[6] Then, after the concluding sentence, he adds: "This is excellent; we still retain this in philosophy. This diremption which proceeds from Plato is the syllogism [*der Schluss*], which is known from the realm of logic [*der aus dem Logischen bekannt ist*]. This syllogism retains the form, as it appears in the familiar syllogistic [*gewöhnlichen Syllogismus*], but as the rational [*als das Vernünftige*]" (Hegel 1970–1: 19:90). Moreover, after quoting Plato's account of the relations between the three bonded numbers, Hegel inserts the equation "$a : b = b : c$", not only signalling his awareness of the geometric mean, but also identifying it with "the syllogism" which is the genuinely dialectical or

---

[6] I have here used the Moldenhauer and Michel edition of the *Vorlesungen ueber die Geschichte der Philosophie* rather than the text of the 1825/6 lectures as it is more explicit as to where Hegel quotes and where he adds a comment. The translation is my own.

"rational" syllogism and which shares its form with the more familiar *formal* syllogism of Aristotle. Armed with this information, let us now return to the discussion of the Divided Line.

It is well known that there exists a type of contradiction in Plato's account of the Divided Line between the fourfold distinction involved when the line was merely described and the effectively threefold structure produced when the line was *actually* constructed according to Socrates' instructions (Foley 2008). Attempts to resolve this problem have led to the suggestion that the actual proportions produced in the Divided Line were even more specific than the ones described in terms of the "geometric mean", that of "division in extreme and mean ratio"; see Brumbaugh (1954), Gibson (1955) and, more recently, Fossa and Erickson (2005).

This division of a line (henceforth "DEMR"), appearing in Euclid's *Elements*, is what *later* came to be called the "golden section", or "divine proportion", and identified as supposedly embodying some universal aesthetic norm found throughout the universe.[7] A type of mystically motivated interest in the section had developed from the Middle Ages, and enthusiastic affirmations of its properties have recurred through to the present. In classical Greece, the DEMR does seems to have been associated with the Pythagorean cult, especially with its concern with "harmonic" proportions, but it was also a significant mathematical object itself and linked to the discovery of the *irrational* numbers – that is, numbers like $\sqrt{2}$ that cannot be represented as a ratio of two whole natural numbers. Some advocates of the idea that Plato had been alluding to the DEMR in the Divided Line passage point to the role played by the academician Eudoxus in this context (Fossa and Erickson 2005).

As we are interested in Hegel's understanding of Plato, we can disregard the complex interpretative questions as to what *Plato* himself had intended with the Divided Line, but the juxtaposition of the passages from *The Republic* and *Timaeus*, I think, strongly suggests that *Hegel* at least identified the geometric mean as at the heart of the Platonic syllogism in both of its inquisitional and ontological dimensions. It is tempting to think that he might easily have had the DEMR in mind as well.[8] Hegel had been clearly aware of the value placed on musical proportions by the Pythagoreans, and

[7] For a comprehensive account of the DEMR free from the hyperbole that characterizes much of this literature see especially Herz-Fischler (1998).
[8] We know that he was an admirer of Kepler's geometric approach to cosmology, which drew upon the "Platonic solids" – the construction of which was bound up with the DEMR. Indeed, Kepler had been explicit about his own high estimation of the properties of this division (Herz-Fischler 1998: 173).

of the way in which the harmonious idea of beautiful proportion had become central to the "classical" aesthetics of the Greeks.[9] However, there is little to suggest from this that Hegel was an enthusiast for Pythagorean number mysticism. Indeed, in Hegel's account everything hangs on the *shortcomings* of the Parmenidean numerical approach to the world – an approach with which he saw Plato as breaking, although neither completely nor entirely successfully. This was part of the contradiction from which Plato's objective syllogism had to be rescued.

Regardless of whether Hegel had the DEMR in mind, it is significant for his account of Plato's movement beyond Pythagorean numerical metaphysics. The Pythagoreans had, as Hegel points out in his discussion in the *Lectures on the History of Philosophy*, a numerical ontology: "Number is the being of things, and the organization of the universe is a system of numbers and numerical relationships" (Hegel 2006: 38). While Plato and Aristotle had taken much from the Pythagoreans, their "abandonment of determination by number", says Hegel, "is the main thing" (Hegel 2006: 39), and the DEMR was significant in this context.

Pythagoras is typically associated with Pythagoras' Theorem, which states that for a right-angle triangle the square of the hypotenuse is equal to the sum of the squares of the other two sides. From this it can be shown that the length of the hypotenuse is thereby *not commensurable* with the lengths of the other sides of the triangle. For example, for a right-angle triangle with sides of length 1 unit, the hypotenuse will equal $\sqrt{2}$ units, and the Pythagoreans had discovered a proof showing that $\sqrt{2}$ cannot be expressed by a ratio of two natural numbers (Heath 1921: 90–1). But this directly *refuted* the Pythagorean conception of number in which *all* magnitudes were understood as "commensurable" because generated from the monad (or "monas", unit) "1" by which they could be "measured".[10] The same incommensurability of line segments is *also* able to be shown from the DEMR,[11] and some have linked the discovery of incommensurability to *it* rather than "Pythagoras' Theorem" itself (Herz-Fischler 1998: 70).

The discovery of the irrationals was a turning point in Greek mathematics, and it was Eudoxus of Cnidus, a leading member of the Academy and

---

[9] For example, in his discussion of Greek architecture he discusses how it was "kept to the most beautiful proportions" and to the "beautiful mean" (Hegel 1975: II:664–5), and mentions a "secret eurythmy discovered above all by the just sense of the Greeks" (Hegel 1975: II:663).

[10] This is more usually described in terms of the discovery of the "irrational" numbers, but the problem from the point of view of the Pythagoreans was that of commensurability – that is, that two magnitudes could not have a common "measure", the Pythagorean unit or monad.

[11] Written out as a geometric mean (*a:b :: b:c*), the DEMR can be represented thus: $2{:}1 + \sqrt{5} :: 1 + \sqrt{5} :: 3 + \sqrt{5}$.

friend of Plato, who responded to the collapse of the Pythagorean numeri-
cism by *reconceptualizing* the nature of number itself, defining it as the
"determinate magnitude" of "proportion". That is, from the new point of
view, determinate magnitude or "number" could be conceived of as being
determinate *without* being generated from the monad, as demanded by the
Pythagoreans. The ratio of the diagonal of a square of unit sides, for
example, could be thought determinate by being defined *geometrically* by
the ratio existing between those actual line segments conceived as proper
mathematical objects (Heath 1921: 69). This transition from the
Pythagorean to the Eudoxean reconceptualization of number or "quantity"
is treated by Hegel in terms of the distinction between the "quantum" and
"measure" that make up the final categories of the "Logic of Being" in the
Objective Logic and effectively set up the transition from the Logic of
Being to the Logic of Essence. That is, for Hegel its significance was not
restricted to "philosophy of mathematics" in any narrow sense. To the
Pythagoreans numbers were significant because they were conceived as
composed of metaphysically ultimate monads, and so the transition *from*
this restricted conception of magnitude to the broader *comparative* determination had deep metaphysical ramifications. As the Logic of Essence
reflects more the Aristotelian metaphysics, Hegel seems to have thought of
Aristotle's approach as being linked to Eudoxus' criticism of the
Pythagoreans. Indeed, Aristotle had made extensive use of cross-genus
"analogies" seemingly on the basis of Eudoxus' non-Pythagorean use of
proportion (Olshewsky 1968; Heath 1949: 43–4), and had developed his
syllogistic in an intellectual environment drenched in such geometrical
issues (e.g. Lasserre 1964: chapter 5). This move from the Pythagorean to
the Eudoxean conception of magnitude, I suggest, might be understood as
significant for Aristotle's syllogistic as well.

10.2   From Aristotle's Inquisitional Syllogistic to Hegel's Reconstruction of Logic as Rational Science

It is sometimes assumed that the formal syllogistic that Hegel presents in the
Subjective Logic of *The Science of Logic* is simply Aristotle's, but it is not.
Aristotelian syllogisms are inferences from two premises to a conclusion in
which the "mean" or "middle term" of the premises (Aristotle's word is the
same as that found in the "geometric mean") can be thought of as binding,
into the *conclusion*, the subject of one premise and the predicate of the other.
The most obvious way in which Hegel's syllogisms depart from Aristotle's is
that the subject and predicate terms of Hegel's judgements can be determined

as any of *three* "quantities", those of *universality, particularity* and *singularity.*
But *singular judgments* – that is, judgements with a *singular* subject such as
"Socrates runs" – had no legitimate place in Aristotle's syllogisms because the
middle term of syllogisms had to play the role of subject in one premise and
predicate in the other,[12] and singular terms, according to Aristotle, could not
be predicates (Aristotle 1984: *Prior Analytics* Bk I, 43a). That is, the term
'Socrates' could not be predicated *of* some further term in the way that 'runs'
can be predicated of 'Socrates'. Thus "officially" the two premises of
Aristotelian syllogisms must have the form of either a universal judgement
(e.g. "All Greeks are mortal") or a particular judgement (e.g. "Some Greeks
run"), because the subject terms of both contain common, and thus predic-
able, names.[13] This would be seen as a limitation by subsequent logicians,
especially in the Middle Ages, and various ways of bringing reference to *specific*
individuals such as by the use of proper names were employed. One was to
treat such singular terms *as* universals, for example, treating the name
"Socrates", as Quine would later do, as a verb, "socratizes". Another was to
treat singular terms as *particulars,* "Socrates" being treated essentially as "some
Socrates" on the model of "some Greek". But the general point is that, for
Aristotle, the term 'Socrates' did not fit into the dynamics of the syllogistic in
a way that recalls the fact that *Socrates, qua* introducer of the individualistic
principle of subjectivity, did not fit into the dynamics of Greek *Sittlichkeit.*[14]

In particular, it was Leibniz who, building on the work of the nominal-
ists, had fashioned the first "symbolic" or "mathematical" logic, reintrodu-
cing the monadic category of singularity back into the Aristotelian
syllogistic. This was the basis of Gottfried Ploucquet's formal syllogistic

[12] While this is strictly true only of Aristotle's *first figure* syllogisms, because for him the proofs
of second and third figure syllogisms require reduction to syllogisms in the first figure, it is indirectly
true of all syllogisms.

[13] These were later set out in the "square of opposition" based on Aristotle's account in *De*
Interpretatione. Aristotle does occasionally give examples with singular judgements as appearing in
the conclusion, but these are in conflict with the general principles of the syllogistic.

[14] We might see here parallels between Aristotle's logic and Eudoxus' transformed number system as
Aristotle was aware of the general significance of Eudoxus' theory of proportion. Eudoxus' solution
to the Pythagorean problem of incommensurable numbers had been to introduce a conception of
magnitude that was irreducibly *comparative* and that *did not rely* on actual numerical specification.
I suggest that in Aristotle's formal syllogistic judgements with subject terms "all As", "Some As" and
"No As" are to be understood as *internally* related as displayed by the square of opposition. Strictly
considered, such judgements *cannot* be thought of as "commensurable" with singular judgements –
the exclusion of singular judgements eliminating any external *common measure,* as it were, relating
universal and particular judgements. From this point of view, "Some Greeks are philosophers" *could*
not be understood as a shorthand way of expressing a conjunction such as "Thales is a philosopher,
and Socrates is a philosopher, and Plato is a philosopher . . . ." in the way this was understood by
medieval nominalist logicians, for example.

taught at Tübingen when Hegel was a student there with its categories universality, particularity *and singularity* (Ploucquet 2006: §§11–13, 19–21). But in turn this effectively *undermined* the internal relations that allowed the Aristotelian syllogistic to function, as Hegel made clear in his comments on the "mathematical syllogism" (Hegel 2010a: 602–7, 12.104–10). This was the lamentable situation into which logic had fallen about which Hegel had written in the Preface to the *Philosophy of Right*.

These issues are too complex to try to sort out in a context such as this, but what is important to keep in mind is that in his logic Hegel was faced with the problem of making the different "syllogisms" – the ontological syllogism of Plato and Aristotle's syllogism of inquiry – relevant to the ways of thought of a historical community in which the "principle of subjectivity", which appealed to a type of Parmenidean monadic conception of the individual subject, had become a basic principle. The broad question we might consider here is how this was to affect the way in which, from Hegel's point of view, the inquisitional and ontological syllogisms might be conceived and how they might be related.

10.3   Issues of Form and Content in Hegel's *Science of Logic*

Commentators on Hegel's *Science of Logic* standardly warn the reader that by "logic" Hegel does not mean logic in the modern sense of a formal logic concerning judgements capable of truth or falsity and inferences capable of validity or non-validity. Rather, it is usually said, by 'logic' Hegel means 'metaphysics'. This, however, is only partially true. We might say that it focuses on the Platonic "ontological" side of the syllogism at the expense of the Aristotelian inquisitional side. Analogously, many interpreters effectively ignore the significance of Hegel's treatment of formal logic in the Subjective Logic of Volume Two of the *Science of Logic*.[15] But ignoring the question of the role played by any inquisitional syllogistic in Hegel's overall speculative logic can easily lead to misunderstandings of the implications his logic has for his metaphysics or, in this case, political ontology.

The Science of Logic traces the fate of "thought-determinations" that start with the most immediate and obvious – "being" – and the fate of this category can be taken as a general model for how this series of thought-determinations is generated. "Being" can be made determinate only by virtue of its contrasting relation with its opposite, "nothing" (Hegel 2010a:

---

[15] The shortcomings of approaches that ignore or misconstrue Hegel's attitude to formal logic are made clear by Elena Ficara in Ficara (2019).

59, 21.69), but *as* the most fundamental category there is nothing further that can be said of being to *separate it* from nothing. The distinction collapses but is rescued by a further third category, "becoming", understood as containing "being" and "nothing" as its "moments". In relation to this new starting point, "becoming" undergoes the same general fate, leading into a series of thought-determinations in which each is replaced by a successor, the process grinding on until it finally stops at "the Idea", "the *adequate concept*, the objectively *true*, or the *true as such*" (Hegel 2010a: 670, 12.173). From the Idea as the result of the *Logic*, we are now somehow meant to understand how this dialectic progresses into those areas of philosophy with more determinate content, first, the philosophy of nature, and then, the philosophy of spirit, in the middle of which we find "objective spirit", the realm of the political thought with which we are primarily engaged.

One question that divides Hegel interpreters is as follows: are the thought-determinations, such as "being", "becoming" and so on, *basically* determinations of *thought* in the sense in which Kantian "categories" are considered, or determinations of *being*, more or less in the way that Aristotle had thought of his list of categories in *Categories*? Or, if they are *both*, how are these structures related? Effectively, these questions are just ways of asking how we should think of "the syllogism" considered *ontologically* and *inquisitionally*. To answer this we should look to the relation between what Hegel describes as the "objective" and "subjective" logics that make up *The Science of Logic*'s volumes I and II, respectively. Objective Logic, which traces the thought determinations from "being" to "actuality", clearly aligns with the project of ontological logic, and Subjective Logic, which has Hegel's account of concepts, judgements and syllogisms and which starts from broadly Kantian considerations, with inquisitional logic. But Hegel's account of such subjective syllogisms concludes by passing over into a new form of "objectivity", the categories of which then unfold until concluding with "the Idea".

Given Hegel's general framework in which two opposing categories are resolved into some third, we should expect that the concluding account of syllogistic objectivity should hold together the two earlier abstractly opposed versions, and this, I suggest, is just the case. What we need to grasp is exactly how Hegel thinks that an initially *formal* account of judgements and syllogisms can *create* a content, and the general direction of an answer here, I believe, is to be found in the role played by *singular judgements* in the transformed version of the Aristotelian syllogistic found in Hegel's Subjective Logic.

What we see then in the account of judgement and syllogism in the Subjective Logic is a process that Hegel had initially spoken of in terms of the capacity for thought to "*determine* itself, that is to give itself a content" (Hegel 2010a: 42, 21.48). His account of judgements and syllogisms will thus involve an account of the elaboration of *objects* with properties and relations that are made determinate within those structures we call judgements and syllogisms, and that will be determined in terms of the logical forms found there. But in these accounts of judgement we will see how it is not only determinate *objects* that are generated; so too will the process described equivalently determine *intentional subjects* for whom those objects are determinate. That is, while it is true that, as many interpreters of Hegel's logic point out, Hegel will not ultimately mean by "judgement" and "syllogism" what these terms commonly mean in the history of logic, but rather, something like complex worldly arrangements of things, these complex worldly arrangements will nevertheless necessarily include beings – judging and syllogizing agents – who must be considered as an essential part of this objective reality and as given shape within it.

The idea that judgements might have contents that include concrete *objects* can sound mysterious, and even more mysterious is the idea that they may *create* those contents, but I suggest that this is not as strange to logic, nor as counter-intuitive, as it may at first seem. It is strange only against the background of the approach to logic which has become dominant for about the last 100 years. Even Bertrand Russell, for example, in 1904, had believed that a judgement made about Mont Blanc actually contained, as a component, *Mont Blanc*. This had sounded outrageous to his correspondent, Gottlob Frege, for whom what a judgement asserted – its "content" – had to be something *abstract* – a "proposition", *qua* abstract object capable of truth or falsity (Frege 1980: 163). Russell himself would soon adopt an approach closer to Frege, establishing the modern paradigm of formal logic, but in 1904 he didn't think his proposal an outrage to common-sense, regarding the content of the judgement as "a certain complex (an objective proposition, one might say) in which Mont Blanc is itself a component part" (Frege 1980: 169). This is *something like the sense* in which, I propose, Hegel treats some judgements as having *concrete contents*. But Hegel would link these concrete objects to similarly concrete *agents* doing the judging, and a similar move is found more recently within *modal logic*.

Again, it is useful to appeal to Russell who, by 1906, had switched to Frege's view and criticized the idea that objects could be components of judgement contents. This is seen in a review of a book by the logician

Hugh MacColl, who had proposed that some judgements could be some-times true and sometimes false. MacColl gave as an example the everyday judgement "Mrs Brown is not at home", but Russell objected that such a sentence was *not* a proper judgement (Russell 1906: 257). It could be *made* a proper judgement by treating it as a *predicate* that could be said of a time *x* that "is true for some values of *x* and false for others" (Russell 1906: 257).[16] Russell won this battle, but the war was resumed half a century later when the logician Arthur Prior would argue against the elimination of "tensed" judgements, judgements with truth-values relative to a context that included the judge's temporal act of judging (Prior 1957).[17]

Elsewhere I have argued that, in his account of judgements and syllo-gisms, Hegel attempted to give a role to these opposed Priorian (de-re) and Russellian (de-dicto) judgement structures (Redding 2019), and that his accounts of judgement and inference that are woven through the Subjective Logic show the evolution of *concrete contents* that we might think of as something like those object-involving complexes alluded to by Russell in 1904 that are understood as containing places for specifically located "subjects". These complexes are aspects of the objective world in which agents and objects in that world are bound together in those complex but determinate ways Hegel calls "judgements" and "syllogisms". This is the metaphysical content that has been produced by the subjective logic and that will be made more determinate in the following parts of the *Encyclopedia*.

10.4 Conclusion: Necessity and Contingency in the Institutions of the Modern Polity

When the focus is placed unilaterally on Hegel's "ontological" syllogisms it is easy to think of Hegel as, like Plato, treating conceptual structures as somehow "out there", written into the fabric of reality and, in the context of objective spirit, dictating the institutional structures that the evolving forms of social life must take. On such a view, one gets the impression of some type of eternal logical necessity lying behind the institutions which help define us as individuals. But attention to the role of singularity both in the ontological dimension and in the inquisitional dimension of Hegel's logic as well as to the relation of objective and subjective logics in his final

---

[16] Strangely, on Russell's translation, the judgement is no longer *about* Mrs Brown and her where-abouts. It is about a point of time and whether or not it has a particular property – whether or not Mrs Brown is home *at* that time.

[17] On the hidden Hegelian background to Prior's logic see Redding (2017).

conception of "objectivity" shows this common picture to be very misleading. The objective "syllogisms" of modern institutional life are no longer merely universal forces that shape the individuals existing within them as their "particular" moments. Those institutions are *also* created and recreated within the human community in ways that have come to rely on the reasoned evaluations of individuals who grasp themselves not only in terms of their institutional roles but also in their "singular" and "subjective" existences. Thus, in modern life, the increasing tendency has been for such individuals to challenge the normativity of given institutional arrangements in which they exist in response to the inadequacies they experience within them. Modern institutions, *unlike* ancient ones, are thus, in this sense, embedded in the argumentative interactions of those shaped by them but who can also reflect on them, call them into question, propose alternatives and so on. This, I suggest, is not in conflict with Hegel's conception of the relation of logic to objective spirit, but an expression of it.

This means that from Hegel's own *logical* perspective we must regard his concrete suggestions as to the "right" institutions for the modern state as it has continued to take shape as no more than possible exemplifications of its logical structure. Such possibilities are no more than indeterminate specifications awaiting actualization and must stand the actual test of those who come to live within them. Thus, those institutions favoured by Hegel that have come to be challenged, such as the bourgeois family with its gendered division of labour, for example, should not be taken as reflecting a shortcoming of his "system" or the logic on which it is based. Here we might appeal to the type of stance taken by Socrates *the day after* giving his speech on the republic. We must look to the history of our *actual* institutions since Hegel's time to test their adequacy as instantiations of "syllogisms".

CHAPTER 11

Taking the System Seriously
On the Importance of "Objective Spirit" for Hegel's
Philosophy of Right

Thom Brooks

11.1 Introduction

Perhaps the biggest challenge facing Hegel scholars is not grappling with his complex, technical vocabulary, but rather understanding the relevance of the systematic nature of his philosophy. With most philosophers – from Plato to Rawls and beyond – we might find commonalities or changes in view across texts, such as between the earlier or later Platonic writings of the *Crito* versus the *Laws* or Rawls's change of mind about the fact of pluralism leading him to recast *A Theory of Justice* in publishing *Political Liberalism* (see Plato 1997; Rawls 1971, 1993, 2001; Brooks and Nussbaum 2015). In contrast, the lecture outlines that make up Hegel's *Encyclopedia of the Philosophical Sciences* were published throughout his academic career from beginning to end, unfolding a single presentation of his systematic philosophy, with each part a representation of the same, mature overall picture.

This makes the task of interpreting any part of Hegel's philosophy different from other non-systematic philosophers. Each of Hegel's texts making up his *Encyclopaedia* are not intended to be understood separately from this wider philosophical system. This is no less true with Hegel's *Philosophy of Right*, which is explicitly clear from numerous reminders throughout this work (Hegel 1991a: §§2R, 3R, 4R, 7R, 8R, 26R, 31, 31R, 33R, 34R, 48R, 57R, 78, 88, 95, 148R, 161, 163R, 181, 256R, 258R, 270R, 278, 279R, 280R, 281R, 302R, 324R).[1] The frequent mentions of how the system is important for

---

[1] I shall use the conventional abbreviations of "R" for "Remarks" and "A" for "Additions." Remarks refer to comments added in a later edition of both his *Philosophy of Right* and *Philosophy of Mind*. Additions refer to the lecture notes of Hotho and Gans that were inserted by T. M. Knox into different sections of the *Philosophy of Right* and *Philosophy of Mind*.

understanding the *Philosophy of Right* in 'Remarks' published in the final edition of this text underscore Hegel's commitment to how his views should be comprehended. Hegel clearly intended his work – including the *Philosophy of Right* – to have a systematic reading where each part took seriously its place within the larger philosophical system (Brooks 2007, 2012a, 2013).

Yet, there has been a temptation to interpret Hegel's work non-systematically – in other words, reading a text independently of any connection to Hegel's other texts – like we might for most other philosophers. These roots can be found more than half a century ago in the highly influential work of Z. A. Pełczyński. He was central in popularizing the study of Hegel's political thought, and was a founder of the Hegel Society of Great Britain, which originally met at his institutional home of Pembroke College, Oxford. In his preface to the first collection in English of Hegel's political essays, Pełcyński notes that these writings "are a most valuable supplement to the *Philosophy of Right* and the *Philosophy of History* . . . being relatively free from speculative elements and philosophical jargon they provide in some ways a clearer insight into Hegel's basic political ideas than the major works" (Pelczynski 1964: 1). The elements and jargon dismissively characterized refer to Hegel's philosophical system beyond his political treatise the *Philosophy of Right*. Pełcyńzski says: "Apparently, Hegel thought that only by transposing politics to the metaphysical plane and giving his concerns a speculative underpinning could he establish their validity" (Pelczynski 1964: 136). This "speculative underpinning" is the *Encyclopaedia*, including its logic, which Hegel intended to provide a foundation for the unfolding of his philosophical system. For Pełczyński, the *Encyclopaedia* system and metaphysics were essentially synonymous and irrelevant for understanding Hegel's political ideas:

> Hegel's political thought can be read, understood and appreciated without having to come to terms with his metaphysics. Some of his assertions may seem less well-grounded than they might otherwise have been; some of his statements and beliefs may puzzle one; some intellectual curiosity may be unsatisfied when metaphysics is left out; a solid volume of political theory and political thinking will still remain. (Pelczynski 1964: 136–7)

The position is clear. Whatever Hegel's self-understanding or presentation of his project, the wider philosophical system of the *Encyclopaedia* is of no more philosophical interest than "some intellectual curiosity". To understand political writings like the *Philosophy of Right*, we need only go to that text itself. Doing otherwise and engaging with Hegel's metaphysics is unnecessary and unhelpful.

This non-metaphysical perspective has its roots in a non-systematic reading of Hegel's texts, where a work like the *Philosophy of Right* is thought best understood separately from the *Encyclopaedia* system of which Hegel claimed it was a part. The influential position of Pełczyński highlighted above is reproduced by many of the best-known commentators that have followed. In his *Hegel's Ethical Thought*, which popularized Hegel's work for a new generation of scholars (including me), Allen Wood says:

> By "philosophical foundations" I do not mean Hegel's speculative metaphysics ... If you decide to examine *those* foundations more closely, you know before long that you are in for a difficult and generally unrewarding time of it, at least from the standpoint of social and political theory. If you are sensible, you will try to avoid that. If you are not so sensible, you will humbug yourself into thinking there is some esoteric truth in Hegelian dialectical logic, which provides a hidden key to his social thought. (Wood 1990: xii)

While he concedes that Hegel "is the most methodologically self-conscious of all philosophers in the Western tradition", Wood claims there is "nothing" of philosophical interest for the study of his political ideas to be found in his wider system and Hegel's "great positive achievements as a philosopher do not lie where he thought they did, in his system of speculative logic" (Wood 1990: 5).

This chapter focuses on the specific link of the *Philosophy of Right* as an elaboration of the "Objective Spirit" section in the final part ("Philosophy of Spirit") in Hegel's *Encyclopaedia* philosophical system. The aim is to make clear the place of Objective Spirit within the system and how the *Philosophy of Right* further fleshes out this section of the *Encyclopaedia* and, in turn, cements their relation. Moreover, in demonstrating the concrete interconnection between Objective Spirit and the *Philosophy of Right*, it will be shown how the former helps us to better understand the latter. This will demonstrate that the study of Hegel's system – and our approach to a *systematic reading* of Hegel's texts – is neither "some intellectual curiosity" nor "humbug", but rather a more accurate and insightful interpretation of Hegel's political and social thought.

11.2 Where to Begin?

The first place to examine is the beginning of the *Philosophy of Right*. Its first section is a single sentence: "The subject-matter of *the philosophical science of right* is the *Idea of right* – the concept of right and its actualization"

(Hegel 1991a: §1). The second section clarifies this sentence by adding that "the science of right is *a part of philosophy*" where "its deduction is presupposed here and is to be taken as given" (Hegel 1991a: §2).

These first comments from the *Philosophy of Right*'s Introduction make clear that this text is not a stand-alone work. It should be understood in the light of a larger body of work – the *Encyclopaedia* – of which it is a component part and from which its "deduction" is presupposed. This is explicit in the first line that opens the book's Preface:

> This textbook is a more extensive, and in particular a more systematic, exposition of the same basic concepts which, in relation to this part of philosophy, are already contained in a previous work designed to accompany my lectures, namely my *Encyclopaedia of the Philosophical Sciences*. (Hegel 1991a: 9)

Both the *Philosophy of Right* and the *Encyclopaedia* are lecture outlines that Hegel would flesh out live in lectures (Pinkard 2001). In short, the *Philosophy of Right* is essentially a more elaborately detailed outline of a briefer outline found in the relevant section ("Objective Spirit") of the *Encyclopaedia* (see Hegel 1971: §§483–552). Hegel notes that it is from the "point of view" of the *Encyclopaedia* that he wishes the *Philosophy of Right* "to be *understood and judged*" (Hegel 1991a: 10). As a more elaborate outline of an outline, Hegel is also clear that it is a sketch that could be spelled out more than he has done. In his *Science of Logic*, he says: "I could not pretend that the method which I follow in this system of logic . . . is not capable of greater completeness, of much elaboration in detail" (Hegel 1969: 54). A more elaborate outline should be expected to provide additional, not less, development of the briefer outline it fleshed out – and potentially open to further specification and "greater completeness" itself.

In his Introduction to the *Philosophy of Right*, Hegel next clarifies that the idea of right is focused on the "Idea" of right which he explains is a "realm of actualized freedom" (Hegel 1991a: §4). The focus for the *Philosophy of Right* is in freedom in its fullest expression. The next few sections claim that freedom is a freedom of the will developing from a "universal" and "particular" to a will that is "free in itself" (Hegel 1991a: §10). But he also makes clear that such a progression only captures the development of freedom "in its concept" but not in actuality (Hegel 1991a: §10). What is meant is that we need some means of discerning where the exercise of our free will is an expression of our freedom and not an arbitrary impulse (Hegel 1991a: §15). So our aim is to grasp "the free will which wills the free will" (Hegel 1991a: §27). When we can understand this, we gain an understanding of something more concrete – and, for Hegel, more philosophically valuable – which is "right [*Recht*]" (Hegel 1991a: §29).

In turning to the *Philosophy of Spirit*, the first point we should notice is that while the *Philosophy of Right* presupposes there is a free will but seeks to establish how it can be free in "actuality" rather than an expression of animal-like impulse, or slave to one's passions, the section "Subjective Spirit" immediately preceding "Objective Spirit" is where Hegel establishes the arguments for why there is a free will in concept to later be examined in actuality. Hegel summarizes "Subjective Spirit" and its discussion of the free will both in the introduction to the *Philosophy of Right* and in the introduction to "Objective Spirit" – making explicit the systematic connections (Hegel 1971: §483, 1991a: §§4–28, 1995a: §§3–10). To understand why Hegel sets himself the task at hand requires coming to grips with his arguments in the *Philosophy of Spirit*.[2]

11.3 Why This Form – and Content?

After explaining that the aim of the *Philosophy of Right* is to understand "the free will which wills the free will", Hegel proceeds to outline the rest of the *Philosophy of Right* in three sections – Abstract Right, Morality, Ethical Life – saying little more in the Introduction than that this is a part of "the development of the Idea of the will in and for itself" that is "presupposed from speculative logic" (Hegel 1991a: §33, 33R).

Hegel presupposes a wide range of knowledge about other parts of his philosophical system that he treats at greater length elsewhere. This is especially the case with the content of his logic, which is the first part of his system and elaborated substantively in the *Science of Logic*. One aspect easy to overlook is that Hegel assumes his readers are already familiar with a large range of conceptual terminology that is presented and defined *before* the *Philosophy of Right* (and often not defined within the *Philosophy of Right* either). This terminology includes: "universal" (Hegel 1991c: 600–5, 612–18, 1991b: §§163, R, A1), "particular" (Hegel 1991c: 600–1, 605–18, 1991b: §§163, R, A1), "individual" (Hegel 1991c: 600–1, 612–22, 1991b: 163, R, A1), "actuality" (Hegel 1991c: 529–71, 1991b: §§142–59), "the Idea" (Hegel 1991c: 755–844, 1991b: §§213–44) and what has been translated into English as "sublation" (*Aufheben*) (Hegel 1991c: 106–8, 1991b: §§96A) among very many others.

---

[2] It should be noted that Hegel's lectures on the *Philosophy of Spirit* did not always include discussion of "Objective Mind" and material appearing later in that published outline, as evidenced in his lectures of 1827/8 (Hegel 2007b).

This fact raises a crucial point. Any proper grasp of the *Philosophy of Right* (or its outline in "Objective Spirit") simply must take the wider philosophical system seriously, if only as a philosophical dictionary presenting and explaining Hegel's technical vocabulary. If Hegel had not intended progress in the system to have an explanatory role as it develops, we would expect him to deduce concepts and define terms for each part of his system. Yet, he explicitly does not and, instead, presupposes that readers are familiar with earlier deductions and discussions which inform later parts of his system – supported by frequent reminders across his texts like the *Philosophy of Right*. To read the *Philosophy of Right* completely independently of Hegel's system and its logic leaves any interpreter having to work with incomplete definitions and presentations of complex terms from, in the words of Bertrand Russell, "the hardest to understand of all the great philosophers" (Russell 1945: 730). A systematic reading of Hegel's work is indispensable for this reason alone.

In fact, every substantive section raises new terminology. "Objective Spirit" (and the *Philosophy of Right*) is no different. This is where the concept of "right [*Recht*]" is first presented, defined and explained. Later discussions about right post-"Objective Spirit" and the *Philosophy of Right*, such as in the following section on the *Philosophy of History*, assume the reader will be familiar with such concepts as universal, particular, the Idea and now right among others. And so on as we proceed to the final substantive sections of the *Encyclopaedia*'s philosophical system. Each part presupposes a familiarity with the terminology and claims made in every preceding part. Diving in and out of one part to the exclusion of others risks any interpretation being mischaracterized.

Examples abound. For instance, many commentators have treated Hegel's sections entitled "Property", "Punishment" or "Morality" – to take but three – as encompassing his complete views on each. Let me take each in turn briefly to illustrate this point.

Hegel's section on property has been thought to show that property "is freedom" and requires no functional justification (Berry 1980: 97). Yet, Hegel's discussion is notoriously unlike most other defences of a right to property. This point is captured well by John Rawls, who notes correctly that Hegel's treatment is unusual as he "leaves aside any appeal to the advantages of private property . . . Nor does he appeal to what people might want to do with their property . . . Less obviously, Hegel doesn't appeal to a psychological need of persons for private property" – nor does Hegel talk about material needs, the economy or poverty (Rawls 2000: 343).

The reason is that the section "Property" simply introduces the concept; it does not exhaust its treatment. It is introduced as a means of showing the

first steps towards our grounding a free will in the free will of another –
through a mutual recognition of property – as an initial step towards
showing how a free will might will the free will. Later discussions about
material needs and a market economy presuppose this treatment, but they
come later and are too often overlooked (Brooks 2013: 29–38).

The section "Objective Spirit" that the *Philosophy of Right* elaborates
makes this point clear. It starts by noting its aim of realizing freedom "at
home with itself ... shaped into the actuality of a world" (Hegel 1971:
§484). Hegel argues that property "is a means" to an end (Hegel 1971:
§489). In trying to grasp the existence and exercise of my freedom in the
world, my appropriation of possessions external to me is a first, basic step.
But this analysis is limited to understanding "the realization of liberty" in
the world "intrinsically" (Hegel 1971: §§496–7). The discussion remains at
too early a stage for considering issues of needs, wants and labour because
we must first develop an understanding of the individuals in their immediate context as part of a family (see Hegel 1971: §322–4). The section
"Property" is fundamentally about freedom, not possessions or earning
a livelihood. A systematic reading of Hegel's arguments makes this clear by
showing how different parts of Hegel's texts are systematically interlinked.

Hegel's theory of punishment is an even clearer example. The most
influential interpretation is by David Cooper, which is explicit about how
one can grasp Hegel's theory of punishment entirely without going any
further than the section "Wrong [*Unrecht*]" in the *Philosophy of Right*'s first
section (Cooper 1971). Much of the argument for seeing Hegel as
a traditional retributivist is for using his own words – but incorrectly
thinking that Hegel's use of philosophical concepts and meanings is no
different from everyday commonplace usage by everybody else. For
example, Hegel does say that punishments are a "negation of a negation"
whose end is "the restoration of right" (Hegel 1991a: §§97A, 99). This
cancellation of crime is called "retribution" (Hegel 1991a: §101).

There are several reasons to believe Hegel's use of "retribution" is not
traditional – aside from the fact his technical philosophical vocabulary is
rarely orthodox. The first reason is that retribution is traditionally about
punishing criminals for their wrongdoing to the degree it is deserved. The
more evil the act, the greater the severity of punishment (Brooks 2012b).
Yet Hegel's discussion here (in the section "Abstract Right") is logically
prior to the state. It is a hypothetical sphere where there are no laws, no
police, no courts and no prisons.

A second reason to doubt that Hegel's use of the term "retribution" is
traditional is exposed by what he says of his theory that "it is not the crime

or punishments which change, but the relation between the two" (Hegel 1991a: §96A). This is an especially significant departure from mainstream retributivism. Following Kant, most are opposed to consequentialism: the social context is not a factor impacting on an individual's moral responsibility for what is deserved. Telling a lie is wrong whether or not it might save an innocent man's life.

This raises the question of how context matters. It is a point frequently missed as so few writing about Hegel on punishment look beyond that first section on "Wrong"; such is the lasting influence of Cooper's essay. When we look beyond this section, we see Hegel supporting an elaboration on how the relation between crime and punishment might change that is antithetical to retributivism:

> The fact that an injury to *one* member of society is an injury to *all* the others does not alter the nature of crime in terms of its concept, but in terms of its outward existence … its *danger to civil society* is a determination of its magnitude … This quality or magnitude varies, however, according to the *condition* of civil society. (Hegel 1991a: §218R)

Hegel goes on to explain that whether the state is in a time of peace or civil war matters to how crimes will be punished. A crime will receive a greater punishment relative to civil war because the right violated by the crime poses a more serious threat to the overall system of rights a legal order upholds than it would during peacetime. So an offender could receive greater or lesser punishment not according to his or her desert alone, but depending on a social context beyond his or her control. This is not retributivism in any conventional, or unconventional, sense.

Hegel's system and logic help us understand this better. In "Objective Spirit", Hegel is clear in discussing "Wrong" that, in this hypothetical sphere without laws, police, courts or prisons, there is no punishment established – any action taken by a wronged individual is no more than "revenge" (Hegel 1971: §500). The law – and setting punishments for its violation – has its "actuality" only in "the social state" which is to be developed later (Hegel 1971: §§502, 531). Hegel makes clear here, too, that "the greater stability of the legal state … gives rise to greater and more stable liberty" supporting more lenient punishments (Hegel 1971: §539).

But if this is no conventional retributivism, what kind of punishment might it be? Hegel's logic clarifies this point in a rarely cited passage:

> *Punishment,* for instance, has a variety of determinations: that it is retribution; and also a deterrent example, a deterring threat made by the law; and also a contribution to the self-awareness and betterment of the culprit. Each

of these different determinations has been regarded as the *ground of punishment*, on the ground that it is the essential determination, and by default the others, since they are different from it, have been regarded as only accidental. But the one determination which is assumed as ground does not amount to the whole punishment. (Hegel 1969: 405–6)

These comments make clear that Hegel did not believe we must choose between defending retributivism, deterrence or rehabilitation. Instead, each is a part of what a full theory of punishment should be about. The ground of punishment is retributivist insofar as an offender must deserve punishment for it to be justified. But punishment can take different forms, including as a deterrent or rehabilitative project, if this serves a wider aim of protecting and maintaining the wider system of rights (Brooks 2017a: 468). This more accurate, complex and potentially illuminating example of what we might call a "unified theory" of punishment – and not retributivism – is best uncovered through a systematic reading (Brooks 2012b, 2016, 2017b).

Finally, much ink is spilled trying to unpick Hegel's theory of morality – and, most especially, its famous (and famously brief) critique of Kant's theory of morality. A large part of the problem is scholars viewing Hegel's use of the term "morality" as if it were like that of anybody else. But this is far from true. The key distinction is that Hegel sees "morality" as a kind of artificial realm where we consider our relations to others abstractly and not in their concrete reality. Morality is at risk of being "without content" because of its nature (Hegel 1991a: §135).

In essence, his criticism – brief as it is – of Kant's moral law as "empty" singles Kant's moral theory out, but he could have made this criticism against almost anybody else – this is because Hegel does not just have a different view of which moral theory is best, but a different conception of what morality is about that is genuinely unique to him. And it is hardly fair to say that, because Kant sees himself as engaged in moral theorizing, therefore it is by nature inadequate – whereas if Kant had seen the same principled project as a kind of theorizing about "ethical life" (where we conceive of morality in the real world), this would somehow make it less objectionable. And yet that Hegel's project is different, in part, because he understands the entire sphere of morality in a technical, unique way tied to his philosophical system is a point that has gone missing from virtually every scholar touching on this much discussed topic. Hegel's understanding of "the moral point of view" is unique to him (Hegel 1991a: §105; Brooks 2013: 52–61).

"Objective Spirit" helps shed further light on this. Hegel notes there that, in his understanding, morality is a reflection "into itself" (Hegel 1971:

§§408A, 503). Moral thinking is an individual intellectual exercise we engage with in isolation from the world. Hegel describes the situation like this: "the good is thus reduced to the level of a mere 'may happen' for the agent, who can therefore decide on something opposite to the good, can be wicked" (Hegel 1971: §509). Without any mention of Kant directly or indirectly, Hegel says the "utterly abstract semblances" of morality must pass over into a new sphere where an individual's "identity with the good ... actualizes and develops it" (Hegel 1971: §512). The problem with morality is mostly down to the very specific and unique way Hegel characterizes it as a total intellectual endeavour apart from the world – and as a very different enterprise from "Ethical Life", where we weigh up what might happen from our free choices, but in the knowledge that we do so from within a specific context of actuality (Hegel 1971: §514). While Hegel's view on morality might be best known for its brief critique of Kant's empty formalism, it is a critique he might have essentially made of just about any other moral theory *qua* moral theory – and "Objective Spirit" helps us see this point more clearly. There is a systematic connection between logic, morality and ethical life.

All three examples have a common core. Each of them highlights illustrations where our reading of Hegel in a traditional way – either taking a section out of context or considering only the *Philosophy of Right* to the exclusion of its place in the system – leads us to interpretations that fail to acknowledge the meaning that Hegel gives the terms he uses, the structure of his philosophical argumentation and the richness of his thought as he takes concepts like "property", "punishment", "morality" and others, considering and reconsidering them from new perspectives and vantage points. Hegel is a complex philosopher, and this interlocking, dialectical nature of his thought is everywhere acknowledged but all too rarely taken to heart.[3] Only a systematic reading of Hegel's work can bring out the full set of conceptions and connections that will help us properly grasp his

---

[3] As a graduate student attending an author meets critics session at the American Philosophical Association's Eastern Division conference several years ago, I challenged one leading commentator on why he had chosen to interpret Hegel's political thought not only non-metaphysically, but non-systematically. He replied that all we had to do was take seriously Hegel's starting point and go from there following a dialectical structure. I retorted that Hegel isn't like a bus driver letting you off at your stop to just dialectically advance, but that you start with a toolbox of terms from the system and a compass with a map that assumes a familiarity with their use. If we did not know the terms or how and why Hegel's dialectic works in a particular way, then we could never move from our starting point. To be fair to the author, whose book I hugely admire, he agreed but said to do any of this would be to write a book about Hegel's metaphysics or system instead of his political thought. This was part of my inspiration for writing a book to show that this was not necessary.

arguments in their true light. Anything less does an incomplete job. A non-systematic reading not only goes against Hegel's self-understanding, but also fails to grasp the substantive content – not only interpretive nuances – of his philosophical positions.

11.4   What Must Come Next?

A significant issue remaining is what is to come afterwards. If "Objective Spirit" (and the *Philosophy of Right*) are part of a wider system (and they are), then there will be a starting point we have already considered, but they should then also point towards the next step. And they do. This is important to understand as well: not only the need for "Objective Spirit", the terminology and argumentative structure it presupposes, but what it turns our focus to next.

There is perhaps no part of Hegel's philosophy as poorly misunderstood as his views on history, which he believes follows "Objective Spirit". Hegel is widely understood to defend what Francis Fukuyama called "the end of history" thesis that the world has reached the end of ideological evolution (Fukuyama 1992). Hegel does give comments that appear to support such a reading, such as "world history travels from East to West, for Europe is absolutely the end of world history, Asia the beginning" (Hegel 1956: 103). Scholars such as Joseph McCarney observe that, for Hegel, history reaches a point "beyond which there can be no progress" (McCarney 2009: 192).

Some of the clues to correcting this error confront us at the start of the *Philosophy of Right*. Every individual is a "child of his time" and "thus philosophy, too, is its own time comprehended in thoughts" (Hegel 1991a: 21). Philosophy looks to what has happened before and attempts to make the best sense of its rationality. Our perspective is historicized: "it is just as foolish to imagine that any philosophy can transcend its contemporary world as that an individual can overleap his time" (Hegel 1991a: 21–2). Thus, philosophy "always comes too late" and "the owl of Minerva begins its flight only with the onset of dusk" (Hegel 1991a: 23).

The reason why philosophy always comes too late is because it is, as Hegel conceives it, fundamentally "a thinking consideration" of that which appears before thought (Hegel 1991b: §2). It is a "thinking-over" (Hegel 1991b: §5). We might see historical developments as leading to a final, higher stage from our present standpoint. But we lack any philosophical crystal ball to peer into the future – and any judgement tomorrow might lead to very different interpretations of our past and present as time unfolds. Of course, America is a land of the future pointing beyond the present, as Hegel saw it in his time, which should give us reason enough to dismiss the idea that he held to any fixed end of history view. This is further reinforced when we consider that it runs counter to his entire project to make future predictions, as he is limited in rational construction of the present in the light of the past – and no more.

Besides, if Hegel believed the end of history was the epitome of civilization, this view fails to account for the fact that the end of Hegel's discussion of history might end "Objective Spirit" and the *Philosophy of Right*. However, the further development of his philosophical system is far from over – including Hegel's views on the progress of civilizations. This analysis extends into art and music, religion and philosophy itself – all presented in outline within the *Philosophy of Spirit*, as anyone reading "Objective Spirit" or taking his system seriously would know.

To be fair, Hegel says little about the transition from politics to history within "Objective Spirit" – and little more in the *Philosophy of Right* (Hegel 1971: §§548–52, 1991a: §§341–60). After completing his discussion of how we should conceive the ideal, or "Idea", of the state, Hegel proceeds to consider the interrelation of states across the world and over time. This leads Hegel to draw conclusions – given his views on how we should understand the past – about the relative merits and demerits of different civilizations. The discussion is key to understanding his position on war and other matters, best understood through a systematic reading.

11.5 Conclusion

Hegel intended his *Philosophy of Right* to serve as an elaboration of the outline for "Objective Spirit" within his *Encyclopaedia* philosophical system. This is important because understanding the need for "Objective Spirit" within the system helps us better grasp the starting point for the *Philosophy of Right*, such as why the challenge of how the free will can will the free will is the central question. It does not come from nowhere and it serves a purpose. Likewise, the dialectical structure of the *Philosophy of Right* is imported from the system and it is only in the latter that its full justification can be found – in addition to key terminology used throughout the *Philosophy of Right*. The core problem, the structure of the arguments used to grapple with it and the language employed to make the case are largely presupposed and imported from outside the *Philosophy of Right*. Hegel offers only brief summaries with frequent reminders to look back at the system for his complete and substantive account. The system plays an explanatory role in understanding Hegel's political and social ideas: it is not mere "intellectual curiosity" or "humbug" as some have claimed.

When I first argued for a systematic reading of Hegel's philosophy as more accurate and illuminating nearly twenty years ago, mine was a relatively lone voice amidst the then raging debate between the so-called metaphysical and non-metaphysical approaches (Brooks 2004). Two decades later there is a new orthodoxy among Hegel scholars where the system is now widely accepted to have an explanatory importance (Brooks and Stein 2017). Recently, Wood has made clear he too accepts this perspective:

> To appropriate Hegel, you have to understand *Hegel*: that means, *of course*, understanding the system and method through which he thought . . . There is no choice between reading Hegel "systematically" and reading him in response to our questions. There are only different ways of doing both at once. (Wood 2017: 83)

This puts things right. Hegel's philosophy is no less controversial, including what importance the system has for our understanding any part of his philosophy as developed in the *Philosophy of Right* or elsewhere. But progress has been made in this now more firmly established position that there is no choice but to adopt a systematic reading of Hegel's texts even if how such an approach might be employed will still be subject to debate.

Reading the *Philosophy of Right* as an elaboration of "Objective Spirit" is both more in keeping with Hegel's explicit intentions and also helps explain the need for the *Philosophy of Right*, its unique structure of its arguments and how it fits within Hegel's works. A systematic reading of these texts achieves this best – and this chapter has been an attempt to show why and how.

CHAPTER 12

§§556–63: Art as a Form of Absolute Spirit
The Discursive, the Non-discursive, the Religious, and the Political

Terry Pinkard

12.1 The Background

When one turns from the collected volumes of Hegel's lectures on the philosophy of art to the eight (mostly one-paragraph) sections on the subject in his final version of the *Encyclopedia*, the obvious difference in size and detail of course clearly stands out. The lectures are voluminous, include many examples, and discuss many matters not even hinted at in the *Encyclopedia*. Going from the lecture transcripts that we still have, we can see that Hegel was working out his views on the rather thin basis he had outlined in the *Encyclopedia* in a way that far outstripped the latter. Whereas in many of the other lectures (for example, on the *Logic*, the philosophy of nature, or the philosophy of objective spirit), one can get a sense of the general shape of the whole just from the outline given in the *Encyclopedia*, one cannot do so with the philosophy of art. If Hegel had not given those lectures, and all we had to go on was his 1807 *Phenomenology of Spirit* and the 1830 *Encyclopedia*, it is hard to imagine that anybody with just that to go on could have constructed the shape of his final views on the subject.

Without those lectures, what could we have thought about those paragraphs? We know that in the *Phenomenology*, there is no separate entry for the philosophy of art. Instead, art is discussed in the section on the "Art-Religion" (*Kunstreligion*), where it is clearly restricted to the religion of the ancient Greeks which he argues was left behind by the later revealed religion (of Christianity). After the disappearance of polytheistic Greek religion in the wake of monotheistic Christianity, it seemed from the standpoint of the *Phenomenology* that art played a much lesser role in the life of *Geist* than religion or philosophy. This 1807 categorization remained intact for Hegel's 1817 first edition of the *Encyclopedia*, in which the categories of absolute spirit are those of "the religion of art, revealed religion, and philosophy." By 1827 and 1830, however, absolute spirit had taken on its canonical form of "art, religion and philosophy." Without the lectures, we might have wondered why Hegel decided to give art its own section. We would speculate: what had he changed his mind about?

We also know that Hegel obsessed about getting everything in his system into the right order since if it were not, it would not really be a *Wissenschaft*, and for it to play the social role as the modern intellectual discipline par excellence in the modern "teaching and research" university, it either had to be "science" or not be there at all. No doubt part of that was Hegel's reason for meticulously recategorizing the place of art in the system. However, that only scratches the surface of Hegel's worry.

What we now have as the lectures on the philosophy of art is an edited compilation of both student lecture notes and Hegel's own notes for his lectures (all now lost) by H. G. Hotho, who, following the guidelines for the compilers of Hegel's collected works after Hegel's death, rewrote all the assembled material into a volume that was supposed to look as if it had been written by Hegel himself. Later generations with different philological ethics have chafed under this ever since. (Any professor who would be told that her reputation would rest entirely on somebody assembling her views out of student notes would have reason to worry.) This way of doing things also made it impossible to see whether Hegel was developing or changing his views on the subject matter. We do know that Hegel was already lecturing on the philosophy of art in Heidelberg in 1818 and then started again anew in Berlin in 1820. By the 1820 lectures, he had adopted his new ordering system and categories for the philosophy of art that marked the shift from the treatment in the *Phenomenology* and the 1817 *Encyclopedia*. The later published student notes from the different years the course was offered have also shown that Hegel did indeed change his views over the period, although how much remains a matter of scholarly debate.

In the course of his later lectures on the topic, Hegel said that for us (his contemporaries), art was a "thing of the past,"[1] a view that nicely fits with the *Phenomenology*'s restriction of art in its full sense to the life of the ancient Greeks. Hegel's statement can also be taken to announce – as some have – a thesis about the coming crisis of modern art itself, something that, so it has been argued, only really shows up in the art after Hegel's death, especially in the revolutionary work by Manet and Cézanne.[2]

---

[1] Hegel (2004: 7); the passage appears in Hotho's edition in Hegel (1970–1: 13:25).
[2] Pippin (2014).

It should be the case that whatever Hegel says in the *Encyclopedia* should therefore be consistent with what he was saying in the lectures, and what is in the *Encyclopedia* should be more or less foundational for what appears in the lectures. But how do the paragraphs serve as the foundation? There are three matters to consider here, and they are all interrelated. One is the condition of the times in which Hegel was making the change, the other had to do with how he conceived of the relation between his philosophy and those times, and the third, of course, is what the paragraphs have to do with the overall Hegelian project.

12.2   From the *Phenomenology* to the *Encyclopedia*: Religion and Art

One of the things that was on Hegel's mind when he sketched out the initial paragraphs on the "religion of art" for the 1817 *Encyclopedia* was the status of religion in his system. By the time he moved on to giving art its own separate category in "absolute spirit" in the 1827 and 1830 versions, the worry about religion had become even more pronounced. In the later editions, in the last section on "objective spirit," he launched into a long discussion of the role of religion in the life of *Geist* and in particular on the role of religion in the state. In the system, the idea is that in ascending to the level of different "peoples" in the progression of the philosophy of history (from one, to some, to all are free), we, the readers, are now moving in the direction of looking at spirit itself rather than any particular actualization of the concept, that is, thinking about the status of humanity in general rather than about the way in which particular formations of humanity play a role in world history. The reflection of spirit on what it means to be spirit is just what "absolute" spirit is supposed to indicate. More colloquially put, it is humanity's reflection on what it is to be the minded creature it is.

Hegel's worries here were both systematic and bound to his own time. On the one hand, he was concerned with elaborating the relation between art and religion (or, more generally, between beauty and partial truth) and concerned with what role, if any, art could play in the development of a fully modern social and political order in which he was determined to have his own philosophy play a leading role. These worries were coming to a head in the years between finishing the *Phenomenology* and his assuming his position, first in Heidelberg in 1816 and then finally in Berlin in 1818. In 1812, Napoleon had been defeated by the reactionary alliance and sent into exile, but then he staged a surprising return, only to be defeated again and exiled for good in 1815. The Congress of Vienna in 1815 threatened to turn the clock back to pre-Revolutionary days but did not succeed, and Hegel more or less breathed a large sigh of relief and immediately began to think through the implications for modern life in his own thought. It was against this background that he began to have second thoughts about the role of art in the modern world and its relation to religion. Unlike in the *Phenomenology*, he began to think about what he decided to call "Romantic" art, which was to encompass all of art in the Christian era (or, put negatively, in the era that succeeded classical art). This leads to the great change from the first part of absolute spirit ceasing to be the "religion of art" and becoming simply "art" itself. It was also, he noted in his late lectures, a "transitional phase."

In the *Phenomenology*, the section right before the long chapter, "Religion," concerns the confession and forgiveness of two beautiful souls who have become the "acting" and the "judging" consciousness. Each is the actualization of a kind of Kantian and Fichtean conception of self-consciousness in which the true motives of a moral agent must by metaphysical necessity be invisible in the social world. Kant argued that a genuinely virtuous action had to be carried out in light of an act of freedom that itself required a form of causality that could have no appearance as the causality it was in the phenomenal world. There could be no empirical test, and thus not even an introspective one, that could determine whether the cause of the action was a freely willed choice or some arbitrary inclination.

Hegel dramatized that into a story about the breakdown of the kind of moralism that follows in practice from any such conception. It concerns two agents, each of whom is obsessed with the purity of their motives and their own unconditional freedom. One claims never to act until he has gathered all the salient facts at that time, so even if bad things result from his action, he is nonetheless blameless since his motive was as pure as any motive could be: he acted fully on principle in light of all the salient facts available. The other holds the same view but, believing that he never has all the salient facts, never acts; and his motives are therefore as pure as any motives could be: he acts only on principle when all the salient facts are available. Each accuses the other of deception, of lying, of hypocrisy, and each vehemently rejects the imputation that the other–accuser could have the standing to know his motives. It is only on seeing the irrationality of such a view that each shifts instead into confessing to their own stiff-necked stance and forgiving the other for the harsh accusations that were made.

This is to make good – some several hundred pages later – the problem posed earlier in the *Phenomenology* about the way in which demands for and struggles for recognition from another agent collapse into the irrationality of relations of mastery and servitude. Two self-conscious agents confront each other. In being self-conscious, they each know what they are doing when they act, and each is capable of redeeming their act by appeal to reasons. They are each moments of a social whole, each is an "I" that is also a "We." Just as we can imagine that each speaks the same language as the other, so that the whole (the language) is given concrete form in the express speech-acts of both of them, each also claims therefore to have a kind of immediate knowledge of what counts as the appropriate manifestation of the language. Each claims an immediate – a non-inferential, non-empirical – knowledge of what it is to be a speaker of that language in a way that is different from more external ways of identifying oneself as a "We" (such as, for example, noting that one is carrying an umbrella just like everyone else in line, which is an external, empirical self-observation).[3] Each therefore claims an authority to speak for the whole – this is similar to when one says, "We English speakers say ... " – and each does so in what Hegel calls "self-certainty" (again similar to when one says that "We English speakers would never say ... "). Whenever there is a dispute about whether some act corresponds to this collective authority, there is a dispute over such "self-certainty," over who speaks for the whole, and, when one of the agents is willing to stake his life on possessing that authority, the relation spirals downward into a struggle for recognition with one of them compelling the other to submit to his authority, with the result that out of their original unity comes disunity, and out of shared meanings comes an inegalitarian, unjust relation. Such a compelled form of recognition is, of course, deeply irrational: the master must demand recognition from somebody whom he denies has the authority to bestow it since if he had the authority to bestow it, he would also have the authority to withhold it.

As he wrote that in the *Phenomenology*, Hegel thought the resolution of that contradiction lay in recognizing the rule of reason as that which binds the two together and of submitting all such inegalitarian claims to reason's tribunal (where they would fail). As he wrote the book, however, he changed his mind about the feasibility of doing that in the way he originally intended, and he added the chapter on "Spirit" and "Religion" to the book.[4] As he brought the book to its penultimate stage in the discussion of beautiful souls several hundred pages later, he made good on the idea that the dead end reached in the section on mastery and servitude was to be transcended by appeal to the idea that in a fully individualistic, even moralistic, society, the impasse reached by the

---

[3] See Haase (2016) and Fisher (2019).   [4] On the details of that change, see Förster (2012).

beautiful souls could be resolved by acts of confession and forgiveness in which each intuits (Hegel's word) himself in the other.

Again, the analogy of shared language as the "We" throws some light on this. Just as one does not (normally) infer the meanings of the words of the shared language – as if when one heard, "this is red," one inferred to "He probably means this is red" or anything like that – the two beautiful souls immediately see in their own distorted self-certainty that they are doing the same thing and that it is senseless. The medium in which they make their accusations against each other is that of language, which, as Hegel says (more than once in the *Phenomenology*), is the existence (*Dasein*) of spirit. Language is a practice which shows itself in the particular utterances of its speakers and which is real ("actual," *wirklich* in Hegel's technical terminology) only in its being manifested by the speakers. As a practice, language has no actuality beyond its practitioners, and the practitioners are practitioners only in manifesting the language.

The setting for the encounter between the beautiful souls is that of Hegel's own day. The kind of self-reflexiveness that he thought had come to be the necessary form of self-conscious modernity seemed to find its expression in an attractive but ultimately senseless conception of freedom that made us all invisible to each other and invisible to ourselves. However, both ideas, of the full invisibility of the inner life as well as of the full visibility of the inner life, are each as one-sided as the other, and are as one-sided as the idea that we are all either independent autonomous individuals or the otherwise empty placeholders for anonymous social forces. The modern form of life – the *Geist* of modernity – is reflected in the self-certainty of the individuals who are exhibiting it in their language and actions as well as the way in which the form of life is manifesting itself in them. Hegel ends the section on beautiful souls in the moment of reconciliation in which he says, perhaps a bit puzzlingly: "The reconciling *yes*, in which both I's let go of their opposed *existence*, is the existence of the *I* extended into two-ness, which therein remains the same as itself and which has the certainty of itself in its complete self-relinquishing and in its opposite. – It is the God that appears in the midst of those who know themselves as pure knowing."[5]

This means that at that stage in the development of the *Phenomenology*'s account, one of the basic problems – maybe even *the* basic problem of the whole book – which has to do with the status of self-conscious subjectivity

---

[5] Hegel (2018a: §671, 389).

had been resolved but only in a non-discursive way. After the completion of his *Logic*, this issue of the role, if any at all, of non-discursive thought had become critical for Hegel, since the *Logic* was so clearly an argument for the absolute status of discursive, judgmental, and inferential thought. This was, he thought, the role that religion had to play, and as Hegel came to see sometime around 1817, one of the biggest issues concerned the role that art was to play in the modern world and in the philosophy of *Geist* in general.

12.3   Art as Absolute Spirit

The passage from objective spirit to absolute spirit has to do with the way in which practical reason as embedded in the institutions and practices of ethical life (*Sittlichkeit*, or what we might also call "moral ethos") requires a move that focuses not just on doing the right thing but on understanding why it would matter at all. (The basic distinction between "morality" and "ethical life" is that between the relations between and among subjects being conceived along the lines of monadic subjects relating to each other as mediated by a system of moral rules and that in which the subjects are not conceived monadically but rather as essentially involved in the relation itself, as in love and friendship and in citizenship in the state.) Religion therefore forms the basic ethical bond among the people of a political community in that it provides the motivation and principles of a life that actually has a grip on the people involved. As Hegel tells his story, religion begins as the non-discursive grasp among the people of a given community about what holds them together, and as such, it is as much immediate knowledge as is the knowledge of the shared language. As religion develops, it becomes more and more discursive (especially among the "people of the book," for which reason Hegel assigns special importance to Christianity). In its further development, religion (as Christianity) develops out of itself a theology which, by submitting the claims of religion to reflective rational inquiry, itself necessarily transforms itself into philosophy, the *Wissenschaft* of pure reason itself. Thus, the "Christian" form of life transforms itself into a more philosophically inclined form of life.

In Hegel's original formulation in the *Phenomenology*, the introduction of religion showed how the inherently dyadic (and thus not monadic) structure of two agents engaged in recognition–confession–forgiveness is made real (and this is where Hegel's dense phrase "the appearing god" stages its entrance). As he moves to the "religion of art," he is concerned to show that the religion and ethical life of the ancient Greeks was united in the experience of beauty. Hegel accepted what he took to be Herodotus' claim that it was the poets (in particular, Hesiod) who gave the Greeks their gods (in light of later philology, that claim is rather dubious). Since, on that view, the Greek gods were essentially aesthetic creations, attending to them tied the Greeks together into what was essentially an aesthetic unity, but which was fated to fall apart on its own terms. The *Phenomenology*'s account (which is still the case in the 1817 *Encyclopedia* account) thus argues that the deficiencies of a purely aesthetic conception of ethical life carry within themselves a logical push to develop the more discursive account that culminates in absolute knowing in which the possibility of art serving any kind of ethical function is over.

By the time he began to lecture on the subject, Hegel had developed a way of marking that division, which also appears in the 1830 *Encyclopedia*. Art, religion, and philosophy are now ordered in terms of non-discursive (art), a mixture moving toward the discursive (religion developing a theology), and fully discursive ideas (philosophy), or, as Hegel expresses it there, in terms of intuition (*Anschauung*), representation (*Vorstellung*), and thought. In the terms of the 1830 *Encyclopedia*, art is the way in which an element of sensibility is transformed into a "sign" (*Zeichen*) of the Idea. In Hegel's terminology, the Idea is what he calls the unity of the concept and reality (or the concept and objectivity, as he also sometimes says). In the terms in which we have interpreted him here, the Idea is thus the term for the unity of a practice and its practitioners, that is, the way in which a general practice (such as a language) shows itself in the actions of the practitioners (in speech acts), who in turn exhibit the practice in their actions. Hegel's philosophical account is thus not that of practices producing the practitioners (as in the various forms of accounts of individual and collective action in terms of social forces and power), nor of the practitioners producing the practice (as in all individualist conventionalist or contractarian accounts), nor even that of the co-production of practice and practitioner (which would be what he calls *Wechselwirkung* in the *Logic*, the final stage of "Essence" and thus inappropriate for accounts of agency that by and large are to be framed in the teleological terms of the "Concept").

The way that Hegel sets up his account of art therefore has to do with its ethical and political role. After the breakdown of the "political work of art" and the "art-religion" of ancient Greece, art would seem no longer to have an essential role to play. This obviously posed a problem for Hegel as he was fundamentally rethinking his philosophy of art after 1817.

Art thus presents an intuition of the "so-called *unity* of nature and spirit,"[6] in which the truth of spirit – that its meanings are not in fact products of nature to be explained in terms of the categories of "force, ground and consequence," which for the moderns are the paradigms for explanation of natural events[7] – emerges only after the breakdown of the more intuitive, immediate form. In its most immediate form, in this self-certainty "burdened with immediacy, the freedom of the subject is only a customary ethic (*nur Sitte*) without the infinite reflection into itself, without the subjective inwardness of *conscience*."[8] In the cases where the particular sensuous content is itself in its particularity a "sign of the Idea" (as might be the case with, for example, a piece of sculpture that expressed the way a god might look), one has the aesthetic phenomenon of beauty (which itself has only a weak connection to the experience of natural beauty, which has to do more with certain inbuilt dispositions and the like).[9] An individual work of art is thereby like an individual action that manifests the general practice in the way it exemplifies the practice, as when one shows somebody, for example, how to do a dance step or how to do it with finesse. ("This is how it's done," says the dance teacher, making the move.) The individual work of art likewise is more or less a version of "This is what it is to be a minded creature, maybe a god, with all its ramifications, in this context." The work of art thus condenses a set of complex meanings into one "sign" of the Idea, unlike a discursive judgment which breaks them up and combines them.

Since the basic determination of human agency is freedom, the true work of art would be a "sign" of freedom, a kind of individual sign of "This is what it means to be free" but in a condensed and non-discursive manner. Discursively, we would say that freedom is acting without there having to be one element in the agent as the ruler or another element as the ruled in one's actions (and, if one is Hegelian, to add that one is acting in terms of a shared sense of meaning with an other so that each can, like the two beautiful souls confessing to and forgiving each other, understand the unity of self and other; or even more concretely, acting in terms of love or friendship, or acting in terms of justice as constituting the virtues of citizenship). Following some of the usage of his day, Hegel calls this the "ideal" of art: an individual work that shows, but does not necessary discursively say, what it is to be free. If it has to make itself discursive to do so, it ceases to be art.[10]

---

[6] Hegel (1970–1: 10:367, §557) (Er enthält die sogenannte *Einheit* der Natur und des Geistes, – d. i. die *unmittelbare*, die Form der Anschauung).
[7] Hegel (2004: 27–8).   [8] Hegel (1970–1: 10:369, §557).   [9] Hegel (1970–1: 10:367, §556).
[10] Hegel is particularly explicit on this point in the last series of lectures on the subject (in 1828/9). See Hegel (2017: 27).

12.4 The Historicity of the Arts

In the lectures series from 1820 onward, Hegel made it clear that "since the history of religions coincides with world history,"[11] the progress of art in history could itself be divided into three stages. In its earliest stage, art is at one with religious self-consciousness, but neither art nor religious self-consciousness could at that stage have developed any distinct theological understanding of divinity. Instead, all of the energy for art and religion would be absorbed into art itself. The "need for art" as he calls it would in those cases exist since art is the "only organ in which the abstract, in itself unclear and confused content, which is taken from natural and spiritual elements, can strive to bring itself to consciousness."[12] He decided to call this "symbolic" art and put just about every form of art prior to the Greeks (and for the most part, all art outside of Western art) into this category. This is art that does not yet determinately know what it wants to express and manifest for the reason that, as it were, it does not know what it wants to say, and, not knowing that, it thus can have no real sense of what would count as the best way to say it, except to craft a work of beauty and point to it. Art and religion at that point would have only the vaguest sense of what, outside of the conditions of natural beauty (symmetry, harmony, and the like) could count as an adequate expression. However, in the *Encyclopedia*, the historical ordering of the progress from symbolic (pre-Greek) to classical (Greek) to romantic art (all art after the triumph of Christianity in the Roman empire) is only implicit, unlike in the lecture series from 1820 onward. On the whole, the *Encyclopedia* treats the three as three simple possibilities for art as a mode of absolute spirit, whereas the lecture series treats them as each flourishing in specific historical periods.

Interestingly, Hegel calls this most direct form of art the art of sublimity, not of beauty itself. Sublimity points beyond itself to something like "the infinite" which cannot be aesthetically grasped, and, in these earlier forms of collective self-formation, cannot be adequately conceptualized in any form. In the art of the sublime, the "sign" in effect says that what it is to be a minded, *geistig* creature is "this," the inexpressible. Symbolic art thus can have no particular direction to itself, since all attempts to express the inexpressible fail for the same obvious reason, and there can be no progress in symbolic art other than in technique and materials. Therefore, the failures of symbolic art cannot be written off as an indication of lack of aptitude on the symbolic artist's part. Its failures are instead expressions of

---

[11] Hegel (1970–1: 10:371, §562).   [12] Hegel (1970–1: 10:371, §562).

deeper conceptual impasses not so much in art as in a certain kind of
religion (and thus in a certain way of living). The sublime is not the
beautiful. It is the "other" to human life which sets human life apart by
showing its insignificance in relation to the sublime and thereby also
spurring reflection on what might be of redeeming value in human life
which otherwise might seem so insignificant. The gods of the religions and
art of sublimity inspire awe but cannot reconcile people and gods.

On the other hand, beauty, which occurs at a later stage of collective self-
formation, would be the "sign" of *Geist* comprehending itself in which the
collectivity takes itself to have perfectly expressed itself. In such art, there is
a standard of progress inherent to it since there can be better and worse
ways of presenting what Hegel calls "humanity's highest vocation"[13] in
beautiful form for the reason that only the most beautiful form would be
adequate to that "highest vocation." A less beautiful presentation of the
god would be inferior to a more beautiful presentation since the latter
would be in fact a more truthful presentation. In giving this account, Hegel
seems to follow in the wake of Kant's conception of natural beauty as the
spontaneous harmonization of intellect ("the understanding") and imagination, when the prosaic world we grasp discursively (in the intellect)
spontaneously harmonizes with the world as we might imagine it to be
(in the imagination). Since the intellect is guided by concepts, which are
rules (for the synthesis of representations), and the imagination has no
rules, spontaneous harmony of rule-guided and non-rule-guided faculties
can itself have no rules. The Greek world was like that, so Hegel thought.
In it, the gods and men functioned together, and when everybody fulfilled
the requirements of their place in the whole, the result was a spontaneous
harmonization. (In his later lectures on the philosophy of history, he
referred to ancient Greek political life as the "political work of art.")

In Hegel's presentation, when the archaic Greeks thought about what
the world meant as a whole, they thought it through in aesthetic terms (by
way of statues, poems, pictures, music) and not in discursive terms.
However, that form of life was fated to break down as the contradictions
which were only implicit in the aesthetic fusion of singular lives and the
world as a whole began themselves to be aesthetically presented to the
Greek audience (paradigmatically, in the tragedies). Those contradictions
appearing in tragic plays pushed the Greeks into a more discursive,
philosophical mode (which was incompatible with the absolute claims
made by their earlier, aesthetic mode), and as that happened, the older

---

[13] Hegel (1970–1: 10:371, §562).

classical arts began to be displaced. The older Greek temples, once the beautiful houses of the gods, became merely beautiful buildings, items in the future to be copied and imitated for their beauty but not, as it were, for their truth about the relation between gods and people.

For the Greeks the whole constituted by people, gods, and earth supposedly had an aesthetic unity, and as it began to unravel, so did the unity.[14] When the unity fully came apart, so did the religion and the form of life oriented around it. Rather than returning to a religion of sublimity, the Mediterranean world (in this case in Roman form) pushed onward to a non-aesthetic unity based on more prosaic matters such as the power of the legions coupled with Rome's often deft and pragmatic diplomacy in dealing with its conquered peoples. The non-aesthetic unity of empire replaced the aesthetic unity of the political work of art and expanded its scope. There were many reasons to be a Roman (wealth, power, peace, protection, etc.), but they were not immanent to the self-certainty of the people it ruled.

With Christianity, a new spiritual unity was established that purported to fill in the gaps left by imperial unity but also not in any necessarily beautiful way. With that, art also necessarily had to change. When it comes to portraying the divine or "humanity's highest interests," Romantic art, as the art following in the wake of the widespread acceptance of Christianity, "gives up portraying it as such in an external shape and thus of showing it by means of beauty; it exhibits the divine as only condescending to appearance. It shows the divine as inner intimacy (*Innigkeit*) in externality."[15]

Hegel's changing reflections on the topic emerged gradually in the lecture series. In 1820, in keeping with his earlier assessment in the *Phenomenology* and the 1817 *Encyclopedia*, he told his students that "our relationship to art indeed no longer has the high seriousness and significance that it earlier had."[16] By 1823, he was saying that "the work of art cannot fulfill our final absolute need, we no longer worship an art-work, and our relationship to the art-work is of more reflectively circumspect sort."[17] By 1826, he had changed that to "the highest vocation (*Bestimmung*) for art is a thing of the past," leaving open the idea that art might still have a role to play in modern life.[18] By 1828 Hegel had sharpened his view to the claim that "we no longer bend the knee to God the Father and Pallas (Athena) no matter how excellently they may be presented" (i.e., neither to the sparse Enlightenment deist god

[14] Hegel (1970–1: 10:32, §384).   [15] Hegel (1970–1: 10:370, §362).
[16] Hegel and Schneider (1995: 38).   [17] Hegel, Hotho, and Gethmann-Siefert (1998: 6).
[18] Hegel (2004: 7); the passage appears in Hotho's edition in Hegel (1970–1: 13:25).

nor to Greek religion) and, putting it even more strongly, he claimed "the bounds of art do not lie in art but lie in us,"[19] and "our time" is described as the period "after art."[20]

12.5   Art, Religion, Politics: Absorption in the Non-absorptive

In his earlier days, first in Tübingen with Schelling and Hölderlin, then later at Frankfurt with Hölderlin, and then even later in Jena with Schelling, Hegel was consumed with the issue about the relation between art and philosophy. By the writing of the *Phenomenology*, however, Hegel had firmly come down against the idea that the truth about *Geist* was in its highest form an aesthetic, non-discursive matter. Philosophy as the "science of reason" triumphed over the non-discursive intuition of the absolute that Schelling had defended in his early work, and especially in *The System of Transcendental Idealism* of 1800. But at least by the beginning of his stay in Berlin in 1818, Hegel was convinced that there also had to be a place for modern art in the world after the Congress of Vienna had not reversed the basic gains of the Revolution. By the lectures of 1820, he thought he had found this in Italian and Dutch painting, where the "magic of seeming-to-be (*Schein*)" so perfected by Dutch painters indicated the place of art in a world in which a certain kind of self-distancing reflection was more of a basis for shared life and religion rather than the more immediate absorption that he thought the ancient Greek cults had practiced. This "magic of seeming-to-be" was as it were the "music of painting,"[21] and it was in this

---

[19] Hegel (2017: 26). This is a passage that throws some doubt on Hotho's version of the lectures. In the Hotho edition, Hegel seems to be responding to Christian ideas in the passage about "bending the knee," where Hotho has him speaking of presentations of "Gottvater, Christus, Maria." However, the 1828 version speaks only of "Gottvater" – which Hegel characterizes as the Enlightenment's abstract view of God, see Hegel (1970–1: 10:31) – and "Pallas" (Athena), which he says is not yet the "genuine God" (*wahrhafte Gott*). That this should also extend to Christian art is, I think, the right inference to draw, but Hegel does not draw it in Heimann's notes of the 1828 lectures. Hegel is also speaking, likely, of his opposition to the worship of images in non-Protestant Christianity, when he says in the *Encyclopedia* that "the reverently revered images are non-beautiful idols, (serving) as miraculous talismans that extend into an other-worldly spiritless objectivity, and bones do the same or even better service than such images" (Hegel (1970–1: 10:372, §562).

[20] Hegel (2017: 26). The phrase "das *Nach* der Kunst" also appears in Hotho's edition, Hegel 1970–1: 10:142).

[21] Hegel and Schneider (1995: p. 277). It is striking that Hotho did not include any of the passages about the magic of *Scheinen* in his version of the lectures on aesthetics, since it is crucial to understanding what Hegel's insight into the status of modern art was. Hegel repeats the 1820 theme about the magic of *Scheinen* in the 1828/9 lectures in even greater detail. He uses it to make the transition into music and a discussion of its elementary power. On Hegel's mature views on the "elementary power" of music, see Pinkard (2011). On the discussion of the "magic of Scheinen," see the helpful account in Rutter (2011).

absorption in what is reflectively taken as "seeming-to-be" – an absorption in an almost paradigmatically non-absorptive state – that the power of modern art was to lie.

What was most striking about the art-religion of the Greeks was its "liveliness" (*Lebendigkeit*), the way in which the Greeks were both self-conscious and absorbed in the religious cults.[22] At first, Hegel suspected that the liveliness of art had to go missing in modern art, but, after his discovery after 1818 of the way in which to understand the absorption in the non-absorptive reflective act on absorptive action and thought – as captured in a Dutch genre painting or still life – Hegel did more or less about an about face. By the 1828 lectures, he seemed to have found a place for modern art as a mode of collective and personal self-reflection. The absorption of non-absorptive reflection on the ordinary objects of life enables a kind of intimacy (an *Innigkeit*) with the world that is the result of an activity, which Hegel (adapting a Lutheran term) calls *Verinnigung*, a kind of "making oneself intimate" with the object, an active losing oneself in the world as one lets the world, as it were, roll over oneself (a *Sichergehen*, as Hegel calls it), all moved by the "character of freedom and intimacy."[23]

This discussion of *Verinnigung* does not appear in the 1827 and 1830 versions of the *Encyclopedia*. Instead, the discussion of art is still framed on both sides (beginning and end) by religion and the political and social role of religion and art. In the transition and run-up to the discussion of art (§552), Hegel speaks in the concluding section on states and world history about how the social and political community can be held together only by an ethos (a *Sitte*), and that this ethos must be internal to the religious consciousness of the people. He says that "the state rests on ... ethical dispositions, and these rest on religious dispositions,"[24] and therefore, if the religion is not true, the ethical dispositions will also be false. What he calls the "monstrous error of our times" consists in thinking that the ethical bond of the political community can be severed from the religious bond even though clearly the two are to be analytically distinguished.[25] He notes that "there cannot be two kinds of conscience, one religious and another ethical which is distinct from it in substance and content,"[26] and that it is simply useless to organize the state along ethical lines if the (religious) dispositions of the people are at odds with it.[27]

---

[22] This theme of liveliness is developed in great insight and detail in Rutter (2011), and it forms one of the key elements in the Hegelian style account of art in Pippin (2014).
[23] Hegel (2017: 127).   [24] Hegel (1970–1: 10:355, §552).   [25] Hegel (1970–1: 10:355, §552).
[26] Hegel (1970–1: 10:355–6, §552).   [27] Hegel (1970–1: 10:360, §552).

He uses those thoughts to launch into an attack on Catholicism. Hegel
had long had an anti-Catholic edge to him, but even he had been taken
aback at the ferocity of the Church's reaction to the Revolution in 1789 and
even more so at the full-throated attempt to undo the Revolution and wipe
out its memory after Napoleon's defeat. He ridiculed as a farce the "Charter"
(instead of a constitution) chosen for the French after 1814 that reinstated the
Catholic church as the established religion, kept intact many of the
Revolutionary and Napoleonic reforms (such as the Napoleonic Code of
law), yet pretended that nothing had happened and Louis XVIII had been
ruling since 1789. Although the regime had the external trappings of
a constitutional monarchy, it was really an absolute monarchy since the
limits to the king's authority could be lifted at any time, basically by the king
himself. Hegel blamed this state of affairs on the Catholic church and its
authoritarian structure distorting the religious consciousness of the people.
He in turn was shocked and disturbed by the French Revolution of 1830,
which swept that away – disturbed, if for no other reason than that it seemed
to show that the hold of the Church was not as rigid as he thought. It was
also becoming a bit more clear to him during the 1820s that the Prussian
Protestant church was actually not that much better.

His next to the last discussions of art in the *Encyclopedia* therefore have to
do with how the philosophy of religion needs to see how the moral ethos –
the *Sittlichkeit* of a people – coheres with the principles of its laws. What is
stressed in the lectures and plays an implicit role in the *Encyclopedia* is, as we
noted, the political role that art played in ancient Greek life and how that is
impossible for modern life. Modern art, even though it has its essential role
to play in freeing people in the otherwise alienating, "prosaic" modern
world, is very secondary to religion. Religion held things together for the
Greeks, and it has to do it also for the moderns. Art did that for the Greeks,
but it cannot do that for the moderns. Hegel's own political philosophy
(appearing in published form in 1820 but in effect finished by 1817) laid out
the baselines of this new order as resting on the systematic combination of
the Lockean rights to life, liberty, and property, the post-Christian moral
scheme of treating people with dignity and acting only in terms of reasons
about which one could exercise one's own insight, a "moral ethos"
(*Sittlichkeit*) of the bourgeois family, a civil society with a market embedded
in it (and not vice versa), and a constitutional monarchy topping it off. None
of this will work unless, or so he thought, a kind of enlightened, heavily
reinterpreted Protestant form of Christianity became the new moral ethos.

However, as the 1820s wore on, Hegel seemed to become more pessimistic about that possibility, although he never abandoned his faith in the

power of reason to force progress. The conclusion which Hegel did not want to draw from his own thought would be that if in fact, and against his own theory, Protestant Christianity failed to hold things together, then the future might well just be an unending cycle of the search for absolute freedom, followed by chaos and Jacobin terror, and then followed by revanchist restoration leading to reformist politics, which then falls apart into chaos following the demand for absolute freedom, *ad infinitum*. If he had lived to see the promise followed by the collapse of 1848, he might have been even more pessimistic.

A large strand of contemporary Hegel scholarship tends to elevate his later philosophy of art and his philosophy in terms of its secular nature and to ignore or denigrate the religious dimension. In the *Encyclopedia*, Hegel gives little place to art but a lot to religion. In the lectures based on the *Encyclopedia*, however, he went much further in developing a philosophy of modern art as having a secular importance distinct from that of religion. Behind it all was his attempt to make his philosophy into his own times grasped in thought. However, his own time was at odds with itself, and some of the strains within those times appear in his thought.

CHAPTER 13

The Stubbornness of Nature in Art
A Reading of §§556, 558 and 560 of Hegel's
Encyclopedia

Ioannis Trisokkas

Speight (2019: 235) has recently raised the question, which he himself leaves
unanswered, of how naturalism relates to spirit in Hegel's philosophy of
art.[1] 'Naturalism' denotes an explanation that invokes aspects of nature
that are (allegedly) irreducible or resistant to thought. I call nature 'stubborn' insofar as it evinces resistance to its being formed *by thought* and
hence to its being united with it. This chapter argues that §§556, 558 and
560 of Hegel's *Encyclopedia of the Philosophical Sciences* (hereafter
Encyclopedia) answer Speight's question by specifying three elements of
nature that, first, are present in art and, second, are resistant to thought.
These are *materiality*, *natural form* and *genius*. They exhibit nature's
stubbornness *in art*. This stubbornness, I argue, is what justifies Hegel's
claim that art is absolute spirit *only implicitly* (§556), which leads to the
claim that art needs to be *superseded* by religion and philosophy. In this
way, Speight's question receives a precise answer.

I proceed as follows. *First*, I discuss the merit of the *Encyclopedia*'s philosophy of art in contradistinction to Hegel's lectures on the same topic (Section
13.1). This discussion is propelled by the fact that the *Encyclopedia*'s section on
art has been largely overlooked in favour of these lectures, which, despite being
sometimes helpful in deciphering some of the concepts and claims Hegel
employs in the *Encyclopedia*, are not as reliable a guide to Hegel's own
thinking about art's place in the *system* as the *Encyclopedia*. Even Gethmann-
Siefert's (1991, 2000, 2005) celebrated work on Hegel's philosophy of art reads
the *Encyclopedia*'s section on art through the lenses furnished by the lectures.
Contra standard practice, the present chapter advances an interpretation of
Hegel's philosophy of art based entirely on the *Encyclopedia*.

---

[1] All in-text stand-alone paragraph numbers refer to Hegel (1970–1: vol. 10). Most translations are
mine; if they are taken from Hegel (2007c), I indicate it accordingly. I refer only to the paragraph
numbers (not to the pages) of the *Encyclopedia*.

Second, since art is placed in the system and, more precisely, determined as absolute spirit, I sketch the basic picture of the system and absolute spirit's status in it (Section 13.2).

Third, I interpret §556 in terms of Hegel's understanding of intuition, the ideal and beauty. I argue that, for Hegel, there are moments in the *reception* of art when material givenness or sheer *materiality* (a manifestation of what Hegel calls "natural immediacy") nullifies the experience of the unity of thought and nature or "the idea" (Section 13.3).

Fourth, I analyse §558, arguing that, for Hegel, what is *received* in art is not only materiality but also a *natural form* which is distinct from the idea (and hence another manifestation of "natural immediacy"). *Pace* Peters (2015), I contend that this paragraph leaves the issue of whether this natural form is exclusively the human form unsettled (Section 13.4).

Fifth, I turn to §560, and argue that, for Hegel, there are moments in the *production* of art when the artist's *genius* (another manifestation of "natural immediacy") liquidates the idea's universality (Section 13.5).

These discussions are meant to reinforce the following two claims. First, *pace* Adorno (2002: 61–78), natural immediacy or *sheer* nature (i.e. nature as being resistant to thought, nature's stubbornness) is, for Hegel, essential to art. Second, art's natural immediacy is the exact reason why art is *not fully* or *explicitly* absolute spirit: art is *only partially* or *implicitly* absolute spirit. Since nature does not yield completely to the idea (the unity of thought and nature) in art, thought must move on to religion and philosophy in order to *fully* become absolute spirit.

13.1   The Textual Locus of Hegel's Philosophy of Art

Comments about art occur in the whole of the Hegel corpus, but the main discussion transpires in two places: (a) in his various lectures on the philosophy of art (hereafter *Lectures*) and (b) in the "Philosophy of Spirit," the *Encyclopedia*'s third part. Hegel delivered five lecture series on the philosophy of art, the first in Heidelberg in 1818 and the rest in Berlin: in 1820/1, 1823, 1826 and 1828/9. No lecture text penned by Hegel himself has survived (save a few fragments), but lengthy student manuscripts (transcripts and lecture notes) are available. Depending on the manuscript one surveys, one can enjoy detailed reflections on art's value, its historical development and the individual arts.

In contrast to the *Lectures*' lengthy expositions, the *Encyclopedia*'s consideration of art is only a few pages long. Hegel published the *Encyclopedia* three times in his lifetime (in 1817, 1827 and 1830), and each subsequent version contains a modification of the section on art; see Gethmann-Siefert (2000) and Speight (2019) for details. I will concentrate on the 1830 version, which submits Hegel's final word on the philosophy of art.

Length is not the sole difference between the *Encyclopedia*'s and the *Lectures*' philosophy of art. Whereas the *Encyclopedia* spotlights art's systematic relation to thought, nature and spirit, the *Lectures* focus instead on unsystematic questions concerning art's value, its relation to morality, its historical development and the individual arts. But despite these variations there is no discrepancy between them. They are rather complementary, each shedding light both on the same and on different aspects of art. The *Lectures* can be helpful in unravelling some of the concepts and claims Hegel utilizes in the *Encyclopedia*.

Nevertheless, it should be emphasized that we cannot fathom Hegel's conception of art by staying only within the *Lectures*, for art's *systematic* character is addressed properly only in the *Encyclopedia*. Thus, I find Gethmann-Siefert's take on the relation between the *Lectures* and the *Encyclopedia* somewhat precarious. She advocates that each edition of the *Encyclopedia*'s philosophy of art is *nothing but* a summary of "the essential thoughts" of the preceding lecture series (Gethmann-Siefert 2000: 317). She does not, however, make a compelling case for such a strong claim (Gethmann-Siefert 2000: 322–9). In my view, the *Encyclopedia*'s section on art tends towards a systematic exposition that is foreign to the *Lectures*.

It is true that the *Encyclopedia* was meant to operate as a textbook for Hegel's lectures, but it does not hold, as Gethmann-Siefert conjectures, that it was meant as a textbook for his lectures on the philosophy of art. The *Encyclopedia*'s goal was to give a concise presentation of Hegel's *system*, not of his philosophy of art. Because she takes the *Encyclopedia*'s section on art to be a summary of Hegel's lectures on the philosophy of art, Gethmann-Siefert makes no effort to decipher that cryptic section *on its own terms*. Relying heavily on the *Lectures*, the early Jena writings and the 1807 *Phenomenology of Spirit*, she ends up paying only minimal attention to the *Encyclopedia*'s passages and, especially, *their own* systematic interconnection. She certainly does not perceive them as *fundamental* for understanding Hegel's philosophy of art. *Contra* Gethmann-Siefert's work, the present chapter focuses exclusively on the *Encyclopedia*'s philosophy of art, hence on Hegel's concern about art's role in the *system*. *This is why I will make only scarce use of the* Lectures *and illuminate the* Encyclopedia*'s section on art by drawing heavily on preceding sections of the* Encyclopedia.

Finally, it should be mentioned that, in the English-speaking world, the bulk of scholarly work on Hegel's philosophy of art is based almost uniquely on H. G. Hotho's posthumous three-volume edition of Hegel's lectures on the philosophy of art published in 1842 (i.e. Hegel 1970–1: vols. 13–15). A translation in exquisite English was published by T. M. Knox in 1975 under the title *Hegel's Aesthetics: Lectures on Fine Art*. Aside from a few notable exceptions (see especially James 2000; Peters 2015; and Speight 2015, 2019), the *Encyclopedia*'s section on art has hardly ever been given a central place in accounts of Hegel's philosophy of art in the English-speaking world. As Gaiger (2006: 160) observes, Hotho's 1842 edition and the Knox translation have long been treated as "the standard edition" by Pippin, Houlgate and other leading Hegel scholars.

Since well-grounded doubts about the validity of Hotho's work were raised by Gethmann-Siefert as early as 1991, the continued usage of Hotho's edition in the English-speaking world is problematic. For instance, Hotho approached the student manuscripts of these lectures as nothing but "sketches and observations" requiring expansion and reorganization. In his *Vorrede* he writes that his goal is to restore the *Lectures'* "animating inner life" by "structuring the whole", adding missing "dialectical transitions", tightening up "loose connections" and increasing the number of examples (Gaiger 2006: 162–3; Gethmann-Siefert 1991: 93). Hotho also augmented the text with thoughts that were meant "to demonstrate the superiority of Hegel's aesthetics in face of [. . .] rival systems" (Gaiger 2006: 163). The outcome of this "restoration" was a massive expansion of the student manuscripts, the most detailed of which does not exceed 300 pages; Hotho's edition, in contrast, runs to nearly 1,600 pages. As Gaiger (2006: 163) notes, "it is now almost impossible to work out exactly what belongs to Hegel and what was introduced by Hotho", and hence Hotho's edition belongs to the corpus of the reception history of Hegel's ideas rather than to the Hegel corpus itself (cf. Speight 2019: 226 n. 4). Given these reasons and that English-speaking scholarship on Hegel's aesthetics has in the main treated Hotho's edition as "the standard text", it would not be an exaggeration to suggest that this scholarship should seek a new beginning.

13.2   The System

The *Encyclopedia* gives a comprehensive, but terse, presentation of Hegel's account of "the absolute". The absolute is the whole of being and has three fundamental dimensions: "thought", "nature" and "spirit". Thought is studied by logic, nature by the philosophy of nature and spirit by the philosophy of spirit. Each fundamental dimension is constituted by an array of lesser dimensions. Specifying the relations between the various lesser dimensions within a fundamental one, as well as between the three fundamental dimensions themselves, is the *Encyclopedia*'s task.

Thought consists of categories or concepts, which are mental or "inner" elements generating *meaning*. Hegel, *contra* Kant, believes categories induce meaning even when they are unrelated to materiality, externality or sensibility. Logic demonstrates how this is done. Thus, in logic thought proves to be an *immaterial structure*.

Nature has two components. On the one hand, it consists of categories and concepts (i.e. thought) *as they apply*, as functions of *organization*, to materiality, externality or sensibility. There is, then, a facet of nature appearing as an organized and hence meaningful structure. On the other hand, nature consists of elements *given* to the categories and concepts of nature *by* materiality, externality or sensibility. This second facet of nature, which is unorganized and hence meaningless, is what I call "*sheer* nature". Although Hegel's *Naturphilosophie* is interested mainly in showing how thought shapes materiality into meaningful structures of nature, it acknowledges sheer nature's existence.

Spirit differs from both thought and nature, yet it involves them both. It is not simply the concepts and categories organizing nature and it is not simply organized materiality. Spirit, rather, is thought's *consciousness* of its finding or "knowing" *itself* in nature, or, more specifically, thought's *consciousness* of its being the *organizing* element in nature. Philosophy of spirit narrates the emergence of such consciousness.

Spirit has three dimensions: subjective, objective and absolute spirit. As *subjective* spirit, thought thinks of itself in nature as an organizing material structure (either as organ(s) or as physical process(es), such as perception and intuition). This form of thought's self-consciousness in nature is defective: by reducing itself to materiality, what thought encounters in nature is only sheer nature. As *objective* spirit, thought *posits* itself in nature and thereby becomes an object *for itself*. Thought's *self-positing* in nature contrasts with *its already being in nature as a material thing*. The problem with *objective* spirit is that nature vanishes and *all* that appears is thought. Finally, as *absolute* spirit, thought can be neither its self-positing in nature *alone* nor a material structure *alone*. The challenge for absolute spirit is to find a way to *combine* thought with nature without annihilating any one of these *at any moment*.

Art is one of *absolute* spirit's three dimensions, the other two being religion and philosophy. It follows (1) that art, religion and philosophy are modes of thought's self-consciousness in nature that, *contra objective spirit*, allow nature's otherness. It also follows (2) that they are modes of thought's self-consciousness in nature that, *contra subjective spirit*, do not reduce thought to a material thing. In the remainder of the chapter I focus on §§556, 558 and 560 of the *Encyclopedia*, seeking to explain how exactly these two fundamental characterizations of absolute spirit apply specifically to *art*.

13.3 Intuition, Ideal and Beauty (§556)

In §556 Hegel lays out art's minimum, most superficial structure. There is (a) the *artwork*, a *Dasein* external to cognizing subjects and open to common appreciation; (b) the subject *producing* it, the artist; and (c) the subject(s) *receiving* it, the audience. As soon as this structure is laid out, Hegel qualifies it significantly. First, he declares that the artwork's reception has the character of *intuition* (*Anschauung*). Second, he asserts that what is intuited is *the ideal* (*das Ideal*). Third, he maintains that what is intuited has "the shape of *beauty*" (*die Gestalt der Schönheit*). In the present section I unpack these three statements.

13.3.1 Intuition

In §449 Hegel defines intuition, a form of subjective spirit, as thought's "recollecting" itself in an externally existing material in which it remains *sunk* (*versenkt*). Thought's *remaining sunk* in externality is crucial, as suggested by its being repeated in the *Zusatz* of §450.

The *Zusatz* of §449 clarifies this definition by differentiating intuition from representation and sensation. On the one hand, while both in representation and in intuition "the object *is* both separate from me and simultaneously mine", *that* the object is mine is *explicit* in representation but only *implicit* in intuition. The object's "mineness", i.e. thought's self-recollection in it, is *suppressed* in intuition because "in intuition the *object-hood* (*Gegenständlichkeit*) of the content predominates (*überwiegt*)" (Hegel 2007c). This "objecthood" is the object's material givenness. Thus, in intuition thought sees itself in the object but it is unaware of this because the object's material givenness predominates in the subject's experience of the object.

On the other hand, while both in sensation and in intuition a manifoldness of individual features comes to the fore, it is only in intuition that this manifoldness appears as "a totality, an abundance of determinations being held together". Sensation does not *unite* the determinations, intuition does. In

Hegel's words, "in immediate intuition I do have the whole object before me". By uniting the determinations, intuition "grasps the *solid substance* of the object", something that sensation cannot do because it presents us only with an aggregate, a disjointed plurality. This "solid substance" of the object is its *meaning*.

By unifying an object's manifold determinations, intuition generates meaning in nature. This unifying function, Hegel believes, cannot belong to material givenness, to sheer nature, but can only belong to thought. It is the thought-in-intuition, not the nature-in-intuition, that generates meaning in nature. Yet, it is intuition's peculiarity that in it thought is *unaware* of its own unifying function. The material givenness "predominating" in intuition does not allow thought to realize that the unifying element in nature is thought itself, an immaterial, non-natural element. Because of this deficiency, Hegel writes that "intuition is [. . .] only the beginning of cognition" and that "it is a blatant error to believe that one has already true knowledge of the thing when one has an immediate intuition of it". Absolute spirit, which sublates subjective spirit and hence intuition, cannot be "an immediate intuition", to wit, it cannot be *just* intuition. Nevertheless, *insofar as absolute spirit is intuition*, thought is dominated by sheer nature and thereby fails to behold itself as the unifying element in nature.

Since intuition characterizes art's reception, art is located in materiality, externality and sensibility. Art is determined fundamentally by a material external object's being given to the audience's senses. Yet, given the nature of intuition, what the audience receives is not only a manifoldness of determinations, but also a unified manifoldness, a "totality". The audience thus finds *meaning* in the artwork. This meaning, as we know, cannot derive from the artwork's material givenness – it is thought's work. Yet, insofar as art's reception is determined by intuition, the audience does not recognize this: they see that the artwork has meaning, but they do not espy thought as that meaning's generator. They assume this meaning is *in* the artwork's material givenness, *in* its colours, weight, lines, texture, sounds and so on. In art's reception thought's function as the unifying element in nature remains hidden from thought.

Crucially, however, art is not "an *immediate* intuition"; it is *absolute spirit*. *Insofar as it is absolute spirit*, art enables thought to *recognize* itself in the artwork as the unifying element in nature. Thought *does* see the artwork as its own product, as what *it* "has posited". In Desmond's words, art indeed is, for Hegel, "a form of sensuous *self-knowledge*" (Desmond 1986: 2).

Since art's reception is both intuition and absolute spirit, it is determined as a 'conjunction' of (a) thought's being dominated by material givenness (sheer nature) and hence being *unaware* of its presence in nature and (b) thought's *self-recognition* in nature. These two, though, cannot exist simultaneously: they cancel each other out. Given that they both determine art's reception, they must exist in the latter *but not simultaneously*. Art's reception is a structure of fluctuation, of *becoming*: thought moves from self-recognition to annihilation, from recognizing itself as the unifying function in nature to being dominated by material givenness, and *vice versa* (Trisokkas 2012: 110–16). Because of this fluid structure art is *not fully* absolute spirit; it is, rather, as Hegel notes in §556, absolute spirit only *implicitly*, "[art] is the concrete intuition [. . .] of the *implicitly* absolute spirit [. . .]" (Hegel 2007c).

This, then, is art's *implicitness* as absolute spirit: in art thought finds itself as the unifying force in nature, *but not constantly*. It is art's distinctiveness that there are *moments* when the artwork's materiality or "objecthood" – its colours, sounds, lines, texture, mass, weight and so on – "predominates" in the audience's experience. Being fundamentally a realm of intuition, art constantly *relapses* into the dominance of nature over thought. Regardless of how hard we try, we cannot avoid being hit by the artwork's material constitution. The *problem* is that when this happens in art's reception, *thought loses itself* in nature. So, art's reception is determined fundamentally by *two* phenomena: (a) thought "recollecting" itself in materiality, externality and sensibility as the unifying element in nature; and (b) this self-recollection being constantly interrupted by raw materiality, by a dominant nature that leads thought into (momentary) vanishing.

13.3.2 The Ideal

Hegel's second statement in §556 is that what is intuited in the artwork is absolute spirit *as the ideal*. Hegel there defines the ideal as "the concrete shape born of subjective spirit" in which "natural immediacy is only a sign of the idea" (Hegel 2007c). On the one hand, being born of *subjective* spirit, the ideal is a *material external shape* given to the senses. On the other hand, as a sign, this shape expresses the *idea*. What is intuited, then, is a material shape that expresses the idea.

The idea is defined in §213 as "the absolute unity of concept and objectivity" (Hegel 1970–1: 8:§213). "Concept" is another name for "thought" and "objectivity" is another name for "nature", so the idea is the unity of thought and nature. Hegel writes that objectivity is the idea's "real content" and has "the form of external *Dasein*" (Hegel 1970–1: 8:§213). The idea is not about "this" or about "representations" or about "external *things*" (Hegel 1970–1:

8:§213). It is not an "idea of *something*", a particular idea (Hegel 1970–1: 8:§213). The idea, most generally, is the presence of thought ("the concept") in externality, in nature.

The definition of the idea as the unity of thought and nature determines the idea as a genus and can be qualified in many ways. The idea's qualification creates its species, which express it in subtly different ways (Hegel 1970–1: 8:§214). The *ideal* is one of the idea's species. As ideal, the idea's concreteness is specifically a material-sensory shape. Since, however, the idea is not only concreteness but also the unity of thought and nature, *the ideal is an expression of this unity in a material-sensory shape*. The unity of thought and nature is another name for thought's being the unifying function in nature.

What is intuited in the artwork, therefore, is the unity of thought and nature (the unification of nature by thought), which is the idea. Yet, in art's reception absolute spirit is bound to sensibility and materiality. In Hegel's own words, "art displays the genuine universal or the *idea* in the form of *sensory reality*" (§456 *Zusatz*; Hegel 2007c). *This* display *is* the ideal.

13.3.3   Beauty

Hegel holds that what is intuited in the artwork's reception has "the shape of beauty". *The ideal*, then, has the shape of beauty. This means that art *as absolute spirit* is exclusively *beautiful* art. In §556 "the shape of beauty" as the ideal's shape has a twofold determination. On the one hand, it is "a *sign* of the idea". On the other hand, it is specified "that *nothing else* [other than the idea] is shown in the shape".

"Sign" (*Zeichen*) is discussed in §§457–8. In the Remark to §457 signs are described as "unifications of what is the spirit's own or its interior with the *intuitive*" (Hegel 2007c). A sign connects material-sensory concreteness, natural immediacy, with a meaning, an inner element. Crucially, the meaning and the sign have a relation of *otherness*: the sign does not signify itself – it is *not* a structure of *self*-signification – but, rather, something *alien* to it. In Hegel's own words, "when intelligence has designated something [as a sign], it has finished with the content of intuition and has given the sensory material an *alien* meaning as its soul" (§457 *Zusatz*; Hegel 2007c).

This interpretation is confirmed by what Hegel writes next in §458:

> In this unity, stemming from intelligence, of an *independent representation*
> and an *intuition*, the matter of the intuition is of course initially something

received, something immediate or given (e.g. the colour of the cockade, etc.). But in this identity the *intuition* does not count as positive or as representing itself, but as representing *something else*. It is an image that has received into itself as its soul an *independent* representation of the intelligence, its *meaning*. This intuition is the *sign*. (§458; Hegel 2007c)

Sign, then, is a given *material* designating a *meaning* that is an *other* to it. The meaning becomes the material's "soul" but is "something else" other than it. In the Remark to §458 Hegel repeats that "in the sign [. . .] the intuition's own content and the content of which it is a sign have nothing to do with each other" (Hegel 2007c).

This description of "sign" is greatly illuminating regarding Hegel's characterization of "the shape of beauty" in §556. His statement that the beautiful shape is "a *sign* of the idea" can only mean that a given sensory material designates an element that is *not* such a material. This element is the idea, the unity of thought and nature or, if you will, thought's unifying function in nature. So, in §556 Hegel states that the beautiful artwork is a natural immediacy, a sensory concreteness, opening up this unity. The artwork's materiality, being a *sign*, is totally distinct from the idea. In art, nature maintains its independence, but thought, nature's other, is able to encounter itself in nature as the unifying force therein. Art creates a "space" for the idea's "posited" appearance *without* losing its naturalness, its givenness, its sensibility *altogether*.

In addition to describing "the shape of beauty" as "a *sign* of the idea", Hegel stipulates "that *nothing else* [other than the idea] is shown in the shape". This means that it is a peculiarity of artistic beauty that nothing else, other than the unity of thought and nature, is brought to the audience's awareness. Art as absolute spirit opens up a "space" *only* for the reception of such a unity. All other features of thought and nature disappear from awareness. Thus, a beautiful artwork is able to suppress natural elements resisting nature's unity with thought, to wit, elements exemplifying the dominance of material givenness.

But we must be very careful here. Given the *intuitive* character of art's reception, that suppression is only *implicit* or *momentary*. *Necessarily*, then, there are moments when beautiful artworks succumb to the brutal forces of material givenness. There are moments when the spectator of Praxiteles's *Apollo Sauroktonos* does not experience it as the presence of divinity (thought) in an anthropomorphic body (nature) but *only* as a piece of bronze. Beautiful art cannot escape from *this* experience. As Hegel elsewhere puts it, "in beauty the natural element – its [i.e. the idea's] sensuous coefficient – *remains*" (Hegel 1956: 261, 1970–1: 12:308).

On the whole, §556 stresses the presence of two conflicting elements in art's reception: intuition and the ideal. As intuition, art suppresses the idea and appears as material givenness. As the ideal, art brings to awareness the idea and suppresses material givenness. The audience's experience fluctuates from the one to the other situation. Art is essentially a becoming (*Werden*). As much as we are enthralled by the idea's presence in the artwork, as much as we see it as a sign of thought's being the unifying force in nature, as much as we feel "at home" in art, we will always be met with the harsh realization that the artwork is simply a natural immediacy, a raw materiality, an aggregate of colours, sounds, weight, mass, texture, hardness and so on. In the domain of art as absolute spirit brutal naturalism will always come back to haunt spirituality. This is why thought eventually must move on to religion and philosophy to become fully spiritual.

13.4   Art and Natural Form (§558)

We have seen that art's reception is partially determined by material givenness, which is a species of natural immediacy. What is received in this way is a material (colours, texture, lines, sounds and so on) destitute of thought and hence of meaning. Thus, insofar as art is specified as material givenness, thought disappears from art. Hegel insists that natural immediacy is present in art's reception not only as material givenness but also as *natural form*. Natural form is the theme of §558, to which I now turn.

As seen, what is received in the beautiful artwork is not only material givenness but also a *unified* material givenness. It is in such a unified structure, resulting from thought's unifying function, that thought finds itself in the artwork. In §558 Hegel identifies the unified material givenness with a *natural* form. This means that, on the one hand, what is presented in the artwork is thought's work but, on the other hand, thought unifies the material *in order to present a natural immediacy*. Apparently, Hegel thinks that only by presenting (*darstellen*) a *natural* form can beautiful art bring to awareness the unity of thought *and nature*.

Hegel endorses H1 ('H' stands for 'Hegel'), which is a passage from §558:

H1: Art also needs, for the expression of spiritual content, the given forms of nature together with their meaning, which art must discern and appropriate (cf. §411). (§558; Hegel 2007c)

Immediately before H1, Hegel repeats that "art [...] needs, for the intuitions to be produced by it, an external given material" (§558; Hegel

2007c). The "also" in H1 thus specifies that, *in addition* to "an external given material", art needs "the given forms of nature". Crucially, *they are needed "for the expression of spiritual content", for the expression of the idea.*

These *Naturformen* have meaning and are therefore distinct from natural immediacy as a simply "external given material". Yet, as we have seen, beautiful art has meaning as absolute spirit by being a *sign*, which is a structure of *other*-signification. The beautiful artwork, then, is a natural immediacy consisting of (a) an external given material and (b) a natural form signifying something alien to it. This alien element is, as we already know, the idea. *But what are these* Naturformen *which beautiful art presents and which function as signs of the idea?*

At the end of H1, Hegel refers to §411 as a text which should illuminate H1. §411 discusses "the actual soul". The *actual* soul, he informs us, is the soul (or thought or intelligence) permeating a *body* so fully that this body's appearance immediately shows *it* as having a soul, as being a body that thinks, or, again, as being a unity of soul (thought) and body (nature). This does not mean that *the body* collapses into the unity of body and soul. Hegel writes that in actual soul the "externality [of bodiliness] represents not itself, but the soul of which it is the *sign*" (§411; Hegel 2007c). Given Hegel's definition of "sign", this means there is still a distinction between the body, as the signifier, and the unity of body and soul, as the signified.[2]

The body as natural immediacy remains devoid of thought. Nevertheless, even though the body *is* sheer nature, it is *also* pervaded by the soul, an element of thought. Our senses are affected by sheer bodiliness, but insofar as it is part of the actual soul, the body acts as a sign, bringing forth the soul pervading it. Given Hegel's reference to §411 in H1, it is justifiable to interpret "the given forms of nature" as instances of the actual soul: *bodies* appearing as *signs* of the *soul*. If this holds, then, solely on the basis of H1, one understands that beautiful art presents *any* body immediately expressing its unity with soul. The presented body would be "the given form of nature",

---

[2] Peters (2015: 33) argues that the actual soul is a *self*-signifying sign: "Hegel holds that the actual soul constitutes an *identity* of inner and outer; hence the actual soul as sign does not signify something other than itself." To square her interpretation with Hegel's divergent account of "sign" Peters simply discards it and suggests that regarding the actual soul Hegel has in mind "a peculiar kind of sign", "a special kind of sign", a sign that "cannot be understood as a sign in the narrow sense of the term" (Peters 2015: 32–4, 40). The problem is that Hegel never talks of *kinds* of sign, something that eventually leads Peters to describe his statement that the body is a sign of the soul as "odd" (Peters 2015: 33). My interpretation saves Hegel's account from oddity since it takes the actual soul as being an *other*-signifying structure, not a self-signifying structure: the body signifies the unity of body and soul, which is distinct from the signifying body.

that species of natural immediacy (distinct from the artwork's material givenness) acting as a sign of the unity of thought and nature.

In the Remark of §558 Hegel declares that H1 "takes care of the principle of the *imitation of nature* in art" (Hegel 2007c), namely, that an item is an artwork if, and only if, it imitates nature. In Hegel's view, this principle is not completely true because beautiful art should "imitate" only that dimension of nature acting immediately as a "sign" of its unity with thought (cf. Peters 2015: 41–42; Desmond 1986: 1–13). Nature "taken *only* in its externality" (my emphasis), as an element devoid of thought, offers nothing to art as absolute spirit. It is only when nature becomes a "meaningful natural form signifying the spirit" that nature has value for art as absolute spirit, for it is only in this case that thought can find itself in nature. Beautiful art should "imitate" bodies, but only bodies that are actual souls.

This interpretation of §411 and hence of H1 can be partially challenged. Hegel concludes §411 by stating that the actual soul has "human [. . .] expression". If the actual soul has *only* a human form, H1 must be understood as saying that beautiful art presents – not *any* body, but – solely the *human* body. This claim, however, does not fit with passage H2, which immediately follows H1:

H2: Among such formations (*Unter den Gestaltungen*) the human is the highest (*die höchste*) and truthful (*wahrhafte*) formation [. . .]. (§558)

If we identify "such formations" with H1's "the given forms of nature" *that "art needs for the expression of spiritual content"*, which is the obvious option, H2 clearly forbids the identification of the given natural forms with *solely* the human form. It refers to a plurality of natural forms that express "spiritual content" and states that the human is only *one* of these forms. The combination of H1 and H2 characterizes beautiful art as an activity presenting not only the human form but also other natural forms that are actual souls (whatever these may be).

Yet, H2 does inform us that the human form is the highest of those forms and the "truthful" one. This creates a hierarchy of natural forms, at the top of which sits the human form. If beautiful art covers the whole spectrum of this hierarchy, it is divided into "the highest art," which presents the human form, and lower species of art, presenting non-human natural forms. In this case, beautiful art as a whole would not be anthropocentric, but the *highest* beautiful art would be.

Yet again, this interpretation is undermined by passage H3, immediately following H2 (I repeat H2 in the brackets):

H3: [Among such formations the human is the highest and truthful formation] because only in the human formation can spirit have its bodiliness and hence its intuitable expression. (§558)

H3 undermines H2 because whereas H2 informs us that spiritual content is "expressed" by *both* non-human natural forms *and* the human natural form, H3 tells us that *only* the human form can express it. We have reached an interpretative impasse that §558 leaves unresolved.

Peters (2015: 9, 17–38, 49) utilizes evidence from the *Lectures* and the "Anthropology" section of the *Encyclopedia* in order to defend her thesis that, for Hegel, the human form is the sole "shape of beauty". I find Peters's arguments convincing, especially those based on Hotho's 1823 text (i.e. Hegel 2003: 36, 157–8), and hence I agree with her thesis. Nevertheless, *pace* Peters (2015: 41–2), §558 does *not* support this thesis. Since the present chapter focuses on the *Encyclopedia*'s section on art, it is certainly important to know that it allows for a (lower) *beautiful* art that presents non-human natural forms.

Independently of how this issue could be resolved, Peters is, in my view, mistaken to present the human form as a *self*-signifying sign (Peters 2015: 40). For Hegel, the human form is a *sign* of the idea in the precise sense that the human body, *a natural immediacy, a natural form devoid of soul*, brings forth what is *other* than it, the unity of body and soul. The beautiful artwork, by presenting the human form, allows thought (the soul) to "see" *itself* in what is *other* than itself. In art *as absolute spirit* the otherness of the presented body (sheer nature) appears equally as strongly as the idea signified by it. *Thus, nature is stubborn in art not only as material givenness but also as a presented natural form, as a depicted sheer (human) body.*

In his *Aesthetic Theory*, Adorno criticizes Hegel for treating art in such a way that nature loses therein all its independence. In his view, Hegel develops a "language of art" that replaces the "language of nature" (Adorno 2002: 77). Nature is "repressed" in art (Adorno 2002: 61), being subsumed under the influence of the "subject", "spirit" or "thought". For Adorno, Hegel thinks that in art "nothing in the world is worthy of attention except that for which the autonomous subject has itself to thank" (Adorno 2002: 62). In this way, in art nature is ruled by "the dark shadow of idealism" (Adorno 2002: 62). Art has been "liberated" "from the heteronomy of the material, especially of natural objects" and has "expunged" from itself "the rawness of what is unmediated by spirit" (Adorno 2002: 63). Adorno's message is clear: Hegel treats art as a domain in which nature is completely subordinated to thought.

Our discussion has shown the mendacity of Adorno's critique. For Hegel, although nature is not thoroughly dominant in art, it is partially or momentarily dominant. For him, in art nature is *not* fully sublated by thought. While art *is* absolute spirit, it is not *fully* or explicitly absolute spirit, since there are *moments* when thought is dominated by nature: there are moments when thought vanishes completely in art. As Desmond remarks, in art nature "refuses to be appropriated without residue" (Desmond 1986: 5–6). This "residue" is nature's material givenness, the given natural forms and, as we shall now witness, the artist's genius.

13.5   Beauty and Genius (§560)

In the previous two sections, I discussed the twofold manifestation of nature's stubbornness ("natural immediacy") in Hegel's conception of art's reception: even though the audience does experience the idea in the artwork and thereby thought finds itself therein as the unifying function in nature, this finding is only implicit (i.e. momentary), since there are moments when *material givenness* and the presented *natural form* interrupt that experience. In §560 Hegel turns his attention from art's reception to its *production*: besides being received by an audience, the artwork is "something *made* by the artist" (§560; Hegel 2007c). In the present section I argue that, analogously with art's reception, which is determined by "the one-sidedness of [natural] immediacy in the ideal" (§560), namely by material givenness and natural form, art's production is marked by a similar stubbornness or "one-sidedness". *This* "one-sidedness" is owed to the artist's *genius*.

We have seen that in art *as absolute spirit*, the artwork is received as "the shape of beauty" and that an inherent determination of this shape is that it exemplifies *only* the idea. It is in this way that the beautiful shape is a *perfection*. It has also been ascertained that, regarding at least the highest beautiful art, the beautiful shape is the human form. Since what the audience must receive from the highest beautiful art is the human form *exclusively* as the unity of thought and nature (the idea), *the artist*, who "transfigures" the idea in the shape, must ensure "that nothing else is shown in the shape" other than that unity (§556).

For Hegel, "thought" is a *universal* structure (Trisokkas 2009). For this reason, when thought is united with nature, what is *presented* is universal, an element devoid of particularities, individual feelings, eccentricities and so on. So, in the beautiful artwork, as Wicks (1993: 367) puts it, "all contingencies in appearance must be eliminated to the greatest extent such as to allow the universality of this content to exhibit itself through the image". In the *Encyclopedia* Hegel relates this demand for universality in beautiful art with the fact that it is presented and addressed to a *community*. Beautiful art must be able to "speak" to *all* in a community, so the artist must seek to express a universal idea, an idea that can "touch" and be significant for everyone (cf. Hegel 1975: I:7, 11, 30). Precisely because the beautiful artwork is "a work of external *common* reality" (§556; Hegel 2007c), the idea the artist "builds into" (*einbilden*) it must be a *universality*, an idea the whole community will recognize as the unity of thought and nature.

In the most beautiful artworks the idea is expressed through the human form. It follows that the human form presented by the most beautiful artworks must not include elements destroying the idea's universality. The artist, therefore, should not simply choose an actual human being and present her in the artwork; she must rather *purify* actual beautiful human forms, *abstract* from their deficiencies, and thereby present a *perfect* human form as a sign of the idea (Peters 2015: 45, 48, 57; Wicks 1993: 366–8). According to Peters (2015:44), for Hegel, such perfect human forms would be the figures of Greek gods and Christian saints.

This is how Hegel expresses this demand for universality (or perfection) in art in §560:

> The subject is the formality of activity and the artwork is an expression of God *only when there is no sign of subjective particularity in it*, and the content of the indwelling spirit has conceived and brought itself forth into the world, *without admixture and unsullied by its contingency*. (§560; Hegel 2007c, my emphasis)

The expression "the subject is the formality of activity" has a twofold sense. On the one hand, the subject, namely the artist, is the "formal" cause of the artwork in that she builds a natural *form* into a material. On the other hand, she is a "formality" in that what is built into the material is *universal*, an idea devoid of particularities and contingencies. The word "God", I maintain, is equivalent to the expression "the absolute", which denotes a structure defined by the idea. God, simply, is, for Hegel, the unity of thought and nature. So, when he writes that "the [beautiful] artwork is an expression of God", he claims that the beautiful artwork expresses the unity of thought and nature.

Since this unity is a universal structure, the beautiful artwork can express it only if the artist can manage to remove any "sign of subjective particularity in it". If, contrastingly, the artwork becomes a sign of "subjective particularity", of peculiarities belonging to the artist who produced it, it stops being "the shape of beauty" and expressing "God" or the idea. Nothing other than the idea must be shown in the artwork, and the artist's subjective particularity, upon entering the artwork, blocks that showing. Subjective particularity generates "contingency", which destroys the idea's universality, and, therefore, the artist must build the idea into the artwork "without admixture" and "unsullied" by the contingency of her own subjective particularity.

In my understanding of §560, Hegel is adamant that this goal of the creator of beautiful artworks, the creation of a perfection, *never* materializes. Unlike the philosopher and, to a lesser degree, the genuine believer, the artist lacks the capacity to free herself completely from her subjective particularities. The freedom of thinking or genuine faith is higher than the freedom of artistic production. When Hegel writes that "freedom only advances as far as thinking" (§560; Hegel 2007c), he implies that freedom *from subjective particularity* follows a progression from art to religion to philosophy: only in philosophy this freedom maximizes itself and in art it remains limited by the artist's subjective particularity.

What is it that limits the artist's freedom from subjective particularity? Hegel could not be any clearer: this obstructive element is her "inspiration", which derives from her "genius". The beautiful artwork is permeated *not only* by the idea or the rational thinking the artist employs in order to build the idea into the artwork, *but also* by "the *inspiration* of the artist", which is "an *unfree* passion, like an alien power within the artist" (§560; Hegel 2007c). "Inspiration" is a source of "subjective particularity" and hence affects the artwork as an expression of absolute spirit negatively. This is so because it interrupts the expression of a universality (the idea) with expressions of peculiarities belonging to the artist.

Hegel writes that inspiration is "an alien power within the artist". By this he means it cannot be controlled by thought: it is *stubborn*. While the artist is indeed able to create an artwork that expresses an idea that "speaks" to all in the same way, this is *not always* so: there are *moments* when her inspiration does not succumb to thought, presenting elements that are peculiar, emotive and contingent. Just as material givenness and natural form undermine thought in art's reception, so does inspiration in art's production.

Hegel's aim is to make us realize the stubbornness of nature in art's production. It is a *fundamental* trait of art's production that the artist cannot remove her "subjective particularity", her "inspiration", from "the shape of beauty" she produces. The artist's "labour" is torn between (a) an application of what Hegel calls "technical intelligence and mechanical externalities" (§560; Hegel 2007c), which are rational tools enabling the expression of a universality, and (b) an application of elements that are peculiar to the artist's character or craftsmanship. The inspired artist, the creator of beautiful artworks, mixes rational thinking and skilled workmanship with her individual passions and cosmotheory in the process of artistic *production*. This becomes a problem for art *as absolute spirit*, precisely because the latter discloses a universal structure, a structure that does not permit, *even momentarily*, the *complete* annihilation of universality by the particular, the emotive and the contingent.

Hegel concludes §560 with the following:

> [T]he *producing* has in itself the form of *natural* immediacy, it belongs to the *genius* as this *particular subject* [. . .]. The artwork therefore is just as much a work of free arbitrariness (*freien Willkür*), and the artist is the master of God. (§560; Hegel 2007c)

Hegel uses "genius" as an umbrella term incorporating subjective particularity, inspiration and passion. He suggests that, when the artist produces a beautiful artwork, she is both a genius and a skilled worker guided by her rationality (note the "just as much" in the quotation). The crucial point is the link between genius and natural immediacy. The artwork cannot escape particularity and arbitrariness precisely because genius infiltrates it with *natural immediacy*. Genius is the reason why art is absolute spirit only *implicitly* from the side of art's *production* as well.

I have claimed that genius is what interrupts the expression of the unity of thought and nature in art's production by allowing *nature* to stand alone therein, cut off from thought (even if momentarily). This reading is ratified by what Hegel says about "genius" in the *Zusatz* of §395. This *Zusatz* presents genius as a "natural determinacy" of the individual soul. The latter has a variety of natural determinacies, but genius is the lowest or *most natural*. In contrast to temperament, character and idiosyncrasy, genius involves nothing extraneous to sheer nature, nothing coming from *thought*: it is a physical processing, an instance of *subjective* spirit. Genius, Hegel claims, is "a determinate direction which the individual spirit has acquired *from nature*." For this reason, genius appertains wholly to "the sphere of the accidental". One artist differs from another precisely because each is determined by a different genius, a peculiar element *given* to them at their birth. Consequently, each beautiful artwork contains something differentiating it from another: the accidentality of genius sires the accidental diverse features of beautiful artworks.

All in all, §560 attests that art's *production* is not fully absolute spirit: it is not a *perfect* expression of *the unity of thought and nature*. It does express absolute spirit but only *implicitly*. The artist, equipped with "technical intelligence and mechanical externalities", builds into the artwork the principles of her community that allow its members to experience the idea. But it is an attribute of great artists that they are geniuses. Genius functions as a source of natural immediacy, of sheer nature: it infiltrates the artwork with the artist's subjective particularity, her passions, feelings and eccentricities. This does *not* mean that the beautiful artwork cannot open up a "space" for the ideal; it only means that there are *moments* when the audience's experience of the idea is interrupted by impressions of the peculiarities the artist has built into the artwork. The experience of the artwork fluctuates between the experience of the universal idea and the experience of the artist's subjective particularity; it is a *becoming*. *This is caused by the fact that the artist is both a rational craftsman and a genius.* This makes art absolute spirit only implicitly, for there are moments when sheer nature (genius) dominates the unity of thought and nature. Exactly in these moments, Hegel exclaims, "the artist is the master of God".

13.6   Conclusion

This chapter has given a precise answer to Speight's question of how naturalism (nature's stubbornness) relates to spirit in Hegel's philosophy of art: the stubbornness of nature (a) is present in art as material givenness, natural form and genius; and (b) is the exact reason why art is absolute spirit only implicitly and must therefore be superseded by religion and philosophy.

CHAPTER 14

The Encyclopedia*'s Notion of Religion*

Roberto Vinco

14.1 Introduction

The main purpose of this chapter is to offer an analysis of the chapter of Hegel's *Encyclopedia* on religion. This analysis will be embedded in a broader religious-oriented presentation of the *Encyclopedia of the Philosophical Sciences*. In order to introduce this topic, I shall begin with the first paragraph of the chapter on revealed religion in which Hegel presents the theme he intends to develop:

> It lies essentially in the concept of genuine religion, i.e. the religion whose content is absolute spirit, that it is *revealed*, and in fact revealed *by God*. For since knowledge, the principle by which the substance is spirit, is, as the infinite form that is for itself, *self-determining* knowledge, it is *manifestation* pure and simple; the spirit is only spirit in so far as it is *for* the spirit, and in the absolute religion it is the absolute spirit that no longer manifests abstract moments of itself, but its very self. (Hegel 2007c: §564, 263)[1]

The fundamental idea used by Hegel to introduce the concept of religion is that of *manifestation*. Because of its pre-eminence, this concept will also be granted centre stage within this chapter.

Manifestation is crucial, on the one hand, because it is the characteristic through which religion gains its fullest meaning, that is its being *revealed*. On the other hand, manifestation also expresses the fundamental nature of Spirit in general and of absolute Spirit in particular. For Spirit, as Hegel argues, differentiates itself from a mere substance, because of its self-disclosing nature.

These two forms of manifestation are, however, not unrelated. On the contrary, revealed religion is to be regarded as a climax on the Spirit's path towards self-disclosure.

---

[1] I have slightly modified the translation. The German words "Geist" and "absoluter Geist" have been translated as Spirit and absolute Spirit here and throughout.

On the basis of this idea of manifestation, we can distinguish three steps, which will constitute the three main sections of the chapter at hand:

(1) The first part, Section 14.2, will be devoted to an analysis of the absolute Idea and absolute Spirit as self-manifestation. This section constitutes an historic-systematic reconstruction of the metaphysical background of the religious worldview according to Hegel.
(2) In the second part, Section 14.3, we shall analyse the sense in which the elaborated self-manifesting nature of absolute Spirit is concretely articulated in revealed religion.

Religion is, however, not the last word; it is not the fullest explication of Spirit and its self-manifesting nature. The pinnacle is, on the contrary, constituted by philosophy.

(3) In the third part, Section 14.4, we shall therefore consider in which sense philosophy might be understood as a higher expression of self-manifesting Spirit and thus as a sublation of religion.

From a methodological point of view, the present contribution considers religion as a sort of "focal point" through which it is possible to develop a general perspective of the encyclopaedic project. In other words, it is with "religious eyes" that we should look at the *Encyclopedia*. At the same time, religion and its worldview are considered *philosophically*. The assumption of this viewpoint is not arbitrary. On the contrary, it aligns well with the Hegelian approach, for Hegel assumes a fundamental content-related unity between religion and philosophy, and argues, at the same time, for a philosophical elaboration and transformation of the content supplied by religion. Furthermore, a religious reading of the Hegelian text enables us to shed some light on a dimension of Hegel's thinking which the more recent "secular-oriented" scholarship has often neglected.[2]

14.2   The Idealistic Character of the Religious Worldview

14.2.1   Some Introductory Remarks

We begin with the philosophical implication of a religious worldview.[3] The question that immediately arises is the following: what kind of philosophy

---

[2] This "hermeneutical blind spot" has been emphasized by Beiser (2008: 5). There are, of course, notable exceptions, for example Williams (2017).

[3] The expression "religious worldview" does not refer to a particular religion, but rather denotes a very broad outlook that reality assumes if considered with religious eyes. The two main features of this

is involved? We may summarize the answer by saying that the philosophical background of the religious *Weltanschauung* is an *idealistic* one.
Hegel writes:

> The idealism of philosophy consists in nothing else than in the recognition that the finite is not truly an existent. Every Philosophy is essentially idealism or at least has idealism for its principle, and the question then is how far this principle is carried out. *This applies to philosophy just as much as to religion*, for religion also, no less than philosophy, will not admit finitude as a true being, an ultimate, an absolute, or as something non-posited, uncreated, eternal. (Hegel 2010b: 124; emphasis added)[4]

What is the meaning of the term "idealism" in this context and to what kind of philosophy does it refer? The first point that needs to be emphasized is the fact that it does not denote a particular theory, and, more specifically, it does not refer to the conception according to which "everything is my representation".

Idealism, conceived as the fundamental link between religion and philosophy, refers rather to a new way of looking at reality in its entirety (a *metanoia*). This, in turn, might be summarized in the following way: sensuous experience is not to be taken as a point of departure. On the contrary, it is something that needs to be depotentiated and criticized in order to *enter* into the domain of philosophy.[5] The *philosophical* starting point is, in other words, the pure object of the intellect, i.e. fundamental unity. Expressed in other terms, this new viewpoint emphasizes the precedence of the unifying nature of the *Logos*[6] over the manifold experience. This dimension of philosophy expresses, according to Hegel, a central congruity with religion. For it explicates a fundamental tenet of religious consciousness, namely, the fact that God (unity) and not the world (plurality) is the fundamental and certain reality.

---

outlook (which will appear more clearly in the following) are: (1) the ontological and epistemological priority of the divine principle and (2) its all-embracing and all-permeating nature. Now, according to Hegel this religious approach is shared also by philosophy and constitutes the core of its idealistic nature. *Absolute* idealism is, in this context, the philosophy that not only assumes the premises of this viewpoint but also completely articulates it.

[4] I chose this quote from the Greater Logic because of its incisiveness. There are, however, numerous passages in which Hegel emphasizes the same point.

[5] The same movement can be described *a parte subjecti* as an "elevation" of the Spirit to God. For an interesting analysis of this concept, see Williams (2017: chapter 2).

[6] The Greek term "logos" is commonly translated as speech, language and thought. It has, however, also a more "objective" meaning that refers to the character of unity that reality assumes if it is considered from a perspective of pure thinking. Thus, Heraclitus (DK 22B50) writes, for example, "Listening not to me, but to the logos it is wise to agree that all things are one." In other words, from the non-subjective point of view of pure thinking reality manifests itself as a fundamental unity. It is this latter meaning of logos which is intended here.

What we have described up to this point is, however, only the negative side of the idealistic worldview. It further entails a positive dimension, for the primacy of the *Logos* and the intellect does not imply an exclusion of the sensuous and manifold world. Idealization is not therefore a destruction of the finite entities of sensuous experience. Idealism is rather the view that is capable of attributing to finite entities their proper ontological status.

Expressed in more precise terms, to state that "finite entities are ideal" means that they are sustained and governed by the absolute unity and that they are therefore its *manifestation.*[7] This ultimately implies that the philosophical unity is to be conceived of not as an abstract and unarticulated unity, but as a concrete one.

This, according to Hegel, also conforms to the religious mindset, for the divine principle of religious consciousness is not just a separated entity, but one which causes and sustains the finite world.[8] In other words, the religious God is an entity which is involved in worldly events and, more specifically, comes into contact with religious consciousness. He is therefore, once again, *manifest* in the world.

Now, this approach entails an important hermeneutical consequence, because the pre-eminence attributed to intellect and *Logos* implies that the Hegelian philosophy is to be understood as a *metaphysical* one. But this would imply, in turn, that the religious-oriented perspective excludes the line of interpretation which tends to read the Hegelian philosophical project in a non-metaphysical way – for example, in continuity with a Kantian position[9] – for this kind of reading attributes a fundamental primacy to finite experience.[10]

---

[7] This point has been clearly emphasized by Houlgate (2006: 428–32) and Williams (2017: 80).

[8] This continuity between religion and philosophy is expressed by Hegel also in the context of philosophy of history. According to the German philosopher, the presupposition for a philosophical analysis of history is the basic thought that *reason governs the world* and, therefore, that the world is the manifestation of the divine Idea. This principle is in turn the philosophical articulation of the religious doctrine of ruling providence. See Hegel (1984: 27–43).

[9] The term "Kantian" is not employed here in the strict sense of affiliation with Kant, but rather refers, in accordance with the Hegelian view, to a particular position of thought towards reality.

[10] Redding (2018) has distinguished three main views of Hegel's philosophy: the traditional/metaphysical view, the post-Kantian/non-metaphysical view and the revised metaphysical view. The traditional metaphysical view offers an account of Hegel's philosophy according to the line of a pre-Kantian (dogmatic) quasi-religious perspective. The post-Kantian/non-metaphysical view interprets Hegelian thought as a more developed and concrete form of Kantianism. Finally, the revised metaphysical view presents the re-establishment of a metaphysical programme that is capable, at the same time, of taking the Kantian critique into account. This "purified" metaphysics is free from exaggerated and unwarranted dogmatic assumptions.

To which view does this interpretation incline? On the one hand, it is a post-Kantian view, for it conceives the Hegelian position as one integrating the empiricist and Kantian critique. At the same time, it is also a traditional view, for it maintains the religious aspect of Hegel's thinking.

The importance of this religious outlook for the structure of Hegelian philosophy can be better understood if we consider the preliminary conceptions that Hegel outlines at the outset of his *Encyclopedia*, for these considerations can be regarded as a sort of methodological introduction to the encyclopedic project. There, he distinguishes three main positions of thought towards reality: (1) metaphysics; (2) empiricism and critical philosophy; and (3) immediate knowing (Hegel 2010a: §§26–78, 67–125).

Interestingly enough, metaphysics is described by Hegel not only as the first approach, but also as the fundamental one. It is, as we mentioned before, the necessary point of departure.[11]

At the same time, it must also be added that the metaphysical approach towards reality is not the last word, for this intellectual point of view is in itself too abstract. The other perspective, namely the one emphasizing the existence of the manifold world of sensuous experience, should also be taken into account. This second position is represented primarily by empiricism and critical philosophy, inasmuch as both share the same fundamental premise according to which sensuous experience is the real point of departure. According to this view, the unifying activity of the intellect is, on the contrary, something exterior and supervening. The third position (immediate knowing) also shares the premise of the second one, while deducing at the same time a different consequence, namely the necessity of a completely different type of knowing, i.e. an immediate one. We have therefore once again two poles: one attributing pre-eminence to the primordial unity (metaphysics) and the other attributing pre-eminence to the manifest manifold reality (explicitly empiricism and critical philosophy and implicitly immediate knowing).

These two poles are not to be considered as completely equivalent. Metaphysics is, in the context of the Hegelian perspective, the fundamental position of thought towards reality. The point of departure is therefore the object of the intellect. However, the pole of experience has to be *integrated*. Empiricism, and especially critical philosophy, have therefore a *corrective* function. This ultimately means that Hegel develops a metaphysics which is capable of fully including the dimension of experience, and therefore of

Furthermore, this interpretation emphasizes the difference between dogmatic metaphysics (an abstract position that needs to be overcome) and classical metaphysics (a position that, on the contrary, needs to be unfolded and explicated completely).

[11] Hegel (2010a: §26, 67): "All philosophy in its beginnings, all the sciences, and even the daily doings and dealings of consciousness, live in this belief."

grasping absolute reality (fundamental unity) as something that manifests itself in the world (plurality).

The question remaining at this juncture is whether the Hegelian metaphysics is a fundamentally new one, or, on the contrary, continuity with tradition prevails. The religious-oriented approach outlined here favours the more conservative, second reading.[12] This means, as the previous quote also suggests, that the Hegelian absolute idealism is to be understood as the complete expression of a viewpoint that characterizes philosophy *from its very inception*.[13]

To summarize: *every* philosophy is a form of idealism and this means that every philosophy has a religious nature. However, only absolute idealism is the complete expression of this nature, for only absolute idealism is capable of *fully* articulating the all-embracing nature of the divine principle that characterizes the religious worldview. Hegel's absolute Idea and absolute Spirit (the two pinnacles of the Hegelian system) are therefore to be conceived of as the final and complete expression of the religious dimension of philosophy.

This fundamental continuity with the metaphysical tradition needs, however, to be further clarified.[14]

14.2.2   The Idea as Absolute Spirit

The metaphysical point of view considers the object of the intellect as the starting point. The first object of the pure intellect, the *primum cognitum*, is, in turn, Parmenidean being. This constitutes therefore the first expression of the Hegelian Idea (the subject matter of the *Encyclopedia*), and thus also the point of departure for the system.

This Parmenidean being is, however, an abstract unity, which does not include the phenomenal world, the world of sensuous experience. It is therefore an incomplete expression of the Idea.[15] Hence, the dialectical development

---

[12] In this regard the position presented in this chapter distinguishes itself from the one presented by Williams (2017).

[13] In the quote that we mentioned above Hegel explicitly observes that even Thales' water is also a primordial expression of the idealistic perspective.

[14] In this sense, it is also important to distinguish between the metaphysical approach towards reality presented in the introduction to the *Encyclopedia Logic* and epitomized by pre-Kantian metaphysics, and the classical metaphysical enterprise represented by philosophies such as those developed by Plato, Aristotle and Spinoza. For whereas the first is an abstract and objectifying way of thinking, which is intrinsically unstable, the second is an expression of the concrete and speculative manner of thinking that needs only to be fully explicated.

[15] To use the expressions of the preliminary considerations discussed above: Parmenidean being is pure abstract metaphysics (the first position) without any reference to the second position.

can be understood as a dynamic that adheres to the Parmenidean conception and, at the same time, does not exclude the world of the *doxa* (the phenomenal world).[16]

Parmenidean being as such is, however, a pure abstraction. It is to be regarded therefore more as a logical vanishing point than as a concrete point of departure. In fact, Hegel's position at the beginning of his system consists in showing that being itself implies a structural reference to nothing, which, in turn, can be considered as the logical core of phenomenality. This means that the Hegelian Idea is, from its very beginning, not only the fundamental reality, but also a principle that is *manifest* in the world.[17]

This fundamental relation to the manifest world can be expressed by saying that the Hegelian Idea has the nature of a substance. This principle, in turn, is to be conceived of not simply as an abstract substratum, but as a manifest principle. Substance is, in other words, not separated from its accidents (or modi), but is fundamentally connected with them.[18]

This explains why the point of view developed by Spinoza is regarded by Hegel as a necessary standpoint for philosophical thinking. Spinoza's substantialism shares namely the aforementioned point of view according to which finite reality is to be completely depotentiated. Spinoza's substance is, in this respect, comparable to the being of the Eleatics. At the same time, this position is a more developed form of Eleaticism, for it recognizes and partially takes into account the existence of the finite entity (Hegel 1995b: 257–8).[19] Hence, Spinozism is a higher form of idealism, because the monistic substantialism is able to secure the Parmenidean dimension of metaphysics without excluding the manifest world.

This point of view is not, however, the final one, it is not absolute idealism, for substance is not fully concrete; it does not include, according to Hegel, the manifest world entirely. Substance is in fact, in spite of its character of totality, still something "objective". It is, in other words, something that an *exterior* observer can discover and shed light on. This element of abstractness has to be overcome in order to reach the perfect expression of the Idea (absolute idealism).

---

[16] Expressed in other terms: Hegel's system is a continuation of the classical (both Platonic and Aristotelian) project of "saving the phenomena".

[17] In Platonic terms: the world of experience is not, as in the case of Parmenides, simply pure illusion. Rather, it is a reflection of the ideal one.

[18] *Ex negativo* it is possible to say that the position developed by Parmenides is the reduction of a substance to a pure substratum.

[19] Interestingly enough, this element of modernity is described by Hegel as the Christian dimension of Spinozism. In other words, Spinozism can be described as a Christianized Eleaticism.

This dynamic of subjectification, or, to express it in Hegelian terms, the becoming of the substance to subject, can be very broadly articulated in three steps: Concept, Absolute Idea and Absolute Spirit.

The first primordial form of subject is the Concept (*Begriff*). This fundamental category, which marks the transition from the objective to the subjective logic, is characterized by means of a twofold dimension. On the one hand, it is a unity in which every element is a concrete expression of the totality. The difference between the fundament of reality and the surface is therefore fully sublated.[20] On the other hand, this coherent totality is all-embracing. The act of discovery is an integral part of this totality. In a few words: manifestation is self-manifestation.[21]

The development of the Concept culminates in the absolute Idea, which marks the final point of the Logic and thus of the first part of the Hegelian system. This last logical category expresses in a very clear way the aforementioned twofold dimension, for it is presented by Hegel both as the absolute and entire Truth (totality) and as the Idea thinking itself (self-manifesting) (Hegel 2010a: §236, 299). This means that the fully unfolded Idea is not a separated entity, but is an all-embracing principle that integrates the manifest world, including its own "act of disclosure".

The self-manifestation of the absolute Idea is, however, only a "logical one". It is a phenomenon occurring within the context of pure thinking. Or, to put it in other terms, the self-manifestation of the absolute Idea refers to an abstract absolute subject manifesting itself at the expense of nature and particularly of finite subjectivity.

This remaining element of abstractness is fully overcome through Spirit and particularly through absolute Spirit. For Spirit is presented as the return of the Idea to itself from nature. Hence, the self-manifesting divine *Logos* includes, as Spirit, also the element of concrete subjectivity, i.e. the concrete act of manifestation.

In absolute Spirit, finally, this concrete subjectivity is raised up to the level of the Absolute and integrated into its self-manifestation. For this reason, absolute Spirit is also presented as the real knowledge of the absolute Idea (Hegel 2007c: §553, 257).

---

[20] In Hegel's words, "The concept is the *free* [actuality] [*das Freie*], as the *substantial power that is for itself*, and it is the *totality*, since *each* of the moments is *the whole* that *it* is, and each is posited as an undivided unity with it. So, in its identity with itself, it is what is *determinate in and for itself*" (Hegel 2010a: §160, 233).

[21] For this reason, Hegel emphasizes in the Greater Logic that the embodiment of the concept is self-consciousness and the I.

We see, therefore, that the result of the fully unfolded Idea coincides with the position of the idealistic and thus religious worldview, according to which the manifestation of the divine principle is actually all-embracing.

The outcome of the "concretization" of the self-manifesting nature of the absolute can also be described as an intersubjective dynamic in which the divine principle (absolute subjectivity) and concrete human subjectivity exist in a mutual relationship. Absolute Spirit is thus the complete expression of the concept of Spirit formulated in the *Phenomenology*: an I that is a We and a We that is an I.

14.3   Religion in Absolute Spirit

14.3.1   From Art to Religion

After the description of the nature of the philosophical background of religion, we can concentrate on the internal articulation of its "systematic place", i.e. absolute Spirit. A first aspect that needs to be emphasized is the fact that religion plays a fundamental role. This is not only the case because it works as the fundamental link between the first and the third section (i.e. Art and Philosophy), but also, and more fundamentally, because it is the religious sphere which characterizes absolute Spirit as such and is articulated in different forms. Absolute Spirit is therefore a threefold expression of a religious worldview.[22]

At this juncture, in introducing this religious nature of absolute Spirit, Hegel observes also that this topic is to be regarded from an objective point of view (absolute Spirit) and from a subjective one (the religious consciousness). The position under discussion can be explained in the following manner: philosophical reflections on religion can be divided roughly into two main orientations. On the one hand, there is an objective approach, represented by natural theology. This discipline, epitomized by the *Theologia rationalis* of pre-Kantian metaphysics, concentrates on God and His action in relation to the world. This occurs, however, at the expense of religious subjectivity. On the other hand, we have the subjective approach, represented by the so-called "Philosophy of religion" (*Religionsphilosophie*). This discipline considers and analyses religion primarily as an expression of human subjectivity. This line of

[22] In an introductory paragraph on the absolute Spirit, Hegel writes "*Religion*, as this supreme sphere can in general be designated, is to be regarded as issuing from the subject and situated in the subject, but is equally to be regarded as objectively issuing from the absolute spirit, which as spirit is in its community" (Hegel 2007c: §554, 257).

thinking has its roots in the anti-metaphysical Kantian stance, and is represented by philosophies such as the one developed by Schleiermacher.

The central Hegelian point is that an isolated natural theology or an
isolated philosophy of religion is an abstraction. The genuine philosophical
expression of the religious sphere and thus of the dynamic of absolute
Spirit implies a co-presence of the two poles. Thus, natural theology and
philosophy of religion stand in a mutual relationship.

Hegel's general systematic analysis is focused, however, on the objective
point of view and aims at reaching an expression of absolute Spirit in which
human subjectivity (and thus also the point of view of philosophy of
religion) is completely integrated into the divine nature. In other words,
the point of view of philosophy of religion emerges as an integral moment
of a completely developed rational theology. This co-presence appears,
however, because the divine, as absolute Spirit, is an all-embracing and self-
manifesting nature (and therefore the interaction of divine and human
subjectivity) and not – as in the case of the pre-Kantian *Theologia rationalis* – a single, isolated entity.[23]

Before we move to Hegel's chapter on revealed religion, some introductory words on the chapter on art are in order. This will help us to better
appreciate the structure of Hegel's main argument.

The fact that pure considerations on aesthetics are not the only topics
discussed by Hegel is an interesting aspect of this first section. In fact, it is
the philosophical analysis of the classical conception of the divine that
constitutes a fundamental aspect of this chapter. In other words, the
worldview of the *Kunstreligion* is a central element of the philosophical
analysis and critique.[24]

The divine principle of the *Kunstreligion* is a beautiful one, and this implies
that being and manifestation coincide in it. This aspect is also reflected in the
fact that the God of this religion has a human form. At the same time, classical
art and its worldview include also a subjective reconciliation between the divine
and the human. The harmony generated by beauty purifies subjectivity and
also opens up a world in which it can "be at home". Thus, Greek beauty
produces a harmonious way of living (of producing and enjoying beauty itself).
Divine principle and concrete human manifestation are therefore united.

This position is not, however, the last word:

---

[23] The integration of the second position of thought towards reality (critical philosophy) into the first
one (metaphysics) – and thus the development of a complete metaphysics articulating the religious
worldview – is therefore relevant also in this context.

[24] According to Peperzak, the theme of this section is not aesthetics, but a philosophy of Greek
religion. See Peperzak (1987: 91).

Beautiful Art (like the religion peculiar to it) has its future in genuine religion. The restricted content of the Idea passes over in and for itself into the universality identical with the infinite form, – intuition, immediate knowledge bound to sensoriness, passes over into self-mediating knowledge, into a reality which is itself knowledge, into *revelation*; so that the content of the Idea has as its principle the determination of the free intelligence, and, as absolute *spirit, is for the spirit.* (Hegel 2007c: §563, 262)

On the one hand, we have a finite content. The absolute of art is not really all-embracing, and this means, from a religious and historical viewpoint, that the Greek God has structurally a finite and local character.

On the other hand, manifestation maintains – at least partially – an element of exteriority. It is something that has to be activated from the outside and therefore something remaining at the surface. It is not therefore completely embedded into the ground of reality. This is reflected, from a religious point of view, in the fact that the "Apollinian" dimension of the Olympic Gods is local and is subject to the blind necessity which is at the same time *ananke* (necessity) and *tyche* (chance).[25]

The artistic worldview is therefore not the perfect expression of the idealistic perspective. The result is a passage to a higher position (the revealed religion), which is at the same time more general and deeper.

A last aspect needs to be mentioned. According to the previous quotation, genuine religion is also the future of art and of its religious perspective.

This implies from an historical-systematic perspective that Christianity is primarily a development not of abstract monotheism, but of the classical Greek and polytheistic perspective. Manifested religion seems therefore to be closer to Athens than to Jerusalem. Why is this the case? Because it is once again the character of manifestation of the divine principle and thus the humanity of the divine principle that is central in this context.

This element characterizes, at least partially, the classical worldview, but it is rejected by the "viewpoint of sublimity" which, on the contrary, highlights the element of divine transcendence and separates the reality of the Absolute from its manifestation, the divine from the human subjectivity.

Revealed religion is defined, however, as the *future* of art and its religion. This implies that there is also a new element that comes into play through revealed religion, i.e. the accentuation, both on a human and on a divine level, of the role and the value of individual subjectivity that tend to be neglected in the classical worldview. This new element is interpreted,

---

[25] For an insightful reflection on these aspects, see for example Inwood (2010: 627).

however, in line with what we said above, as an integration and complete explication of the classical worldview.

14.3.2   Hegel's Revealed Theology

Manifested religion is Spirit for Spirit. The divine principle is fully self-manifesting, and this implies that it includes in itself the element of human subjectivity, which is only superficially present in the classical conception of the divine. In the context of religion, there are two ways of looking at this self-manifesting divine principle: (1) on the one hand, we have the proper perspective of religious consciousness; and (2) on the other, we have the philosophical consideration of the religious perspective itself, which is implemented in the *Encyclopedia*. What is the difference between these two points of view? Religious consciousness considers the divine content according to the mode of representation. This means, on the one hand, that the different moments of the divine content are separate from each other. On the other, it also implies a separation between the consciousness and the content itself.

In the philosophical consideration the element of unity prevails, and thus also the all-encompassing and self-manifesting nature of the divine principle. This last element emerges in its fullest form in the last chapter on philosophy, but it is foreshadowed in the philosophical analysis developed in the chapter on religion. Given the fact that the analysed content is divine revelation (i.e. that which religious consciousness believes in), and that this analysis is a rational and philosophical one, it is possible to state that a major part of the chapter on religion pivots on a dialectical version[26] of traditional Christian revealed theology.[27]

Some explanatory words are required. For the traditional point of view, the content of revelation is an object of faith. This does not mean, however, that it is irrational. On the contrary, although this content cannot be accounted for in a completely rational manner, it is an object of rational analysis that aims at exposing its internal consistency.

Regarding the content itself, we may say that Christian revealed theology strives to give a rational account of reality in the light of revelation. More

---

[26] The systematic dimension lies at the centre of the chapter on religion in the *Encyclopedia*. A more historically oriented approach is presented by Hegel in his *Lectures on the Philosophy of Religion*. Concerning the latter approach, see, for example, Stewart (2018). On Hegel's view on Christian theology, see, for example, Hodgson (2007).

[27] With the use of this term "traditional revealed Theology", I refer to the articulation of the Christian faith along lines that can broadly be defined as Thomistic. For a clear presentation of Saint Thomas Aquinas' revealed theology in the context of the *Summa theologica*, see Aquinas (2006: 153–75).

specifically, it is primarily an articulation of the Christian conception of God (Trinitarian theology). Secondly, it is an explication of the movement of *exitus* of all entities from God, culminating in the creation of the human being (theology of creation). Finally, it is an explication of the human being's return and with them of the entirety of creation to the divine origin through Christ (Christology and soteriology). In a few words, the central topic of this discipline is God, not just as a single and separated entity, but as the cause and goal of all things. The human being plays, however, a central role in this context. The goal of revelation is the glory of God, but this glory is expressed in its highest form as the reconciliation between the Trinitarian divine origin and humanity itself. Furthermore, this reconciliation is attained through the Incarnation (i.e. *Mensch*werdung Gottes).

Turning now to the Hegelian text, we can observe a continuity both in form and in content.

Concerning the form, according to Hegel, revelation is articulated by a threefold syllogism. This form constitutes, in turn, the nature of rationality itself. Revealed theology is therefore an expression of rationality. Concerning the content, the first syllogism (syllogism of universality) is an explication of the Christian dogma of the Trinity (God is one in nature and at the same time three persons). In this context, the one nature of God articulates itself through three persons. The relational dynamic is both a differentiation, because the divine principle, as Father, generates the Son, and a unification, for Father and Son are unified through their mutual love expressed in the Holy Spirit (since the Spirit proceeds from the Father and the Son).

The second syllogism (syllogism of particularity) considers the dynamic of creation through the Son (the element of difference). It is first the creation of nature, and secondly the creation of the finite spirit and of its self-assertion.

Finally, the third syllogism (syllogism of individuality) is the return of the finite natural spirit (human being) to God. This occurs through a mediator, i.e. the incarnate Logos, which assumes negativity upon himself and redeems it.

We notice therefore that the philosophical articulation of the revealed content unfolds in line with a traditional schema: a circular dynamic in which the human subjectivity is reconducted and reconciled with its divine origin. This continuity can also be expressed by saying that Hegel assumes and deepens the traditional idea of *theosis* (deification) according to which God became man so that man might become a god.

In spite of these central points of continuity, there is at least a basic element of differentiation. Both the traditional and the Hegelian approach are in agreement on the fact that revealed theology is not the perfect disclosure of rationality and thus not the perfect expression of the reconciliation between the divine and human Spirit. However, according to the traditional view this imperfection arises from the fact that reason operating in revealed theology is only a reflection of the superhuman divine *Logos*, which transcends our powers and is accessible only to God Himself and the blessed in heaven.

In the case of the Hegelian approach, the reason operating in revealed theology is imperfect because it is only an imperfect expression of speculative philosophy, which is divine and human at the same time, and thus accessible to us all. Expressed in negative terms, for Hegel, traditional revealed theology is still too closely linked with the finite perspective of representation, and is therefore incapable of articulating the divine content. Revealed theology is therefore not the last word. It is not the perfect expression of idealism and therefore it is not the reconciliation between divine and human subjectivity.

There is, however, also another form of reunification and reconciliation, which begins this time from the interior religious perspective. Religious consciousness is, as was pointed out above, in a situation of separation. However, through faith and especially through the cultus, it is capable of gaining a reconciliation and a reunification with the revealed divine content.[28]

Namely, faith, devotion and cultus have a twofold effect. (1) Through cultic activity the finitude of subjectivity and its self-centredness are overcome and purified, for the finite subject transcends itself and is integrated into a set of norms that characterizes its community. (2) At the same time, through faith and cultus the divine revealed content is appropriated and interiorized by the religious subject. Divine manifestation becomes man's own manifestation, and this means that the Spirit is in truth for the spirit.[29]

In Hegel's words:

> The three syllogisms, which constitute the one syllogism of the absolute mediation of Spirit with itself, are the revelation of Spirit, a revelation that

---

[28] Hegel (2007c: §555, 257–8): "The subjective consciousness of the absolute spirit is essentially a process within itself, a process whose immediate and substantial unity is *belief* through the witness of the spirit as *certainty* of the objective truth. Belief – at once this immediate unity and containing this unity as the relationship of these different determinations – has, in *devotion*, in the implicit or explicit *cult*, passed over into the process of sublating the contrast up to spiritual liberation, the process of *verifying* that initial certainty by this mediation, and of gaining the concrete determination of this certainty, namely the reconciliation, the actuality of the spirit." For a clear analysis of Hegel's conception of cultus, see, for example, Lewis (2011: 169–78).

[29] Concerning this twofold dimension of Hegel's conception of cultus, see also Williams (2017: 286–7).

explicates the life of spirit in the cycle of concrete shapes of representation. In its result, the joining of spirit together with itself, the unfolding of the mediation pulls itself together out of its dispersal and out of its temporal and external succession, not only to the simplicity of faith and devotional feeling, but also to *thinking*. In the immanent simplicity of thinking the unfolding likewise has its expansion, but known as an inseparable connection of the universal, simple and eternal spirit within itself. In this form of truth, truth is the object of *philosophy*. (Hegel 2007c: §571, 265–6)

This quotation is important not only because it confirms the role of faith and devotion, but also because it serves as a transition to the following chapter on philosophy.

The cultic appropriation of the divine content and the reconciliation that proceeds from it do not constitute Hegel's final position. Rather, they pave the way for a new and reflected form of reconciliation, i.e. the one generated by philosophical thinking.

This passage emphasizes therefore the aforementioned basic relation existing between religion and philosophy and simultaneously the sublation of religion into philosophy.

14.4   From Religion to Philosophy

The transition from religion to philosophy will be articulated according to three models.[30] The first model interprets the idea of sublation as a substitution. Philosophy is conceived of as the new, secular religion substituting the old, representational one. The second model emphasizes the co-presence of the two different articulations of absolute Spirit. The third and final model conceives the sublation of religion into philosophy as a transfiguration of the religious way of life.

14.4.1   Substitution of Religion

The first line of interpretation can be defined as broadly left-Hegelian and can be summarized by the famous quote formulated by Ludwig Feuerbach: "God was my first thought, reason the second, the human being my third and last thought" (Feuerbach 1959: 388–9).[31]

---

[30] For a "typological presentation" of the relationship between religion and philosophy, see Fackenheim (1970), particularly chapter 4.
[31] "Gott war mein erster Gedanke, die Vernunft mein zweiter, der Mensch mein dritter und letzter Gedanke" (my translation).

This passage can be read, in the light of the present analysis, as a progressive emphasis on the immanent character of the real divine principle leading to a divinization of humanity.

How is this movement to be explained? The meaning of cultus consists, as already mentioned, in the reconciliation of God and human being. This reconciliation, in turn, manifests itself through the presence of Spirit in the community. Expressed in other terms, it is through human intersubjectivity that God is made manifest.

Now, if philosophical sublation means a negation of the elements of transcendence connected with representation, we can conclude that the sublation operating through philosophy implies that the real and only Spirit keeping reality united and completely manifest is not a transcendent one but is rather present in human Spirit.

The real intersubjective bond is not between divine and human subjectivity; it is the relation between human beings. It is therefore humanity that deserves the predicate of divinity. Hence, the sublation of religion into philosophy is to be conceived in terms of a philosophical religion of humanity, in which every human being is a God for the other human being.

This perspective is, however, not free of difficulties. If this religion of humanity is the philosophical heir of revealed religion, it also inherits the all-embracing character of revealed religion. In other words, this secularized religion expressed through philosophy implies a world in which the representational view of reality and the transcendent dimension which is connected with it are abandoned and the "philosophical gospel of humanity" has become a mass phenomenon.

This result seems, however, to run contrary to the idea expressed by Hegel in the previous citation. For the philosopher suggests a coexistence of religious and philosophical reconciliation.

14.4.2   Co-presence of Philosophy and Religion

In order to save this co-presence, the following possible alternative might be proposed. Hegelian philosophy – conceived once again as a religion of humanity – is a path for those capable of elevating themselves to the dimension of pure thinking. Traditional religion remains, on the contrary, a path for those living in the world of representation. This standpoint can also be articulated through a reformulation of Nietzsche's expression that Christianity is "Hegelianism for the masses".

This position is, however, also problematic, because it implies an element of "esotericism", which does not seem to fit into the idealistic worldview. According to this perspective, God is to be conceived of as complete manifestation, and therefore as entirely accessible. The differentiation between the esoteric and exoteric spheres fits more closely to a Platonic mindset, in which the ground of reality is separated from the phenomenal word and is accessible only to philosophers who are capable of attaining the level of pure thinking.[32] Furthermore, if philosophy maintains a religious character, it also involves a practical and existential aspect. If this is the case, this means that it is difficult to conceive of the same person simultaneously living both the philosophical and the religious way of life. We know, however, that Hegel considered himself a Lutheran and lived as one.

A possible reaction to this impasse might be the following. Human beings (concrete subjectivities) are not constituted merely by pure thinking. They have also an emotional component. Hence, if they want to develop a complete human relationship to absolute truth, it is not enough for them to know it only philosophically. They also have to nourish a religious sense of gratitude and trust in God (i.e. absolute Truth).[33] According to this interpretation, philosophy and religion are thus conceived of as two separate, but also integral, elements of a concrete relationship with the Absolute.

But this position is also not without difficulties. For, in this context, philosophy seems to lose, at least partially, its religious dimension and, more specifically, its practical and existential character. If, however, speculative philosophy reaches a form of reconciliation that is, *mutatis mutandis*, comparable to the one attained through cultic action, this means that it is also a way of *living*. In other words, in the light of this position, philosophy can be conceived of as the expression of the absolute, but not as the *absolute expression* of the absolute, for at least an element – i.e. the emotional dimension of concrete subjectivity – is not integrated into philosophy itself.

Finally, a viewpoint that emphasizes the difference between the religious approach and the philosophical one, but also takes into account the practical and existential dimension of Philosophy, is suggested by Friedrich Hermanni (2013). Hermanni distinguishes between the theoretical and the practical side of religion. The first side is shaped by representation and is overcome in philosophical thinking. Concerning the practical dimension, there is, however, a sort of equivalence between the two approaches, for religion is able, to

---

[32] This position does not seem to work even from an historical point of view, for traditional Christianity presents itself as a position that is opposed to "Gnostic tendencies" emphasizing a form of esotericism.

[33] Concerning this position, see Houlgate (2015).

the same extent as philosophy, to reach a reconciliation, namely through cultus. This implies also that philosophy is a praxis and is therefore comparable to religion, but is superior to the latter due to its higher level of reflection.

A problematic aspect related to this point of view is, however, given by the fact that the reconciliation obtained through philosophy consists also in a sublation of the separation of theory and praxis. In other terms, philosophy can be regarded as the perfect expression of free Spirit, and therefore of the unity of theory and praxis. This ultimately means that philosophy is the better religion also from a practical standpoint; it is the better way of living.

14.4.3   The Philosophical Transfiguration of Religion

This position might be described as one opposed to the left-Hegelian one, since it interprets speculative philosophy not as a sort of top-down dynamic reducing God to humanity, but rather as a bottom-up movement of purification that elevates humanity to the self-manifesting dynamic of the divine principle. In so doing, it remains in contact with the traditional religious point of view and is therefore closer to a right-Hegelian position.

This element of continuity with religion is underpinned by, among other things, the fact that philosophy is defined by Hegel explicitly as a "divine service" (*Gottesdienst*) and as continual cultus. Now, the idea of philosophy as divine service implies that God is Philosophy's

> [...] one and only object [...]. [Its concern is] to occupy itself with God, to apprehend everything in him, to lead everything back to him, as well as to derive everything particular from God and to justify everything only insofar as it stems from God, is sustained through its relationship with him, lives by his radiance and has [within itself] the mind of God. (Hegel 2007a: 84)[34]

In other words, the idea of philosophy as divine service entails a twofold implication. It means, on the one hand, that philosophy has a theocentric character, and, on the other, that the divine principle is conceived as an all-embracing and omnipresent one.

The aforementioned continuity is related therefore to the fact that philosophy embodies the idealistic point of view that constitutes the background of a religious worldview. Furthermore, if philosophy is divine

---

[34] An interpretation of this idea of Philosophy as "divine service" that emphasizes at the same time the mutual relationship between religion and philosophy is given by Desmond (1992, 2017). On this theme see also Vinco (2015).

service, this implies that it is not just abstract theory, but has a fundamental practical and existential character.

In which sense is it possible, however, to say that philosophy transfigures[35] religion? The service celebrated in and through philosophy is deeper and more general than the religious one, for thinking is at the same time the most human (and therefore the most intimate) and the most divine (and therefore most general) activity. In other words, the omnipresence of the divine principle that characterizes religious consciousness is perceived and expressed in a more intense way by philosophical consciousness.

Expressed in religious vocabulary, while it is true that religious cultus makes explicit the actual presence of God in the world, it is also true that in the context of religion the celebration of the divine mysteries remains only a reflection of the divine service that takes place in heaven. In other terms, the human celebration of divine glory is only a partaking in the transcendent divine Liturgy. The difference between *Ecclesia militans* and *Ecclesia triumphans* is not completely overcome through religious cultus.

This complete sublation is, however, the result of philosophical cultus. Philosophy is thus the real expression of the "beatific vision", which representational religious thinking tends to conceive of as transcendent and separated.

The *Encyclopedia* system appears therefore, from this point of view, as the real and complete manifestation of the all-embracing manifestation of the divine principle, as an expression of the beatific vision.

This approach is not, of course, exempt from difficulty. Amongst other problems, it seems to abuse and overstretch[36] the meaning and the role of philosophy. It is, however, the one that most clearly emphasizes the continuity between philosophy and traditional religion and, for this reason, it is also the closest to the line of interpretation assumed in this chapter.

---

[35] The term "transfiguration" has been used in a similar context by Fackenheim (1970: chapter 6).

[36] According to this view, philosophy would seem to be not simply the highest form of life, but life itself ("life of life").

CHAPTER 15

Absolute Geist *or Self-Loving God?*
Hegel and Spinoza on Philosophy

Sebastian Stein[1]

Wisdom is the oneness
of mind that guides
and permeates all things.

Heraclitus[2]

15.1   Introduction

Observers of recent debates about the relationship between Hegel's and
Kant's idealisms have witnessed the emergence of naturalist and essentialist
interpretations of Hegel.[3] Some of these paint Hegel in a seemingly pre-
Kantian, rationalist or anti-individualist light.[4] Meanwhile, metaphysical
Spinozism enjoys the reputation of being the most systematic, monist
rationalism and is taken as either the greatest challenge or the most
promising complement to Kant's subjectivity-centred project. This raises
the following question: how much of a Spinozist is Hegel? The following
investigation into Hegel's and Spinoza's notions of philosophy attempts to
go some way towards an answer.

The resulting enquiry shows that (1) Spinoza and Hegel agree that
philosophy is best thought of as universal truth's self-reference but that
(2) both ground their claims on diverging metaphysical foundations that
(3) enable Hegel to argue that particular philosophers are free to control
their own thought, whereas this might not be the case with Spinoza.

The chapter is structured as follows. Section 15.2 analyses the similarity
between Hegel's and Spinoza's accounts of philosophy, finding that, in
their own way, both define philosophy as universal truth's self-reference.

[1] The author would like to express his deeply felt gratitude (in alphabetical order) to Ansgar Lyssy,
Felix Stein, Ioannis Trisokkas and Joshua Wretzel for commenting on earlier drafts of this chapter.
[2] Fragment 19 in Heraclitus (2001).
[3] For example Knappik (2016), McDowell (1994) and Kreines (2015).   [4] Halfwassen (2006: 106).

However, the investigation into the authors' ontological foundations in Section 15.3 shows that Hegel's account is based on a kind of concept-metaphysics that profoundly differs from Spinoza's substance-monism. Section 15.4 describes the consequences of this for the roles that particular philosophers are able to play in the act of articulating unconditioned truth.

15.2 Hegel's Account of Philosophy

How does Hegel define philosophy? In the early paragraphs of the *Encyclopedia*, he states that "philosophy replaces representations [...] with concepts" (Hegel 2010a: 30, 31): the philosophical thinker has intuition- and cognition-based representations about finite phenomena, thinks about these and comprehends that there are 'eternal' (Hegel 2010a: 299) and unconditioned concepts at work within these phenomena (Hegel 2010a: 62). The philosophical thinker not only understands how the world works and has valid representations about its conditioned and temporal events and entities, but also is able to trace these to the determinations of the most fundamental, unconditioned ontological principle that 'freely causes' – that is, 'posits' (Hegel 2010b: 528) – the entire finite natural and spiritual (henceforth *geistige*) world, including time and space (Hegel 2010a: 46). Hegel calls this principle 'the concept' (Hegel 2010a: 233).[5]

The concept is also the principle at work within the finite subject's and thus the philosophical thinker's own mind: both world and cognizing mind originate in the concept that has taken its more concrete form as *Geist* (Hegel 1986: 229). The concept-based identity between finite mind and world explains their compatibility: the cognizing subject can learn about the objective world because ultimately, within the concept as *Geist*, they are one (Hegel 2007c: 173).

The same applies to the finite philosopher and the object of his enquiry: his mind is just as *geistig* and thus concept-structured as the philosophical truth that it comprehends (Hegel 2007c: 267). However, while the cognizing subject learns about *Geist* in the form of a presupposed objective world, the finite, *geistige* philosopher comprehends the concept and its categorial shapes in its own form: as immaterial and conceptual. In doing philosophy, the concept-posited, finite thinker thus comprehends the unconditioned concept and its categorial shapes in their distinctly non-material form.

---

[5] The concept is deduced by showing that all more abstract categories are forms of the concept, and it thus provides the most fundamental metaphysical blueprint for all higher-order claims in Hegel's philosophical system.

Philosophy is accordingly something that finite thinkers do: they comprehend the concept at work within themselves and reality by having an "intellectual [*geistige*] intuition" (Hegel 2007c: 267), that is, a unified
comprehension of the concept's unconditioned, conceptual truth (Hegel
2010a: 28, 2007c: 267).

15.2.1   Philosophy as the Idea's Self-Thinking

However, Hegel goes on to argue that this is not the only or ultimate way
to think about philosophy (Hegel 2010a: 45, §17). In the final paragraphs of
the outline of the *Encyclopedia*, he provides his philosophy of philosophy,
arguing that the philosophical thinking undertaken by particular thinkers
is the unconditioned *Geist*'s self-comprehension (Hegel 2007c: 267).

The finite philosopher thus comprehends that particular, finite subjects
that think philosophically *are* unconditioned *Geist* that knows itself (Hegel
2007c: 259). This makes philosophy 'absolute *Geist*': it is *Geist* that is self-
comprehending (Hegel 2007c: 276). And the particular acts of philosophical thinking undertaken by finite, self-conscious subjects qualify as the
'appearance' (Hegel 2007c: 276) of *Geist*'s absolute comprehension.[6]

Geist is thus the knower and the known of philosophy. However, if *Geist*
can only know itself, and pure logic and nature are not *Geist*, how is it
possible that philosophy includes knowledge about pure logic and nature
in the way the *Encyclopedia* states? Hegel argues that these are accessible to
philosophy because, just like *Geist*, they are ultimately forms of the
concept-engendered idea (Hegel 2007c: §577, 276): by uniting itself with
a self-posited objective dimension, the concept turns itself into idea and
ultimately into the *Logic*'s 'absolute idea' (Hegel 2010a: 299, §236). This
absolute idea then takes an objective form as nature and subjective form of
Geist:

> The [final] syllogism [of philosophy] is the Idea of philosophy, which has
> self-knowing reason [i.e. the absolute idea], the absolutely universal, for its
> middle, a middle that divides into mind and nature, making mind the
> presupposition, as the process of the Idea's subjective activity, and nature
> the universal extreme, as the process of the Idea that is in itself, objective.
> (Hegel 2007c: 276, §577)

In philosophy, the idea as *Geist* thus knows itself in its forms as logical idea,
nature and *Geist*. The philosopher, as *geistiges* being, is part of the idea that

---

[6] Cf. Hegel (2008b: §8, 33).

knows itself in its three forms (Hegel 2007c: 276, §576). So when *Geist* comprehends itself, it also comprehends that it is the subjective form of the same idea that defines nature as its objective form and that determines (onto)logical thought and knowledge as such.

As part of *Geist*, the finite philosopher thus comprehends (1) that nature is the objective form of the idea, (2) that *Geist* is the idea's subjective form and (3) that it is the logical idea that takes subjective form in *Geist* and objective form in nature. Throughout, the subject of philosophical knowledge is thus the same as the object: the idea (Hegel 2007c: 276, §577):

> The eternal Idea, the Idea that is in and for itself, eternally remains active, engenders and enjoys itself as absolute [*Geist*]. (Hegel 2007c: 276)

Since the idea originates in 'the concept',[7] philosophy is ultimately the comprehension *of* the unconditioned, independent and free concept and its categorial determinations *by* the concept.[8]

15.2.2 Philosophy and Absolute Idea

Crucially, the structure of Hegel's description of philosophical thinking is modelled on the *Logic*'s account of the 'absolute idea' (Hegel 2010b: 735ff.). Like the absolute idea, the structure of 'philosophy' as activity of absolute *Geist* is 'free' in the sense that it is exclusively self-referential, independent and spontaneous: philosophy's idea as *Geist* knows *itself* as it truly is; it is knowledge as complete congruence of subjectivity and objectivity without external conditioning:

> The idea as the unity of the subjective and the objective idea is the concept of the idea, for which the idea as such is the object [. . .] – an object into which all determinations have gone together. This unity is accordingly the *absolute and entire truth,* the idea thinking itself, and here, indeed, *as* thinking, as the *logical* idea. (Hegel 2010a: 299)

In absolute and thus self-referential knowledge, the knowing subject and the known object are thus always already one and their difference is accommodated within a unity (Hegel 2010a: 299–300, §237). The subject can know the object because they are the same in being different. This entails that the difference between the *Logic*'s absolute idea and absolute *Geist*'s definition of philosophy is merely one of concreteness: the latter

---

[7] It is the unity of the concept's subjective and objective forms (Hegel 2010a: 282).
[8] Halfwassen (2006: 327).

SEBASTIAN STEIN

contains all the features of nature[9] and *Geist*[10] and thus involves *geistige* beings and a philosophical comprehension of the ontological structures of nature and of *Geist* in its self-comprehension.

As *geistige* entity, the philosophical thinker thus comprehends the structure of the logical realm, of nature and of *Geist*. In contrast, the logical idea as subject and object of knowledge is purely logical without external natural or *geistige* manifestation or knowledge thereof. And yet, while the self-reference of absolute *Geist* in philosophy is categorically richer and thus more concrete than that of the merely logical, absolute idea, their structures are fundamentally the same.

The most basic reason for this congruence lies at the root of Hegel's description of philosophy as the self-knowing of the absolute (logical) idea ('the idea') in its forms as natural and *geistige* idea. Since the absolute idea defines the structure of knowledge as such, the manner in which the unconditioned idea of philosophy knows itself as nature and as *Geist is the idea's own form*: the unity of *Geist* and nature within the philosophical self-knowing of the unconditioned idea *is itself ideal*.[11] This defines philosophy as the unconditioned idea that knows itself as nature and *Geist* in its own form. To Hegel, philosophy thus means that the concept-based, unconditioned idea knows itself as *Geist* and nature *in accordance with its own structure* (Hegel 2007c: 577, §276).

15.2.3   Spinoza's Notion of Philosophy

How does this compare with Spinoza's account of philosophy? A similar sequence of the definitions of philosophy can be observed in Spinoza's *Ethics*. He there differentiates between three kinds of knowledge that a finite thinker can have and associates philosophy with the third:

> [I]t is clear that we perceive many things and form universal notions: 1. from singular things which have been represented to us through the senses in a way which is mutilated, confused, and without order for the intellect [. . .] 2. from signs, for example, from the fact that, having heard or read certain words, we recollect things, and form certain ideas of them, like those through which we imagine the things [. . .] 3. finally, from the fact that we have common notions and adequate ideas of the properties of things [. . .] This I shall call reason and the second kind of knowledge. [4.] In addition to these two kinds of knowledge, there is [. . .] another, third kind, which we

---

[9] Mechanics, physics, organics.

[10] Subjective (cognition), objective (action) and absolute (art, religion, philosophy).

[11] Cf. Halfwassen (2006: 9).

shall call intuitive knowledge. And this kind of knowing proceeds from an adequate idea of the formal essence of certain attributes of God to the adequate knowledge of the [NS: formal] essence of things. (Spinoza 1994: *Ethics* II, p40, schol. 2: 141)

Philosophy is thus something finite thinkers do, relying on reason and intuition. And it provides immediate knowledge about universal truth. However, Spinoza provides a further, seemingly more fundamental definition of philosophy. Towards the end of the *Ethics* and in accord with his commitment to the notion of god's/substance's all-embracing, necessary universality, Spinoza argues that the finite philosopher employs reason in a manner reminiscent of the third kind of knowledge to see things as necessary and thus as if from god's own timeless, eternal perspective:

> It is of the nature of reason to perceive things under a certain species of eternity. Dem.: It is of the nature of reason to regard things as necessary and not as contingent. [. . .] But [. . .] this necessity of things is the very necessity of God's eternal nature. Therefore, it is of the nature of reason to regard things [from the standpoint] of eternity. (Spinoza 1994: *Ethics* II p44 dem: 144)

. . . and . . .

> Whatever the mind conceives under the guidance of reason, it conceives under the same species of eternity, *or* necessity [. . .] and is affected with the same certainty. (Spinoza 1994: *Ethics* IV p62 dem: 233)

It is by virtue of the eternity of our own minds that we can participate in god/substance's eternity (Spinoza 1994: *Ethics* V p30: 33). Taking the intellectual perspective of eternity, and thus the perspective of universal substance/god itself, amounts to participating in god's intellectual self-love, only from the finite point of view:

> *God loves himself with an infinite intellectual love.* [. . .] God is absolutely infinite [. . .] that is [. . .] the nature of God enjoys infinite perfection, accompanied [. . .] by the idea of himself, that is [. . .], by the idea of his cause. And this is what we said [. . .] intellectual love is. [. . .] *The mind's intellectual love of God is the very love of God by which God loves himself, not insofar as he is infinite, but insofar as he can be explained by the human mind's essence, considered under a species of eternity; that is, the mind's intellectual love of God is part of the infinite love by which God loves himself.* (Spinoza 1994: *Ethics* V p36: 260)

However, since the finite philosophers and their activity of reasonable and intuitive thought as well as their intellectual love are modes of god/substance (Spinoza 1994: *Ethics* I D5: 85) and therefore *are* substance, their thinking and loving of substance is substance's thinking and loving of itself. Philosophy is thus substance's self-reference.

So while Hegel's self-referential (and subjectivity-implying) idea defines his model of knowledge and determines philosophy as its own most concrete instance, the structure of Spinoza's (purely objective) substance's self-reference provides the framework for the philosophical thinking by the philosophers as modes.

15.2.4 Spinoza's Philosopher

This raises the question about the role of the particular philosopher in this process: does Spinoza mean to say that the universal and unconditioned substance 'thinks' itself? Can substance be defined as a 'self-thinking subject' – as appears to be the case with Hegel's account of absolute *Geist*? It seems not. Spinoza explicitly opposes the attribution of subjectivity or personhood to universal god/substance:

> So in whatever way [the will] is conceived, whether as finite or as infinite, it requires a cause by which it is determined to exist and produce an effect. And so [...] it cannot be called a free cause, but only a necessary or compelled one [...] From this it follows, first, that God does not produce any effect by freedom of the will. (Spinoza 1994: *Ethics* I p32 cor. 1: 106)

... and ...

> [N]either intellect nor will pertain to God's nature. Of course I know there are many who think they can demonstrate that a supreme intellect and a free will pertain to God's nature. For they say they know nothing they can ascribe to God more perfect than what is the highest perfection in us. (Spinoza 1994: *Ethics* I p17 schol: 98)

In doing philosophy, the finite thinker may thus take substance's own eternal and unconditioned perspective onto itself. But does the particular thinker cause this 'action' or is it explicable with reference to substance's necessary self-causing and thus no 'action' after all? Bracketing this complication within Spinoza's account for now, it can be said that, despite the substantive and methodological differences between Hegel and Spinoza, both define philosophy as universal truth's[12] reference to itself.

15.2.5 Reasons for Defining Philosophy as Truth's Self-Reference

What motivates the two thinkers to define philosophy in this way? Spinoza's account seems to follow consistently from his commitment to the priority[13]

---

[12] That is, the idea/Geist's or god/substance's. [13] Spinoza (1994: *Ethics* I p1: 86).

and unconditionality of universal god/substance: since substance's self-causing is all there is, any finite subject or object must ultimately be – and be explicable with reference to – substance. However, Hegel's endorsement of the self-referentiality of the unconditioned idea in its three forms might seem odd, given Hegel's self-identification as part of the post-Kantian idealist tradition that is explicitly committed to the irreducibility of individual autonomy (Hegel 2010b: 515). It might thus appear that Hegel contradicts his idealist heritage and sacrifices the independence of the particular philosophical thinker for the sake of defining philosophy as unconditioned truth's self-reference.

However, the two philosophers' motives might seem less mysterious if one considers two problems that are encountered by accounts that define philosophy exclusively as an activity of finite thinkers. The first problem is the metaphysical inexplicability of finite subjects. For accounts that posit finite subjectivity as fundamental – for example Kant's and Fichte's – there is no higher-order explanation of finite subjectivity's existence. Particular subjects and thus also the particular philosophers simply exist, and any universal principle is explained in terms of their self-conscious thought and activity.

For example, the universality of 'reason' (Kant) or 'universal consciousness' or 'I' (Fichte)[14] is something that presupposed individuals have or participate in. The sequence of ontological deduction proceeds from them to a universal principle and not from a principle to them. The finite subjects are the irreducible condition sine qua non, they are the ground for everything (else). While universality might be found within them with necessity – that is, they must have universal reason to qualify as rational individuals in the first place[15] – universality remains explained *in their terms*: universal reason is something *they* have.[16] Finite subjectivity is thus ontologically first; universal reason is a function of it and is therefore 'second'.

This is problematic insofar as, without a universal ontological principle that explains the existence of particular subjects, they are mere 'givens' and contradict the requirement for ontological explanation: if giving a reason amounts to identifying a universal, ontological principle for the existence of something or someone, then mind-possessing, finite subjects are *inexplicable* for finitude-centred accounts. Instead, finite subjects' existence conditions the demand for explanation: an ontological explanation is

---

[14] See Moyar (2012).   [15] See Jarrett (2009).
[16] See Kant (1989, 1991) and Fichte (2005a, 2005b).

something finite mind-possessing beings think without themselves being subjects to it.

Spinoza and Hegel consider this to be problematic. To them, any kind of entity must be standing in some explicatory relation to a universal principle in order to count as justified. In Spinoza's case, this means tracing every determination, that is, modes and attributes, to substance's universality.[17] In Hegel's case, it means tracing everything to the 'free' (Hegel 2010a: §158, 230) self-positing of the concept that manifests itself as logical idea and in the forms of nature and *Geist* (Hegel 2010a: §18, 46). Without a universal principle, there is no rational reason for particular subjects' existence. According to both thinkers, assuming finite, mind-possessing subjects at best courts the charge of dogmatically asserting finite subjectivity and at worst entails self-contradiction: particular thinkers are intelligible only in contrast to the universality of the principle that posits their particularity. If particulars are first, there is no sufficiently equal universality to contrast them with or to explain them by.

The second problem concerns the status of the philosophical definition of philosophy and its property of being a part of philosophy in general. Both Spinoza and Hegel seem to think that in order for philosophical statements to be true – and thus also for a philosophical account *of philosophy* to be true – both the thinking subject and the thought object must be defined as truthful; that is, they must be aspects of or participate in the same unconditioned truth. For if the subject were merely a particular thinker instead of the universal truth itself, the particular thinker's statements *could* be untrue. They might just be the particular thinker's opinions rather than representing universal truth *and* the thinker's opinion. Similarly, if the content of thought were defined as particular thoughts and not as universal truth, the thoughts could be untrue. They might be *just* particular thoughts without universal import rather than particular *and* universal thoughts. In either case, philosophical thought would not be universally true *by definition*. To both Spinoza and Hegel, if particularity is defined as the prime feature of either the philosophical thinker or the thought content (or both at once), philosophical thought's claim to being universally true is undermined.

To avoid this, they argue that the subject that thinks philosophical knowledge must be as universal as the knowledge itself: philosophy is

---

[17] On the relationship between attributes, finite mind-possessing beings and substance, see Trisokkas (2017).

universal truth that is referred to by universal truth. This also reveals truth to be its own criterion: philosophical thought is true because in it, the truth – rather than just a particular thinker – refers to itself. Or, expressed in the subjectivity-implying terms of Hegel's *Geist*: the *Geist* is able to judge the truthfulness of philosophical thought because it is the same as the truth that is thought. The universal truth of *Geist* thus comprehends itself in philosophical thought. This relieves the particular thinker of the duty of being the criterion of truth: what is thought is not true because the particular thinker judges and thinks it. It is true because the truth is both judging subject and judged object.

Both Spinoza and Hegel harness these conceptual benefits when they describe philosophy as unconditioned truth's self-reference.

15.2.6   The Criterion of Truth

This definition of philosophy also has a self-reinforcing effect on Hegel's and Spinoza's own definitions of philosophy. They can argue that, insofar as they are successfully doing philosophy, their philosophies report on truth's self-reference *by definition*. Truthfulness is an always already implied feature of their philosophical accounts. Crucially, this also enables them to argue that the very claim that philosophy describes the truth *is itself true* because it is part of the philosophical truth that they report. In contrast, if philosophy were defined as particular subjects' attempts to describe truth or as their 'striving' for truth, the truthfulness of their philosophical claims or of their definition of philosophy would not be guaranteed: if philosophy is philosophically defined as *striving* for truth rather than as reporting on truth, the claim that philosophy is striving for truth is itself not philosophically proven to be true: a contradiction.

And yet, while both Spinoza and Hegel lay claim to articulating the one universal truth's self-reference, their philosophical accounts differ. How could their conflict be adjudicated? Who can decide which of these thinkers does indeed articulate truth's self-thinking properly – or at least more properly than his rival? Both thinkers would maintain that the only criterion that enables a decision on this matter must be the universal truth itself: if either account is true, the truth refers to itself – and thus within the truth-tracking, particular thinker – through Spinoza's account or through Hegel's. In them as well as in their readers, it must be the truth that recognizes its own self-articulation if their accounts are to live up to their own definition of philosophy. The particular thinker would be able to recognize the truth in either account only because she or he participates in truth's self-comprehension.

To both, truth's self-tracking thus takes place to a larger degree within that particular thinker within which reason and intellectual/*geistige* intuition are more effective. While Spinoza argues that the most developed possible intellectual intuition and reasoning reveal that there can be no more truthful account than his own,[18] Hegel maintains that intellectual intuition and concept-based reasoning establish that everything that is true about Spinoza's account is accommodated within his own.[19]

In either case, the question remains to what degree the finite philosophical thinker has any agency or control over her or his philosophical thought according to either Spinoza or Hegel. Can the thinker actively and spontaneously decide to channel and think truth and thus to prefer a more truthful account over a lesser one? Is the truth simply present within the thinker's mind by virtue of its own nature, or is it the truth that 'decides' to use the thinker and comprehend itself through him or her? A clue about answers to these questions can be found in the most basic conceptual commitments that inform Spinoza's and Hegel's accounts of philosophy.

15.3   Hegel's Concept-Metaphysics

Hegel's fundamental ontological commitment to 'the concept' (Hegel 2010a: 233) implies that he differentiates himself from what he calls 'essentialist' (Hegel 2010a: 173ff.) thinkers, amongst whose ranks he also places Spinoza (Hegel 2010a: 244). To Hegel, all essentialists are committed to 'objectivist' metaphysics and argue that mind and world are both functions of an ultimately determined[20] ontological principle, usually labelled 'substance', 'essence' or 'nature'.[21] Since to these thinkers, everything – and thus also the mind of a thinking and acting, particular subject – is explicable with reference to an objective principle, minds are as determined as the principle itself. Hegel's essentialists thus assume determined objectivity *and then* explain particular subjective minds with reference to it.

In contrast, Hegel's concept-metaphysics are distinctly non-objectivist.[22] They are not based on a notion of essence or nature but instead are grounded in what he calls 'the freedom' of 'the concept' (Hegel 2010b: 505). In its role

[18] Spinoza (1994: 142).
[19] For example, Hegel would argue that the ontological truth of his 'concept' has sublated the necessity of Spinoza's substance (Hegel 2010b: 513).
[20] And thus an 'objective' rather than 'subjective' principle   [21] Hegel (2010a: 223).
[22] And non-necessitarian insofar as necessity is associated with substance-metaphysics.

as ultimate, ontological principle, the concept's free – rather than necessary – structure unites the dimensions of subjectivity and objectivity when it posits itself as *Geist* (Hegel 2007c: 9, §381). The resulting unity of mind and world within *Geist* is both irreducibly subjective *and* objective at once: while the objective world is determined, the mind's irreducibly undetermined subject-ivity is always already related to it (Hegel 2007c: 165). Where essentialists explain mind and world with reference to objective determinacy, Hegel's concept-metaphysics explains world and mind with reference to *Geist*'s internally differentiated unity of undetermined subjectivity *and* determined objectivity (Hegel 2007c: 173).[23]

To Hegel, this also means that *Geist*'s dimension of indeterminacy is out of reach for all essentialists because they logically prioritize the deter-mined principle over all particularity, including undetermined particulars such as subjects' minds.[24] This, however, undermines the prioritized notion of objectivity because it requires the contrast to subjectivity to be what it is *on the same ontological level*: objectivity has to be 'non-subjectivity' to have any conceptual determinacy itself. So if essentialism argues that all subjectivity ultimately *is* determined and is thus truly objectivity – and Hegel thinks essentialism has to argue this to be consist-ent (Hegel 2010a: 224–5) – then this 'ultimate objectivity' has nothing to contrast itself with *on its own ontological level*. Without subjectivity, object-ivity cannot be what it is supposed to be (Hegel 2010b: 735).

Hegel admits that some essentialist thinkers such as Aristotle attempt to avoid this self-undermining by trying to shield the indeterminacy of particular subjectivity against objectivity – for example by insisting that the soul is non-material (Hegel 1986a: 200) and thus contains an undeter-mined dimension. However, ultimately, also the soul's indeterminacy is a form of substance and thus determinacy (Aristotle 1984: 900). Alternatively, if it is to be a form of substance but is still to be undeter-mined, its indeterminacy must come at the cost of its compatibility with determinacy: if all substance is determined and the soul is undetermined, how can it be part of substance? If the soul's – and thus the mind's – subjectivity is irreducibly undetermined in the face of substance's universal determinacy, it is unintelligible how they can be compatible at all.

On Hegel's reading, Aristotle's at least implied insistence on the moments' irreducible difference thus undermines their unity.[25] Hegel accordingly

---

[23] Cf. Hegel (2010a: 223ff.).
[24] In Spinoza's case, substance is prior to the modes and attributes (Spinoza 1994: *Ethics* I p1: 86).
[25] "The soul is substance" (Hegel 1970: 201).

maintains that mostly reflection-oriented essentialists like Spinoza are more consistent when they prioritize (substance's) determinacy over particularity than their speculative counterparts (Hegel 1990a: 154). Nonetheless, the former still lose subjectivity within objectivity, with self-contradictory consequences.

15.3.1 The Unity of Hegel's Concept

However, if both Hegel and Spinoza agree on the importance of unity, what motivates Hegel's reliance on 'the concept' and its 'idea' – especially in contrast to Spinoza's account of substance?

According to Hegel, the concept unites the dimensions of universality and particularity within individuality in such a manner that neither dimension is reducible to the other:

> [The concept's] universal is what is identical with itself *explicitly in the sense* that at the same time the particular and the individual are contained in it. Furthermore, the particular is what has been differentiated or the determinacy, but in the sense that it is universal in itself and as an individual. Similarly, the individual has the meaning of being the *subject*, the foundation which contains the genus and species in itself and is itself substantial. This is the *posited* inseparability of the moments in their difference [. . .], the *clarity* of the concept in which no difference interrupts or obscures the concept, but in which each difference is instead equally transparent. (Hegel 2010a: 238–9)

While universality seems to take precedence by virtue of representing the active dimension of the concept's triad, universality's activity is freely self-negating:

> But the "I" is *in the first place* purely self-referring unity, and is this not immediately but by abstracting from all determinateness and content and withdrawing into the freedom of unrestricted equality with itself. As such it is *universality*, a unity that is unity with itself only by virtue of its *negative* relating, which appears as abstraction, and because of it contains all determinateness within itself as dissolved. (Hegel 2010b: 514)

The concept's universality thus freely posits itself as particularity and then negates this determination to unite particularity with universality to form individuality:

> For in its absolute negativity the universal contains determinateness in and for itself, so that, when speaking of determinateness in connection with the universal, the determinateness is not being imported into the latter from outside. As negativity in general, that is, according to the *first immediate*

negation, the universal has determinateness *in it* above all *as particularity*; as
a second universal, as the negation of negation, it is *absolute determinateness*,
that is, [*individuality*] and *concreteness*. (Hegel 2010b: 532)

In positing itself as particularity and individuality, the concept's universality thus posits itself and in so doing remains unconditioned, independent
and self-referential. Insofar as it is in the very 'nature' of the concept's
universality to freely posit itself as particularity and individuality, the
concept's universality would not exist and is neither thinkable nor explicable without them. It could not be undetermined and self-referential
activity (i.e. universality) because there would be no determinacy and
dependence (i.e. particularity) to contrast it with.

The concept's undetermined universality thus ensures its independence,
self-referentiality and unconditionality. Meanwhile, particularity's determinacy enables the concept to be contentful and determined, and to relate
to other particulars and their determinacy: the concept's particulars are
other-relational and mutually define and limit each other (Hegel 2010b: 534).

Within the concept's individuality, particularity thus obtains universality's feature of independence and self-positing *whilst* universality receives
particularity's determinacy and relationality. Universality and particularity
are one and the same within individuality whilst retaining and bestowing
unto each other their distinct characteristics. Neither moment is prioritized over the respective other because they are simultaneous: universality
has always already been particularity and particularity has always already
been universality.

15.3.2   *Hegel's Spinoza*

In contrast, Hegel argues that Spinoza's essentialist substance-metaphysics
frames the relationship between extended and non-extended[26] substance
and universal substance and finite, particular modes in a determined,
objectivist manner: the unity of substance and modes is itself as determined
and necessary as substance's self-causing. This interpretation seems to be
supported by passages like these:

> Whatever is, is in God, and nothing can be or be conceived without God.
> [. . .] Except for God, there neither is, nor can be conceived, any substance
> [. . .], that is [. . .], thing that is in itself and is conceived through itself. But
> modes [. . .] can neither be nor be conceived without substance. So they can

---

[26] Cf. Spinoza (1994: 94).

be in the divine nature alone, and can be conceived through it alone. But except for substances and modes there [...] is nothing [...]. Therefore, [NS: everything is in God and] nothing can be or be conceived without God. (Spinoza 1994: *Ethics* I p15: 94)

A substance is prior in nature to its affections. (Spinoza 1994: *Ethics* I p1: 86)

For a mode is in another, through which it must be conceived [...], that is [...], it is in God alone, and can be conceived through God alone. (Spinoza 1994: *Ethics* II p47 schol: 102)

From the necessity of the divine nature there must follow infinitely many things in infinitely many modes. (Spinoza 1994: *Ethics* I p16: 97)

God is the efficient cause, not only of the existence of things, but also of their essence. (Spinoza 1994: *Ethics* I p25: 102)

God is the immanent, not the transitive, cause of all things. (Spinoza 1994: *Ethics* I p18: 100)

A substance which is absolutely infinite is indivisible. (Spinoza 1994: *Ethics* I p13: 93)

God acts from the laws of his nature alone, and is compelled by no one. (Spinoza 1994: *Ethics* I p17: 97)

To Hegel, this entails that Spinoza is committed to the singularity and absolute priority of substance, thus making it *the* all-determining principle. Within substance's self-causing activity, negation-defined modes[27] constitute its determinacy and thus particularity.[28] Substance's self-causing thus exerts necessary causality over its particular modes, inducing the modes' total ontological dependence (Hegel 2010b: 473).

Against Spinoza's explicit statements to the contrary, Hegel thus argues that the modes' particularity disappears in substance's necessary universality:[29] since, ultimately, all modes *are* substance, their particularity truly is substance's sublime and strictly 'non-determined' universality. So, from the ultimately true point of view of prioritized substance, the modes' particularity and their contingency is but an illusion:[30]

Substance ought not to remain Spinoza's substance, the sole determination of which is the negative one that everything is absorbed into it. Differentiation occurs with Spinoza quite empirically – attributes (thought and extension) and then modes, affects, and all the remaining. *The differentiation falls to the [finite] intellect, itself a mode*; the connection of the attributes to substance and to each other *says no more* than that they express the whole of substance, that their content, the order of things as

---

[27] Martin (2012: 76–8).   [28] Bowman (2013: 221ff.).
[29] Against this, see Luckner and Ostritsch (2019: 15–27).
[30] Against this, see Melamed (2010: 89ff.).

extended and as thoughts, is this same substance. (Hegel 2010b: 333, first italics added by author)

Forced to decide whether particular modes are independent from and thus limiting to substance or whether they ultimately are aspects of and thus 'within' substance,[31] Hegel's Spinoza renders them substance-internal and thus reducible to substance.[32] Spinoza seems to want both: on the one hand, substance is unconditional, independent and self-referential; on the other hand, the modes are contingent and determinate. However, the former requires that the modes be reducible to substance and thus identical with it. Meanwhile, the latter requires their irreducibility to substance and thus their difference from it. Hegel's Spinoza suggests that both are real but is *conceptually* forced to decide for the former when he declares that the latter is merely attributable to the finite mind that is itself a mode of substance and thus not to substance *as it truly is*.

In so doing, Spinoza protects substance's eternal independence: there is nothing on substance's ontological level to limit it. But this also undermines the reality of the modes and thus the determinacy of substance itself. Since substance is defined as the opposite of the determined modes and thus as *un*determined, the disappearance of modes within substance entails the disappearance of substance's indeterminacy: it deprives substance of its own means of contrast *on its own ontological plane*. To Hegel, substance's universal indeterminacy can thus only be what it is in negation of the modes' particular determinacy: substance is 'non-modes'. However, without modes, substance is not even this indeterminacy, as indeterminacy is itself a determination that requires determination through contrast.

On Hegel's reading, Spinoza's approach thus forces a choice: either the modes are first or substance is. Either substance can be explained with reference to the modes or the modes can be explained with reference to substance. Hegel's Spinoza resolves this tension in favour of prioritizing substance so that the differentiation of substance into particular modes comes 'too late': logically, modes are introduced *after* substance is already established as ultimate and all-encompassing principle so that modes must be thought of as substance's particular form, which in turn undermines the modes' definition as irreducibly particular. So, while Hegel's Spinoza states that substance is first and modes are second but the latter are irreducible aspects of how we must think

[31] DellaRocca (2008: 62).   [32] Against this reading, see Melamed (2012).

and experience substance, Hegel argues that the modes' irreducibility cannot be justified by virtue of substance's priority.

This helps uncover Hegel's main reason for endorsing the meta-physics of the concept: he thinks that the concept is able to avoid this undermining of the determinations. When the concept speculatively defines universality and particularity as simultaneous and as mutually irreducible on the same logical level *from the beginning*, it enables their mutual determination within individuality instead of sacrificing one for the sake of the other. Individuality's priority over universality and particularity does not demand a decision in favour of one element over the other. Instead, it accommodates the elements without redu-cing them.

This difference between Hegel's commitment to speculative concept-metaphysics and Spinoza's substance essentialism grounds a difference of profound relevance for the roles they assign to particular thinkers in the process of philosophizing.

15.4   The Role of the Particular Philosopher: Thinkers in Spinoza's Substance

Spinoza's basic commitment to necessary substance and Hegel's preference for the 'free' concept thus also entail different definitions of the relation-ship between universal truth and particular thinker. These two accounts give varying answers to the question of whether the finite philosopher is determined by the universal, self-comprehending truth in a manner that renders him or her a passive aspect or tool of truth or whether the particular thinker remains a spontaneous and active part of philosophical thinking. Stated as a question, what remains of the particular thinker's spontaneity and control over philosophical thought in the face of philosophy's defin-ition as truth's self-reference?

According to the *Ethics*, Spinoza seems to think of particular thinkers as 'individual' (Spinoza 1994: *Ethics* II L3 CorA3: 126) in some sense. Despite substance's all-embracing universality, the thinkers remain what they are: finite, particular entities (Spinoza 1994: *Ethics* I D5: 85). Furthermore, Spinoza's twofold manner of describing philosophy as (1) an intellectual intuition of finite thinkers and (2) universal truth's self-reference suggests that, to him, both substance and thinkers as modes are real: philosophy might be universal substance referring to itself. But if it is, it must do so via the activity of the modes that are particular thinkers. It seems that, without particular thinkers, universal substance could not refer to itself. Substance's philosophical self-reference would not be intelligible without the finite thinkers' thinking. Substance's self-causing might thus have to include the modes' finitude so that universal substance can be what it is: substance's self-reference might have to imply the thinking undertaken by finite philosophers.

And yet, the inclusion of the modes would have to work in such a manner that substance's unconditionality remains untouched: its universality must not depend on the particular modes as this would undermine its independence (Spinoza 1994: *Ethics* I D7: 86).

To Hegel the subordination of the modes to substance's universality includes the subordination of the particular philosophical thinkers since these are equally modes of substance. If, ultimately, everything that determinately exists is within the parameters of universal substance's eternal self-causing, then all particular modes and their activities are reducible to substance. This includes the activity of philosophical thinking by particular thinkers.

This would mean that the only 'freedom' (Spinoza 1994: *Ethics* I D7: 85) that Spinoza allows to exist is substance's unconditional, independent self-causing (Spinoza 1994: *Ethics* I p17 cor2: 97–8). And because of the priority of substance over the modes, this freedom exists *at the expense* of the particular thinkers' freedom.[33] This would explain Spinoza's adamant rejection of Cartesian freedom of the will[34] and thus individual agents' and thinkers' autonomy: by virtue of being aspects of substance, they are reduced to it. Their self-determination is surrendered to substance's self-causing. Hegel's Spinoza thus realizes that he cannot have both (1) substance's priority and thus self-sufficiency and (2) modes' independence. Forced to choose, he opts for the former.

Since the identity of substance (from here on just 'substance') and modes logically precedes their difference in the sense that substance causes itself and the modes are a part of this self-causation *before* the modes are defined as 'non-substance', the differentiation of the mental activities of particular philosophers is parasitical on their identity with substance.[35] If substance did not have priority over all modes and thus the particular philosophers, the thinkers as particular modes could engage in activity

---

[33] See Spinoza (1994: *Ethics* II p35 schol: 137) and Melamed (2017).
[34] Cf. Spinoza (1994: *Ethics* I p32).
[35] Hegel disqualifies the third option of the modes' priority over substance on the grounds of Spinoza's commitment to substance's unifying universality and independence.

independently from the universality of substance's self-causing. The modes and their thinking of substance could be used to explain substance *while* substance would be used to explain them. However, this would undermine substance's unconditionality:[36] substance could be explained with reference to something else and thus depend on and be limited by this 'other'.

In order to make good on his insistence on substance's independence, self-sufficiency and self-referential causality,[37] Hegel's Spinoza thus has to reduce the modes – and therefore also the finite thinkers' philosophical activity – to substance's self-causing:[38] ultimately and truly, there are no independently active, self-deciding particular philosophical thinkers. Instead, there is only universal substance causing itself in both material and non-material form. And in so doing, it causes particular thinkers' intellectual 'activity', undermining them in their reality as agents, thinkers and even particular entities. According to Hegel's Spinoza, whether we reason and intuit truthfully, whether we intellectually love god or not, is not up to us but is up to god, since all we are is god.[39]

15.4.1   Spinoza's Reply to Hegel

However, from Spinoza's perspective, Hegel's account of the logical sim-ultaneity of universality and particularity within *Geist*'s individuality discloses a self-undermining weakness within Hegel's account: the univer-sality of Hegel's *Geist* is limited by its contrast with particularity. Hegel's universality is thus dependent on particularity and vice versa.

To Spinoza, such a universality is no true universality at all because it loses its properties of independence, unconditionality and pure self-reference. Hegel's individuality might assume these. But since it is 'contaminated' by

---

[36] Cf. "This is why substance is eternally present in its affections and cannot be thought outside of them, no more than they can be thought without it" (Macherey 2011: 210).

[37] "We have before us two determinations, the universal or what has being in and for itself, and secondly the determination of the particular and singular [or individual], that is, individuality. Now it is not hard to demonstrate that the particular or the singular is something altogether limited, that its concept altogether depends upon an other, that it is dependent, does not truly exist for itself, and so is not truly actual. With regard to the determinate, Spinoza established this thesis: omnis determinatio, est negatio [all determination is negation]. Hence only the nonparticularized or the universal is. It alone is what is substantial and therefore truly actual. As a singular thing, the soul or the mind is something limited. It is by negation that – a singular thing is. – . . . Therefore – it [the singular thing] does not have genuine actuality" (Hegel 1990a: 154).

[38] "The substance of this system is *one substance*, one indivisible totality; there is no determinateness which would not be contained in this absolute and be dissolved into it" (Hegel 2010b: 472 remark).

[39] Cf. Nadler (2018: 305).

particularity, it is no proper universality at all. Insofar as Spinoza identifies substance with non-particularity and thus with *pure* universality, Hegel's transfer of universality's properties onto individuality with the simultaneous accommodation of particularity within individuality reduces universality to being an abstract moment of individuality instead of defining it as the ultimate truth itself.

Hegel would reply to this charge that Spinoza's insistence on the priority of strictly non-particular substance/universality is self-undermining because its absorption of particularity deprives it of determination by contrast. To retain substance's unconditionality, self-referentiality and independence, it has to be comprehended as *individuality*. In this form, it is *'true'* (Hegel 2010b: 569) or 'concrete' (Hegel 2010b: 656) universality, that is, a universality informed by particularity that is unconditioned, self-referential and, in contrast to Spinoza's substance, contains the particularity that is required for determinacy and for defining universality on the same logical plane whilst retaining its properties.[40]

15.4.2 *Hegel: Particular Thinkers and Absolute* Geist

Hegel's concept-based and philosophy-defining category of absolute *Geist* is supposed to avoid this: *Geist*'s universality is part of the same individuality that also accommodates the philosophical thinkers' particularity. Since universality *is* particularity within *Geist*'s individuality, universality's properties of unconditionality, self-determination and independence are transferred from universality onto particularity. Meanwhile, particularity's determinateness is transferred onto universality. Since the particular philosophers participate in *Geist*'s universality-informed individuality, they are independent and spontaneous. Meanwhile, *Geist*'s individuality is irreducibly determined because of the philosophers' particularity.

Since the particular philosopher is able to self-determine thanks to her or his participation in universality-informed individuality, universality provides a reason for her and his thought: Hegel's particular philosophers comprehend the philosophical truth because they freely decide to do so and they can do so because they participate in universality. Meanwhile, universality is real because it manifests in form of the thinkers' particularity: without the thinkers, *Geist* would be merely abstractly universal.

---

[40] While I will not try to comment on this dispute here, an answer might lie in a reading of both accounts that disregards the letter of their writings in favour of their conceptual essence.

The finite philosophers' particular decisions to think philosophically can thus be explained with reference to *Geist*'s universality: they think because *Geist* thinks. At the same time, *Geist*'s universality can be explained only with reference to the thinkers' particularity: *Geist* thinks because the finite philosophers think. Both express the same: since they are *Geist* and *Geist* is them, its self-determination is theirs and theirs is its. In being different, they are one and the same. Individual *Geist*'s decisions are the choice of one and the choices of many.

So when Hegel talks of *Geist* in singular fashion, for example in the lectures on the philosophy of history,[41] he implies that *Geist*'s individuality means that particular thinkers' actions and thoughts determine its content just as much as its universality determines them:

> This vast conglomeration of volition, interests, and activities is the sum total of instruments and means which the world spirit (Welstgeist) employs to accomplish its end, to make this end conscious and to give it reality; and its end is simply that of finding itself, of coming to terms with itself, and of contemplating its own actuality. All these expressions of individual and national life, in seeking and fulfilling their own ends, are *at the same time* the means and instruments of a higher purpose and wider enterprise of which they are themselves ignorant and which they nevertheless unconsciously carry out. (Hegel 1984: 74, author's italics)

Talking of individual *Geist* as if it is something different from the particular agents is thus at best metaphorical. Individual *Geist* differs from the primarily particular agent only insofar as individual *Geist* is also universal. However, the particular agent participates in the same universality as *Geist* since the agent is a part of *Geist*'s individuality.

Instead of misleadingly juxtaposing, for example, individual *Weltgeist* with a particular agent, arguing that *Weltgeist* uses him/her as a means, one should say: 'individual *Geist*'s particular agent x does y'. Since the particular agent is able to self-determine by virtue of participating in *Geist*'s universality and *Geist* is determined only by virtue of the particular individuals, *Geist* cannot use the particular agent as if it were something different from itself.

What does this mean for the difference between Hegel's account of philosophy and Spinoza's? Since *Geist* contains and preserves the dimensions of universality and particularity, the definition of philosophy as *Geist*'s absolute and thus self-referential activity entails that *Geist*'s

---

[41] "The world spirit is the spirit of the world as it reveals itself through the human consciousness; the relationship of men to it is that of single parts to the whole which is their substance" (Hegel 1984: 52).

individuality expresses itself in the particular thoughts of finite thinkers *whilst* these retain universality's ability to self-determine. Through the thoughts of finite philosophers, absolute *Geist* is determined *and* the finite philosophers are self-determining by virtue of *Geist*'s universality. So, within *Geist*'s individuality, the particular philosophers are 'universalized' and are therefore as self-causing and independent as *Geist*'s universality. The philosophers' decision to replace representations with concepts, to have an intellectual intuition and thus to open themselves to philosophical truth is thus not determined by a prioritized universal *Geist* that differs from them. Instead, their thinking *is* the universal, albeit in particular form. They are authors and owners of the decision to think philosophically and thus to comprehend truth because they participate in *Geist*'s universality. Their ability to author philosophical thought is rooted in the same universality as that to which their particularity gives concrete content within individuality's unity.

In potential contrast to Spinoza's particular, mode-like and substance-accommodated thinkers, Hegel's particular philosophers thus determine *Geist*'s universality *while* this universality's self-positing is articulated in their particular existence and activity: "The end of the [*Weltgeist*] is realised in substance through the freedom of each individual" (Hegel 1984: 55).

15.5 Conclusion

Despite their common rejection of individuality-based accounts of philosophy and what they perceive as their self-contradictory destabilization of philosophical truth, Spinoza and Hegel profoundly differ on the form that the ontological foundation of philosophy should take. While Spinoza focuses on the pure universality, independence and unconditionality of substance, Hegel speculatively unites universality's indeterminacy with particularity's determinacy within the concept's individuality. In contrast to Spinoza, who rejects the notion of modes' and thus particular thinkers' causal powers on the most profound possible level, Hegel argues that the particular philosopher does have a universality-informed say in the form and content of his thoughts.

Whether Hegel succeeds in his attempt to unite Kantian/Fichtean individual autonomy with the overarching universal dimension of *Geist* or whether Spinoza's monist naturalism is ultimately preferable might depend on whether one primarily subscribes to the thinking-method of reflection or speculation.[42] In either case, these two philosophers' commitment to a unified, universality-based philosophical science that is able to self-justify and to provide an all-the-way-down explanation of all reality might be one of the most meaningful commonality two metaphysical thinkers could possibly share.

---

[42] Cf. Hegel (1991b: §§79–82, 125ff.).

Bibliography

Adorno, T. (2002). *Aesthetic Theory*. Trans. R. Hullot-Kentor. New York: Continuum.

Alznauer, M. (2015). *Hegel's Theory of Responsibility*. Cambridge: Cambridge University Press.

Ameriks, K. (1990). "Kant, Fichte, and Short Arguments to Idealism," *Archiv für Geschichte der Philosophie*, 72(1), pp. 63–85.

Ameriks, K. (2000). *Kant and the Fate of Autonomy: Problems in the Appropriation of the Critical Philosophy*. New York and Cambridge: Cambridge University Press.

Aquinas, T. (2006). *The Treatise on the Divine Nature: Summa Theologiae I*, 1–13. Trans. B. J. Shanley. Indianapolis: Hackett.

Aristotle (1984). *The Complete Works of Aristotle: The Revised Oxford Translation*, 2 vols. Edited by J. Barnes. Princeton: Princeton University Press.

Beiser, F. C. (2008). "Introduction: The Puzzling Hegel Renaissance," in F. C. Beiser, ed. *The Cambridge Companion to Hegel and Nineteenth-Century Philosophy*. New York: Cambridge University Press, pp. 1–14.

Bernasconi, R. (1998). "Hegel at the Court of the Ashanti," in S. Barnett, ed. *Hegel after Derrida*. New York: Routledge, pp. 41–63.

Bernasconi, R. (2000). "With What Must the Philosophy of World History Begin? On the Racial Basis of Hegel's Eurocentrism," *Nineteenth-Century Contexts*, 22(2), pp. 171–201.

Berry, C. (1980). "Property and Possession: Two Replies to Locke – Hume and Hegel," in J. R. Pennock and J. W. Chapman, eds. *Property*. New York: New York University Press, pp. 89–100.

Berthold-Bond, D. (1995). *Hegel's Theory of Madness*. Albany: State University of New York Press.

Biard, J., et al. (1987). *Introduction à la lecture de la* Science de la Logique *de Hegel*, vol. 3: *La doctrine du Concept*. Paris: Aubier.

Bonsiepen, W. (1997). *Die Begründung einer Naturphilosophie bei Kant, Schelling, Fries und Hegel: Mathematische versus spekulative Naturphilosophie*. Frankfurt am Main: Klostermann.

Blackburn, S. (1990). "Filling in Space," *Analysis*, 50(2), pp. 62–5.

Bowman, B. (2013). *Hegel and the Metaphysics of Absolute Negativity*. New York and Cambridge: Cambridge University Press.

Brinkmann, K. (2011). *Idealism without Limits: Hegel on the Problem of Objectivity.* Dordrecht: Springer.

Brinkmann, K. (2016). "Hegel on Translating Representations: Rethinking the Task of Philosophy," in L. Fonnesu and L. Ziglioli, eds. *System und Logik bei Hegel.* Hildesheim: Olms, pp. 43–61.

Brooks, T. (2004). "Taking the System Seriously: Themes in Hegel's *Philosophy of Right*," Ph.D. dissertation, Department of Philosophy, University of Sheffield.

Brooks, T. (2007). *Hegel's Political Philosophy: A Systematic Reading of the Philosophy of Right.* Edinburgh: Edinburgh University Press.

Brooks, T. ed. (2012a). "Hegel and the Unified Theory of Punishment," in T. Brooks, ed. *Hegel's Philosophy of Right.* Oxford: Blackwell, pp. 103–23.

Brooks, T., ed. (2012b). *Hegel's Philosophy of Right.* Oxford: Blackwell.

Brooks, T. (2012c). *Punishment.* London: Routledge.

Brooks, T. (2013). *Hegel's Political Philosophy: A Systematic Reading of the Philosophy of Right*, 2nd edition. Edinburgh: Edinburgh University Press.

Brooks, T. (2016). "In Defence of *Punishment* and the United Theory of Punishment: A Reply," *Criminal Law and Philosophy*, 10, pp. 629–38.

Brooks, T. (2017a). "Hegel on Crime and Punishment," in T. Brooks and S. Stein, eds. *Hegel's Political Philosophy: On the Normative Significance of Method and System.* Oxford: Oxford University Press, pp. 202–21.

Brooks, T. (2017b). "Hegel's Philosophy of Law," in D. Moyar, ed. *The Oxford Handbook of Hegel.* Oxford: Oxford University Press, pp. 453–74.

Brooks, T., and M. C. Nussbaum, eds. (2015). *Rawls's Political Liberalism.* New York: Columbia University Press.

Brooks, T., and S. Stein, eds. (2017). *Hegel's Political Philosophy: On the Normative Significance of Method and System.* Oxford: Oxford University Press.

Brumbaugh, R. S. 1954. *Plato's Mathematical Imagination: The Mathematical Passages in the Dialogues and Their Interpretation.* Indiana: Indiana University Press.

Buchwalter, A. (2009). "Is Hegel's Philosophy of History Eurocentric?," in W. Dudley, ed. *Hegel and History.* Albany: State University of New York Press, pp. 87–110.

Burbidge, J. W. (2006). *The Logic of Hegel's Logic: An Introduction.* Peterborough, Ontario: Broadview Press.

Carlson, L. (2009). *The Faces of Intellectual Disability: Philosophical Reflections.* Bloomington: Indiana University Press.

Carlson, L., and E. F. Kittay, eds. (2010). *Cognitive Disability and Its Challenge to Moral Philosophy.* Malden: Wiley-Blackwell.

Ciavatta, D. (2005). "Hegel on Owning One's Body," *The Southern Journal of Philosophy*, 43, pp. 1–23.

Clare, E. (2017). *Brilliant Imperfection: Grappling with Cure.* Durham: Duke University Press.

Cooper, D. E. (1971). "Hegel's Theory of Punishment," in Z. A. Pelczynski, ed. *Hegel's Political Philosophy: Problems and Perspectives.* Cambridge: Cambridge University Press, pp. 151–67.

Corti, L. (2016). "Conceptualism, Non-conceptualism, and the Method of Hegel's *Psychology*," in S. Herrmann-Sinai and L. Ziglioli, eds. *Hegel's Philosophical Psychology*. London and New York: Routledge, pp. 228–50.

Cramer, K. (1999). "Peripetien der Ontologie – Wolff, Kant, Hegel," in R. Bubner, ed. *Die Weltgeschichte – das Weltgericht?* Stuttgart: Klett Cotta, pp. 176–207.

De Laurentiis, A. (2014). "Race in Hegel: Text and Context," in M. Egger, ed. *Philosophie nach Kant: Neue Wege zum Verständnis von Kants Transzendental- und Moralphilosophie*. Berlin: De Gruyter, pp. 591–624.

DellaRocca, M. (2008). *Spinoza*. New York: Routledge.

Desmond, W. (1986). *Art and the Absolute: A Study of Hegel's Aesthetics*. Albany: State University of New York Press.

Desmond, W. (1992). *Beyond Hegel and Dialectic: Speculation, Cult, and Comedy*. Albany: State University of New York Press.

Desmond, W. (2017). *Hegel's God: A Counterfeit Double?* Abingdon and New York: Routledge.

DeVries, W. (1988). *Hegel's Theory of Mental Activity*. Ithaca and London: Cornell University Press.

DeVries, W. (2016). "Hegel's Account of the Presence of Space and Time in Sensation, Intuition, and the World: A Sellarsian View," in S. Herrmann-Sinai and L. Ziglioli, eds. *Hegel's Philosophical Psychology*. London and New York: Routledge, pp. 214–27.

Dryden, J. (2013). "Hegel, Feminist Philosophy, and Disability: Rereading Our History," *Disability Studies Quarterly*, 33(4), http://dsq-sds.org/article/view/38 68/3407 (accessed 9 February 2021).

Dryden, J. (2016). "Digestion, Habit, and Being at Home: Hegel and the Gut as Ambiguous Other," *PhaenEx*, 11(2), pp. 1–22.

Düsing, K. (2016). *Das Problem der Subjektivität in Hegels Logik*. Hamburg: Meiner. (First published Bonn: Bouvier, 1976.)

Fackenheim, E. L. (1970). *The Religious Dimension in Hegel's Thought*. Boston: Beacon Press.

Falk, H. P. (1983). *Das Wissen in Hegels* Wissenschaft der Logik. Freiburg: Alber.

Ferrarin, A. (2019). *Thinking and the I: Hegel and the Critique of Kant*. Evanston: Northwestern University Press.

Feuerbach, L. (1959). *Grundsätze der Philosophie der Zukunft*, in *Sämtliche Werke*, Vol. 2. Edited by W. Bolin and F. Jodl. Stuttgart-Bad Cannstadt: Frommann.

Fichte, J. G. (1971a). *Die Wissenschaftslehre* (1804), in *Fichtes Werke*, Vol. 10. Edited by I. H. Fichte. Berlin: De Gruyter.

Fichte, J. G. (1971b). *Einige Vorlesungen über die Bestimmung des Gelehrten, 1794*, in *Fichtes Werke*, Vol. 6. Edited by I. H. Fichte. Berlin: De Gruyter.

Fichte, J. G. (1971c). *System der Sittenlehre nach den Principien der Wissenschaftslehre, 1798*, in *Fichtes Werke*, Vol. 4. Edited by I. H. Fichte. Berlin: De Gruyter.

Fichte, J. G. (1971d). *Zweite Einleitung in die Wissenschaftslehre* (1797), in *Fichtes Werke*, Vol. 1. Edited by I. H. Fichte. Berlin: De Gruyter.

Fichte, J. G. (1988). *Early Philosophical Writings*. Trans. and edited by D. Breazeale. Ithaca and London: Cornell University Press.

Fichte, J. G. (2005a). *The Science of Knowing: J. G. Fichte's 1804 Lectures on the Wissenschaftslehre*. Trans. W. E. Wright. New York: State University of New York Press.

Fichte, J. G. (2005b). *The System of Ethics*. Trans. and edited by D. Breazeale and G. Zöller. Cambridge: Cambridge University Press.

Ficara, E. (2019). "Empowering Forms: Hegel's Conception of 'Form' and 'Formal.'" in P. D. Bubbio, A. De Cesaris, M. Pagano, and H. Weslati, eds. *Hegel, Logic and Speculation*. London: Bloomsbury, pp. 15–26.

Findlay, J. N. (1962). *Hegel: A Re-examination*. New York: Collier Books.

Fisher, Q. A. "Being-Together: An Essay on the First-Person Plural," Ph.D. dissertation, Georgetown University.

Foley, R. (2008). "Plato's Undividable Line: Contradiction and Method in Republic VI," *Journal of the History of Philosophy*, 46, pp. 1–24.

Förster, E. (2012). *The Twenty-Five Years of Philosophy: A Systematic Reconstruction*. Cambridge: Harvard University Press.

Fossa, J. A., and G. W. Erickson (2005). "The Divided Line and the Golden Mean," *Revista Brasileira de História da Matemática*, 5(9), pp. 59–77.

Frege, G. (1980). *Philosophical and Mathematical Correspondence*. Trans. H. Kaal. Edited by B. McGuinness. Chicago: University of Chicago Press.

Fukuyama, F. (1992). *The End of History and the Last Man*. New York: Free Press.

Fulda, H. F. (1999). "Die Ontologie und ihr Schicksal in der Philosophie Hegels. Kantkritik in Fortsetzung kantischer Gedanken," *Revue Internationale de Philosophie*, 210, pp. 465–84.

Fulda, H. F. (2003). *Georg Wilhelm Friedrich Hegel*. Munich: C. H. Beck.

Fulda, H. F., R. P. Horstmann, and M. Theunisen (1980). *Kritische Darstellung der Metaphysik: Eine Diskussion über Hegels Logik*. Stuttgart: Suhrkamp.

Furlotte, W. (2018). *The Problem of Nature in Hegel's Final System*. Edinburgh: Edinburgh University Press.

Gaiger, J. (2006). "Catching Up with History: Hegel and Abstract Painting," in K. Deligiorgi, ed. *Hegel: New Directions*. Chesham: Acumen, pp. 159–76.

Gerhard, M. (2015). *Hegel und die logische Frage*. Berlin: De Gruyter.

Gethmann-Siefert, A. (1991). "Ästhetik oder Philosophie der Kunst: Die Nachschriften und Zeugnisse zu Hegels Berliner Vorlesungen," *Hegel-Studien*, 26, pp. 92–110.

Gethmann-Siefert, A. (1992). "Das 'moderne' Gesamtkunstwerk: Die Oper," in A. Gethmann-Siefert, ed. *Phänomen versus System: Zum Verhältnis von philosophischer Systematik und Kunsturteil in Hegels Berliner Vorlesungen über Ästhetik oder Philosophie der Kunst*. Bonn: Bouvier, pp. 165–230.

Gethmann-Siefert, A. (2000). "Die Kunst (§§556–563): Hegels systematische Begründung der Geschichtlichkeit der Kunst," in H. Drüe et al., eds. *Hegels "Enzyklopädie der philosophischen Wissenschaften" (1830): Ein Kommentar zum Systemgrundriß*. Franfurt am Main: Suhrkamp, pp. 317–74.

Gethmann-Siefert, A. (2005). "Die systematische Bestimmung der Kunst und die Geschichtlichkeit der Künste: Hegels Vorlesung über 'Aestheticen sive philosophiam artis' von 1826," in G. Hegel, *Philosophie der Kunst: Vorlesung von 1826*.

Edited by A. Gethmann-Siefert, J.-I. Kwon, and K. Berr. Frankfurt am Main: Suhrkamp, pp. 9–44.

Gibson, A. B. (1955). "Plato's Mathematical Imagination," *Review of Metaphysics*, 9, pp. 57–70.

Ginsborg, H. (1997). "Aesthetic and Biological Purposiveness," in A. Reath, B. Herman, and C. M. Korsgaard, eds. *Reclaiming the History of Ethics: Essays for John Rawls*. Cambridge: Cambridge University Press, pp. 329–60.

Ginsborg, H. (2001). "Kant on Understanding Organisms as Natural Purposes," in E. Watkins, ed. *Kant and the Sciences*. Oxford: Oxford University Press, pp. 63–78.

Greene, M. (1972). *Hegel on the Soul: A Speculative Anthropology*. The Hague: Martinus Nijhoff.

Haase, M. (2016). "Three Forms of the First Person Plural," in G. Abel and J. Conant, eds. *Rethinking Epistemology*, Vol. 1. Berlin and Boston: De Gruyter, pp. 229–56.

Hackenesch, C. (2000). "Die Wissenschaft der Logik (§§ 19–244)," in H. Drüe et al., eds. *Hegels "Enzyklopädie der philosophischen Wissenschaften" (1830): Ein Kommentar zum Systemgrundriß*. Frankfurt am Main: Suhrkamp, pp. 87–138.

Halbig, C. (2002). *Objektives Denken: Erkenntnistheorie und Philosophy of Mind in Hegels System*. Stuttgart: Frommann-Holzboog.

Halfwassen, J. (2005). *Hegel und der spätantike Neuplatonismus: Untersuchungen zur Metaphysik des Einen und des Nous in Hegels spekulativer und geschichtlicher Deutung*. Hamburg: Meiner.

Halfwassen, J. (2006). *Der Aufstieg zum Einen: Untersuchungen zu Platon und Plotin*. Munich: Saur.

Harris, E. E. (1983). *An Interpretation of the Logic of Hegel*. Lanham: University Press of America.

Hartmann, K. (1972). "Hegel: A Non-metaphysical View," in A. MacIntyre, ed. *Hegel: A Collection of Critical Essays*. Notre Dame: University of Notre Dame Press, pp. 101–24.

Hartmann, K. (1999). *Hegel's Logic*. Berlin and New York: De Gruyter.

Heath, T. (1921). *A History of Greek Mathematics. Volume 1, From Thales to Euclid*. Oxford: Clarendon Press.

Heath, T. (1949). *Mathematics in Aristotle*. Oxford: Oxford University Press.

Hegel, G. W. F. (1894). *Philosophy of Mind* (Volume 3 of Hegel's *Encyclopedia*). Trans. W. Wallace. Oxford: Clarendon Press.

Hegel, G. W. F. (1956). *The Philosophy of History*. Trans. J. Sibree. New York: Dover.

Hegel, G. W. F. (1968). *Philosophy of Nature* (Volume 2 of Hegel's *Encyclopedia*). Volume 1. Trans. M. J. Petry. London: Humanities Press.

Hegel, G. W. F. (1968–). *Gesammelte Werke*. Edited by the Rheinisch-Westfälische Akademie der Wissenschaften. Hamburg: Felix Meiner.

Hegel, G. W. F. (1969). *Science of Logic*. Trans. A. V. Miller. Amherst: Humanity Books.

Hegel, G. W. F. (1970). *Hegel's Philosophy of Nature, Part Two of the Encyclopædia of the Philosophical Sciences (1830)*. Trans. A. V. Miller. Oxford: Oxford University Press.

Hegel, G. W. F. (1970–1). *Werke.* Edited by E. Moldenhauer and K. Michel. Frankfurt am Main: Suhrkamp.

Hegel, G. W. F. (1971). *Hegel's Philosophy of Mind: Part Three of the Encyclopaedia of the Philosophical Sciences (1830).* Trans. W. Wallace, together with the *Zusätze* in Boumann's text (1845), trans. A. V. Miller. Oxford: Oxford University Press.

Hegel, G. W. F. (1975). *Aesthetics: Lectures on Fine Art,* 2 vols. Trans. T. M. Knox. Oxford: Clarendon Press.

Hegel, G. W. F. (1977). *The Phenomenology of Spirit.* Trans. A. V. Miller. New York: Oxford University Press.

Hegel, G. W. F. (1984). *Lectures on the Philosophy of World History: Introduction.* Trans. H. B. Nisbet. Cambridge: Cambridge University Press.

Hegel, G. W. F. (1986). *The Philosophical Propadeutic.* Trans. A. V. Miller. Edited by M. George and A. Vincent. Oxford: Blackwell.

Hegel, G. W. F. (1988a). *Introduction to the Philosophy of History.* Trans. L. Rauch. Indianapolis and Cambridge: Hackett Publishing Company, Inc.

Hegel, G. W. F. (1988b). *Lectures on the Philosophy of Religion: One Volume Edition, The Lectures of 1827.* Trans. R. F. Brown, P. C. Hodgson, and J. M. Stewart, with the assistance of H. S. Harris. Edited by P. C. Hodgson. Berkeley: The University of California Press.

Hegel, G. W. F. (1990a). *Encyclopedia of the Philosophical Sciences in Outline and Critical Writings.* Edited by E. Behler. New York: Continuum.

Hegel, G. W. F. (1990b). *Lectures on the History of Philosophy: The Lectures of 1825–1826: Volume III Medieval and Modern Philosophy.* Trans. R. F. Brown, J. M. Stewart, and H. S. Harris. Edited by R. F. Brown. Berkeley: University of California Press.

Hegel, G. W. F. (1991a). *Elements of the Philosophy of Right.* Trans. H. B. Nisbet. Edited by A. Wood. Cambridge: Cambridge University Press.

Hegel, G. W. F. (1991b). *The Encyclopedia Logic.* Trans. T. F. Geraets, W. A. Suchting, and H. S. Harris. Indianapolis: Hackett Publishing.

Hegel, G. W. F. (1991c). *Science of Logic.* Trans. A. V. Miller. Atlantic Highlands: Humanities Press International.

Hegel, G. W. F. (1992). *Vorlesungen über Logik und Metaphysik. Heidelberg 1817.* Co-written by F. A. Good. (*Vorlesungen. Ausgewählte Nachschriften und Manuskripte,* Vol. II). Hamburg: Meiner.

Hegel, G. W. F. (1994). *Hegels Vorlesungen über die Philosophie des Geistes 1827/28.* Edited by F. Hespe and B. Tuschling, with an introduction by B. Tuschling. Hamburg: Meiner.

Hegel, G. W. F. (1995a). *Lectures on Natural Right and Political Science: The First Philosophy of Right.* Trans. J. M. Stewart and P. C. Hodgson. Berkeley: University of California Press.

Hegel, G. W. F. (1995b). *Lectures on the History of Philosophy,* 3 volumes, volume 3 *Medieval and Modern Philosophy.* Trans. E. S. Haldane and F. H. Simson, with introduction by F. C. Beiser. Lincoln: University of Nebraska Press.

Hegel, G. W. F. (2001). *Vorlesungen über die Logik. Berlin 1831. Nachgeschrieben von Karl Hegel*, in *Vorlesungen: Ausgewählte Nachschriften und Manuskripte*, Vol. 10. Edited by U. Rameil in collaboration with H.-C. Lucas. Hamburg: Meiner.

Hegel, G. W. F. (2002a). *Vorlesungen über die Philosophie der Natur. Berlin 1819/20.* Co-written by Johann Rudolf Ringier. (*Vorlesungen. Ausgewählte Nachschriften und Manuskripte*, Vol. 16). Hamburg: Meiner.

Hegel, G. W. F. (2002b). *Vorlesung über Naturphilosophie. Berlin 1821/22.* Postscript Boris von Uexküll. Edited by G. Marmasse and T. Posch. Frankfurt am Main: Peter Lang.

Hegel, G. W. F. (2003). *Vorlesungen über die Philosophie der Kunst: 1823.* Edited by A. Gethmann-Siefert. Hamburg: Meiner.

Hegel, G. W. F. (2004). *Philosophie der Kunst oder Ästhetik: Nach Hegel, im Sommer 1826; Mitschrift Friedrich Carl Hermann Victor von Kehler.* Munich: Fink.

Hegel, G. W. F. (2006). *Lectures on the History of Philosophy 1825–6. Volume II: Greek Philosophy.* Trans. R. F. Brown and J. M. Stewart with the assistance of H. S. Harris. Edited by R. F. Brown. Oxford: Clarendon Press.

Hegel, G. W. F. (2007a). *Lectures on the Philosophy of Religion: Volume I: Introduction and the Concept of Religion.* Trans. R. F. Brown, P. C. Hodgson, and J. M. Stewart. Edited by P. C. Hodgson. Oxford: Oxford University Press.

Hegel, G. W. F. (2007b). *Lectures on the Philosophy of Spirit 1827–8.* Translated by R. R. Williams. Oxford: Oxford University Press.

Hegel, G. W. F. (2007c). *Philosophy of Mind (Part III of the Encyclopædia of the Philosophical Sciences).* Trans. W. Wallace and A. V. Miller, revised by M. Inwood. Oxford: Oxford University Press.

Hegel, G. W. F. (2007d). *Vorlesungen über die Philosophie der Natur. Berlin 1825/26.* Co-written by Heinrich Wilhelm Dove. (*Vorlesungen. Ausgewählte Nachschriften und Manuskripte*, Vol. 17). Hamburg: Meiner.

Hegel, G. W. F. (2008a). *Lectures on Logic. Berlin, 1831. Transcribed by Karl Hegel.* Trans. C. Butler. Bloomington: Indiana University Press.

Hegel, G. W. F. (2008b). *Outlines of the Philosophy of Right.* Trans. T. M. Knox. Edited and introduction by S. Houlgate. Oxford: Oxford University Press.

Hegel, G. W. F. (2010a). *Encyclopedia of the Philosophical Sciences in Basic Outline. Part One: The Science of Logic.* Trans. and edited by K. Brinkmann and D. O. Dahlstrom. Cambridge: Cambridge University Press.

Hegel, G. W. F. (2010b). *The Science of Logic.* Trans. G. di Giovanni. Cambridge: Cambridge University Press.

Hegel, G. W. F. (2015). *Hegel's Philosophy of Nature.* 1st ed. Trans. M. J. Petry. London: Routledge.

Hegel, G. W. F. (2017). *Vorlesungen zur Ästhetik: Vorlesungsmitschrift Adolf Heimann (1828/1829).* Edited by A. P. Olivier and A. Gethmann-Siefert. Paderborn: Wilhelm Fink, Brill Deutschland.

Hegel, G. W. F. (2018a). *The Phenomenology of Spirit.* Trans. T. Pinkard. Cambridge: Cambridge University Press.

Hegel, G. W. F. (2018b). *The Phenomenology of Spirit.* Trans. with introduction and commentary by M. Inwood. Oxford: Oxford University Press.

Hegel, G. W. F., and H. Glockner (1927). *Sämtliche Werke. Jubiläumsausgabe. Auf Grund des von Ludwig Boumann* [et al.] *besorgten Originaldruckes im Faksimileverfahren.* Stuttgart: Frommann.

Hegel, G. W. F., and H. Schneider (1995). *Vorlesung über Ästhetik: Berlin 1820/21: Eine Nachschrift.* Frankfurt am Main and New York: Lang.

Hegel, G. W. F., H. G. Hotho, and A. Gethmann-Siefert (1998). *Vorlesungen über die Philosophie der Kunst: Berlin 1823.* Hamburg: Meiner.

Heidegger, M. (1985). *Schelling's Treatise: On the Essence of Human Freedom.* Trans. J. Stambaugh. Athens: Ohio University Press.

Heidemann, D. (2018). "Die Lehre vom Wesen. Zweyter Abschnitt. Die Erscheinung," in M. Quante and N. Mooren, eds. *Kommentar zu Hegels Wissenschaft der Logik.* Hamburg: Meiner, pp. 325–86.

Heidemann, D. (2019). "Hegel: Ein Rationalist?," in D. Emundts and S. Sedgwick, eds. *Internationales Jahrbuch des Deutschen Idealismus/International Yearbook of German Idealism* 14. Berlin: DeGruyter, pp. 235–64.

Henrich, D. (1971). "Hegels Theorie über den Zufall," in D.Henrich, *Hegel im Kontext.* Frankfurt: Suhrkamp.

Henrich, D., ed. (1986). *Hegels* Wissenschaft der Logik*: Formation und Rekonstruktion.* Stuttgart: Klett-Cotta, 1986.

Heraclitus (2001). *Fragments: The Collected Wisdom of Heraclitus.* Trans. B. Haxton. New York: Viking Press.

Herrmann-Sinai, S. (2016). "Subjective Action," in S. Herrmann-Sinai and L. Ziglioli, eds. *Hegel's Philosophical Psychology.* London and New York: Routledge, pp. 127–52.

Herrmann-Sinai, S., and L. Ziglioli (2016). *Hegel's Philosophical Psychology.* London and New York: Routledge.

Hermanni, F. (2013). "Kritischer Inklusivismus: Hegels Begriff der Religion und seine Theorie der Religionen," *Neue Zeitschrift für Systematische Theologie und Religionsphilosphie,* 55(2), pp. 136–60.

Herz-Fischler, R. (1998). *A Mathematical History of the Golden Number.* New York: Dover.

Hobbes, T. (1994). *Leviathan, with Selected Variants from the Latin Edition of 1668.* Edited by E. Curley. Indianapolis: Hackett.

Hodgson, P. C. (2007). *Hegel and Christian Theology: A Reading of the Lectures on the Philosophy of Religion.* Oxford: Oxford University Press.

Houlgate, S. (2005). *An Introduction to Hegel: Freedom, Truth, and History,* 2nd ed. Malden: Blackwell.

Houlgate, S. (2006). *The Opening of Hegel's Logic: From Being to Infinity.* West Lafayette: Purdue University Press.

Houlgate, S. (2009). "Hegel's Logic," in F. C. Beiser, ed. *The Cambridge Companion to Hegel and Nineteenth-Century Philosophy.* Cambridge: Cambridge University Press, pp. 111–34.

Houlgate, S. (2011), "Essence, Reflexion, and Immediacy in Hegel's *Science of Logic,*" in S. Houlgate and M. Baur, eds. *A Companion to Hegel.* Oxford: Wiley-Blackwell, pp. 139–58.

Houlgate, S. (2015). "Glaube, Liebe, Verzeihung: Hegel und die Religion," in F. Hermanni, B. Nonnenmacher, and F. Schick, eds. *Religion und Religionen im deutschen Idealismus: Schleiermacher – Hegel – Schelling*. Tübingen: Mohr Siebeck, pp. 253–74.

Houlgate, S. (2018). "Thought and Being in Hegel's Logic: Reflections on Hegel, Kant and Pippin," in L. Illetterati and F. Menegoni, eds. *Geist und Geschichte*. Frankfurt am Main: Klostermann, pp. 101–18.

Hutchings, K., and T. Pulkinnen, eds. (2010). *Beyond Antigone: Hegel's Philosophy and Feminist Thought*. London: Palgrave Macmillan.

Iber, C. (1990). *Metaphysik absoluter Relationalität: Eine Studie zu den beiden ersten Kapiteln von Hegels Wesenslogik*. Berlin: De Gruyter.

Iber, C. (2002). "Hegels Konzeption des Begriffs," in A. F. Koch and F. Schick, eds. *G. W. F. Hegel: Wissenschaft der Logik*. Berlin: Akademie, pp. 181–201.

Ikäheimo, H. (2017). "Hegel's Psychology," in D. Moyar, ed. *The Oxford Handbook of Hegel*. Oxford: Oxford University Press, pp. 424–49.

Illetterati, L., and F. Menengoni, eds. (2018). *Wirklichkeit: Beiträge zu einem Schlüsselbegriff der Hegelschen Philosophie*. Frankfurt am Main: Klostermann.

Inwood, M. (2010). *A Commentary on Hegel's Philosophy of Mind*. Oxford: Oxford University Press.

Jaeschke, W. (1999). "Einleitung," in G. W. F. Hegel, *Wissenschaft der Logik. Erster Band: Die objektive Logik. Zweites Buch: Die Lehre vom Wesen (1813)*. Edited by H.-J. Gawoll. Hamburg: Meiner, pp. ix–xxxv.

James, D. (2009). *Art, Myth and Society in Hegel's Aesthetics*. London: Continuum.

Jarrett, C. (2009). "Spinoza on Necessity," in O. Koistinen, ed. *The Cambridge Companion to Spinoza's Ethics*. Cambridge: Cambridge University Press, pp. 118–39.

Kang, S.-J. (1999). *Reflexion und Widerspruch: Eine entwicklungsgeschichtliche und systematische Untersuchung des Hegelschen Begriffs des Widerspruchs*. Bonn: Bouvier.

Kant, I. (1968). *Kants Werke*. Berlin: De Gruyter.

Kant, I. (1969). *Kritik der reinen Vernunft*, in I. Kant, *Gesammelte Schriften*. Edited by the Preußische Akademie der Wissenschaften. Berlin and New York: De Gruyter.

Kant, I. (1989). *Critique of Pure Reason*. Trans. P. Guyer and A. W. Wood. Cambridge: Cambridge University Press.

Kant, I. (1991). *The Metaphysics of Morals*. Trans. M. Gregor. Cambridge: Cambridge University Press.

Kant, I. (2000). *Critique of the Power of Judgment*. Trans. P. Guyer and E. Matthews. New York and Cambridge: Cambridge University Press.

Kaufmann, R. M., and C. Yeomans (2017). "Math by Pure Thinking: R First and the Divergence of Measures in Hegel's Philosophy of Mathematics," *European Journal of Philosophy*, 25(4), pp. 985–1020.

Kittay, E. (1999). *Love's Labor: Essays on Women, Equality, and Dependency*. New York: Routledge.

Knappik, F. (2016). "Hegel's Essentialism: Natural Kinds and the Metaphysics of Explanation in Hegel's Theory of 'the Concept,'" *European Journal of Philosophy*, 24(4), pp. 760–87.

Koch, A. F. (2003). *Der Begriff als die Wahrheit: Zum Anspruch der Hegelschen "subjektiven Logik."* Paderborn: Schöningh.

Koch, A. F. (2014a). "Subjektivität und Objektivität: Die Unterscheidung des Begriffs," in A. F. Koch, F. Schick, K. Vieweg, and C. Wirsing, eds. *Deutsches Jahrbuch Philosophie: Hegel – 200 Jahre Wissenschaft der Logik.* Hamburg: Meiner, pp. 209–21.

Koch, A. F. (2014b). *Die Evolution des logischen Raumes: Aufsätze zu Hegels Nichtstandard-Metaphysik.* Tübingen: Mohr Siebeck.

Koch, A. F., and F. Schick, eds. (2002). *G. W. F. Hegel: Wissenschaft der Logik.* Berlin: Akademie, pp. 181–201.

Koch, A. F., F. Schick, K. Vieweg, and C. Wirsing, eds. (2014). *Deutsches Jahrbuch Philosophie: Hegel – 200 Jahre Wissenschaft der Logik.* Hamburg: Meiner.

Kolb, D. (2010). "The Necessities of Hegel's Logics," in A. Nuzzo, ed. *Hegel and the Analytic Tradition.* London: Continuum, pp. 40–60.

Kosman, A. (2013). *The Activity of Being: An Essay on Aristotle's Ontology.* Cambridge: Harvard University Press.

Kreines, J. (2007). "Between the Bounds of Experience and Divine Intuitions: Kant's Epistemic Limits and Hegel's Ambitions," *Inquiry*, 50, pp. 306–34.

Kreines, J. (2008). "The Logic of Life: Hegel's Philosophical Defense of Natural Teleology," in F. C. Beiser, ed. *The Cambridge Companion to Hegel*, 2nd ed. Cambridge: Cambridge University Press, pp. 344–77.

Kreines, J. (2015). *Reason in the World: Hegel's Metaphysics and Its Philosophical Appeal.* Oxford: Oxford University Press.

Lakebrink, B. (1979). *Kommentar zu Hegels "Logik" in seiner "Enzyklopädie" von 1830. Band I: Sein und Wesen.* Freiburg and Munich: Alber.

Lasserre, F. (1964). *The Birth of Mathematics in the Age of Plato.* London: Hutchinson.

Lewis, T. A. (2011). *Religion, Modernity, and Politics in Hegel.* Oxford: Oxford University Press.

Longuenesse, B. (2007). *Hegel's Critique of Metaphysics.* Trans. N. J. Simek. Cambridge: Cambridge University Press.

Luckner, A., and S. Ostritsch, eds. (2019) *Philosophie der Existenz: Aktuelle Beiträge von der Ontologie bis zur Ethik.* Berlin: Springer.

Lumsden, S. (2013). "Between Nature and Spirit: Hegel's Account of Habit," in D. Stern, ed. *Essays on Hegel's Philosophy of Subjective Spirit.* Albany: State University of New York Press, pp. 121–37.

Mabille, B. (1999). *Hegel: L'épreuve de la contingence.* Paris: Aubier.

Macherey, P. (2011). *Hegel or Spinoza.* Trans. S. M. Ruddick. Minneapolis: University of Minnesota Press.

Martin, C. "Our Three Attitudes towards Nature" (unpublished manuscript).

Martin, C. (2012). *Ontologie der Selbstbestimmung: Eine operationale Rekonstruktion von Hegels »Wissenschaft der Logik«.* Tübingen: Mohr Siebeck.

Martin, C. (2014). "Die Idee als Einheit von Begriff und Objektivität," in A. Koch, ed. *200 Jahre Wissenschaft der Logik.* Hamburg: Meiner, pp. 223–42.

Martin, C. (2017a). "Das Logische und der Raum," in J. Noller, ed. *Wozu Metaphysik? Historisch-systematische Perspektiven.* Freiburg: Alber, pp. 151–81.

Martin, C. (2017b). "Hegel on Truth and Absolute Spirit," *Idealistic Studies*, 47, 191–217.

Martin, C. (2019). "G. W. F. Hegel: Die Verwandlung von Metaphysik in Logik," in J. Urbich, ed. *Metzler Handbuch Ontologie*. Darmstadt: Metzler.

Martin, C. (2020). *Die Einheit des Sinns: Untersuchungen zur Form des Denkens und Sprechens*. Münster: Mentis.

McCarney, J. (2009). *Hegel on History*. London: Routledge.

McCumber, J. (1990). "Hegel on Habit," *The Owl of Minerva*, 21(2), pp. 155–65.

McDowell, J. (1994). *Mind and World*. Cambridge: Harvard University Press.

McDowell, J. (2017). "Why Does It Matter to Hegel That Geist Has a History?," in R. Zuckert and J. Kreines, eds. *Hegel on Philosophy in History*. Cambridge: Cambridge University Press, pp. 15–32.

McWhorter, L. (1999). *Bodies and Pleasures: Foucault and the Politics of Sexual Normalization*. Bloomington: Indiana University Press.

Melamed, Y. Y. (2010). "Acosmism or Weak Individuals?: Hegel, Spinoza, and the Reality of the Finite," *Journal of the History of Philosophy*, 48(1), pp. 77–92.

Melamed, Y. (2012). "'Omnis determinatio est negatio': Determination, Negation, and Self-Negation in Spinoza, Kant, and Hegel," in M. Förster and Y. Melamed, eds. *Spinoza and German Idealism*. Cambridge: Cambridge University Press, pp. 175–96.

Melamed, Y. Y. (2017). *The Causes of Our Belief in Free Will: Spinoza on Necessary, "Innate," yet False Cognition in Spinoza's Ethics: A Critical Guide*. Cambridge: Cambridge University Press, pp. 121–41.

Merleau-Ponty, M. (2012). *Phenomenology of Perception*. Trans. D. A. Landes. London and New York: Routledge.

Michalko, R. (1999). *The Two-in-One: Walking with Smokie, Walking with Blindness*. Philadelphia: Temple University Press.

Mills, P. J., ed. (1996). *Feminist Interpretations of Hegel*. University Park: Penn State University Press.

Moland, L. (2003). "Inheriting, Earning, and Owning: The Source of Practical Identity in Hegel's 'Anthropology,'" *Owl of Minerva*, 34(2), pp. 139–70.

Molas, A. (2019). "The Compatibility of Hegelian Recognition and Morality with the Ethics of Care," *Journal of the British Society for Phenomenology*, 50(4), pp. 285–304.

Mowad, N. (2019). *Meaning and Embodiment: Human Corporeity in Hegel's Anthropology*. Albany: State University of New York Press.

Moyar, D. (2007). "Urteil, Schluss und Handlung: Hegels logische Übergänge im Argument zur Sittlichkeit," *Hegel-Studien*, 42, 51–80.

Moyar, D. (2012). "Thought and Metaphysics: Hegel's Critical Reception of Spinoza," in M. Förster and Y. Melamed, eds. *Spinoza and German Idealism*. Cambridge: Cambridge University Press, pp. 197–213.

Moyar, D. (2018). "Die Lehre vom Begriff. Zweiter Abschnitt. Die Objektivität," in M. Quante and N. Mooren, eds. *Kommentar zu Hegels Wissenschaft der Logik*. Hamburg: Meiner, pp. 559–650.

Mure, G. (1940). *An Introduction to Hegel's Logic*. Oxford: Oxford University Press.

Nadler, S. (2018). "The Intellectual Love of God," in M. DellaRocca, ed. *The Oxford Handbook of Spinoza*. Oxford: Oxford University Press, pp. 295–313.

Ng, K. (2016). "Life and Mind in Hegel's *Logic* and Subjective Spirit," *Hegel Bulletin*, 39(1), pp. 23–44.

Ng, K. (2019). "Life and the Space of Reasons: On Hegel's Subjective Logic," *Hegel Bulletin*, 40(1), pp. 121–42.

Novakovic, A. (2017). "Hegel's Anthropology," in D. Moyar, ed. *The Oxford Handbook of Hegel*. New York and Oxford: Oxford University Press, pp. 407–23.

Nuzzo, A. (2013). "Anthropology, *Geist*, and the Soul–Body Relation: The Systematic Beginning of Hegel's *Philosophy of Spirit*," in D. Stern, ed. *Essays on Hegel's Philosophy of Subjective Spirit*. Albany: State University of New York Press, pp. 1–17.

Nuzzo, A. (2018). *Approaching Hegel's Logic Obliquely*. Albany: State University of New York Press.

Okochi, T. (2008). *Ontologie und Reflexionsbestimmungen: Zur Genealogie der Wesenslogik Hegels*. Würzburg: Königshausen & Neumann.

Olshewsky, T. M. (1968). "Aristotle's Use of Analogia," *Apeiron*, 2(2), pp. 1–10.

Parekh, S. (2009). "Hegel's New World: History, Freedom, and Race," in W. Dudley, ed. *Hegel and History*. Albany: State University of New York Press, pp. 111–31.

Pelczynski, Z. A. (1964). "An Introductory Essay," in G. W. F. Hegel, *Hegel's Political Writings*. Trans. T. M. Knox. Oxford: Clarendon Press, pp. 1–137.

Peperzak, A. (1987). *Selbsterkenntnis des Absoluten*. Stuttgart: Frommann-Holzboog.

Peters, J. (2015). *Hegel on Beauty*. London: Routledge.

Petry, M. (1970). *Hegel's Philosophy of Nature*. London: Allen and Unwin.

Pillow, K. (2002). "Hegel and Homosexuality," *Philosophy Today*, 46 (5, SPEP Supplement), pp. 75–91.

Pinkard, T. (1996). *Hegel's* Phenomenology: *The Sociality of Reason*. New York and Cambridge: Cambridge University Press.

Pinkard, T. (2001). *Hegel: A Biography*. Cambridge: Cambridge University Press.

Pinkard, T. (2011). "Freedom and Necessity. And Music," in A. Honneth and G. Hendrichs, eds. *Freiheit: Stuttgarter Hegelkongress*. Frankfurt: Klostermann, pp. 313–29.

Pinkard, T. (2013). *Hegel's Naturalism: Mind, Nature, and the Final Ends of Life*. Oxford: Oxford University Press.

Pippin, R. B. (1989). *Hegel's Idealism: The Satisfactions of Self-Consciousness*. New York and Cambridge: Cambridge University Press.

Pippin, R. (2008). *Hegel's Practical Philosophy: Rational Agency as Ethical Life*. Cambridge: Cambridge University Press.

Pippin, R. B. (2014). *After the Beautiful: Hegel and the Philosophy of Pictorial Modernism*. Chicago and London: The University of Chicago Press.

Pippin, R. B. (2019). *Hegel's Realm of Shadows: Logic as Metaphysics in* The Science of Logic. Chicago and London: The University of Chicago Press.

Plato (1997). *Complete Works*. Edited by J. M. Cooper. Indianapolis: Hackett.

Plevrakis, H. (2018). "Übergang von der Logik in die Natur aus ‚absoluter Freiheit'? Eine argumentanalytische Rekonstruktion des letzten Satzes der enzyklopädischen Logik Hegels," *Hegel-Studien*, 52, pp. 103–38.

Ploucquet, G. (2006). *Logik*. Edited, translated, and with an introduction by M. Franz. Hildesheim: Olms.

Prior, A. N. (1957). *Time and Modality: Being the John Locke Lectures for 1955–6 Delivered in the University of Oxford*. Oxford: Clarendon Press.

Quante, M., and N. Mooren, eds. (2018). *Kommentar zu Hegels* Wissenschaft der Logik. Hamburg: Meiner.

Rademaker, H. (1979). *Hegels "Wissenschaft der Logik": Eine darstellende und erläuternde Einführung*. Bonn: Bouvier.

Rand, S. (2007). "The Importance and Relevance of Hegel's 'Philosophy of Nature,'" *The Review of Metaphysics*, 61(2), pp. 379–400.

Rawls, J. (1971). *A Theory of Justice*. Cambridge: Harvard University Press.

Rawls, J. (1993). *Political Liberalism*. New York: Columbia University Press.

Rawls, J. (2000). *Lectures on the History of Moral Philosophy*. Edited by B. Herman. Cambridge: Harvard University Press.

Rawls, J. (2001). *Justice as Fairness: A Restatement*. Edited by E. Kelly. Cambridge: Harvard University Press.

Redding, P. (2017). "Findlay's Hegel: Idealism as Modal Actualism," *Critical Horizons*, 18(4), pp. 359–77.

Redding, P. (2018). "Georg Wilhelm Friedrich Hegel," in E. N. Zalta, ed. *The Stanford Encyclopedia of Philosophy*, https://plato.stanford.edu/archives/su m2018/entries/hegel (accessed 10 February 2021).

Redding, P. (2019). "Time and Modality in Hegel's Account of Judgment," in B. Ball and C. Schuringa, eds. *The Act and Object of Judgment: Historical and Philosophical Perspectives*. New York: Routledge, pp. 91–109.

Rohs, P. (1982). *Form und Grund: Interpretation eines Kapitels der Hegelschen Wissenschaft der Logik*, 3rd ed. Bonn: Bouvier.

Rosen, S. (2014). *The Idea of Hegel's* Science of Logic. Chicago and London: The University of Chicago Press.

Russell, B. (1906). "Review of *Symbolic Logic and Its Applications* by Hugh MacColl," *Mind*, New Series, 15(58), pp. 255–60.

Russell, B. (1945). *A History of Western Philosophy*. New York: Simon & Schuster.

Rutter, B. (2011). *Hegel on the Modern Arts*. Cambridge: Cambridge University Press.

Schelling, F. W. J. (1975). *Zur Geschichte der neueren Philosophie: Münchener Vorlesungen*. Darmstadt: Wissenschaftliche Buchgesellschaft.

Schelling, F. W. J. (1982). *Philosophische Briefe über Dogmatismus und Kritizismus*, in *Historisch-kritische Ausgabe F. W. J. Schelling*, Vol. I/3. Edited by H. Buchner, W. G. Jacobs, and A. Pieper. Stuttgart: Frommann-Holzboog.

Schelling, F. W. J. (1985). *Ausgewählte Schriften*. Edited by M. Frank, 6 vols. Frankfurt am Main: Suhrkamp.

Schelling, F. W. J. (2005). *System des transcendentalen Idealismus*, in *Historisch-kritische Ausgabe F. W. J. Schelling*, Vol. I/9-1. Edited by H. Korten and P. Ziche. Stuttgart: Frommann-Holzboog.

Schelling, F. W. J. (2009). *Darstellung meines Systems der Philosophie*, in *Historisch-kritische Ausgabe F. W. J. Schelling*, Vol. I/10. Edited by M. Durner. Stuttgart: Frommann-Holzboog.

Schick, F. (1994). *Hegels Wissenschaft der Logik: Metaphysische Letztbegründung oder Theorie logischer Formen?* Freiburg and Munich: Alber.

Schick, F. (2012). "Logik, Wirklichkeit und ihre Verwechslung. Schellings Hegel-Kritik," in F. Hermanni, ed. *"Der Anfang und das Ende aller Philosophie ist – Freiheit!": Schellings Philosophie in der Sicht neuerer Forschung*. Tübingen: Attempto, pp. 383–401.

Schick, F. (2018). "Die Lehre vom Begriff. Erster Abschnitt. Die Subjectivität," in M. Quante and N. Mooren, eds. *Kommentar zu Hegels* Wissenschaft der Logik. Hamburg: Meiner, pp. 457–558.

Schmidt, K. J. (1997). *G. W. F. Hegel: "Wissenschaft der Logik – Die Lehre vom Wesen." Ein einführender Kommentar*. Paderborn: Schöningh.

Schmidt am Busch, H.-C. (2010). "What Does It Mean to 'Make Oneself into an Object'? In Defense of a Key Notion of Hegel's Theory of Action," in A. Laitinen and C. Sandis, eds. *Hegel on Action*. London: Palgrave, pp. 189–211.

Siebers, T. (2019). "Returning the Social to the Social Model," in D. T. Mitchell, S. Antebi, and S. L. Snyder, eds. *The Matter of Disability: Materiality, Biopolitics, Crip Affect*. Ann Arbor: University of Michigan Press, pp. 39–47.

Sheppard, A. (2014). *Embodied Virtuosity: Dances from Disability Culture*. Emory University YouTube channel, www.youtube.com/watch?v=c-qfZA1V7Y0 (accessed 14 November 2019).

Speight, A. (2015). "Hegel's Philosophy of Art," in M. Baur, ed. *Hegel: Key Concepts*. London: Routledge, pp. 103–15.

Speight, A. (2019). "Art as a Mode of Absolute Spirit: The Development and Significance of Hegel's *Encyclopaedia* Account of the Philosophy of Art," in M. F. Bykova, ed. *Hegel's Philosophy of Spirit: A Critical Guide*. Cambridge: Cambridge University Press, pp. 225–42.

Spinoza, B. de (1994). *Ethics*, in *A Spinoza Reader*. Trans. and edited by E. Curley. Princeton: Princeton University Press.

Stekeler-Weithofer, P. (1992). *Hegels analytische Philosophie: Die* Wissenschaft der Logik *als kritische Theorie der Bedeutung*. Paderborn: Schöningh.

Stern, R. (2009). *Hegelian Metaphysics*. Oxford: Oxford University Press.

Stewart, J. (2018). *Hegel's Interpretation of the Religions of the World: The Logic of the Gods*. Oxford: Oxford University Press.

Stone, A. (2018a). "Matter and Form: Hegel, Organicism and the Difference between Women and Men," in A. Stone, *Nature, Ethics and Gender in German Romanticism and Idealism*. London: Rowman and Littlefield, pp. 191–205.

Stone, A. (2018b). *Nature, Ethics and Gender in German Romanticism and Idealism*. Lanham: Rowman & Littlefield.

Stone, A. (2020). "Hegel and Colonialism," *Hegel Bulletin*, 41(2), pp. 1–24.

Testa, I. (2013). "Hegel's Naturalism or Soul and Body in the *Encyclopedia*," in D. Stern, ed. *Essays on Hegel's Philosophy of Subjective Spirit*. Albany: State University of New York Press, pp. 19–35.

Theunissen, M. (1980). *Sein und Schein: Die kritische Funktion der Hegelschen Logik*. Stuttgart: Suhrkamp.

Trisokkas, I. (2009). "The Speculative Logical Theory of Universality," *The Owl of Minerva*, 40, pp. 141–74.

Trisokkas, I. (2012). *Pyrrhonian Scepticism and Hegel's Theory of Judgement*. Leiden: Brill.

Trisokkas, I. (2017). "The Two-Sense Reading of Spinoza's Definition of Attribute," *British Journal for the History of Philosophy*, 25(6), pp. 1093–115.

Vinco, R. (2015). "Philosophie ist Gottesdienst: Zum liturgischen Charakter des hegelschen Philosophieren," in F. Hermanni, B. Nonnenmacher, and F. Schick, eds. *Religion und Religionen im deutschen Idealismus: Schleiermacher – Hegel – Schelling*. Tübingen:Mohr Siebeck, pp. 233–51.

Wandschneider, D. (2004). "Zur Dialektik des Übergangs von der absoluten Idee zur Natur. Eine Skizze," in H. Schneider, ed. *Sich in Freiheit entlassen: Natur und Idee bei Hegel*. Frankfurt am Main: Peter Lang, pp. 107–24.

Wandschneider, D. (2016). "Die Entäußerung der Idee zur Natur bei Hegel und ihre ontologische Bedeutung," in W. Neuser, ed. *Natur zwischen Logik und Geschichte: Beiträge zu Hegels Naturphilosophie*. Würzburg: Königshausen und Neumann, pp. 61–71.

Watson, G. (2004). *Agency and Answerability: Selected Essays*. Oxford: Clarendon Press.

Wendte, M. (2012). "To Develop Relational Autonomy: On Hegel's View of People with Disabilities," in B. Brock, ed. *Disability in the Christian Tradition: A Reader*. Grand Rapids and Cambridge: Wm. B. Eerdmans, pp. 251–85.

Whitehead, A. N. (1997). *Science and the Modern World*. New York: Free Press.

Wicks, R. (1993). "Hegel's Aesthetics: An Overview," in F. C. Beiser, ed. *The Cambridge Companion to Hegel*. Cambridge: Cambridge University Press, pp. 348–77.

Williams, R. R. (2007). "Translator's Introduction," in G. W. F. Hegel, *Lectures on the Philosophy of Spirit 1827–8*. Oxford: Oxford University Press, pp. 1–56.

Williams, R. R. (2017). *Hegel on the Proofs and Personhood of God: Studies in Hegel's Logic and Philosophy of Religion*. Oxford: Oxford University Press.

Wong, S. (2002). "At Home with Down Syndrome and Gender," *Hypatia*, 17(3), pp. 89–117.

Wolff, M. (2013). "The *Science of Logic*," in A. De Laurentiis and J. Edwards, eds. *The Bloomsbury Companion to Hegel*. London and New York: Bloomsbury Academic.

Wood, A. W. (1990). *Hegel's Ethical Thought*. Cambridge: Cambridge University Press.

Wood, A. W. (2017). "Method and System in Hegel's *Philosophy of Right*," in T. Brooks and S. Stein, eds. *Hegel's Political Philosophy: On the Normative Significance of Method and System*. Oxford: Oxford University Press, pp. 82–102.

Wretzel, J. (2018). "Organic Imagination as Intuitive Intellect: Self-Knowledge and Self-Constitution in Hegel's Early Critique of Kant," *European Journal of Philosophy*, 26(3), pp. 958–73.

Wretzel, J. I. (2020). "Constraint and the Ethical Agent: Hegel between Constructivism and Realism," in J. Gledhill and S. Stein, eds. *Hegel's Practical Philosophy*. New York: Routledge, pp. 88–106.

Yeomans, C. (2012). *Freedom and Reflection: Hegel and the Logic of Agency*. New York and Oxford: Oxford University Press.

Yeomans, C. (2019). "Perspective and Logical Pluralism in Hegel," *Hegel Bulletin*, 40(1), pp. 29–50.

Index

Note: *Main headings capitalized and in quotation marks may refer to parts of the* Encyclopedia.

CAMBRIDGE CRITICAL GUIDES

Titles published in this series (continued):

For EU product safety concerns, contact us at Calle de José Abascal, 56–1°,
28003 Madrid, Spain or eugpsr@cambridge.org.

www.ingramcontent.com/pod-product-compliance
Ingram Content Group UK Ltd.
Pitfield, Milton Keynes, MK11 3LW, UK
UKHW020341140625
459647UK00018B/2248